Foundations First

SENTENCES AND PARAGRAPHS

WITH READINGS

Foundations First

SENTENCES AND PARAGRAPHS

WITH READINGS

Laurie G. Kirszner
University of the Sciences in Philadelphia

Stephen R. Mandell
Drexel University

Bedford / St. Martin's
Boston ■ New York

For Bedford/St. Martin's

Senior Editor: Talvi Laev
Senior Production Editor: Shuli Traub
Senior Production Supervisor: Dennis J. Conroy
Marketing Manager: Brian Wheel
Art Direction and Cover Design: Lucy Krikorian
Text Design: Wanda Kossak
Copy Editor: Alice Vigliani
Cover Photos: left to right: Photo Researchers, Inc.; Daemmrich Photography, Inc.; Corbis Stock Market; Corbis Stock Market; David Young-Wolff/PhotoEdit.
Photo Research: Alice Lundoff
Composition: Monotype Composition Company, Inc.
Printing and Binding: R. R. Donnelly & Sons Company

President: Charles H. Christensen
Editorial Director: Joan E. Feinberg
Editor in Chief: Nancy Perry
Director of Marketing: Karen R. Melton
Director of Editing, Design, and Production: Marcia Cohen
Managing Editor: Erica T. Appel

Library of Congress Control Number: 2001097009

Manufactured in the United States of America.

7 6 5 4 3
f e d c

For information, write: Bedford/St. Martin's, 75 Arlington Street, Boston, MA 02116 (617-399-4000)

ISBN: 0-312-39423-3 (Instructor's Annotated Edition)
0-312-39076-9 (Student Edition with Readings)
0-312-39077-7 (Student Edition)

Acknowledgments
Acknowledgments and copyrights appear at the back of the book on pages 517–18, which constitute an extension of the copyright page.

Preface for Instructors

When we wrote our paragraph-to-essay developmental writing text, *Writing First: Practice in Context,* we wanted it to be consistent with our priorities as teachers as well as with the realities of college. We believe that in college, writing comes first, and that students learn writing skills most meaningfully in the context of their own writing. *Foundations First: Sentences and Paragraphs* adapts the "practice in context" approach used in *Writing First* to the sentence-to-paragraph course, giving students the practice they need in order to become better writers.

More important, *Foundations First* is the only developmental writing text to offer not just grammar and writing help but a complete collection of resources for developmental students entering college. By providing unique coverage of study skills, vocabulary development, ESL issues, and critical reading, we strive in *Foundations First* to give students the support and encouragement they need to build a solid foundation for success in college and beyond.

In *Foundations First,* as in the classroom—and, we believe, in everyday life—writing is essential. In our text, writing comes first chronologically: the book begins with thorough coverage of the writing process, and most chapters begin with a writing prompt. Writing is also first in importance: extensive writing practice is central to the "grammar chapters" as well as to the "writing chapters" of the text. Throughout the book, students learn to become better writers by applying each chapter's concepts to writing, revising, and editing their own writing.

We wrote this book for adults—our own interested, concerned, and hardworking students—and we tailored the book's approach and content to them. We avoided exercises that reinforce the idea that writing is a dull, pointless, and artificial activity. Instead, we chose fresh, contemporary examples (both student and professional) and worked hard to develop interesting exercises and writing assignments. In the book's style and tone, we aim to show our respect for our audience (as well as for our subject matter), and so we try to talk *to* students, not *at* or *down* to them. Throughout, we strive to be concise without being abrupt, thorough without being repetitive, direct without being rigid, specific without being prescriptive, and flexible without being inconsistent. Our most important goal is a simple one: to create an appealing, engaging text that motivates students to improve their writing and that gives them the tools they need to do so.

Organization

Foundations First: Sentences and Paragraphs has a flexible organization that lets instructors teach various topics in the order that works best for them and their students. The book opens with a unique chapter on academic survival skills, which is followed by coverage of three major areas: the writing process, sentence grammar, and the reading-writing connection. Unit One provides a comprehensive discussion of the writing process. Units Two through Five present a thorough review of sentence skills, grammar, punctuation, mechanics, and spelling. Unit Six, included only in *Foundations First with Readings,* introduces students to critical reading skills and includes twenty essays (five by student writers). Finally, two appendixes provide additional enrichment for students. Appendix A, "Building Word Power," reviews the vocabulary highlighted in the text and gives students practice exercises and other opportunities for expanding their vocabulary further. Appendix B, "Picture Gallery," provides a collection of images, drawn mainly from fine art, with accompanying discussion questions and writing prompts.

For instructors wishing to emphasize the patterns of development, an Index of Rhetorical Patterns points to essays and other writing samples exemplifying particular modes. (Most of the patterns are covered in Chapter 4, and the essays in Unit Six include at least one example of each pattern.)

Features

We have worked hard to make *Foundations First* the most complete sentence-to-paragraph text available for developmental writers. In addition, recognizing that writers at this level often need help not just with grammar and writing but also with making a successful transition to college, we include unique coverage of study skills and related issues. Finally, as in *Writing First,* we support our "students first" philosophy with innovative features designed to make students' writing practice meaningful, productive, and enjoyable.

A Complete Resource for Developmental Writers

Using a process approach, the text provides comprehensive coverage of the writing process in a flexible format. Chapters 2, "Writing a Paragraph," and 3, "Fine-Tuning Your Paragraph," cover the steps in the process, from invention to final draft, and include all the stages of a model student paper. Chapter 4, "Patterns of Paragraph Development," covers the most frequently taught patterns. For programs that require students to write an essay by the end of the term, Chapter 5, "Moving from Paragraph to Essay," offers more in-depth coverage of the essay than any competing text, including multiple drafts of an actual student paper.

Unique "practice in context" activities let students apply each new concept to their own writing. Chapters begin with a ***Seeing and Writing*** activity that asks students to write a response to a prompt based on a photo or other visual. At the end of the chapter, a ***Revising and Editing*** activity helps students fine-tune their Seeing and Writing response using what they have learned in the chapter. ***Self-Assessment Checklists*** in Unit One guide students as they revise and edit their own writing.

Each chapter offers numerous opportunities for practice, revision, and review. Easy-to-grade ***Practices*** following each section of each chapter form a strand of workbook-style mastery exercises that let students hone specific skills. (These Practices can supplement or replace the Seeing and Writing strand, depending on an instructor's preference.) Three kinds of ***Chapter Review*** activities provide additional practice opportunities: an ***Editing Practice*** featuring a full-length passage gives students an opportunity to edit to eliminate a specific writing problem; ***Collaborative Activities*** offer creative options for student-centered classroom learning; and a ***Review Checklist*** recaps the main points of each chapter for quick review. Finally, ***Answers to Odd-Numbered Exercises*** at the end of the book let students check their own work as they practice and review.

An appendix features additional visuals for writing assignments and in-class discussion. *Appendix B, "Picture Gallery,"* gathers twelve images, each followed by two discussion questions and a writing prompt. This appendix encourages students to use their own observations and insights in their writing.

More Than Just a Grammar Text

Unique coverage of academic survival skills. Chapter 1, "Strategies for College Success," provides support not found in any competing text, helping students develop effective strategies for adjusting to college, taking notes, completing homework assignments, doing well on exams, and managing time efficiently. A section on Internet strategies shows students how to find and evaluate Web sources—a skill that will help them beyond the composition classroom. Throughout the chapter, exercises encourage students to practice and individualize the strategies presented in the chapter.

A unique integrated approach to building vocabulary in context. *Foundations First* helps students develop their vocabulary with features that are unique among sentence-to-paragraph books: ***Word Power*** boxes in every chapter help students master specific new words in context, while ***Appendix A, "Building Word Power,"*** provides opportunities for additional practice.

The most extensive help for ESL students. Chapter 21, "Grammar and Usage Issues for ESL Writers," discusses in detail concerns of particular interest to nonnative writers. ***ESL Tips*** in the Instructor's Annotated Edition guide instructors in helping these students get the most out of the text.

The most comprehensive coverage of critical reading. Chapter 27, "Becoming an Active Reader," guides students step by step through the reading process and includes a sample annotated reading as well as a series of exercises. Chapter 28, "Readings for Writers," contains twenty engaging, often provocative readings, five of them by students. Questions following each reading test comprehension and offer topics for writing.

A "Students First" Approach

Students' writing concerns get serious attention. The tone and level of explanatory material, as well as the subject matter of examples and exercises, acknowledge the diverse interests, ages, and experiences of developmental writers. *Writing Tips* in the margins provide additional information, address common problem areas, and draw connections between chapter topics and nonacademic writing situations. *Computer Tips* give helpful advice for writers working online.

Numerous examples of student writing provide realistic models for students. The text features multiple stages of a paragraph as well as six complete essays. *Student Voices* in the margins communicate the experiences of actual student writers.

The engaging full-color design supports the text's pedagogy and helps students find information quickly. *Focus boxes* highlight key concepts and important information throughout the book, *quick-reference corner tabs* make the book easy to navigate, and *marginal cross-references* to other parts of the text help students find and review key information quickly.

Ancillaries

Foundations First is accompanied by a comprehensive teaching support package that includes the following items:

Print Resources

- The *Instructor's Annotated Edition* features numerous teaching tips in the margins, including many ESL tips designed especially for instructors teaching nonnative speakers. The book's annotations include answers to all the Practices in *Foundations First.*
- *Classroom Resources for Instructors Using* FOUNDATIONS FIRST offers extensive advice for teaching developmental writing as well as chapter-by-chapter pointers for using *Foundations First* in the classroom. Also included are sample syllabi, answers to all the grammar Practices in *Foundations First* (in a format suitable for distribution to students), and sample answers to essay questions.
- *Teaching Developmental Writing: Background Readings* offers nearly three dozen professional articles on topics of interest to developmental writing instructors, accompanied by suggestions for practical applications to the classroom.

- *Supplemental Exercises to Accompany* FOUNDATIONS FIRST offers additional grammar exercises (including material from Exercise Central).
- *Diagnostic and Mastery Texts to Accompany* FOUNDATIONS FIRST complements the topic coverage in *Foundations First.*
- *Transparency Masters to Accompany* FOUNDATIONS FIRST includes student examples of the stages of paragraph and essay writing (from Chapters 2 and 5) and uncorrected essays from the Chapter Reviews to be used for in-class editing activities. The transparency masters are available as a printed package and as files downloadable from the *Foundations First* Web site.

Online Resources

- **The *Foundations First Web site*** <www.bedfordstmartins.com/foundationsfirst> offers downloadable forms (including all the transparency masters); a PowerPoint presentation that instructors can customize for the classroom; links to other useful materials; and a link to Exercise Central.
- **Exercise Central,** the largest collection of grammar exercises available with any writing text, includes multiple exercise sets on every grammar topic that give students all the practice they need. Exercise Central can be accessed via the *Foundations First* Web site.

Acknowledgments

In our work on *Foundations First,* we have benefited from the help of a great many people.

Franklin E. Horowitz of Teachers College, Columbia University, drafted an early version of Chapter 21, "Grammar and Usage Issues for ESL Writers," and his linguist's insight continues to inform that chapter. Linda Stine of Lincoln University devoted energy and vision to the preparation of *Classroom Resources for Instructors Using* FOUNDATIONS FIRST. Linda Mason Austin of McLennan Community College drew on her extensive teaching experience to contribute teaching tips and ESL tips to the *Instructor's Annotated Edition.* Susan Bernstein's work on the compilation and annotation of *Teaching Developmental Writing: Background Readings* reflects her deep commitment to scholarship and teaching. We are very grateful for their contributions.

We thank Kristen Blanco, Stephanie Hopkins, Judith Lechner, and Carolyn Lengel for their contributions to the exercises and writing activities in the text, and Linda Stine for developing the PowerPoint presentation featured on the *Foundations First* Web site.

Foundations First could not exist without our students, whose words appear on almost every page of the book, whether in sample sentences, paragraphs, and essays, or as Student Voices. Our thanks go to Jessi Allender, Trina Andras, Theresa Armetta, Joellen Baird, Kristin Barnett, Becky Bentzel, Shaun Berry, Heather Blaine, Jen Borowski, Miriam Bravo, Kevin Cao, Margaret Caracappa, Iris Colon, Din Ngoc Dang, Cynthia

Dankanis, Hector de la Paz, Megan Diamond, Melissa Donnell, Lenny Fox, Erin Franks, Ashley Johns, Carmen Johnson, Alana Krakov, Lisa Liebman, George Lin, Krishna Mahajan, Joe McVay, Brigid Mitchell, Victoria Nasid, Chuck Newman, John Palcza, Frank Palmer, Mike Paparone, Amit Parmar, Nirav Patel, Agaja Reddy, Rachel Reilly, Julia Reyes, Pete Rubbo, Stacie Sasinowsky, Haley Sav, Vanessa Scully, Geraldine Smith, Ben Stein, Cheng Tang, Amanda Thomas, Trui Trong, Nicole Walsh, Molly Ward, David Weaver, Delaine Weaver, Forrest Williams, Lisa Wy, Vanessa Young, and Mike Zink.

Instructors throughout the country have contributed suggestions and encouragement at various stages of the book's development. For their collegial support, we thank Jessica Carroll, Miami-Dade Community College; Reginald Gerlica, Henry Ford Community College; Thomas Halverson, Edmonds Community College; Stephen Holland, Muscatine Community College; Dennis Keen, Spokane Community College; Miriam Markus, Broward Community College; Marie Nigro, Lincoln University; Michael Ritterbrown, Glendale College; Linda Robinett, Oklahoma City Community College; Margaret Sokolik, University of California, Berkeley; and Teresa Ward, Butte College.

At Bedford/St. Martin's, we thank Chuck Christensen, president of Bedford/St. Martin's, and Joan Feinberg, editorial director, who believed in this project and gave us support and encouragement from the outset. We thank Nancy Perry, editor in chief and our longtime friend, who continues to earn our respect as well as our affection. We also thank Sara Billard and Nicholas Wolven, editorial assistants, for helping with numerous tasks, big and small; Erica Appel, managing editor, and Shuli Traub, senior project editor, for guiding the book ably through production; and Lucy Krikorian, art director, for once again overseeing a beautiful and innovative design. Thanks also go to Dennis Conroy, senior production supervisor; Karen Melton, director of marketing; and Brian Wheel, marketing manager. Finally, we thank our editor, Talvi Laev, whose attention to detail and commitment to our book simply astound us. She is truly one of a kind, and we consider ourselves lucky to have worked with her.

We are grateful, too, for the continued support of our families—Mark, Adam, and Rebecca Kirszner, and Demi, David, and Sarah Mandell. Finally, we are grateful for the survival and growth of the writing partnership we entered into in 1975, when we were graduate students. We had no idea then of the wonderful places our collaborative efforts would take us. Now, we know.

Laurie G. Kirszner
Stephen R. Mandell

Contents

A Student's Guide to Using Foundations First

What *Foundations First* Can Do for You

It's no secret that writing is essential in most of the courses you will take in college. Whether you write a lab report or an English paper, a midterm or a final, your ability to organize your ideas and express them in writing will affect how well you do. In other words, succeeding at writing is the first step toward succeeding in college. Even more important, writing is a key to success outside the classroom. On the job and in everyday life, if you can express yourself clearly and effectively, you will stand a better chance of achieving your goals and influencing the world around you.

Whether you write as a student, as an employee, as a parent, or as a concerned citizen, your writing almost always has a specific purpose. When you write an essay, a memo, a letter, or a research paper, you are writing not just to complete an exercise but to give other people information or to tell them your ideas or opinions. That is why, in this book, we don't ask you simply to do grammar exercises and fill in blanks; in each chapter, we also ask you to apply the skills you are learning to a piece of your own writing.

As teachers—and former students—we know how demanding college can be and how hard it is to juggle assignments with work and family responsibilities. We also know that you don't want to waste your time or money. That is why in *Foundations First* we make information easy to find and use and provide many different features to help you become a better writer.

The following sections describe the key features of *Foundations First*. If you take the time now to familiarize yourself with these features, you will be able to use the book more effectively later on.

How *Foundations First* Makes Information Easy to Find and Use

Brief table of contents Inside the front cover is a brief table of contents that summarizes the topics covered in this book. The brief contents can help you find a particular chapter quickly.

Detailed table of contents The table of contents that starts on page xi provides a detailed breakdown of the book's topics. Use this table of contents to find a specific part of a particular chapter.

Index The index, which appears at the back of the book starting on page 519, lets you find all the available information about a particular topic. The topics appear in alphabetical order, so, for example, if you wanted to find out how to use commas, you would find the *C* section and look up the word *comma*. (If the page number following a word is **boldfaced,** then on that page you can find a definition of the word.)

List of Self-Assessment Checklists On page xxvi is a list of checklists designed to help you write, revise, and edit paragraphs and even essays. Use this list to find the checklist that is most useful for the particular writing task you are working on.

A handy cross-referencing system Often, an *italicized* ***marginal cross-reference*** will point you to another section of the book (for example, "See 2C"). At the tops of most pages of *Foundations First,* you'll find ***quick-reference corner tabs*** consisting of green-and-blue boxes, each containing a number and a letter. This information tells you which chapter you have turned to and which section of that chapter you are looking at. Together, the cross-references and the tabs help you find information quickly. For example, if a note in the text suggested, "For more on topic sentences, see 3A," you could use the tabs to quickly locate section 3A.

34 **2 C**

WRITING EFFECTIVE PARAGRAPHS

For more on topic sentences, see 3A.

Understanding Paragraph Structure

A **paragraph** is a group of related sentences. A paragraph usually begins with a **topic sentence**, a single sentence that states the paragraph's main idea. This first sentence is **indented,** written or typed about one-half inch (five spaces) from the left margin. The other sentences in the paragraph provide **support** for this main idea: explanations, reasons, description, examples, and so on. (Often, a paragraph ends with a final sentence that acts as a conclusion.) A paragraph looks like this:

How *Foundations First* Can Help You Become a Better Writer

Preview boxes Each chapter starts with a list of key concepts that will be discussed in the chapter. Looking at these boxes before you skim the chapter will help you get an overview of the material that will be covered.

Seeing and Writing activities Most chapters include a two-part writing activity that helps you apply specific skills to your own writing. Each chapter starts with a ***Seeing and Writing*** exercise that asks you to write about a particular topic. Later, a ***Revising and Editing*** exercise guides you in fine-tuning your writing.

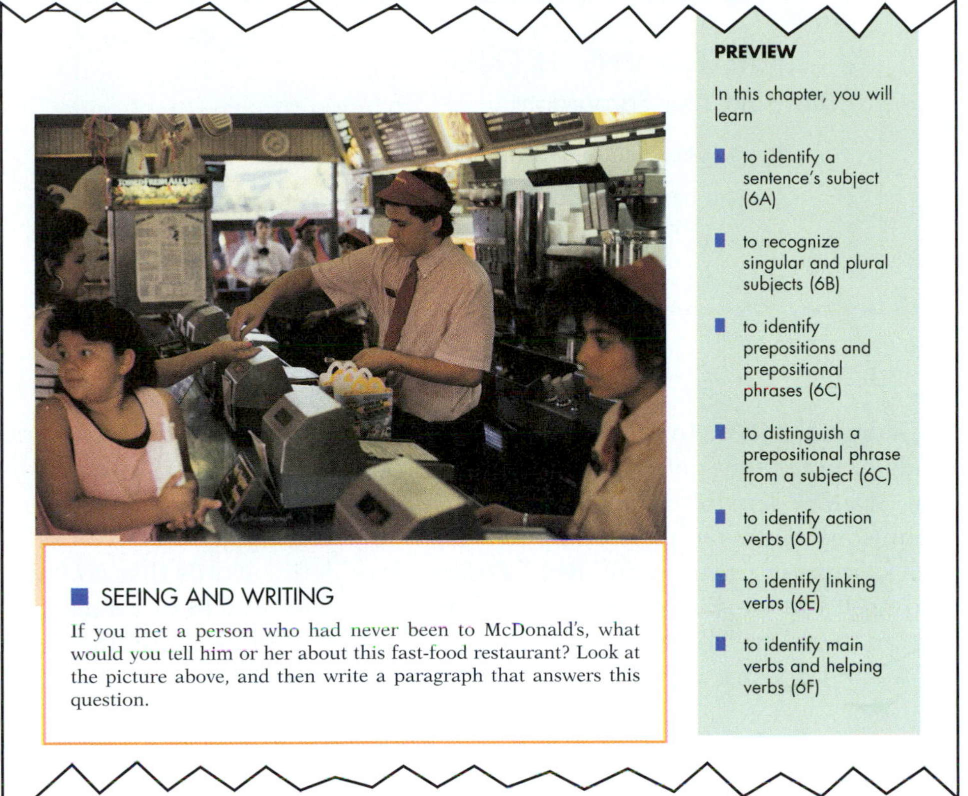

PREVIEW

In this chapter, you will learn

- to identify a sentence's subject (6A)
- to recognize singular and plural subjects (6B)
- to identify prepositions and prepositional phrases (6C)
- to distinguish a prepositional phrase from a subject (6C)
- to identify action verbs (6D)
- to identify linking verbs (6E)
- to identify main verbs and helping verbs (6F)

■ SEEING AND WRITING

If you met a person who had never been to McDonald's, what would you tell him or her about this fast-food restaurant? Look at the picture above, and then write a paragraph that answers this question.

Focus boxes Throughout the book, boxes with the word *Focus* in a red banner highlight useful information, identify key points, and explain difficult concepts.

FOCUS Identifying Sentence Fragments

In paragraphs and longer pieces of writing, sentence fragments sometimes appear next to complete sentences. You can often correct a sentence fragment by attaching it to a nearby sentence that includes the missing subject or verb. Here, a fragment appears right after a complete sentence.

COMPLETE SENTENCE / FRAGMENT

Okera majored in two subjects. English and philosophy.

To correct the fragment, simply attach it to the complete sentence that contains the missing subject (*Okera*) and verb (*majored*).

Okera majored in two subjects, English and philosophy.

Self-Assessment Checklists Chapters 2, 4, and 5 include Self-Assessment Checklists that give you a handy way to check your work and measure your progress. Use these checklists to revise your writing before you hand it in.

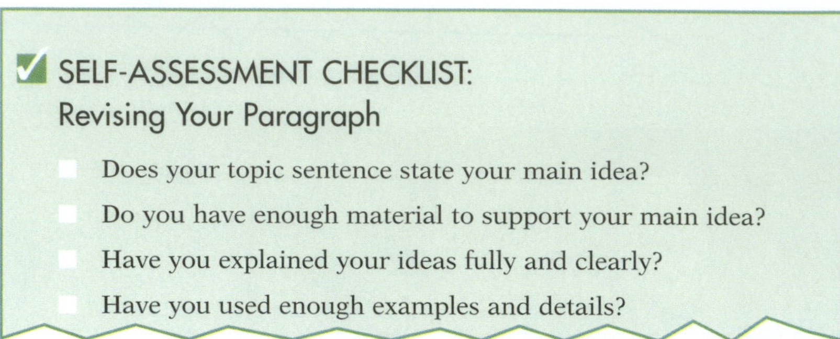

SELF-ASSESSMENT CHECKLIST:
Revising Your Paragraph

- Does your topic sentence state your main idea?
- Do you have enough material to support your main idea?
- Have you explained your ideas fully and clearly?
- Have you used enough examples and details?

Marginal notes In the margins of *Foundations First,* you'll find several kinds of notes that give you additional information in an easy-to-read format. ***Writing Tips*** offer practical information and helpful hints, including definitions and examples. ***Computer Tips*** help you make effective use of your computer as you write. ***Word Power*** boxes define words that you may find useful in working with a particular writing assignment or reading selection. ***Student Voices*** present the words of real students telling what works and doesn't work for them when they write.

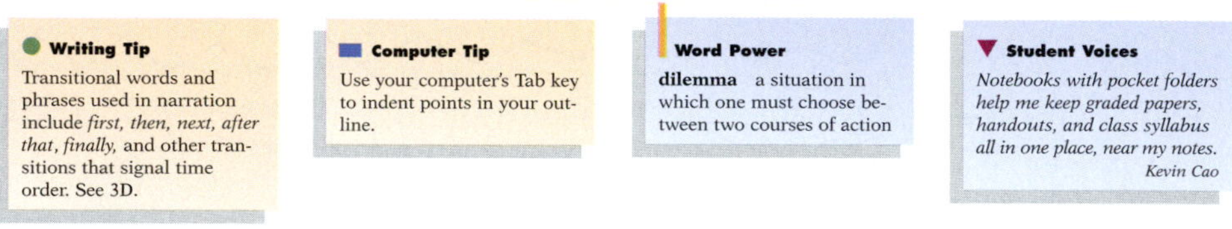

Writing Tip
Transitional words and phrases used in narration include *first, then, next, after that, finally,* and other transitions that signal time order. See 3D.

Computer Tip
Use your computer's Tab key to indent points in your outline.

Word Power
dilemma a situation in which one must choose between two courses of action

Student Voices
Notebooks with pocket folders help me keep graded papers, handouts, and class syllabus all in one place, near my notes.
Kevin Cao

Review Checklists Each chapter ends with a summary of the most important information in the chapter. Use these checklists to review material for quizzes or to remind yourself of the main points in the chapter you've been studying.

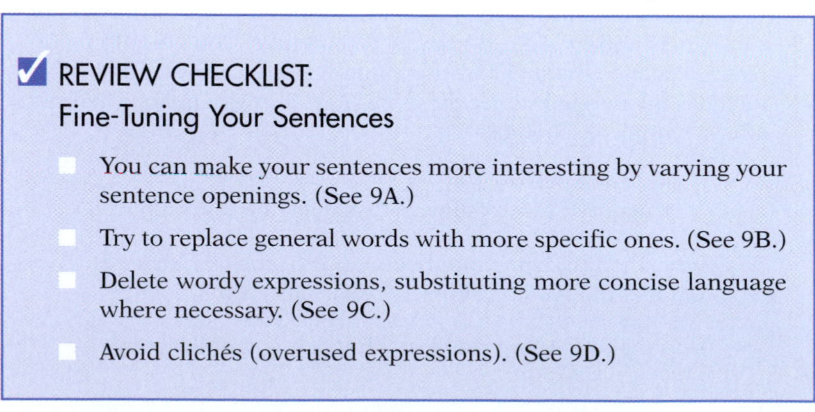

REVIEW CHECKLIST:
Fine-Tuning Your Sentences

- You can make your sentences more interesting by varying your sentence openings. (See 9A.)
- Try to replace general words with more specific ones. (See 9B.)
- Delete wordy expressions, substituting more concise language where necessary. (See 9C.)
- Avoid clichés (overused expressions). (See 9D.)

Answers to Odd-Numbered Exercises Starting on page 505, you'll find answers for some of the Practice items in the book. When you need to study a topic independently, or when your instructor has you complete a Practice but not hand it in, you can consult these answers to see if you're on the right track.

How *Foundations First* Can Help You Succeed in Other Courses

In a sense, this whole book is all about succeeding in other courses. After all, as we said earlier, writing is the key to success in college. But *Foundations First* also includes sections that you may find especially useful in courses you take later on in college. We have designed these sections so you can use them either on your own or with your instructor's help.

Chapter 1, "Strategies for College Success" Here you'll find tips for making your semester (and your writing course) as successful as possible. Included are effective strategies for taking notes, completing homework assignments, doing well on exams, and managing your time efficiently. A section on Internet strategies shows you how to find and evaluate Web sources—a skill that will be useful in all your courses.

Appendix A, "Building Word Power" This practical guide tells you how to get the most out of your dictionary. It also offers tips for building your vocabulary and gives you opportunities to practice using the words you've encountered in the Word Power boxes.

We hope *Foundations First* will help you become a better writer and student. If you have suggestions for improving this book, please send them to: Laurie Kirszner and Stephen Mandell, c/o Bedford/St. Martin's, 33 Irving Place, New York, NY 10003.

Self-Assessment Checklists for Improving Your Writing

Unit One of *Foundations First* includes a series of Self-Assessment Checklists to help you write, revise, and edit paragraphs and essays. You can use these checklists in your writing course and in other courses that include written assignments. The page number for each checklist is included here.

CHAPTER

1

Strategies for College Success

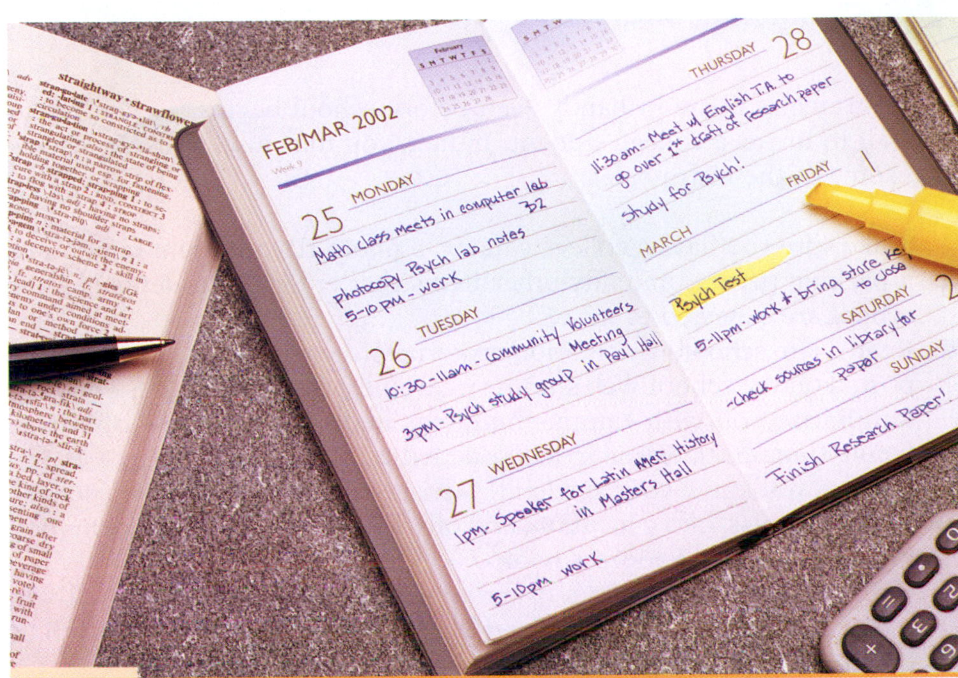

PREVIEW

In this chapter, you will learn

- orientation strategies (1A)
- first-week strategies (1B)
- day-to-day strategies (1C)
- note-taking strategies (1D)
- homework strategies (1E)
- exam-taking strategies (1F)
- time-management strategies (1G)
- Internet strategies (1H)

SEEING AND WRITING

How do you manage to fit everything you need to do into the limited time you have? Look at the picture above, and then write a few sentences that answer this question.

By deciding to go to college, you have decided to make some important changes in your life. In the long run, you will find that the changes will be positive, but there will be some challenges as well. One way in which your life will change is that now, perhaps more than ever, you will find yourself short of time. Life will become a balancing act as you juggle classroom time, commuting time, work time, and study time, along with family responsibilities and time for yourself. The strategies discussed in this chapter can help make your life as a college student less stressful and more productive.

◆ PRACTICE 1.1

List the number of hours per day that you expect to spend on each of the following activities while you are a college student: reading, attending class, sleeping, working at a job, fulfilling family commitments, relaxing, commuting, studying. (Be sure you have a total of twenty-four hours.) When you have finished your list, trade lists with another student, and compare your daily activities. Should any other activities be added? If so, from which activities will you subtract time?

Word Power

orientation adjustment to a new environment

orient to adjust

▼ **Student Voices**

Stay away from tables that offer free credit cards!

Megan Diamond

A Orientation Strategies

Some strategies come in handy even before school begins, as you orient yourself to life as a college student. In fact, you may already have discovered some of these strategies.

- Make sure you have a college catalog, a photo ID, a student handbook, a parking permit, and any other items that entering students at your school are expected to have.
- Read your school's orientation materials (distributed as handouts or posted on the school Web site) very carefully. These materials will help familiarize you with campus buildings and offices, course offerings, faculty members, extracurricular activities, and so on.
- Be sure you know your academic adviser's name (and how to spell it), e-mail address, office location, and office hours. Copy this information into your personal address book.
- Get a copy of the library's orientation materials. These will tell you about the library's hours and services and explain procedures such as how to use an online catalog.
- Be sure you know where things are—not just how to find the library and the parking lot, but also where you can do photocopying or buy a newspaper. You might as well learn to find your way around before things get too hectic.

◆ PRACTICE 1.2

Visit your school's Web site. List the three most useful pieces of information you find there. Now, compare your list with those of other students in your class. Did reading their lists lead you to reevaluate your own? Do you still think the three items you listed are the most useful?

1. ______________________________

2. ______________________________

3. ______________________________

◆ PRACTICE 1.3

Working in a group of three or four students, draw a rough map of your school's campus, including the general locations of the following: the library, the financial aid office, the registrar's office, the cashier, the cafeteria, the bookstore, the computer lab, the campus police, the student health office. Now, make up a quiz for another group of students, asking them to locate three additional buildings or offices on their map.

B First-Week Strategies

College can seem like a confusing place at first, but from your first day as a college student, there are steps you can take to help you get your bearings.

1. ***Make yourself at home***. Find places on campus where you can get something to eat or drink, and find a good place to study or relax before or between classes. As you explore the campus, try to locate all the things you need to feel comfortable—for example, pay phones, ATMs, and rest rooms.
2. ***Know where you're going and when you need to be there***. Check the building and room number for each of your classes and the days and hours the class meets. Copy this information onto the front cover of the appropriate notebook. Pay particular attention to classes with irregular schedules (for example, a class that meets from 9 a.m. to 10 a.m. on Tuesdays but from 11 a.m. to 12 noon on Thursdays).
3. ***Get to know your fellow students***. Get the name, phone number, and e-mail address of two students in each of your classes. If you miss class, you will need to get in touch with someone to find out what material you missed.
4. ***Familiarize yourself with each course's syllabus***. At the first meeting of every course, your instructor will hand out a **syllabus**. (The syllabus may also be posted on the course's Web page.) A syllabus gives you three kinds of useful information.

   - Information that can help you plan a study schedule—for example, when assignments are due and when exams are scheduled
   - Practical information, such as the instructor's office number and e-mail address and what books and supplies to buy
   - Information about the instructor's policies on absences, grading, class participation, and so on

   Read each syllabus carefully, ask questions about anything you don't understand, refer to all your course syllabi regularly—and don't lose them.
5. ***Buy books and supplies with care***. When you buy your books and supplies, be sure to keep the receipts, and don't write your name in your books until you are certain that you are not going to drop a course. (If you write in a book, you will not be able to return it.) In fact, if your roster of courses is not definite, you should wait a few days to buy your texts. You should, however, buy some items right away: a separate notebook and folder for each course you are taking, a college dictionary, and a pocket organizer (see 1G). In addition to the books and other items required for a particular course (for example, a lab notebook, a programmable calculator, art supplies), you should buy pens and pencils in different colors, blank computer disks, paper clips or a stapler,

Student Voices

I'm not a morning person, so I try not to take 8 o'clock classes.

Joe McVay

Word Power

syllabus an outline or summary of a course's main points (the plural form is *syllabi*)

Student Voices

I check out each of my classes before I buy my books, to make sure I want to stay in the class.

Kristin Barnett

Post-it notes, highlighter pens, and so on. (Don't forget to buy a backpack or bookbag in which to keep all these items!)

▼ Student Voices

I like using an online dictionary because I don't have to leave the computer to find out what a word means.

Amit Parmar

FOCUS Using a Dictionary

Don't think that you do not have to buy a dictionary just because you use a spell checker. A college dictionary tells you not only how to spell words but also what words mean and how to use them.

For more on using a dictionary, see Appendix A.

6. ***Set up your notebooks***. Establish a separate notebook (or a separate section of a divided notebook) for each of your classes. Copy your instructor's name, e-mail address, phone number, and office hours and location into the inside front cover of the notebook; write your own name, address, and phone number on the outside.

▼ Student Voices

Notebooks with pocket folders help me keep graded papers, handouts, and class syllabus all in one place, near my notes.

Kevin Cao

◆ PRACTICE 1.4

Set up a notebook for each course you are taking. Now, exchange notebooks with another student, and review each other's work.

C Day-to-Day Strategies

As you get busier and busier, you may find that it's hard to keep everything under control. Here are some strategies to help you as you move through the semester.

1. ***Find a place to study***. As a college student, you will need your own private place to work and study. Even if it's just a desk in one corner of your dorm room (or, if you are living at home, in one corner of your bedroom or at the back of your garage), you will need a place that is yours alone, a place that will be undisturbed when you leave it. (The kitchen table, which you share with roommates or family members, will not work.) This space should include everything you will need to make your work easier—quiet, good lighting, a comfortable chair, a clean work surface, storage for supplies, and so on.
2. ***Set up a bookshelf***. Keep your textbooks, dictionary, calculator, supplies, and everything else you use regularly for your coursework in one place—ideally, in your own work space. That way, when you need something, you will know exactly where it is.
3. ***Set up a study schedule***. Identify thirty- to forty-five-minute blocks of free time before, between, and after classes. Set this time aside for review. Remember, studying should be part of your regular routine, not something you do only the night before an exam.
4. ***Establish priorities***. It's very important to understand what your priorities are. Before you can establish priorities, however, you have to know which assignments are due first, which ones can be done in

Word Power

priorities things that deserve extra attention

FOCUS Skills Check

Don't wait until you have a paper to write to discover that you don't know how to use a computer well enough. Be sure your basic word-processing skills are at the level you need for your work. If you need help, get it right away.

Computer Tip

Your school's computer lab should be the first place you turn for help with word processing, but writing lab and library staff members may also be able to help you.

steps, and which tasks or steps will be most time consuming. Then, you must decide which tasks are most pressing. For example, studying for a test to be given the next day is more pressing than reviewing notes for a test scheduled for the following week. Finally, you have to decide which tasks are more important than others. For example, studying for a midterm is more important than studying for a quiz, and the midterm for a course you are in danger of failing is more important than the midterm for a course in which you are doing well. Remember, you can't do everything at once; you need to know what must be done immediately and what can wait.

5. ***Check your mail***. If you have a campus mailbox or e-mail account, check it regularly—if possible, several times a day. If you miss a message, you may miss important information about changes in assignments, canceled classes, or rescheduled quizzes.
6. ***Schedule conferences***. Try to meet with each of your instructors during the semester even if you are not required to do so. You might schedule one conference during the second or third week of school and another a week or two before a major exam or paper is due. Your instructors will appreciate and respect your initiative.
7. ***Become familiar with the student services available on your campus***. College is hard work, and you can't do everything on your own. There is nothing shameful about getting help from your school's writing lab or tutoring center or from the center for disabled students (which serves students with learning disabilities as well as physical challenges), the office of international students, or the counseling center, as well as from your adviser or course instructors. Think of yourself as a consumer. You are paying for your education, and you are entitled to—and should take advantage of—all the services available to students.

FOCUS Asking for Help

Despite all your careful planning, you may still run into trouble. For example, you may miss an exam and have to make it up; you may miss several days of classes in a row and fall behind in your work; you may have trouble understanding the material in one of your courses; or a family member may get sick. Don't wait until you are overwhelmed to ask for help. If you have an ongoing personal problem or a family emergency, let your instructors know immediately.

◆ PRACTICE 1.5

Try to figure out how and when you study best. Do you do your best studying in the morning or late at night? In complete silence or in a busy library? When you have answered these questions, set up a weekly study schedule. Begin by identifying your free time and deciding how you can use it most efficiently. Next, discuss your schedule with a group of three or four other students. How much time does each of you have available? How much time do you think you need? Does the group consider each student's study schedule to be realistic? If so, why? If not, why not?

D Note-Taking Strategies

Learning to take notes in a college class takes practice, but taking good notes is essential for success in college. Here are some basic guidelines that will help you develop and improve your note-taking skills.

During Class

1. ***Come to class***. If you miss class, you miss notes—so come to class, and come on time. In class, sit where you can see the board and hear the instructor. Don't feel you have to keep sitting in the same place in each class every day; change your seat until you find a spot that's comfortable for you.

> **FOCUS Classroom Behavior**
>
> College instructors know their students are adults, and they expect them to behave like adults. Instructors expect you to pay attention, look alert (and stay awake!), and listen politely (and without interrupting) when classmates speak. They also expect you not to talk among yourselves, not to make unnecessary noise (for example, rustling papers or dropping books), and not to eat or drink in class. In addition, they expect you to turn off cell phones and pagers. Finally, instructors expect you to bring the appropriate books and supplies to class and to come to class prepared to discuss the assigned reading. In short, college instructors expect students to come to class ready to learn.

2. ***Date your notes***. Begin each class by writing the date at the top of the page. Instructors frequently identify material that will be on a test by dates. If you do not date your notes, you may not know what to study.
3. ***Know what to write down***. You can't possibly write down everything an instructor says. If you try, you will miss a lot of important information. Listen carefully *before* you write, and listen for cues to what's important.

For example, sometimes the instructor will tell you that something is important, or that a particular piece of information will be on a test. Sometimes he or she will write key terms and concepts on the board. If the instructor emphasizes an idea or underlines it on the board, you should do the same in your notes. Of course, if you have done the assigned reading before class, you will recognize important topics and know to take especially careful notes when these topics are introduced in class.

4. ***Include examples.*** Try to write down an example for each general concept introduced in class—something that will help you remember what the instructor was talking about. (If you don't have time to include examples as you take notes during class, add them when you review your notes.) For instance, if your world history instructor is explaining *nationalism,* you should write down not only a definition but also an example, such as "Germany in 1848."
5. ***Write legibly, and use helpful signals.*** Use dark (blue or black) ink for your note-taking, but keep a red or green pen handy to highlight important information, jot down announcements (such as a change in a test date), note gaps in your notes, or question confusing points.
6. ***Ask questions.*** If you do not hear (or do not understand) something your instructor said, or if you need an example to help you understand something, *ask!* But don't immediately turn to another student for clarification. Instead, wait to see if the instructor explains further, or if he or she pauses to ask if anyone has a question. If you're not comfortable asking a question during class, make a note of the question and ask the instructor—or send an e-mail—after class.

After Class

1. ***Review your notes.*** After every class, try to spend ten or fifteen minutes rereading your notes, filling in gaps and examples while the material is still fresh in your mind.
2. ***Recopy information.*** When you have a break between classes, or when you get home, recopy important pieces of information from your notes.

   - Copy announcements (such as quiz dates) onto your calendar.
   - Copy reminders (for example, a note to schedule a conference before your next paper is due) into your organizer.
   - Copy questions you have to ask the instructor onto the top of the next blank page in your notes.

> **Student Voices**
> *I recopy all my notes after every class. Writing things down is how I learn.*
> *Delaine Weaver*

> **Student Voices**
> *After each class, I give the day's notes a title so I can remember the topic of each class. This helps me find information when I study.*
> *Lisa Liebman*

Before the Next Class

1. ***Reread your notes.*** Leave time to skim the previous class's notes once more just before each class. This strategy will get you oriented for the class to come and will remind you of anything that needs clarification or further explanation.
2. ***Ask for help.*** Call a classmate if you need to fill in missing information; if you still need help, see the instructor during his or her office hours, or come to class early so you can ask your question before class begins.

◆ PRACTICE 1.6

Compare the notes you took in one of your classes with notes taken by another student in the same class. How are your notes different? Do you think you need to make any changes in the way you take notes?

E Homework Strategies

Doing homework is an important part of learning in college. Homework gives you a chance to practice your skills and measure your progress. If you are having trouble with the homework, chances are you are having trouble with the course. Ask the instructor or teaching assistant for help *now;* don't wait until the day before the exam. Here are some tips for getting the most out of your homework.

1. ***Write down the assignment***. Don't expect to remember an assignment; copy it down. If you are not sure exactly what you are supposed to do, check with your instructor or another student.
2. ***Do your homework, and do it on time***. It is easy to fall behind in college, and trying to do three—or five—nights' worth of homework in one night is not a good idea. Teachers assign homework to reinforce classwork, and they expect homework to be done on a regular basis. If you do several assignments at once, you not only overload yourself, you also miss important day-to-day connections with classwork.
3. ***Be an active reader***. Get into the habit of highlighting your textbooks and other material as you read. (See Chapter 27 for specific strategies for active reading.)
4. ***Join study groups***. A study group of three or four students can be a valuable support system for homework as well as for exams. If your schedule permits, do some homework assignments—or at least review your homework—with other students on a regular basis. In addition to learning information, you will learn different strategies for doing assignments.

◆ PRACTICE 1.7

Working in a group of three or four students, brainstorm about how a study group might benefit you. How many students should be in the group? How often should they meet? Should the group include students whose study habits are similar or different? What kind of help would you need? What kind of help could you offer to other students?

F Exam-Taking Strategies

Preparation for an exam should begin well before the exam is announced. In a sense, you begin this preparation on the first day of class.

Before the Exam

1. ***Attend every class***. Regular attendance in class—where you can listen, ask questions, and take notes—is the best possible preparation for exams. If you do have to miss a class, arrange to copy (and read) another student's notes *before the next class* so you will be able to follow the discussion.
2. ***Keep up with the reading***. Read every assignment, and read it before the class in which it will be discussed. If you don't, you may have trouble understanding what is going on in class.
3. ***Take careful notes***. Take careful, thorough notes, but be selective. If you can, compare your notes on a regular basis with those of other students in the class; working together, you can fill in gaps or correct errors. Establishing a buddy system will also force you to review your notes regularly instead of just on the night before the exam.
4. ***Study on your own***. When an exam is announced, adjust your study schedule—and your priorities—so you have time to review everything. (This is especially important if you have more than one exam in a short period of time.) Review all your material (class notes, readings, and so on), and then review it again. Make a note of anything you don't understand, and keep track of topics you need to review. Try to predict the most likely questions, and—if you have time—practice answering them.
5. ***Study with a group***. If you can set up a study group, you should certainly do so. Studying with others can help you understand the material better. However, don't come to group sessions unprepared and expect to get everything from the other students. You must first study on your own.
6. ***Make an appointment with your instructor***. Set up an appointment with the instructor or with the course's teaching assistant a few days before the exam. Bring to this conference any specific questions you have about course content and about the format of the upcoming exam. (Be sure to review all your study material before the conference.)
7. ***Review the material one last time***. The night before the exam is not the time to begin your studying; it is the time to review. When you have finished your review, get a good night's sleep.

During the Exam

Like an athlete before a big game or a musician before an important concert, you will already have done all you could to get ready for the test by the time you walk into the exam room. Your goal now is to keep the momentum going and not do anything to undermine all your hard work.

1. ***Read through the entire exam***. Be sure you understand how much time you have, how many points each question is worth, and exactly what each question is asking you to do. Many exam questions call for just a short answer—*yes* or *no, true* or *false*. Others ask you to fill in a blank with a few words, and still others require you to select the best answer from among several choices. If you are not absolutely certain what kind of answer a particular question calls for, ask the instructor or the proctor *before* you begin to write. (Remember, on some tests

there is no penalty for guessing, but on other tests it is best to answer only those questions you have time to read and consider carefully.)

FOCUS Writing Essay Exams

If you are asked to write an essay on an exam, remember that what you are really being asked to do is write a **thesis-and-support essay**. Chapter 5 of this text will tell you how to do this.

2. ***Budget your time***. Once you understand how much each section of the exam and each question are worth, plan your time and set your priorities, devoting the most time to the most important questions. If you know you tend to rush through exams, or if you find you often run out of time before you get to the end of a test, you might try putting a mark on your paper when about one-third of the allotted time has passed (for a one-hour exam, put a mark on your paper after twenty minutes) to make sure you are pacing yourself appropriately.
3. ***Reread each question***. Carefully reread each question *before* you start to answer it. Underline the **key words**—the words that give specific information about how to approach the question and how to phrase your answer.

FOCUS Key Words

Here are some helpful key words to look for on exams.

analyze	explain	suggest results, effects, outcomes
argue	give examples	summarize
compare	identify	support
contrast	illustrate	take a stand
define	recount	trace
demonstrate	suggest causes, origins, contributing factors	
describe		
evaluate		

Remember, even if everything you write is correct, your response is not acceptable if you don't answer the question. If a question asks you to *compare* two novels, writing a *summary* of one of them will not be acceptable.

For more on brainstorming, see 2B.

4. ***Brainstorm to help yourself recall the material***. If you are writing a paragraph or an essay, look frequently at the question as you brainstorm. (You can write your brainstorming notes on the inside cover of the exam book.) Quickly write down all the relevant points you can think of—what the textbook had to say, your instructor's comments,

and so on. The more you can think of now, the more you will have to choose from when you write your answer.

5. ***Write down the main idea***. Looking closely at the way the question is worded and at your brainstorming notes, write a sentence that states the main idea of your answer. If you are writing a paragraph, this sentence will be your topic sentence; if you are writing an essay, it will be your thesis statement.

For more on topic sentences, see 3A. For more on thesis statements, see 5D.

6. ***List your main points***. You don't want to waste your limited (and valuable) time writing a detailed outline, but an informal outline that lists just your key points is worth the little time it takes. An informal outline will help you plan a clear direction for your paragraph or essay.
7. ***Draft your answer***. You will spend most of your time actually writing the answers to the questions on the exam. Follow your outline, keep track of time, and consult your brainstorming notes when you need to—but stay focused on your writing.
8. ***Reread, revise, and edit***. When you have finished drafting your answer, reread it carefully to make sure it says everything you want it to say—and that it answers the question.

G Time-Management Strategies

Learning to manage your time is very important for success in college. Here are some strategies you can adopt to make this task easier.

1. ***Use an organizer***. Whether you prefer a print organizer or an electronic one, you should certainly use one—and use it *consistently*. If you are most comfortable with paper and pencil, purchase a "week-on-two-pages" academic year organizer (one that begins in September, not January); the "week-on-two-pages" format (see p. 12) gives you more writing room for Monday through Friday than for the weekend, and it also lets you view an entire week at once.

   Carry your organizer with you at all times. At the beginning of the semester, copy down key pieces of information from your course syllabi—for example, the date of every quiz and exam and the due date of every paper. As the semester progresses, continue to write in assignments and deadlines. Also, enter information such as days when a class will be canceled or will meet in the computer lab or in the library, reminders to bring a particular book or piece of equipment to class, and appointments with instructors or other college personnel. You can also jot down reminders and schedule appointments that are not related to school—for example, changes in your work hours, a dentist appointment, or lunch with a friend. (In addition to writing notes on the pages for each date, some students like to keep a separate month-by-month "to do" list; crossing out completed items can give you a feeling of accomplishment—and make the road ahead look shorter.)

   The first sample organizer (p. 12) shows how you can use an organizer to keep track of deadlines, appointments, and reminders. The second sample organizer (p. 12) includes not only this information but also a study schedule, with notes about particular tasks to be done each day.

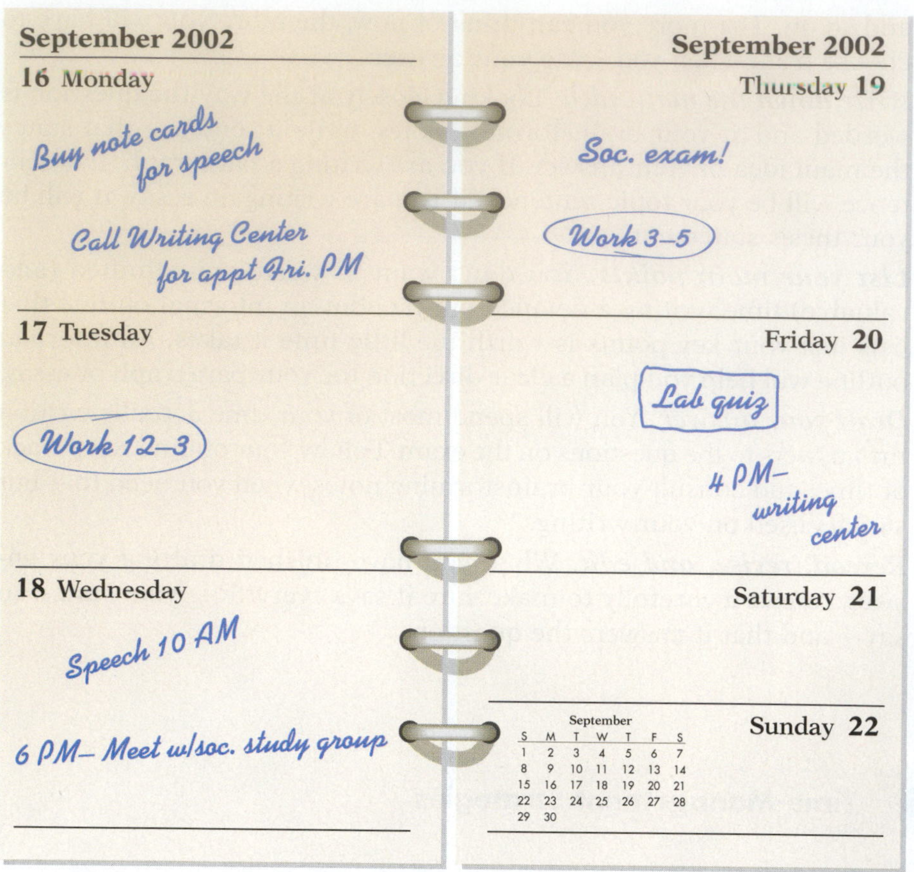

Sample Organizer Page: Deadlines, Appointments, and Reminders Only

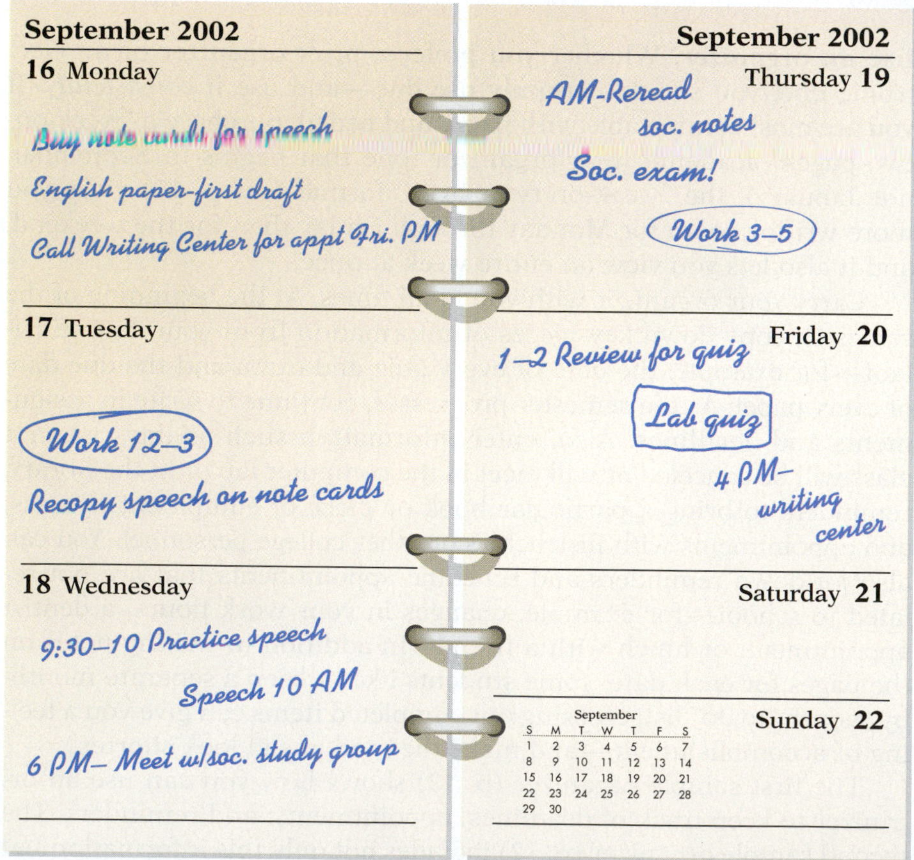

Sample Organizer Page: Deadlines, Appointments, Reminders, and Study Schedule

2. ***Use a calendar***. Buy a large calendar, and post it where you will see it every morning—on your desk, in your car, or on the refrigerator. At the beginning of the semester, fill in important dates such as school holidays, work commitments, exam dates, and due dates for papers and projects. When you get home from school each day, update the calendar with any new information you have entered into your organizer.
3. ***Plan ahead***. If you think you will need help from a writing lab tutor to revise a paper that is due in two weeks, don't wait until day thirteen to make an appointment; all the time slots may be filled by then. To be safe, make an appointment for help about a week in advance.
4. ***Learn to enjoy downtime***. One final—and very important—point to remember is that you are entitled to "waste" a little time. When you have a free minute, take time for yourself—and don't feel guilty about it.

Student Voices

I keep my calendar right next to the hook where I hang my keys and my ID. This forces me to check my calendar every day before I leave home.
Jen Borowski

◆ PRACTICE 1.8

Fill in the blank organizer pages to create a schedule for your coming week. (Enter activities that are related to school as well as those that are not.) Now, trade books with another student, and compare your plans for the week ahead.

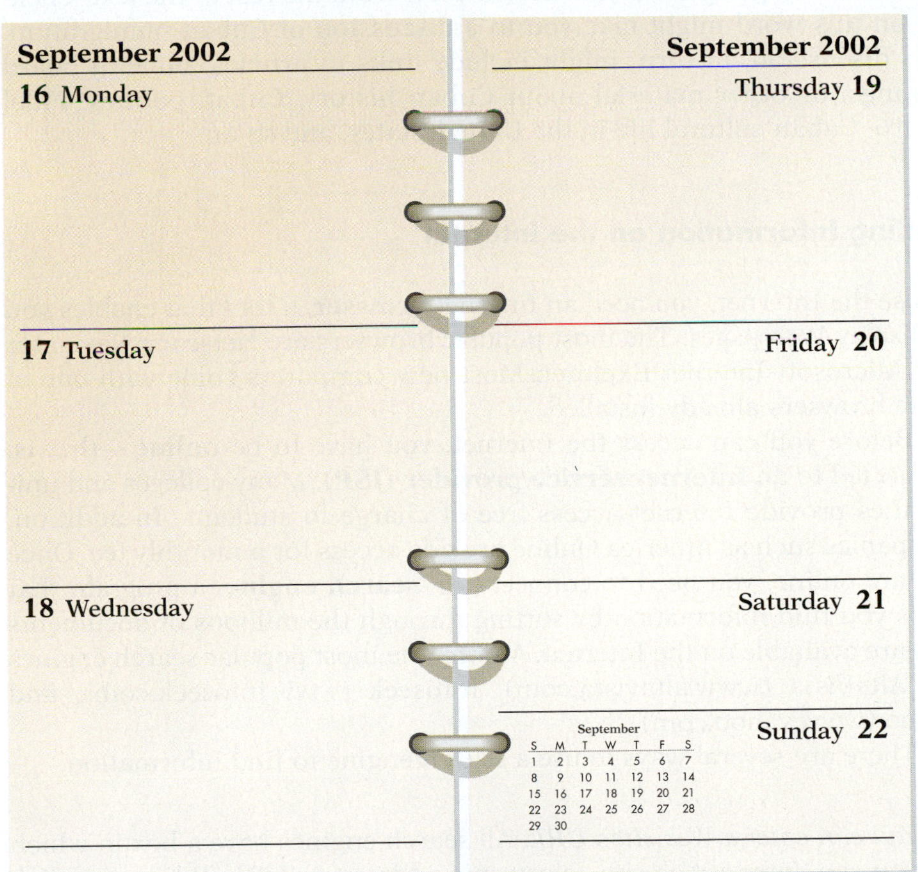

H Internet Strategies

The **Internet** is a network of millions of computers at colleges and universities, government agencies, research institutions, businesses, and libraries all over the world. The Internet can give you access to a world of information—information that can help you in school and in your everyday life. Here are some of the things you can do on the Internet:

- Send and receive messages via e-mail
- Send and receive text files (for example, assignments), graphics, sound, animation, film clips, and live video
- Read articles and other documents about practically any subject, from asteroids to engineering to Zen Buddhism
- Send messages to electronic "bulletin boards" set up for your classes or for other groups, and read messages sent by others

When people refer to the Internet, they often mean the **World Wide Web**. The Web, which forms an important part of the Internet, is a collection of millions of documents on every imaginable topic. The Web relies on **hypertext links**—specially highlighted words and phrases. By clicking your computer's mouse on these links, you can move easily from one part of a document to another, or from one **Web site** (collection of documents) to another.

For example, a Web article discussing immigration might have the word *Cuban* highlighted in a different color from the rest of the text. Clicking on this word might take you to a discussion of Cuban immigration. This discussion, in turn, might include links to articles, bulletin board postings, or other material about Cuban history, Cuban politics, Fidel Castro, Cuban cultural life in the United States, and so on.

Finding Information on the Internet

To use the Internet, you need an Internet **browser**, a tool that enables you to display Web pages. The most popular browsers are Netscape Navigator and Microsoft Internet Explorer. Most new computers come with one of these browsers already installed.

Before you can access the Internet, you have to be **online**—that is, connected to an **Internet service provider (ISP)**. Many colleges and universities provide Internet access free of charge to students. In addition, companies such as America Online provide access for a monthly fee. Once you are online, you need to connect to a **search engine**, a program that helps you find information by sorting through the millions of documents that are available on the Internet. Among the most popular search engines are AltaVista (www.altavista.com), Infoseek (www.infoseek.com), and Yahoo (www.yahoo.com).

There are several ways to use a search engine to find information.

- *You can enter a Web site's URL.* All search engines have a box in which you can enter a Web site's electronic address, or **URL**. When you click on the URL or hit your computer's Enter key, the search engine connects you to the Web site. For example, to find information about family members who entered the United States through Ellis Island, you would enter this URL: *www.ellisislandrecords.com.*
- *You can do a keyword search.* All search engines let you do a **keyword search**: you type a term into a box, and the search engine looks for documents that contain the term, listing all the **hits** (documents con-

taining one or both of these words) that it found. If you type in a broad term like *civil war,* you might get hundreds of thousands of hits—more than you could possibly consider. If this occurs, don't give up. Narrow your search by using a more specific term—*the Battle of Gettysburg,* for example. You can focus your search even further by putting quotation marks around the term (*"Battle of Gettysburg"*). When you do this, the search engine will search only for documents that contain this phrase.

- *You can do a subject search.* Some search engines, such as Yahoo, let you do a **subject search**. First, you choose a broad subject from a list of subjects: The Humanities, The Arts, Entertainment, Business, and so on. Each of these general subjects leads you to more specific subjects, until eventually you get to the subtopic that you want. For example, you could start your search on Yahoo with the general topic Entertainment. Clicking on this topic would lead you to Movies and then to Movie Reviews. Finally, you would get to a list of movie reviews that might link to a review of the specific movie you are interested in.

Computer Tip

It is a good idea to **bookmark** useful sites by selecting the Bookmark or Favorites option at the top of your browser screen. Once you bookmark a site, you can return to it whenever you want.

FOCUS Accessing Web Sites: Troubleshooting

Sometimes, your computer will tell you that a site you want to visit is unavailable or does not exist. When this occurs, consider the following possibilities before moving on to another site.

- *Check to make sure the URL is correct.* To reach a site, you have to type its URL accurately. Do not add spaces between items in the address or put a period at the end. Any error will send you to the wrong site—or to no site at all.
- *Check to make sure you are connected to the Internet.* To reach a site, you have to be connected to the Internet. If you are not properly connected, your computer will indicate this.
- *Check to make sure your computer is connected to your phone line.* A loose connection or an unplugged phone jack will make it impossible for you to access the Internet. If your computer is not connected to a phone line, it will indicate that it is not receiving a dial tone.
- *Check to make sure the site still exists.* Web sites, especially those maintained by individuals, frequently disappear. People either cannot afford to maintain a site or lose interest in doing so. If you entered a URL correctly, your computer is functioning properly, and you still cannot access a site, chances are that the site no longer exists.
- *Try revisiting the site later.* Sometimes Web sites experience technical problems that prevent them from being accessed. Your computer will tell you if a site is temporarily unreachable.

Word Power

skepticism a doubtful or questioning attitude

Evaluating Web Sites

Not every Web site is a valuable source of information. In fact, anyone can put information on the Internet. For this reason, it is a good idea to approach Web sites with skepticism. In a sense, Web sites are like strangers knocking at your door: before you let them in, you need to be sure they are honest and trustworthy. To determine whether information you find on the Internet is believable and useful, you must evaluate the Web site where you found it.

Computer Tip

A Web site's URL can give you information about the site's purpose. For example, the abbreviation *.edu* indicates that the site is sponsored by an educational institution; *.gov* indicates a government agency; *.org* indicates a nonprofit organization; and *.com* indicates a business.

FOCUS Evaluating Web Sites

To decide whether to use information from a particular Web site, ask the following questions:

- *Is the site reliable?* Never rely on information by an unidentified author; always try to determine the author of material on a Web site. Also, try to determine the author's qualifications. For example, say you are looking at a site that discusses Labrador retrievers. Is the author a breeder? A veterinarian? Someone who has had a Lab as a pet? The first two authors would probably be authorities on the subject; the third author might not be.
- *Does the site have a hidden purpose?* When you evaluate a Web site, be sure to consider its purpose. For example, a site discussing the health benefits of herbal medicine would have one purpose if it were sponsored by a university and another if it were sponsored by a company selling herbal remedies. Researchers who post information on a university site are trying to inform others about their findings. Retailers, however, put information online to sell a product; therefore, they sometimes make exaggerated claims about its usefulness.
- *Is the site up-to-date?* If a site has not been recently updated, you should question the information it contains. A discussion of foot-and-mouth disease in England, for example, would be out of date if it were written before the widespread outbreak in 2001. You would have to continue your search until you found a more current discussion.
- *Is the information on the site trustworthy?* A site should include evidence to support what it says. If it does not, consider the information to be unsupported personal opinion. Points are supported with facts, examples, statistics, and expert opinions—not rumors or third-hand opinions.
- *Does the site contain needlessly elaborate graphics?* With Web sites, substance counts more than style. When you come across a site that has slick visuals—animation, bright colors, and lots of pictures—don't be misled. Make sure that these graphic elements do not mask weak logic or uninformed opinion.

Using the Internet to Locate Information for Assignments

You can use the Internet to find information about the subjects you are studying. For example, if in your communication class you were discussing early television situation comedies, you could go to the Internet and find Web sites devoted to this subject. You could also find sites for shows such as *I Love Lucy, The Honeymooners,* and *The Brady Bunch.* The following sites can help you access information that will be useful for many of your courses.

Academic Subjects on the Web

The Humanities

Art history
Art History Resources on the Web
http://witcombe.sbc.edu/ARTHLinks.html

Film
The Internet Movie Database
http://www.imdb.com

History
HyperHistory Online
http://www.hyperhistory.com/online_n2/History_n2/a.html

Literature
The On-Line Books Page
http://digital.library.upenn.edu/books/

Philosophy
Stanford Encyclopedia of Philosophy
http://plato.stanford.edu

The Natural Sciences

Biology
Biodiversity and Biological Collections Web Server
http://biodiversity.uno.edu

Chemistry
WWW Chemistry Resources
http://www.chem.ucla.edu/chempointers.html

Engineering
The Engineer's Reference
http://www.eng-sol.com

Mathematics
Math.com
http://www.math.com

Physics
Web Links: Physics Around the World
http://www.physicsweb.org/resources/

The Social Sciences

Education
Education World®
http://www.education-world.com/

Political science
Political Resources on the Net
http://www.politicalresources.net

Psychology
PsychCrawler
http://www.psychcrawler.com

Sociology and social work
Social Work and Social Services Web Sites
http://gwbweb.wustl.edu/websites.html

FOCUS **Avoiding Plagiarism**

When you transfer information from Web sites into your notes, you may be tempted to "cut and paste" text without noting where the text came from. If you then copy this text into a draft of your paper, you are committing plagiarism—*and plagiarism is the theft of ideas.* Every college has rules that students must follow when using words, ideas, and visuals from books, articles, and Internet sources. Consult your school's Web site or student handbook for information on the appropriate use of such information.

Using the Internet to Improve Your Writing

The Internet has many Web sites that can help you with your writing. Sites like the following ones include links to other useful sites.

Writing Help on the Web

The *Foundations First* site
http://www.bedfordstmartins.com/foundationsfirst

Help with the writing process
Principles of Composition
http://webster.commnet.edu/grammar/composition/composition.stm
The UVic Writer's Guide
http://www.clearcf.uvic.ca/writersguide/Pages/MasterToc.html

Help finding something to say
Paradigm Online Writing Assistant: Choosing a Subject
http://www.powa.org/whtfrms.htm

Help writing paragraphs
Purposes of Paragraphs
http://www.fas.harvard.edu/~wricntr/para.html
Writing Paragraphs
http://www.uottawa.ca/academic/arts/writcent/hypergrammar/paragrph.html

Advice on revision
Paradigm: Global and Local Perspectives
http://www.powa.org/revifrms.htm

Tips on grammar
The Online English Grammar
http://www.edunet.com/english/grammar
Guide to Grammar and Writing
http://webster.commnet.edu/grammar/index.htm

Tips on proofreading
Tips for Effective Proofreading
http://www.ualr.edu/~owl/proof.htm
Proofreading
http://www.bgsu.edu/departments/writing-lab/goproofreading.html

Online writing centers
LEO: Literacy Education Online
http://leo.stcloudstate.edu.
Online Writing Lab
http://owl.english.purdue.edu

Using the Internet to Locate Everyday Information

The Internet can make your daily life easier. For example, you can use the Internet to access news and weather reports, download voter registration forms, get travel information, find directions, obtain consumer information, locate people, find movie reviews—or even find a job. The following sites are just a sample of the many resources available on the Internet.

Everyday Information on the Web

The Bible
The Unbound Bible
http://www.unboundbible.org

Book reviews
The New York Times *on the Web: Books*
http://www.nytimes.com/books/home/

Calendars
Calendar Zone
http://www.calendarzone.com

Census data
U.S. Census Bureau Newsletter: Census and You
http://www.census.gov/prod/www/abs/cen-you.html

City and county data
U.S. Census Bureau: County and City Data Book
http://www.census.gov/statab/www/ccdb.html

Computers
Free On-Line Dictionary of Computing
http://foldoc.doc.ic.ac.uk/foldoc/index.html

Dictionaries
yourDictionary.com™
http://www.yourdictionary.com

Employment
America's Job Bank
http://www.ajb.dni.us/

Encyclopedias
Britannica.com®
http://www.britannica.com

Genealogy
Lineages
http://www.lineages.com

Insurance company ratings
A. M. Best Insurance Information
http://ambest.com/insurance

Law and legal information
American Law Sources On-line
http://lawsource.com/also/

Maps and directions
MapBlast!
http://www.mapblast.com/myblast/index.mb

Movie reviews
The Internet Movie Database
http://www.imdb.com

Newspapers
Newspapers.Com
http://www.newspapers.com

Telephone directories
AnyWho
http://www.tollfree.att.net
Switchboard.com
http://www.switchboard.com

Weather forecasts and information
National Weather Service Home Page
http://www.nws.noaa.gov

◆ PRACTICE 1.9

At home or in your school's computer lab, practice entering five of the URLs listed on pages 17–19. Make sure you enter the URLs exactly as they appear on the page. If a URL you enter does not take you to the appropriate Web site, check to make sure that you entered the URL correctly. (If the site is no longer active, choose another URL from the list.)

◆ PRACTICE 1.10

Working in a group of four students, select one of the Web sites listed on pages 17–19. At home or in your school's computer lab, access the site, and make a list of three things you like and three things you dislike about it. Then, exchange lists with another student in your group. In what ways do you agree? In what ways do you disagree?

◆ PRACTICE 1.11

Access the following Web site, which focuses on evaluating Web resources: *http://www2.widener.edu/Wolfgram-Memorial-Library/webevaluation/webeval.htm.* Do you think this site is useful? Why or why not? Write a few sentences explaining your answer.

◆ PRACTICE 1.12

Working in a group of three or four students, access two or three of the Web sites listed on pages 17–19. Choose one site, and evaluate it according to the guidelines listed on page 16. Present your groups findings to the class.

◆ PRACTICE 1.13

Use one of the search engines listed on page 14 to locate a Web site that focuses on a topic you know a lot about—for example, your hometown, a famous person, or a sport. Evaluate the site according to the guidelines listed on page 16.

■ REVISING AND EDITING

Look back at your response to the Seeing and Writing exercise on page 1. Now that you have read the information in this chapter, you should have a better idea of how to manage your time in the weeks and months to come. How do you think you will fit everything in? Which of the strategies described in this chapter do you think you will find most helpful? Revise your Seeing and Writing response so that it answers these questions.

✓ REVIEW CHECKLIST:
Strategies for College Success

- Some strategies come in handy even before school begins. (See 1A.)
- From your first day as a college student, there are steps you can take to help you get your bearings. (See 1B.)
- Day-to-day strategies can help you move through the semester. (See 1C.)
- Learning to take good notes is essential for success in college. (See 1D.)
- Doing homework gives you a chance to practice your skills and measure your progress. (See 1E.)
- Preparation for an exam should begin well before the exam is announced. (See 1F.)
- Learning to manage your time is very important for success in college. (See 1G.)
- The Internet can help you in school and in your everyday life. (See 1H.)

UNIT ONE

Writing Effective Paragraphs

CHAPTER

2

Writing a Paragraph

PREVIEW

In this chapter, you will learn

- to focus on your assignment, purpose, and audience (2A)
- to use invention strategies (2B)
- to select and arrange ideas (2C)
- to draft a paragraph (2D)
- to revise a paragraph (2E)

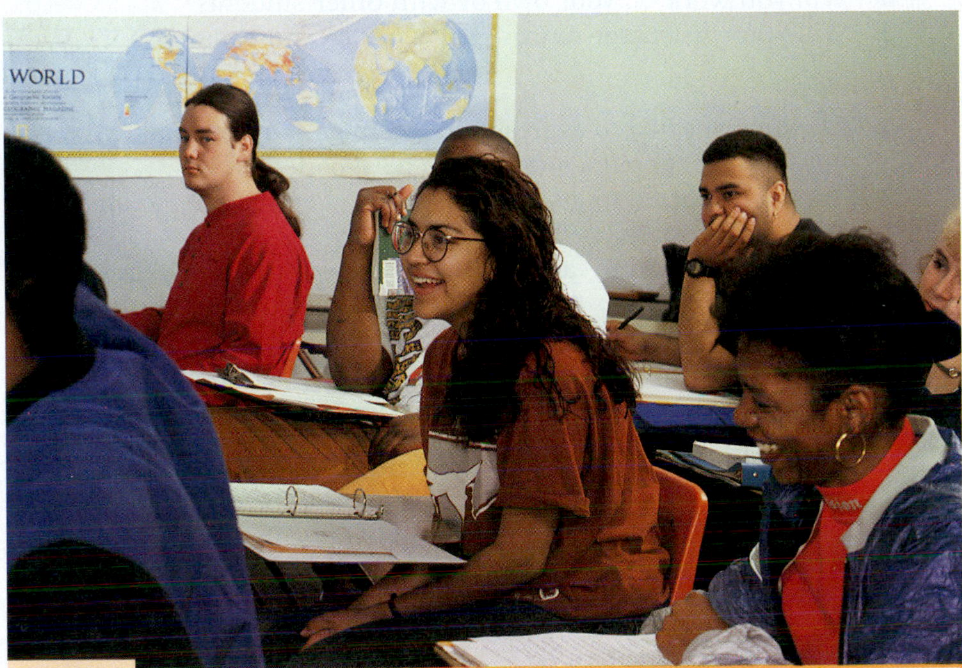

SEEING AND WRITING

Why did you decide to go to college? Look at the picture above, and think about this question carefully before you read the pages that follow. This is the topic you will be writing about as you move through this chapter.

Word Power

self-esteem pride in oneself; self-respect

This chapter will guide you through the process of writing a **paragraph**, a group of related sentences working together to develop one main idea. Because paragraphs play an important part in almost all the writing you do, learning to write a paragraph is central to becoming an effective writer.

A Focusing on Your Assignment, Purpose, and Audience

In college, a writing task almost always begins with an assignment. Before you begin to write, stop to ask yourself some questions about this

assignment (*what* you are expected to write) as well as about your **purpose** (*why* you are writing) and your **audience** (*for whom* you are writing). If you answer these questions now, you will save yourself a lot of time later.

Questions about Assignment, Purpose, and Audience

Assignment

- What is your assignment?
- Do you have a word or page limit?
- When is your assignment due?
- Will you do your writing at home or in class?
- Will you work on your own or with other students?
- Will your instructor return your work so you can revise it?

Purpose

- Are you expected to express your feelings—for example, to tell how you feel about a story in the newspaper?
- Are you expected to give information—for example, to answer an exam question?
- Are you expected to take a position on a controversial issue?

Audience

- Who will read your paper—just your instructor, or other students, too?
- Do you have an audience beyond the classroom—for example, your supervisor at work or the readers of your school newspaper?
- How much will your readers already know about your topic?
- Will your readers expect you to use a formal or an informal style? (For example, are you writing a research paper or a personal essay?)

◆ PRACTICE 2.1

Each of the following writing tasks has a different audience and purpose. On the lines following each task, write a few notes about how you would approach the task. (The Questions about Assignment, Purpose, and Audience above can help you decide on the best approach.) When you have finished, discuss your responses with the class or in a group of three or four students.

1. For the other students in your writing class, describe the best or worst class you have ever had.

____

____

____

____

2. For the instructor of a course in elementary education, discuss how a very good (or very bad) teacher can affect a student's attitude toward school.

3. Write a short letter to your school newspaper in which you try to convince readers that a certain course should no longer be offered at your school.

4. Write a letter applying for a job. Explain how the courses you have taken will help you in that job.

B Using Invention Strategies

Once you understand your assignment, purpose, and audience, you can begin to find ideas to write about. This process of finding material to write about is called **invention**. Invention is different for every writer. You may be the kind of person who likes a structured way of finding ideas, or you may prefer a looser, more relaxed way of finding things to write about. As you gain more experience as a writer, you will learn which of the four invention strategies discussed in the pages that follow (*freewriting, brainstorming, clustering,* and *journal writing*) work best for you.

Julia Reyes, a student in an introductory writing course, was given the following assignment:

> ASSIGNMENT Is it better to go to college right after high school or to wait? Write a paragraph in which you answer this question.

Before she could begin her paragraph, Julia needed to find ideas to write about. She used all four invention strategies to find ideas. The pages that follow explain these four strategies and show how Julia used them.

Word Power

dilemma a situation in which one must choose between two courses of action

Computer Tip

Try doing "invisible free-writing" by turning off your monitor and writing without looking at the screen. When you have finished, turn on the monitor to see what you have written.

Student Voices

When I freewrite, I like to listen to music.

Rachel Reilly

Freewriting

When you **freewrite**, you write whatever comes into your head, and you write for a set period of time without stopping. Grammar and spelling are not important; what is important is to get your ideas down on paper. So, even if your words don't seem to be going anywhere, keep on writing. Sometimes you freewrite to find a topic. Most often, however, you free-write on a specific topic that your instructor gives you. This strategy is called **focused freewriting**.

When you finish freewriting, read what you have written. As you read, try to find an idea you think you might be able to write more about. Underline this idea, and then freewrite again, using the underlined idea as a starting point.

Here is an example of Julia's focused freewriting on the topic "Is it better to go to college right after high school or to wait?"

> *Which is better? To start college right away? To wait? I waited, but last year was such a waste of time. Such a waste. Every job I had was stupid. Telemarketing — the worst worst job. Why didn't I just quit the first day? (<u>Money.</u>) Waitressing was a dumb job. Everybody had an attitude. The customer was always right, blah blah. Another waste of time. Why didn't I just go right to college? I needed money. And I was sick of school. School was hard. I wasn't good at it. But work was boring. But now I hate how all my friends are a year ahead of me. So I guess it's better <u>not</u> to wait.*

Freewriting

◆ PRACTICE 2.2

Read Julia's freewriting. What ideas do you think she should write more about? Write your suggestions on the following lines.

____

____

____

____

____

◆ PRACTICE 2.3

Freewrite about the topic "Why did you decide to go to college?" On a blank sheet of lined paper (or on your computer), write for at least five minutes without stopping. If you can't think of anything to write, just write the last word over and over again until something else comes to mind.

◆ PRACTICE 2.4

Reread the freewriting you did for Practice 2.3. Which sentence expresses the most interesting idea? Use this sentence as a starting point for a focused freewriting exercise.

Brainstorming

When you **brainstorm**, you write down all the ideas you can think of about your topic. Brainstorming is different from freewriting, and it looks different on the page. Instead of writing on the lines, you write all over the page. You can star, check, box, or underline words, and you can ask questions, make lists, and draw arrows to connect ideas.

Here is an example of Julia's brainstorming on the topic "Is it better to go to college right after high school or to wait?"

> ▼ **Student Voices**
> *When I brainstorm, I tape two pieces of paper together so I have lots of room to write.*
> *Pete Rubbo*

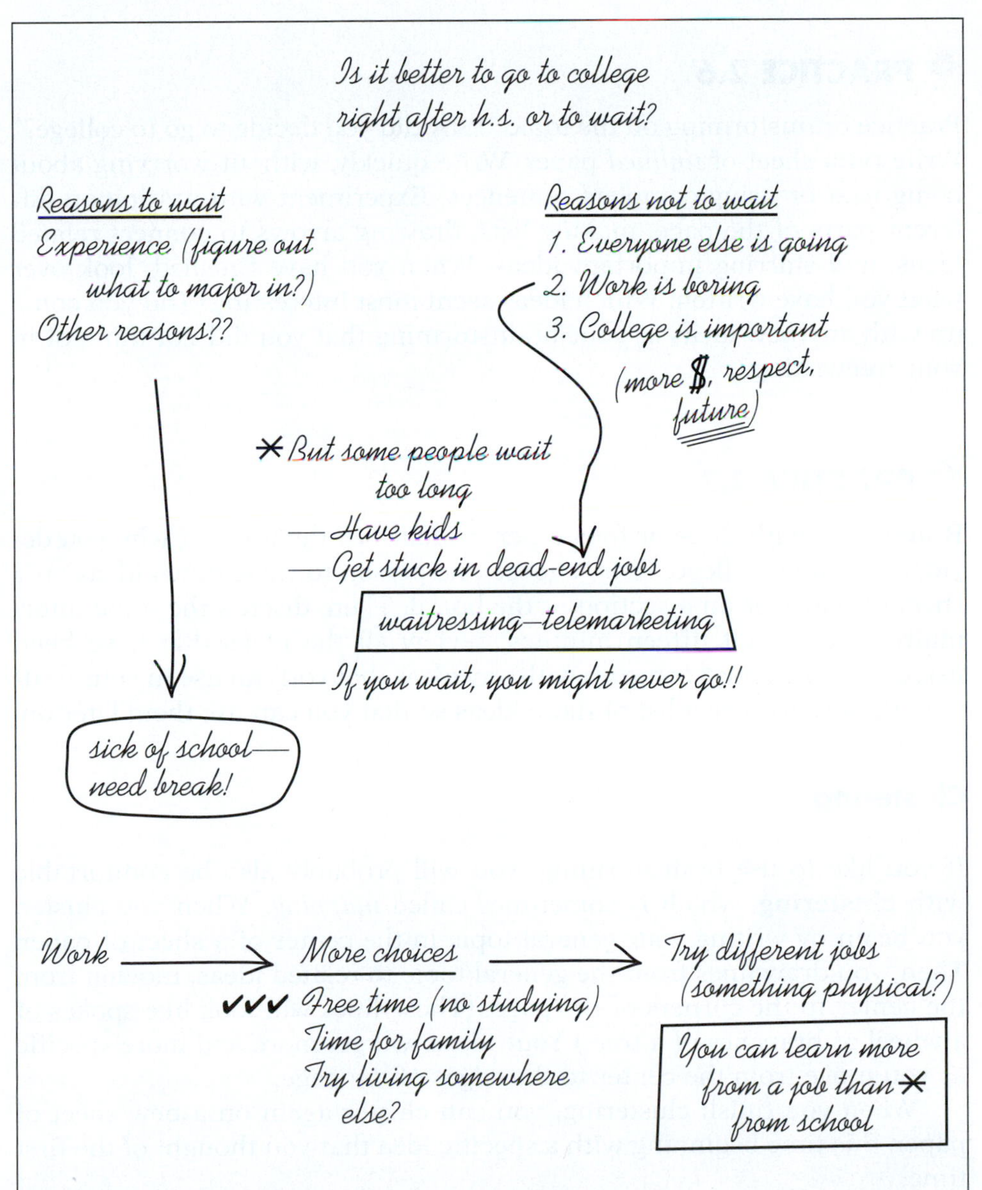

Brainstorming

◆ PRACTICE 2.5

Read Julia's brainstorming notes. How is her brainstorming similar to her freewriting (p. 28)? How is it different? Which ideas do you think she should write more about? Which ones should she cross out? Write your suggestions on the following lines.

____

____

____

____

____

____

◆ PRACTICE 2.6

Practice brainstorming on the topic "Why did you decide to go to college?" Write on a sheet of *unlined* paper. Write quickly, without worrying about being neat or using complete sentences. Experiment with writing on different parts of the page, making lists, drawing arrows to connect related ideas, and starring important ideas. When you have finished, look over what you have written. Which ideas seem most interesting? Did you come up with any new ideas in your brainstorming that you did not think of in your freewriting?

◆ PRACTICE 2.7

Brainstorm with three or four other students on the topic of why you decided to attend college. First, choose one person to write down ideas on a sheet of paper or on a section of the board. Then, discuss the topic informally. After about fifteen minutes, review all the ideas that have been listed. Has the group come up with any ideas that you can use in your writing? Be sure to keep a list of these ideas so that you can use them later on.

Clustering

> ● **Writing Tip**
> If you can find an empty classroom, try using the board for clustering.

If you like to use brainstorming, you will probably also be comfortable with **clustering**, which is sometimes called *mapping*. When you cluster, you begin by writing your general topic in the center of a sheet of paper. Then, you draw lines from the general topic to related ideas, moving from the center to the corners of the page. (These lines will look like spokes of a wheel or branches of a tree.) Your ideas will get more and more specific as you move from the center to the edges of the page.

When you finish clustering, you can cluster again on a new sheet of paper, this time beginning with a specific idea that you thought of the first time.

Here is an example of Julia's clustering on the topic "Is it better to go to college right after high school or to wait?"

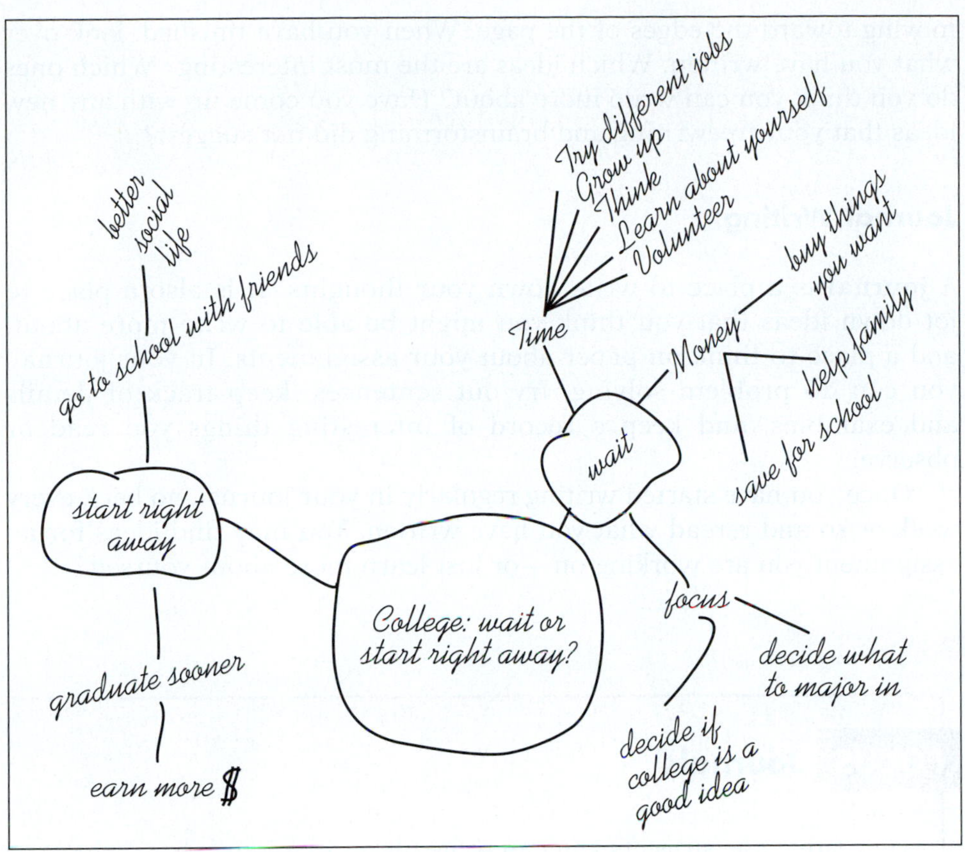

Clustering

◆ PRACTICE 2.8

How is Julia's clustering similar to her brainstorming on the same subject (p. 29)? How is it different? Which branch of her cluster diagram do you think Julia should focus on? Why? Should she add any other branches? Write your suggestions on the following lines. Then, discuss them with the class or in a small group.

____

____

____

____

____

____

____

◆ PRACTICE 2.9

Practice clustering on the topic "Why did you decide to go to college?" Begin by writing this topic in the center of a sheet of unlined paper. Circle the topic, and then draw branches to connect specific ideas and examples, moving toward the edges of the page. When you have finished, look over what you have written. Which ideas are the most interesting? Which ones do you think you can write more about? Have you come up with any new ideas that your freewriting and brainstorming did not suggest?

Journal Writing

Computer Tip

Try keeping a journal on your computer by making entries at set times every day—when you check your e-mail, for example.

A **journal** is a place to write down your thoughts. It is also a place to jot down ideas that you think you might be able to write more about, and a place to think on paper about your assignments. In your journal, you can do problem solving, try out sentences, keep track of details and examples, and keep a record of interesting things you read or observe.

Once you have started writing regularly in your journal, go back every week or so and reread what you have written. You may find ideas for an assignment you are working on—or just learn more about yourself.

FOCUS Journals

Here are some subjects you can write about in a journal.

- *Your schoolwork.* Writing regularly about the topics you are studying in school is one way to become a better student. In a journal, you can explore ideas for writing assignments in your courses. You can also think about what you are learning, ask questions about topics you are having trouble understanding, and examine new ideas.
- *Your job.* You can write about the day-to-day triumphs and frustrations of your job. For example, you can write down conversations with coworkers, or you can list problems and remind yourself how you solved them. Rereading your journal may help you understand your strengths and weaknesses as an employee.
- *Your ideas about your community and your world.* As you learn more about the social and political world around you, you can explore your reactions to new ideas. For example, you may read an interesting story in the newspaper or see something on television that challenges your beliefs. Even if you are not ready to talk to others about what you are thinking, you can still "talk" to your journal.
- *Your impressions of what you observe.* Many writers carry their journals with them and record interesting, unusual, or funny things they notice as they go about their daily business. If you get into the habit of writing down your observations and reactions, you may be able to use them later in your writing.

(continued on the following page)

(continued from the previous page)

- *Personal thoughts.* Although you may not feel comfortable writing about your personal thoughts and experiences—especially if your instructor will read your journal—you should try to be as honest as you can. Writing about relationships with family and friends, personal problems, and hopes and dreams can help you get to know (and understand) yourself better.

Here is an example of Julia's journal entry on the topic "Is it better to go to college right after high school or to wait?"

> This is a hard topic for me to write about. When I finished high school, I never wanted to go to school again. High school was hard. I worked hard, but teachers always said I could do better. Studying was boring. I couldn't concentrate. I never seemed to get things right on homework or on tests. Things seemed easier for everyone else. Sometimes I hated school. So I decided I'd work and not go to college right away, or maybe ever. But after a year, here I am. I'm still not sure why. School always felt hard. Work was easy. For the first time, I could do everything right. I got raises and promotions and better hours because I was a good worker. I wasn't judged by how I did on some dumb test. For once, I had some self-esteem. So why am I here? Good question.

Journal Entry

◆ PRACTICE 2.10

Buy a notebook to use as a journal. Make an appointment with yourself to write for fifteen minutes or so—during lunch, for example, or right before you go to bed—every day. Then, write your first journal entry. Being as honest with yourself as possible, try to explain why you really decided to go to college.

C Selecting and Arranging Ideas

When you think you have enough material to write about, the next step is to find a main idea to develop. Then, you will choose details to support this main idea, and you will organize those details into a paragraph.

Writing Tip

If at any stage in the writing process you run out of ideas, return to the invention strategies you found most helpful and use them to help you come up with more material.

For more on topic sentences, see 3A.

Understanding Paragraph Structure

A **paragraph** is a group of related sentences. A paragraph usually begins with a **topic sentence**, a single sentence that states the paragraph's main idea. This first sentence is **indented,** written or typed about one-half inch (five spaces) from the left margin. The other sentences in the paragraph provide **support** for this main idea: explanations, reasons, description, examples, and so on. (Often, a paragraph ends with a final sentence that acts as a conclusion.) A paragraph looks like this:

Paragraph

The **topic sentence** states the main idea of the paragraph.

Support develops the main idea with explanations, reasons, description, examples, and so on.

Stating Your Topic Sentence

Writing Tip

If your topic is in the form of a question, your topic sentence should answer that question.

To find a main idea for your paragraph, read through all your notes—your freewriting, brainstorming, clustering, and journal entries. Look for the central point or idea that these notes can best support. The phrase or sentence that states this main idea and gives your paragraph its focus will become your topic sentence.

Julia thought most of her notes supported the idea that it was better to wait instead of starting college right after high school. She stated this idea in a sentence.

TOPIC SENTENCE I think it's better to wait a few years instead of beginning college right after high school.

Choosing Supporting Material

After you identify your main idea, review your notes again. This time, you are looking for specific details, facts, and examples to support your topic sentence. Write or type the topic sentence at the top of a sheet of paper. As you review your notes and continue to think about your topic, list all the supporting points you think you might be able to use in your paragraph.

Julia chose the following points from her notes to support her paragraph's topic sentence.

TOPIC SENTENCE I think it's better to wait a few years instead of beginning college right after high school.

- Time to think
- Work experience
- Chance to earn money

- Chance to develop self-esteem
- Time to grow up
- Chance to decide if college is right for you

Ordering Supporting Material

Once you have made a list of supporting points, arrange them in the order in which you think you will discuss them. Julia arranged her supporting points in the following list.

TOPIC SENTENCE I think it's better to wait a few years instead of beginning college right after high school.

1. Waiting gives people time to earn money.
2. Waiting gives people time to think about life and grow up.
3. Waiting helps people decide if college is right for them.
4. Waiting gives people a chance to develop self-esteem.

◆ PRACTICE 2.11

In Practices 2.3, 2.6, 2.9, and 2.10, you practiced freewriting, brainstorming, clustering, and journal writing. Now, you are ready to write a paragraph about why you decided to go to college. Begin by looking over all the work you have done, and then think some more about your topic. What main idea does all your material seem to support? On the following lines, write a topic sentence that expresses this idea.

____

____

____

____

Now, reread your invention exercises, and list below all the points you can use to support your topic sentence. You can also list any new points you think of.

____

____

____

____

____

____

Reread the points you listed above. Does each point support your topic sentence? Cross out any points that do not. On the following lines, arrange the remaining points in the order in which you plan to write about them.

1. ____________________

2. ____________________

3. ____________________

4. ____________________

D Drafting Your Paragraph

So far, you have found a main idea for your paragraph, written a topic sentence, listed supporting points, and arranged them in the order in which you will write about them. Now, you are ready to write a first draft.

Begin drafting your paragraph by stating your topic sentence. Then, referring to your list of supporting points, write down your ideas without worrying about correct sentence structure, word choice, spelling, or punctuation. If you think of an idea that is not on your list, write it down. (Don't worry about where it fits or whether you will keep it.)

You can type your first draft, or you can write it by hand. (Julia wrote hers by hand because it was an in-class assignment.) Remember, though, that your first draft is a rough draft that you will revise. It is all right to be sloppy and to cross out; after all, the only person who will see this draft of your paragraph is you.

When you have finished your rough draft, don't start correcting it right away; take a break. Then, return to your draft and read it.

Here is a draft of Julia's paragraph on the topic "Is it better to go to college right after high school or to wait?"

Writing Tip

If you plan to revise on your handwritten draft, make things easy for yourself by skipping lines so you have room to add ideas.

Waiting

I think it's better to wait a few years instead of beginning college right after high school. Many people start college right after high school just because that's what everybody else is doing. But that's not always the right way to go. Different things are right for different people. There are other possible choices. Taking a few years off can be a better choice. During this time, people can work and earn money. They also have time to think and grow up. Waiting can even help people decide if college is right for them. Finally, waiting gives them a chance to develop self-esteem. For all these reasons, waiting a year or two between high school and college is a good idea.

Draft

◆ PRACTICE 2.12

Read Julia's draft paragraph. What do you think she should change in her draft? What should she add? What should she take out? Write your suggestions on the following lines. Then, discuss your suggestions with the class or in a small group.

____

____

____

◆ PRACTICE 2.13

Using the material you came up with for Practice 2.11, draft a paragraph on the topic of why you decided to go to college. Be sure to state your main idea in the topic sentence and support it with specific points. Leave wide margins; if you like, skip lines. (If you type your draft, you can triple-space.) When you have finished, give your paragraph a title.

E Revising Your Paragraph

Revision means much more than correcting a few commas or crossing out one word and putting another one in its place. Often, it means moving sentences around, adding words and phrases, and even changing the topic sentence. To get the most out of revision, begin by carefully rereading your draft—first aloud, then to yourself. Then, consider each of the questions on the checklist that follows.

✓ SELF-ASSESSMENT CHECKLIST: Revising Your Paragraph

- ☐ Does your topic sentence state your main idea?
- ☐ Do you have enough material to support your main idea?
- ☐ Have you explained your ideas fully and clearly?
- ☐ Have you used enough examples and details?
- ☐ Are all your examples and details necessary?
- ☐ Does every sentence say what you mean?
- ☐ Does the order of your sentences make sense?
- ☐ Is every word necessary?
- ☐ Have you used the right words?

After Julia drafted the paragraph on page 36 by hand, she typed it, triple-spacing to leave room for handwritten changes. Then, she used the Self-Assessment Checklist on page 37 to help her revise her paragraph.

Waiting

For students who are not getting much out of school, it is often ~~I think it's~~ better to wait a few years instead of beginning college right after high school. Many people start college right *away* ~~after high school~~ just because *that is* ~~that's~~ what everybody else is doing. *However, that is* ~~But that's~~ not always the right *thing to do.* ~~way to go~~. ~~Different things are right for different people. There are other possible choices~~. Taking a few years off can *often* be a better choice. During this time, people can work and earn money *for college. Working at different jobs can help them decide on a career.* ~~They also have~~ *Taking a year or two off also gives people* time to think and grow up. Waiting can even help people decide if college is *really* right for them. *Most important of all* ~~Finally~~, waiting gives them a chance to develop self-esteem. *I was a poor student in high school. School always felt hard. When I took a year off, everything changed. In high school, I always saw all the things I couldn't do. At work, I learned what I could do. Now, I think I can succeed.* For *me* ~~all these reasons~~, waiting a year ~~or two~~ between high school and college *was* ~~is~~ a good idea*, and I think it can be a good idea for other students, too.*

Revised Draft

When she revised her paragraph, Julia crossed out sentences, added sentences, and changed the way she worded her ideas. Her biggest change was to add an explanation of how taking a year off had helped her. (Note that she revised her topic sentence to reflect her personal perspective.) Here is the final version of her revised paragraph.

Waiting

For students who are not getting much out of school, it is often better to wait a few years instead of beginning college right after high school. Many people start college right away just because that is what everybody else is doing. However, that is not always the right thing to do. Taking a few years off can often be a better choice. During this time, people can work and earn money for college. Working at different jobs can help them decide on a career. Taking a year or two off also gives people time to think and grow up. Waiting can even help people decide if college is really right for them. Most important of all, waiting gives them a chance to develop self-esteem. I was a poor student in high school. School always felt hard. When I took a year off, everything changed. In high school, I always saw all the things I couldn't do. At work, I learned what I could do. Now, I think I can succeed. For me, waiting a year between high school and college was a good idea, and I think it can be a good idea for other students, too.

FOCUS Editing

Don't confuse revision with editing, which comes *after* revision. When you **edit**, you check for correct grammar, punctuation, and spelling. Then, you proofread your writing carefully for typing errors that a computer spell checker may not identify.

Remember, editing is a vital last step in the writing process. Readers may not take your ideas seriously if there are grammatical or spelling errors in your writing.

For information on editing, see 5G.

◆ PRACTICE 2.14

Read the final version of Julia's revised paragraph (pp. 38–39), and compare it with her draft (p. 36). What specific changes did she make? Which do you think are her best changes? Why? Answer these questions on the following lines. Then, with the class or in a small group, discuss your reaction to the revised paragraph.

____

____

____

____

____

◆ PRACTICE 2.15

Use the Self-Assessment Checklist on page 37 to help evaluate the paragraph you drafted for Practice 2.13. What can you add to support your topic sentence more fully? Should anything be crossed out because it doesn't support your topic sentence? Can anything be stated more clearly? On the following lines, list some of the changes you might make in your draft.

____

____

____

____

■ REVISING AND EDITING

Revise the draft paragraph that you wrote in this chapter. Begin by crossing out unnecessary material and any material you want to rewrite, and then add new and rewritten material. After you finish your revision, edit the paragraph, checking grammar, punctuation, and spelling—and look carefully for typing errors. When you are satisfied with your paragraph, print out a clean copy.

☑ REVIEW CHECKLIST: Writing a Paragraph

- Before you start to write, consider your assignment, purpose, and audience. (See 2A.)
- Use invention strategies—freewriting, brainstorming, clustering, and journal writing—to find ideas. (See 2B.)
- Select ideas from your notes, and arrange them in a logical order. (See 2C.)
- Write a first draft. (See 2D.)
- Revise your draft. (See 2E.)
- Edit your draft. (See 2E.)

CHAPTER

3

Fine-Tuning Your Paragraph

PREVIEW

In this chapter, you will learn

- to write effective topic sentences (3A)
- to write unified paragraphs (3B)
- to write well-developed paragraphs (3C)
- to write coherent paragraphs (3D)

SEEING AND WRITING

Look at the picture above. Then, write a paragraph about an event that you wanted to attend but could not. What was special about the event? What caused you to miss it?

Word Power

venue the scene or location at which something takes place

spectacle a public show or exhibition; an unusual sight

A Writing Effective Topic Sentences

Student Voices

Once I find my topic sentence, the rest is easy.

Jessi Allender

Every paragraph that you write should include a **topic sentence**—a sentence that clearly states the paragraph's main idea. Your topic sentence should be the most general sentence in the paragraph. It is the sentence that the other sentences in the paragraph explain, support, or discuss. In the following paragraph, the topic sentence is the first sentence.

<u>One of my most satisfying experiences occurred when I volunteered at the day-care center at the Whosoever Gospel Mission</u>. Most

of the people who live at the mission are recovering addicts or alcoholics. Some are just down on their luck. Many, however, have small children who must be cared for while their parents are in recovery. These children need a lot of attention, and anyone who gives it to them is rewarded with love and affection. During the summer that I worked at the mission, I grew very attached to the children. I played with them, read to them, and hugged them anytime I could. Although I was sad to leave the mission in September, I was happy that I could make a difference in the children's lives.

Victoria Nasid (student)

FOCUS Writing Effective Topic Sentences

Although a topic sentence can appear anywhere in a paragraph, it is a good idea to place the topic sentence at the beginning of your paragraph. This strategy will tell readers immediately what your paragraph will be about. It will also keep you on track as you write.

Here are two additional things to remember as you write a topic sentence:

1. ***An effective topic sentence should not be a statement of your topic or an announcement of what you plan to write about.***

TOPIC SENTENCE	One of my most satisfying experiences occurred when I volunteered at the day-care center at the Whosoever Gospel Mission.
TOPIC	A satisfying experience
ANNOUNCEMENT	In this paragraph, I will write about a satisfying experience.

2. ***An effective topic sentence should present an idea that you can discuss in a single paragraph.*** If your topic sentence is too broad, you will not be able to discuss it in the limited space of a paragraph. If it is too narrow, you will not be able to think of much to say about it.

TOPIC SENTENCE TOO BROAD	Building a supermarket in my neighborhood will destroy our community.
TOPIC SENTENCE TOO NARROW	If a supermarket is built in my neighborhood, White's market may have to close.
EFFECTIVE TOPIC SENTENCE	The construction of a Giant supermarket in my neighborhood will hurt the community by forcing many small stores out of business.

◆ PRACTICE 3.1

Underline the topic sentence in each of the following paragraphs. Keep in mind that the topic sentence will not always be the first sentence of the paragraph.

Example

How did the Himalayas, the world's tallest mountains, come to exist? They were created the same way the Andes mountains were—by forces that are also responsible for earthquakes in California. The earth's surface is divided into several large masses called plates. The plates are in constant, gradual motion. When two plates push against each other, mountains form. When they slide against each other suddenly, the result is an earthquake. Scientists call such interactions plate tectonics. Many of the world's geographic features have been created by plate tectonics.

1. Having my tonsils removed when I was six was a dramatic event. My overnight stay in the hospital was exciting and strange. I wasn't used to being away from home. The idea of having the operation made me a little nervous, but the nurses explained everything to me. Afterward, my throat was sore for several days. Generous doses of ice cream helped make my recovery bearable.

2. Not long ago, all public schools were run by local governments. Parents relied on government officials to meet their children's needs. However, some public schools seemed to be doing a poor job. Charter schools are changing the way public education works. Charter schools are funded with public money but are run by private groups. They tend to be small and specialized. Some teach moral values as well as reading and math. Supporters believe charter schools will grow in popularity over time.

3. Sunlight travels through space in waves. It contains all the colors of the spectrum, from red to deep blue. When sunlight enters the earth's atmosphere, the light waves run into dust particles. Red light waves, which are long, move around the particles without much trouble. Shorter blue light waves, on the other hand, crash into the particles and are scattered. Those scattered waves reach our eyes from every direction, crowding out other colors. The sky appears to be blue because light waves of different colors react to dust particles in different ways.

◆ PRACTICE 3.2

Read the following items. Put a check mark next to each one that you think would make an effective topic sentence for a paragraph.

Examples

Reviewing a car's service record. ____

Buying a used car requires careful research. _✓_

1. Domestic cats and lions and tigers. ____
2. Domestic cats resemble lions and tigers in several ways. ____
3. Fresh water, a limited resource, is in short supply in some western states. ____
4. In this paragraph, I will discuss hiking. ____
5. Instead of tearing down old factories in the waterfront district, the city should convert them into high-tech office buildings. ____

◆ PRACTICE 3.3

The following sentences are too broad or too narrow to be effective topic sentences. On the line after each sentence, write *Too broad* if the sentence is too broad and *Too narrow* if the sentence is too narrow. Then, rewrite each sentence—making it more specific or more general—so that it could be an effective topic sentence for a paragraph.

Examples

Global warming is a serious issue.

Too broad. Possible rewrite: Global warming could cause dramatic changes to our environment.

Many supermarkets sell more salsa than ketchup.

Too narrow. Possible rewrite: Ethnic foods have become very popular with American consumers.

1. Required courses are a bad idea.

____

____

2. Many jobs require computer skills.

____

____

3. Cigarette smoking is a public nuisance.

____

____

4. Many laws are not properly enforced.

____

____

5. The current campaign for mayor is not fair because one candidate has more campaign funds than the other.

______

______

◆ PRACTICE 3.4

The following paragraphs do not have topic sentences. Think of a topic sentence that sums up each paragraph's main idea, and write it in on the lines above the paragraph.

Example

Possible answer: The risk of heart disease can be lowered in several ways.

One major cause of heart disease is a diet high in fat and cholesterol. Reducing fat and cholesterol, therefore, can reduce the risk of illness. Another way to reduce the risk is to exercise regularly. A third technique for avoiding heart disease is to balance work and recreation.

1. ______

______

The first night, we set up camp and cooked dinner over the fire. I hadn't seen so many stars in years. On Saturday, we hiked five miles to a nearby lookout point. It was so clear that we could see parts of three states. On the way back, we took turns naming different trees and flowers. I slept like a log after all that exercise. Sunday was overcast, so we stayed near the camp and sang songs. It seemed a shame to pack up and come home.

2. ______

______

Taking a warm bath or drinking a cup of hot herbal tea is relaxing for some people. Others prefer to ease tension by doing some form of exercise, such as walking or running. Another soothing activity is meditation, which can be done almost anywhere. But the easiest way to relax is simply to take a series of slow, deep breaths.

3. ______

______

In some cultures, personal space is shared constantly. Men hug each other, women hold hands, and strangers kiss. In other cultures, it is considered impolite to touch someone, even to shake hands. Individuals have different ideas about personal space as well. Some people are comfortable only when they are in physical contact with other people. Others prefer to keep an imaginary bubble around themselves, avoiding contact at all costs.

B Writing Unified Paragraphs

A paragraph is **unified** when all of its sentences focus on the single main idea stated in the topic sentence. A paragraph lacks unity when its sentences wander away from the main idea.

When you write, you may lose sight of your main idea and write sentences that go off in all different directions. You can correct this problem by rereading the topic sentence and crossing out or rewriting any sentences that do not support it.

Writing Tip

Underline the topic sentence of a paragraph before you start to revise.

Paragraph Not Unified

Although applying for a loan can be a nerve-wracking experience, it is really easy. The first step is to determine which bank has the lowest interest rate. There are a lot of banks in my neighborhood, but none of them is very friendly. The last time I went into one, I waited for twenty minutes before anyone bothered to wait on me. Once you have chosen a bank, you have to go to the bank in person and apply, and if the bank isn't friendly, you don't want to go there. This is a real problem when you apply for a loan. If you have any questions about the application, you won't be able to get anyone to answer them. After you have submitted the application comes the hard part—waiting for approval.

This paragraph is not unified. After telling readers that applying for a loan is not a difficult process, the writer wanders from his main idea to complain about how unfriendly the banks in his neighborhood are. Most of the sentences in the paragraph do not support the topic sentence.

The revised paragraph that follows is unified. When the writer reread his paragraph, he deleted the sentences that had nothing to do with the topic sentence. He then added sentences that supported his main idea. The result is a paragraph that supports its main idea: that applying for a loan is easy.

Paragraph Unified

Although applying for a loan can be a nerve-wracking experience, it is really easy. The first step is to determine which bank has the lowest interest rate. Although a half-percent difference in rates may not seem like much, over the course of a four-year loan, the savings can really add up. Once you have chosen a bank, you have to go to the bank in person and apply. Make sure you tell the loan officer exactly what rate you are applying for. Then, take the application home and fill it out, being careful not to omit any important information. If you have any problems with your credit, explain them on the application or in a separate letter. Then, take the application back to the bank, and ask any questions that you might have. (Do not sign the application until all your questions have been answered.) After you have submitted the application comes the only hard part—waiting for approval.

Hector de la Paz (student)

◆ PRACTICE 3.5

Read the following paragraphs. Write *unified* after the paragraphs that are unified and *not unified* after the ones that are not unified.

Example

Pet ownership is a big responsibility. Thousands of families adopt dogs and cats every month. Other family activities include taking vacations and playing sports together. In fact, families who spend time together tend to be happier and communicate more. Most people give little thought to the animals' needs for a proper diet, exercise, company, and veterinary care. In fact, few people realize how much time and money they will spend taking care of their pets. *not unified*

1. Drivers must be careful to avoid road rage incidents. Road rage occurs when a driver loses control over his or her emotions in a stressful situation. Driving in bad weather can be very stressful. A car does not handle as easily on snowy or icy roads as it does on dry ones. Snow tires can make winter driving safer. Even with snow tires, though, driving on slippery roads requires concentration. Road rage can lead to property damage and even injury. Therefore, drivers should always keep their emotions under control. ______________

2. Music can either help or hurt a person's ability to recall information. For example, students who study while listening to loud dance music tend to remember less than those who study in quiet settings. The reason for this is that dance music has a strong rhythm, which tends to distract a person from the material being studied. Classical music, on the other hand, may help improve memory. Research shows that some people remember information more clearly if they listen to quiet classical music while studying. Understanding the link between music and memory can help students make wise choices about listening to music while studying. ______________

3. Georgia O'Keeffe was a bold and influential painter. Her most famous paintings are of flowers and of scenes from the Southwest. Many tourists visit the Southwest to enjoy its beautiful deserts. Taos, New Mexico, is an especially busy tourist spot. O'Keeffe developed a unique painting style. She created dramatic images that went against the artistic fashion of her times. In fact, her rich use of color has inspired many artists. Quite a few artists today work in video and collage as well as in paint. O'Keeffe's work is on display in many of the world's leading museums. ______________

◆ PRACTICE 3.6

Reread the paragraphs in Practice 3.5 that you decided were not unified. Cross out the sentences in each paragraph that do not belong.

Example

Pet ownership is a big responsibility. Thousands of families adopt dogs and cats every month. ~~Other family activities include taking vacations and playing sports together. In fact, families who spend time~~

~~together tend to be happier and communicate more.~~ Most people give little thought to the animals' needs for a proper diet, exercise, company, and veterinary care. In fact, few people realize how much time and money they will spend taking care of their pets.

1. Drivers must be careful to avoid road rage incidents. Road rage occurs when a driver loses control over his or her emotions in a stressful situation. Driving in bad weather can be very stressful. A car does not handle as easily on snowy or icy roads as it does on dry ones. Snow tires can make winter driving safer. Even with snow tires, though, driving on slippery roads requires concentration. Road rage can lead to property damage and even injury. Therefore, drivers should always keep their emotions under control.

2. Music can either help or hurt a person's ability to recall information. For example, students who study while listening to loud dance music tend to remember less than those who study in quiet settings. The reason for this is that dance music has a strong rhythm, which tends to distract a person from the material being studied. Classical music, on the other hand, may help improve memory. Research shows that some people remember information more clearly if they listen to quiet classical music while studying. Understanding the link between music and memory can help students make wise choices about listening to music while studying.

3. Georgia O'Keeffe was a bold and influential painter. Her most famous paintings are of flowers and of scenes from the Southwest. Many tourists visit the Southwest to enjoy its beautiful deserts. Taos, New Mexico, is an especially busy tourist spot. O'Keeffe developed a unique painting style. She created dramatic images that went against the artistic fashion of her times. In fact, her rich use of color has inspired many artists. Quite a few artists today work in video and collage as well as in paint. O'Keeffe's work is on display in many of the world's leading museums.

C Writing Well-Developed Paragraphs

A paragraph is **well developed** when it includes the details, facts, and examples needed to support the topic sentence. Without this material, readers may become confused. As you write, imagine your readers asking, "What do you mean?" or "What support do you have for this statement?" Be sure your paragraph answers these questions.

How do you determine how much support you need? The answer to this question depends on how complicated the idea in your topic sentence is. Remember that the purpose of support is to convince readers that the statement you are making in the topic sentence is believable or reasonable. If your topic sentence is relatively straightforward—for example, "My school's registration process is a nightmare"—two or three well-chosen examples will probably be enough to convince readers. If, however, your statement is more complicated—for example, "The plan that the mayor

Writing Tip

A paragraph can be long but still not well developed. Remember, a well-developed paragraph is one that supports the topic sentence with specific ideas.

has presented for building a new stadium is flawed"—you will have to present more support.

FOCUS Developing Paragraphs with Specific Details

Specific details can make a paragraph interesting and convincing. You can say that many soldiers were killed during the American Civil War. Your paragraph will be far more effective, however, if you say that more than 500,000 soldiers were killed during the Civil War—more than in all the other wars in U.S. history combined.

Student Voices

If I find that I don't have enough to write about, I brainstorm again.

Mike Paparone

When you are checking your paragraphs to make sure they are well developed, look for unsupported general statements. If you find any, add the details, facts, and examples you need to support these statements. The following paragraph is not well developed.

Undeveloped Paragraph

Computerized special effects now bring to the screen things that never could have been shown before. Modern digital technology has created effects that would have been too expensive or too difficult to create in the studio. It is almost certain that in the future, special effects will become even more realistic. They may even blur the line between what the audience believes to be real and what actually is real.

Computer Tip

Hit the Enter or Return key after your topic sentence and after each sentence that follows it. If you highlight each detail, fact, and example, you will find it easier to evaluate the amount and kind of support you have used.

The paragraph above consists of general statements that are not backed up with specific examples. Details, facts, and examples can turn this paragraph into a more interesting and persuasive one.

Well-Developed Paragraph

Computerized special effects now bring to the screen scenes that never could have been shown before. Modern technology has created effects that would have been too expensive or too difficult to create in the studio. With the help of computerized special effects, films can show disasters and re-create the past. For example, in the movie *Titanic*, computerized special effects showed the *Titanic* splitting in half as it sank. Real actors were combined with digitally generated figures to show people falling to their deaths from the upended ship. In *Gladiator*, computerized special effects were used to re-create the ancient city of Rome. In addition, the film was able to show gladiators fighting in a digital re-creation of the Coliseum as it might have appeared two thousand years ago. It is almost certain that in the future, special effects will become even more realistic. They may even blur the line between what the audience believes to be real and what actually is real.

Andrew McGillin (student)

◆ PRACTICE 3.7

Some of the following paragraphs are well developed; others are not. On the line after each paragraph, write *well developed* if the paragraph is well developed and *not well developed* if it is not.

Examples

Genealogy is the study of a family's lineage, or history. Genealogy is an interesting and important field. Some family histories are easier to trace than others. Professional genealogists use both traditional and modern techniques to trace a person's lineage. Many people who research their family histories make surprising discoveries. Everyone should trace his or her family's history at some point. not well developed

Consumer items such as televisions, clothing, and electronics are selling well. One reason they are in such high demand is the growth of the national economy in recent decades. As a result of economic expansion, many people are earning more money than they once did. In addition, families with two incomes are more common than ever. Some couples who spend most of their time working reward themselves by shopping. well developed

1. Caffeinated drinks are very popular, but caffeine has negative effects on some people. Beverages that do not contain caffeine are healthier than those that do. Decaffeinated soda, coffee, and tea are possible options. Herbal tea and juices are other caffeine-free drinks. The best drink of all, though, is plain water. ____________________

2. Last Saturday, the marching band gave an excellent performance at the football game. The musicians were all quite talented and performed with great energy, especially when they played a John Paul Sousa march. The drummers, in particular, were really lively. Their performance during halftime was especially exciting, inspiring fans in the stands to give them a standing ovation. The director should be congratulated for his work with the band. ____________________

3. Shad are fascinating fish. In some ways, they behave like salmon, yet in other ways, they are unique. The behavior of shad is interesting to different groups of people. Their anatomy, too, is of interest. Information about each fish's history is revealed in its anatomy. For generations, people have been intrigued by shad and their behavior. ____________________

◆ PRACTICE 3.8

The following paragraphs are not well developed. On the lines below each paragraph, write three questions or suggestions that might help the writer develop his or her ideas more fully.

Example

Adam Sandler is a wonderful comedian. Some of his movies are absolutely hilarious. He is especially good at using funny voices to express his emotions. I never get tired of watching Adam Sandler's movies. I have seen *The Wedding Singer* and *Water Boy* several times each.

1. *Describe the voices Adam Sandler uses.*
2. *Give an example of a part he has played in one of the movies mentioned.*
3. *Tell about the funny way he talks in this movie.*

1. For me, having a regular study routine is important. I need to do the same things at the same times. If I have important school work to do, I stick to my routine. As long as I follow my schedule, everything works out all right.

1. __________
2. __________
3. __________

2. Religion is a deeply personal issue. Attitudes toward religion vary from person to person. One person I know considers religion an essential part of life. Another feels just the opposite. Because of such differences, it is impossible to generalize about religious attitudes.

1. __________
2. __________
3. __________

◆ PRACTICE 3.9

Choose one of the paragraphs from Practice 3.8. Reread it, and review your suggestions for improving it. Then, rewrite the paragraph, adding any details, facts, or examples you think are needed to make it well developed.

D Writing Coherent Paragraphs

Student Voices

I used to have a lot of problems with coherence. I guess practice pays off.

Cynthia Dankanis

A paragraph is **coherent** when all its sentences are arranged in a clear, logical order. Readers should be able to see the connections between ideas and should not have to guess why one sentence follows another. You can make a paragraph coherent by arranging details in a logical order and by choosing transitional words and phrases to show the connections between sentences.

In general, you can arrange the ideas in a paragraph in three ways: in *time order*, in *spatial order*, or in *logical order*.

Time Order

When you use **time order**, you arrange events in the order in which they occurred. News reports, historical accounts, and process explanations are usually arranged like this.

The following paragraph presents events in time order.

> No other American writer has achieved as great a reputation on the basis of a single book as Ralph Ellison has. Ellison was born in 1914 in Oklahoma City, Oklahoma, and grew up in the segregated South. In 1936, he came to New York City to earn money to pay his tuition at Tuskegee Institute, where he was a senior majoring in music. After becoming friends with many writers who were part of the Harlem Renaissance—a flowering of art, music, and literature among African Americans—he decided to remain in New York. During this period, Richard Wright, author of *Native Son* and *Black Boy*, encouraged Ellison to write his first short story. In the years that followed, Ellison published two collections of essays and some short fiction. Eventually, in 1952, he wrote *Invisible Man*, the novel that established him as a major twentieth-century writer.

Word Power

renaissance rebirth or revival

This paragraph moves in time order, tracing events from Ellison's childhood in the South to his arrival in New York to the publication of *Invisible Man*. Notice that throughout the paragraph, transitional words and phrases that signal time order—*in 1936, after, during this period, in the years that followed,* and *eventually*— help make the paragraph coherent.

Some Transitional Words and Phrases That Signal Time Order

after	later	dates (for example, "in 1920")
afterward	now	
at first	since	
before	soon	
earlier	then	
eventually	today	
finally	when	
first . . . next	while	

◆ PRACTICE 3.10

Read the following paragraphs, whose sentences are organized in time order. Underline the transitional words and phrases that make each paragraph coherent.

Example

Writing a research paper requires several steps. First, you must choose a topic to write about. The topic should be broad enough to allow for an interesting discussion but narrow enough to cover in a few pages. Next, begin researching your topic. Reference sources, books, articles, and Web sites are all good places to look for information. While you are gathering material, you might adjust your topic on the basis of what you are learning about it. When you have finished collecting information, it is time to plan your paper by drafting an outline. Then, it is time to write and to revise. Finally, you will want to add a bibliography or works cited page and proofread your paper.

1. A job interview is most likely to go well when you are prepared for it. The first step is to determine your strengths. Do you have the right level of education for the job? Are you experienced in the field? What special skills do you have? The next step is to research the company and the kind of business it does. If you have a thorough knowledge of the company you will make a good impression and be able to answer many questions. Finally, decide what points you want to emphasize in the interview. Although the interviewer will guide the conversation, you should be ready to offer your own thoughts as well.

2. Filmmaker Spike Lee has had a successful career making unusual movies. Before he started making movies professionally, he was a film student at New York University. In 1986, he released his first feature, *She's Gotta Have It.* Critics praised the low-budget film for its strong characters and clever dialogue. After that, Lee went on to make such acclaimed movies as *Do the Right Thing, Jungle Fever, Malcolm X, Summer of Sam,* and *The Original Kings of Comedy.* Most of Lee's films are made in his signature style, which includes vivid colors and unusual camera angles. To this day, Lee uses his movies to explore ideas about race and class in American society.

◆ PRACTICE 3.11

Arrange the following sentences into a coherent paragraph. Be sure you are able to explain why you arranged the sentences the way you did.

_____ 1. During colonial times, public voice votes were common.

_____ 2. Soon, individual voters may be able to cast ballots on the Internet.

_____ 3. Voting machines, which ensured privacy and accuracy, were common by the early 1900s.

_____ 4. Then, voting became a private matter with the use of secret paper ballots around the time of the Revolutionary War.

____ 5. Until the late 1800s, political parties printed and distributed their own ballots.

____ 6. Voting methods in the United States have changed dramatically in the past 250 years.

____ 7. In recent decades, voting officials have used computers to count votes.

Spatial Order

When you use **spatial order**, you present details in the order in which they are seen—from top to bottom, from right to left, from near to far, and so on. Spatial order is used most often in paragraphs that describe something—for example, in a lab report describing a piece of equipment, or in an art history paper describing a painting.

The following paragraph uses spatial order.

> When I was fourteen, my family and I traveled to Michigan to visit the town where my great-grandmother had lived before she died. Somerset was hardly a town; in fact, it seemed to be just a collection of farms and cow pastures. Scattered among the fields were about twenty buildings. One of them was my great-grandmother's old brick farmhouse. Next to the house were a rusting silo and a faded barn. In front of the house was a long wooden porch that needed painting. On the porch were a potted plant, two white wooden rocking chairs, and a swing. The house was locked, so all we could do was walk around it and look. The lace curtains that my great-grandmother had made before she died still hung in each window. In back of the house was a small cemetery that contained eight graves. There, off in the corner, on the oldest-looking stone, was the name "Azariel Smith"—the name of my great-grandmother's father.
>
> Molly Ward (student)

Notice how the writer moves from far to near as she describes her great-grandmother's farmhouse. She begins by describing the fields around the farmhouse and then moves closer to the house itself. Eventually, she moves behind the farmhouse to the cemetery and then to a specific grave. Notice how transitional words and phrases that signal spatial order—*next to, in front, on the porch, in back,* and *off in the corner*—add to the paragraph's coherence.

Some Transitional Words and Phrases That Signal Spatial Order

above	in front	on the right
behind	inside	on the top
below	near	outside
beneath	next to	over
beside	on the bottom	under
in back	on the left	

◆ PRACTICE 3.12

Read the following paragraphs, whose details are arranged in spatial order. Underline the transitional words and phrases that make each paragraph coherent.

Example

My childhood home was a typical one-story house. The front door opened into a small foyer. Above the foyer and to the right was a carpeted living room shaped like the letter *L*. The short part of the *L* served as our dining room. Behind the living room was the kitchen. A hallway led from the kitchen to a bathroom on the right and then to two bedrooms. Below the bedrooms was a playroom. At the other end of the first floor, beneath the living room, was a garage.

1. The new government building has several security features. Outside, the entire property is surrounded by a security fence. The parking lot to the left of the building is monitored by two guards. Inside, video cameras record all activity in the lobby. Employees must use their badges to enter the elevators at the rear of the lobby. Above the ground floor, guards are posted beside the elevators and stairwells.

2. Room 202 in Phillips Hall is a state-of-the-art classroom. To the right of the door is a dimmer switch for the overhead lights. In the right-front corner of the room, on the wall, is a console with a built-in computer and other electronic equipment. To the left of the console is a large board and, above that, a screen that can be raised and lowered. Computer images are displayed on this screen.

◆ PRACTICE 3.13

Arrange the following sentences into a coherent paragraph. Be sure you are able to explain why you arranged the sentences the way you did.

_____ 1. Next to the video gallery is a display of celebrity portraits.

_____ 2. For example, museum officials have installed a brightly colored fountain on the main lawn in front of the museum.

_____ 3. In a small gallery to the left of the entrance hall, videotapes made by artists play on three monitors.

_____ 4. The Middletown Museum of Art has added several displays designed to attract younger visitors.

_____ 5. Inside the main doors is a large entrance hall, above which hang a dozen large, spinning mobiles.

_____ 6. Officials hope young people will wander behind and above the entrance hall toward the rest of the museum's art exhibits.

_____ 7. A series of small animal sculptures leads from the fountain back toward the main doors.

Logical Order

When you use **logical order**, you present ideas in a sequence that indicates why one idea logically follows another. For example, a paragraph may move from general to specific or from specific to general. In addition, writers may start with the least important idea and end with the most important one, or they may begin with the most important idea and then go on to the less important ones.

The following paragraph presents ideas in logical order.

> As someone who is both a parent and a student, I have had to develop strategies for coping. First, I try to do my studying at night, after I have put my son to bed. I want to give my son all the attention that he deserves, so after I pick him up from day care, I play with him, read to him, and watch a half-hour of TV with him. When I am sure he is asleep, I begin doing my schoolwork. Second, I try to use every spare moment that I have during the day. If I have an hour between classes, I go to the computer lab and do some work. While I eat lunch, I get some of my reading out of the way. When I ride home from work on the bus, I review my class notes. Finally, and most important, I always keep my priorities in mind. My first priority is my son, my second priority is my schoolwork, and my last priority is keeping my apartment clean. If I have studying to do, or if I have promised to take my son to the movies, I will skip housecleaning or doing the wash. Naturally, my apartment can get messy, and occasionally I run out of clean clothes, but that is all right as long as I am able to give my son the attention he deserves.
>
> Vanessa Scully (student)

The writer of this paragraph moves from her least important to her most important point. Notice how transitional words and phrases that signal logical order—*first, second,* and *finally*—add to the paragraph's coherence.

Some Transitional Words and Phrases That Signal Logical Order

also
although
consequently
equally important
finally
first . . . second . . . third
for example
for instance
furthermore
in addition
in fact
last
moreover
not only . . . but also
one . . . another
similarly
the least important
the most important
therefore

◆ PRACTICE 3.14

Read the following paragraphs, whose sentences are organized in logical order. Underline the transitional words and phrases that make each paragraph coherent.

Example

Among the many reasons to support school sports, the most important is the education students get on the playing field. Students in a sports program such as baseball or field hockey learn teamwork, self-confidence, and the value of physical fitness. They also feel a sense of belonging that athletes on a team enjoy. In addition, schools often benefit financially from the sales of tickets to sporting events. Attending a football game may help provide students with new textbooks and other materials. The least important reason to support school sports is the chance that a school athlete could go on to become a famous sports figure. Such success is extremely rare, and most young people should be encouraged to pursue other, more practical careers.

1. The negative effects of illegal drug use are as serious now as they have ever been. First, illegal drug users risk arrest every time they buy, sell, or use drugs. Drug enforcement has become more aggressive over time, and jail sentences are often long. Moreover, drug use is associated with problems such as crime and unemployment. Drug users are more likely to be involved in crimes or to experience periods of unemployment than are people who do not use drugs. But the most important risk to drug users is the physical and mental damage that drugs can cause. Such damage can be life threatening and is often irreversible.

2. I have made some important decisions lately. For example, last year I decided to move from my home in rural Connecticut to an apartment in New York City. This move has had many benefits. For instance, being in the city gave me more career opportunities. It also helped me to meet many more people than I could have in my small Connecticut town. Furthermore, I found plenty of interesting things to do with my time. My new interests include Thai food and modern dance. In fact, I find the cultural mix in the city interesting and exciting.

◆ PRACTICE 3.15

Final Test sentences arranging

Arrange the following sentences into a coherent paragraph. Be sure you are able to explain why you arranged the sentences the way you did.

____ 1. Finally and most important, human beings may one day need to live in space.

____ 2. Velcro, for example, was developed for use in zero-gravity space flights.

____ 3. The exploration of space should continue to be an international priority.

____ 4. For another, the technology used in space travel has other applications.

____ 5. Therefore, space exploration is a vital interest for all nations.

____ 6. A third reason to continue space programs is that they encourage cooperation among nations.

_____ 7. We might need to colonize other planets if the earth becomes too polluted or overcrowded, for instance.

_____ 8. For one thing, scientists learn a great deal about other planets from astronauts' trips into space.

REVISING AND EDITING

Look back at your response to the Seeing and Writing exercise on page 41. First, make sure your paragraph has an effective topic sentence. Then, revise the paragraph so that it is unified, well developed, and coherent.

CHAPTER REVIEW

EDITING PRACTICE

Read the following paragraphs, and evaluate each one in terms of its unity, development, and coherence. First, underline the topic sentence. Next, cross out any sentences that do not support the topic sentence. Then, add transitional words and phrases where needed. Finally, discuss in class what additional details, facts, and examples might be added to each paragraph.

1. At a young age, pirate Anne Bonny traded a life of wealth and privilege for one of adventure and crime. In 1716, she ran away from home to marry a sailor. Sailors passed through the place where she lived, on the East Coast of the United States, on a regular basis. Later, through her husband, she met a pirate named Calico Jack Rackham. Bonny soon left her husband to join Rackham's crew. She developed a reputation as a fierce fighter. In 1720, Bonny met another female pirate named Mary Read. They were captured by authorities. Bonny, who was pregnant, was not sentenced to death because executing a woman criminal who was pregnant was against the law. Read received a death sentence. Before it could be carried out, she died of a fever in prison. No one knows what finally became of Bonny.

2. Over time, attitudes toward the people who live in the Appalachian mountains and their way of life have changed a great deal. At first, in the early days of European settlement, life in Appalachia was difficult. It was hard for people to get across the mountains to trade with or visit their neighbors. Communities were often isolated. Residents developed their own local arts and crafts. The recent television series *Survivor* also shows an isolated community, but it does not accurately depict the challenges people face in a new environment. Its popularity has more to do with sensationalism than fact. Each settlement in Appalachia developed its own forms of entertainment. People invented simple stringed instruments and wrote music for them. They created dances based on earlier English dances. In the middle of the twentieth century, many people considered Appalachian culture to be backward and uninteresting. Many tourists visit the states in Appalachia to enjoy their crafts, art, music, and dance.

3. The number of all-volunteer fire departments has declined for a number of reasons. People have less time than they used to for volunteer activities. Most volunteer fire departments were founded when two-parent, single-income families were the rule. That model is far less common than it once was. Many people have come to expect payment for the work they do. The ideal of community service for its own sake is held by fewer and fewer people. American families are more mobile than they have ever been. Long commutes and frequent moves often mean that people are not strongly connected to their neighborhoods. They are less likely to volunteer time and risk their personal safety for the good of the community.

◆ COLLABORATIVE ACTIVITIES

1. Working in a group, list some reasons why many students find it difficult to perform well in college, and arrange these reasons from least important to most important. Then, create a topic sentence that states the main idea suggested by the reasons. Finally, write your own draft of a paragraph in which you discuss why some students have difficulty in college.
2. Think of a place you know well. Write a paragraph that describes the place so that readers will be able to imagine it almost as clearly as you

can. Decide on a specific spatial order—outside to inside, left to right, front to back, or another arrangement that makes sense to you. Use that spatial order to organize the details in your draft paragraph. When you have finished, trade paragraphs with another student. See if you can sketch the place described in your partner's paragraph. If you cannot, offer suggestions that could improve his or her description.

3. Bring to class a paragraph from a newspaper or a magazine. Working in a group, find the main idea of each paragraph, and underline the paragraph's topic sentence. Then, decide whether each paragraph is unified, well developed, and coherent. If it is not, work together to make it more effective.

✓ REVIEW CHECKLIST: Fine-Tuning Your Paragraph

- ☐ Every paragraph you write should include a topic sentence that states the paragraph's main idea. (See 3A.)
- ☐ A paragraph is unified when it focuses on a single main idea, which is often stated in the topic sentence. (See 3B.)
- ☐ A paragraph is well developed when it contains enough details, facts, and examples to support the main idea. (See 3C.)
- ☐ A paragraph is coherent when its sentences are arranged in a clear, logical order and it includes all necessary transitional words and phrases. (See 3D.)

CHAPTER

4

Patterns of Paragraph Development

PREVIEW

In this chapter, you will learn to write paragraphs using the following patterns:

- exemplification (4A)
- narration (4B)
- description (4C)
- comparison and contrast (4D)
- argument (4E)

CBS PHOTO ARCHIVE. Photo: Monty Brinton/CBS.

SEEING AND WRITING

What skills do you have that would help you survive on a deserted island? Why would these skills be helpful? Look at the picture above, and then write a paragraph that answers these questions.

Word Power

maroon to put ashore on a deserted island

improvise to make do with the tools or resources at hand

As you write paragraphs, you will discover that you present ideas in patterns that reflect the ways in which your mind works. Recognizing these patterns and understanding how they help you communicate your ideas will make you a stronger, more self-confident writer. In this chapter, you will learn about five ways of developing paragraphs—*exemplification, narration, description, comparison and contrast,* and *argument.*

Student Voices

Before I write an exemplification paragraph, I list all the examples I'm going to use.

Theresa Armetta

A Exemplification

An **example** is a specific illustration of a general idea. An **exemplification paragraph** explains or clarifies a general statement or idea—the topic sentence—with one or more specific examples. Personal experiences, class discussions, observations, conversations, and reading (for example, material from newspapers, magazines, or the Internet) can all be good sources of examples.

How many examples you need depends on your topic sentence. A complicated, far-reaching statement might require many examples to convince readers that it is reasonable. A simple, more straightforward statement would require fewer examples.

The following paragraph uses examples to make the point that the English language makes no sense.

> Sometimes you have to believe that all English speakers should be committed to an asylum for the verbally insane. In what other language do people drive in a parkway and park in a driveway? In what other language do people recite at a play and play at a recital? In what other language do privates eat in the general mess and generals eat in the private mess? In what other language do men get hernias and women get hysterectomies? In what other language do people ship by truck and send cargo by ship? In what other language can your nose run and your feet smell?
>
> Richard Lederer, "English Is a Crazy Language"

Notice that the author uses a number of short examples, one after the other, to make his point. Each example supports the statement that Lederer makes in his topic sentence: that sometimes you have to think speakers of English are insane.

Writing Tip
Transitional words and phrases used in exemplification include *for instance, for example,* and *one reason . . . another reason.*

✓ SELF-ASSESSMENT CHECKLIST: Writing an Exemplification Paragraph

- ☐ Does your topic sentence clearly express what the rest of the paragraph is about?
- ☐ Do all your examples support your topic sentence?
- ☐ Have you used enough examples?
- ☐ Have you used appropriate transitional words and phrases?

Writing Tip
Many everyday writing tasks require exemplification. For example, in a memo to your employer, you might give examples of how your department could save money.

◆ PRACTICE 4.1

Read this exemplification paragraph, and answer the questions that follow it.

Squash is a delicious vegetable that comes in many different shapes, sizes, flavors, and colors, but few people are aware of its tremendous variety. Most consumers have encountered the popular types of squash: pumpkin, butternut, acorn, and spaghetti. There are many less popular but equally appealing varieties, however. For example, stripetti squash is yellow with green stripes, has stringy flesh much like the spaghetti squash, and is crisp with a taste somewhat like corn. Another relative unknown, Hubbard squash, is a huge variety, weighing at least ten pounds. It has blue skin and orange flesh, and the flavor, unlike some other types of squash, is not sugary. A few other varieties of squash are also not very well known. Sweet dumplings, for instance, are a small squash with dark green and white striped skin. Their flavor is rich, buttery, and very sweet. Kabochas, another unusual variety of squash, look a lot like a butternut squash and also have a sweet flavor. They have dark green or dark orange skin, sometimes with white stripes. You can experiment with these different kinds of squash by using them as filling in ravioli; making them into soup; stuffing, sautéing, or baking them; or making them into pies. Now that you have learned about the many kinds of squash, explore a few new varieties.

1. Underline the topic sentence of the paragraph.
2. List the specific examples the writer uses to support the topic sentence. The first example has been listed for you.

   Stripetti, yellow and green, tastes like corn
   ____
   ____
   ____
   ____

3. Circle the transitional words and phrases that the writer uses to connect ideas in the paragraph.

◆ PRACTICE 4.2

Following are four topic sentences for exemplification paragraphs. After each topic sentence, list three examples that could support the main idea. For example, if you were writing about the poor quality of food in your school cafeteria, you could give examples of mystery meat, weak coffee, and stale bread.

1. World War II was a conflict of intense and unprecedented destructiveness.

   ____
   ____
   ____

2. Racial conflict is a serious problem in many parts of the country.

   ____
   ____
   ____

3. I have always been very unlucky (or lucky) in love.

___

___

___

4. Although many people criticize television shows as mindless, there are important exceptions.

___

___

___

◆ PRACTICE 4.3

Choose one of the following topics (or one of your own choice) as the subject of an exemplification paragraph. Then, on a separate sheet of paper, list as many examples as you can for the topic you have chosen. Use the invention strategies discussed in 2B to help you think of examples.

Why the Internet is important to you
The importance of family in your life
What made a favorite movie memorable
The benefits of a healthy diet
How not to act on a first date
How your school can be improved
The accomplishments of a historical figure
The difficulty of being young today
The demands of being a parent
Drivers who are a menace
Annoying trends on your college campus
Exercise for busy people
Books that have influenced you the most
The best jobs for a recent college graduate
Ways to organize schoolwork
The consequences of procrastinating (putting things off)

◆ PRACTICE 4.4

On a separate sheet of paper, write an exemplification paragraph on the topic you chose in Practice 4.3. When you have finished, use the Self-Assessment Checklist on page 62 to help you revise your paragraph.

◆ PRACTICE 4.5

On a separate sheet of paper, write a final, edited draft of your exemplification paragraph.

B Narration

Narration is writing that tells a story. Most of the time, a **narrative paragraph** makes a point—for example, that an experience you had as a child changed you, that the life of Helen Keller is inspiring, or that the Battle of Gettysburg was the turning point of the Civil War. The topic sentence states this idea, and the rest of the paragraph develops it, with events and details arranged in time order.

In the following narrative paragraph, the writer tells about the poverty she experienced as a child.

> Like rural Southern gypsies, we moved from one dilapidated Southern farmhouse to another in a constant search for a decent place to live. Sometimes we moved when the rent increased beyond the 30 or 40 dollars my mother could afford. Or the house burned down, not an unusual occurrence in substandard housing. One year, when we were gathered together for Thanksgiving dinner, a stranger walked in without knocking and announced that we were being evicted. The house had been sold without our knowledge and the new owner wanted to start remodeling immediately. We tried to finish our meal with an attitude of thanksgiving while he worked around us with his tape measure.
>
> Melanie Scheller, "On the Meaning of Plumbing and Poverty"

Writing Tip
Transitional words and phrases used in narration include *first, then, next, after that, finally,* and other transitions that signal time order. See 3D.

Notice that the details in the paragraph follow a time sequence: first one thing happens, then another thing happens, and so on. The transitional words and phrases in the paragraph—*sometimes* and *one year*—help make this structure clear.

✓ SELF-ASSESSMENT CHECKLIST: Writing a Narrative Paragraph

- ☐ Does your narrative paragraph make a point?
- ☐ Is your topic sentence specific enough?
- ☐ Does your narrative move clearly from an earlier time to a later time?
- ☐ Have you used appropriate transitional words and phrases?

Writing Tip
Many everyday writing tasks require narration. For example, in a letter to your HMO, you might summarize the history of your claim.

◆ PRACTICE 4.6

Read this narrative paragraph, and answer the questions that follow it.

I've lived in the same house my entire life, and when I was eight years old, I helped to build part of it. Our house was too small, so one summer my father decided to build two new bedrooms for my older brother and me. I remember clearly how we all worked together on the project. Even though I was only eight years old, I was very proud of how I helped carry the heavy concrete blocks that formed the foundation of what would be my new bedroom. After the foundation was built, we had to lay down the wooden floor. I watched with fascination as my father fitted together the planks of pine that he had carefully finished with a deep brown stain. Next, he framed the walls and, with my mother's help, put up wallboard. After that came the ceiling and, finally, the roof. At each stage, my father would give me and my brother a small job to do so that we would feel as if we were constructing along with him. Most often, my brother and I were limited to hammering nails, but we felt that this was a major accomplishment. I was too small to do some of the jobs my brother was permitted to help on, but I felt I was contributing just the same. The whole family spent many happy weekends outside, hammering and sawing, listening to music and telling jokes. After many months, we finished the project, an occasion we celebrated with uncles, aunts, cousins, and grandparents.

1. Underline the topic sentence of the paragraph.
2. List the major events of the narrative. The first event has been listed for you.

   When I was eight, my father decided to add two new bedrooms to our house.

   ______

   ______

   ______

   ______

   ______

3. Circle the transitional words and phrases that the writer uses to link events in time.

◆ PRACTICE 4.7

Following are four topic sentences for narrative paragraphs. After each topic sentence, list four events you could include in a narrative paragraph to support the main idea. For example, if you were telling about a dinner that turned out to be a disaster, you could tell about how the meat burned, the vegetables were overcooked, the cake fell, and the guests arrived late.

1. The day started out normally enough, but before it was over all our lives had been changed forever.

   ______

   ______

   ______

   ______

2. When I was young, my grandmother would tell me stories about her childhood.

____

____

____

____

3. I'll never forget my first college roommate, a person I grew to hate.

____

____

____

____

4. It was a difficult decision for me to make.

____

____

____

____

◆ PRACTICE 4.8

Choose one of the following topics (or one of your own choice) as the subject of a narrative paragraph. Then, on a separate sheet of paper, list as many events and details as you can for the topic you have chosen. Use the invention strategies discussed in 2B to help you think of events and details.

A fairy tale
Your proudest moment
Overcoming an obstacle
A family legend
A great adventure
A fortunate accident
Your first day at school
An important choice
Your most embarrassing moment
Your favorite holiday memory
A terrifying event
Taking a risk
An incredible coincidence
A new experience
A humorous incident
A great loss
A lesson learned

◆ PRACTICE 4.9

On a separate sheet of paper, write a narrative paragraph on the topic you chose in Practice 4.8. When you have finished, use the Self-Assessment Checklist on page 65 to help you revise your paragraph.

◆ PRACTICE 4.10

On a separate sheet of paper, write a final, edited draft of your narrative paragraph.

C Description

▼ **Student Voices**

When I write descriptions, I try hard to choose exactly the right word.

Cheng Tang

When you write a **description,** you rely on your sense of sight, sound, smell, taste, and touch. In a **descriptive paragraph**, you use your senses to paint a word picture of a person, object, or place.

When you write a descriptive paragraph, you try to communicate a single **dominant impression**—a particular mood or quality—in your topic sentence. For example, if you were describing your younger sister's room and wanted to leave readers with the impression that it was a cluttered, messy place, your topic sentence would convey this idea: *My sister's room looks like a place that has just been burglarized.* All the other sentences in the paragraph would include details to support this dominant impression.

FOCUS Description

Good descriptions rely on language that is specific and original. Vague, overused words such as *good, nice, bad,* and *beautiful* do not help readers visualize what you are describing. When you write a descriptive paragraph, try to use specific words and phrases that make your writing come alive.

VAGUE The dogs are following a woman.

SPECIFIC Two dogs are following an old woman in gardening clothes as she strolls along.

● **Writing Tip**

Transitional words and phrases used in description include *in front, in back, next to, near, beyond,* and other transitions that signal spatial order. See 3D.

In the following paragraph, writer Jeanne Wakatsuki Houston, a second-generation Japanese American who along with her family was imprisoned in Manzanar internment camp in 1942, describes the pictures on a page of her high school yearbook.

All the class pictures are there, from the seventh grade through twelfth, with individual head shots of seniors, their names followed by the names of the high schools they would have graduated from on the outside: Theodore Roosevelt, Thomas Jefferson, Herbert Hoover, Sacred Heart. You see pretty girls on bicycles, chicken yards full of fat pullets, patients back-tilted in dental chairs, lines of laundry, and finally, two large blowups, the first of a high tower with a searchlight, against a Sierra backdrop, the next, a two-page endsheet showing a wide path that curves among rows of elm trees. White stones border the path.

Two dogs are following an old woman in gardening clothes as she strolls along. She is in the middle distance, small beneath the snowy peaks. It is winter. All the elms are bare. The scene is both stark and comforting. The path leads toward one edge of the camp, but the wire is out of sight, or out of focus. The tiny woman seems very much at ease. She and her tiny dogs seem almost swallowed by the landscape, or floating in it.

Jeanne Wakatsuki Houston, "Manzanar, U.S.A."

Word Power

stark bare; harsh; grim

Wakatsuki Houston uses vivid language and specific details to convey an unsettling dominant impression: that the innocence of the students' high school yearbook pictures is overshadowed by the picture of a guard tower and the suggestion of barbed wire. The specific details that support this dominant impression are arranged in spatial order, and transitional words and phrases—*the first* and *the next*—reinforce this organization.

✓ SELF-ASSESSMENT CHECKLIST: Writing a Descriptive Paragraph

- Does your topic sentence communicate the paragraph's dominant impression?
- Do all your details support the dominant impression?
- Have you used language that is both specific and original?
- Have you used appropriate transitional words and phrases?

Writing Tip

Many everyday writing tasks require description. For example, in a job application letter, you might describe a piece of equipment you have worked with.

PRACTICE 4.11

Read this descriptive paragraph, and answer the questions that follow it.

When I first moved to New York City, it seemed huge and dirty. In the winter especially, it felt like the entire city was lonely and gray. As I walked to work every day, the glass and steel buildings towered over the street and looked down on me ominously. The concrete sidewalks were cold and gritty under my feet. Everything seemed gray—the massive bridges, the crowded, smelly subways, even the sky. The city teemed with people huddled in their dark coats and hats and scarves, pale from lack of sun. They didn't seem to notice the garbage on the street, the foul odors in the air, or even the people around them. I thought I'd never adjust, but eventually I began to get used to New York.

1. Underline the topic sentence of the paragraph.

2. In a few words, summarize the dominant impression the writer gives of the subject, New York City.

____

____

3. What are some of the details the writer uses to create this dominant impression? The first detail has been listed for you.

   Towering buildings
   ____
   ____
   ____
   ____
   ____

◆ PRACTICE 4.12

Following are four topic sentences for descriptive paragraphs. After each topic sentence, list three details that could help convey the dominant impression. For example, to describe an interesting person, you could tell what the person looked like, how he or she behaved, and what he or she said.

1. It was a long hike, but when we finally got to the top of the mountain, the view was incredible.

   ____
   ____
   ____

2. Every community has one house that all the kids swear is haunted.

   ____
   ____
   ____

3. In every living situation, there is one person who is an unbelievable slob.

   ____
   ____
   ____

4. I'll never forget the first time I met her (him).

   ____
   ____
   ____

◆ PRACTICE 4.13

Choose one of the following topics (or one of your own choice) as the subject of a descriptive paragraph. Then, on a separate sheet of paper, list as many details as you can for the topic you have chosen. Use the invention strategies discussed in 2B to help you think of details.

A childhood hideout
Your first pet
A beautiful view
A memorable gift
A musical or other performance
A favorite childhood toy
The place you feel the most comfortable
Your favorite article of clothing
The face of a loved one
A place you never want to go to again
Your most treasured possession
Your dream car (or the car you already have)
A frightening sight
Your dream house
The best meal you've ever eaten

◆ PRACTICE 4.14

On a separate sheet of paper, write a descriptive paragraph on the topic you chose in Practice 4.13. When you have finished, use the Self-Assessment Checklist on page 69 to help you revise your paragraph.

◆ PRACTICE 4.15

On a separate sheet of paper, write a final, edited draft of your descriptive paragraph.

D Comparison and Contrast

When you **compare** two things, you concentrate on their similarities. When you **contrast** them, you concentrate on their differences. (Sometimes, people use the term *comparison* to refer to both similarities and differences.) When you write a **comparison-and-contrast paragraph,** you examine the similarities or differences (or both) between two people, two things, or two ideas.

FOCUS Topics for Comparison and Contrast

In order to write an effective comparison-and-contrast paragraph, you have to discuss two things that have enough in common so the comparison makes sense. For example, it would be practically impossible to compare dogs and telephones. (They do not share any significant characteristics.) It would, however, be easy to compare dogs and cats. (Both are mammals, both like to play, and both make good pets.)

There are two methods for structuring a comparison-and-contrast paragraph: subject by subject and point by point.

Subject-by-Subject Comparisons

In a **subject-by-subject** comparison, you discuss all the points you are going to make about one subject and then discuss the same points for the second subject. This method of organization works well if you are discussing relatively few points for each subject. A subject-by-subject comparison has the following structure.

> **Writing Tip**
> Transitional words and phrases used in comparison and contrast include *however, in contrast, similarly,* and *on the one hand . . . on the other hand.*

Subject A
  Point 1
  Point 2
  Point 3
Subject B
  Point 1
  Point 2
  Point 3

> **Computer Tip**
> Use your computer's Tab key to indent points in your outline.

In the following paragraph, the writer uses a subject-by-subject comparison to compare two methods of transportation—cars and trains.

> Last year, when I took the train to Boston to visit my sister, I had a chance to compare this method of transportation with the way I usually travel, by car. Driving to Boston from Philadelphia takes about six-and-a-half hours. I often drive alone with only my car radio and CD player for company. By the third hour, I am bored and tired. Traffic is also a problem. The interstate roads I take are crowded and dangerous. If my attention wanders, I can get into serious trouble. If there is an accident, I may have to wait for more than an hour until the police clear the highway. A train ride, however, is a much better experience. Often, I meet other students and get into interesting conversations. If I am tired, I can take a nap, and if I am hungry, I can get a snack. If I really feel motivated, I can even catch up on my schoolwork. Best of all, I never get stuck in traffic, and when I arrive in Boston, I am rested and ready for a day with my sister.
>
> Forest Williams (student)

In his topic sentence, the writer clearly states what two things he will be comparing, and the rest of his paragraph presents the points that support his comparison. In the first half of the paragraph, the writer discusses the disadvantages of driving. In the second half, he discusses the advantages of taking the train. Notice that he signals the shift from his discussion of cars to his discussion of trains with the transition *however.*

Point-by-Point Comparisons

When you write a **point-by-point** comparison, you make a point about one subject and then discuss the same point in relation to another subject. You use this alternating pattern throughout the paragraph. This arrangement is best for a paragraph in which you discuss many points because it helps readers to see the specific points of the comparison as they read. A point-by-point comparison has the following structure.

Point 1
  Subject A
  Subject B
Point 2
  Subject A
  Subject B
Point 3
  Subject A
  Subject B

Notice how the author of the following paragraph uses a point-by-point comparison to compare students who commute to those who live on campus.

> Some people say that there is no difference between students who commute and those who live on campus, but I disagree. Just come to an 8 o'clock class any morning, and the differences are obvious. Commuters are fighting to keep awake after their one-hour ride to school. Dorm students are wide awake after a brisk ten-minute walk to class. As a result of being sleep deprived, commuters are frequently grumpy and irritable. Dorm students, however, are generally alert and in good spirits. After all, they have gotten an extra hour of sleep. The differences between dorm students and commuters do not end in class. After class, the dorm students go back to their rooms to nap before their next class. Commuters must find something to occupy their time before the next class. Often, this means walking around campus trying to find a quiet spot to rest. After classes are finished for the day, the dorm students go back to their rooms. The commuters, who by this time are exhausted, trudge wearily to the bus stop and wait for the process to begin again the next morning.
>
> Margaret Caracappa (student)

This point-by-point comparison begins with a topic sentence that clearly states what two subjects will be compared. The writer goes on to discuss a series of points, making a point about commuters and then a related point about dorm students. She signals shifts from one subject to another by repeating the words *dorm students* and *commuters*.

Writing Tip

Many everyday writing tasks require comparison and contrast. For example, in a letter to your local school board, you might compare two methods of teaching reading before recommending one of them.

✓ SELF-ASSESSMENT CHECKLIST: Writing a Comparison-and-Contrast Paragraph

- ☐ Does your topic sentence indicate what two things you will compare?
- ☐ Do the two things you are comparing have enough in common so the comparison makes sense?

(continued on the following page)

(continued from the previous page)

- Have you used a subject-by-subject or a point-by-point comparison? Why?
- Have you discussed the same or similar points for both subjects?
- Have you used appropriate transitional words and phrases?

◆ PRACTICE 4.16

Read this comparison-and-contrast paragraph, and answer the questions that follow it.

Having been both a smoker and a nonsmoker, I feel qualified to compare the two ways of life. When I smoked, I often found myself banished from public places such as offices, restaurants, and stores when I felt the urge to smoke. I would huddle with my fellow smokers outside, enduring all kinds of weather just for the pleasure of a cigarette. As more and more people stopped smoking, I found myself banished from private homes, too, if I gave in to my craving. I spent a lot of money on cigarettes, and the prices seemed to rise faster and faster. In my sanest moments, I worried about lung cancer and heart disease. My colds lingered and often turned into bronchitis. Climbing stairs and running left me breathless. Now that I have been smoke-free for over a year, I can go anywhere and socialize with anyone. The money I have saved in the last year on cigarettes is going to pay for a winter vacation in sunny Florida. After not smoking for only a few weeks, I could breathe more easily. I had more energy for running and climbing stairs. I have avoided colds so far, and I'm not as worried about lung and heart disease. In fact, I've been told that my lungs should be as healthy as those of a nonsmoker within another year or so. Quitting smoking has proved to be one of the smartest moves I've ever made.

1. Underline the topic sentence of the paragraph.
2. Does this paragraph deal mainly with similarities or differences?

   ____

   How do you know?

   ____

   ____

3. Is this paragraph a subject-by-subject or a point-by-point comparison? How do you know?

   ____

   ____

   ____

   ____

   ____

4. List some of the contrasts the writer describes. The first contrast has been listed for you.

When she was a smoker, she often had to smoke outside of public and private places. As a nonsmoker, she can go anywhere.

______

______

______

______

______

______

◆ PRACTICE 4.17

Following are four topic sentences for comparison-and-contrast paragraphs. First, identify the two things being compared. Then, list three similarities or differences for the two subjects. For example, if you were comparing two authors, you could show the similarities and/or differences in the subjects they write about, their styles of writing, and what kinds of readers they attract.

1. My life plan has changed considerably since I was a child.

______

______

______

2. The media's portrayal of young people has been very negative in recent years, but the true picture is more positive.

______

______

______

3. These two styles of music are very similar.

______

______

______

4. As soon as I get to my job, I become a different person.

______

______

______

◆ PRACTICE 4.18

Choose one of the following topics (or one of your own choice) as the subject of a comparison-and-contrast paragraph. Then, on a separate sheet of paper, list as many similarities or differences as you can for the topic you have chosen. Use the invention strategies discussed in 2B to help you think of similarities and differences.

- Two different parts of the country
- The differences between two political candidates
- What you thought college would be like before you started, and what it actually is like
- Two different sports
- How you and your best friend or sibling are alike (or different)
- Horror movies and comedies
- Writing letters and sending e-mail
- The music you listen to and the music your parents listen to
- Technology today and 100 years ago
- How people see you and how you really are
- Dog owners and cat owners
- The work of two different authors or musicians
- Differences in the lives of the rich and poor in the United States
- Two different jobs you've had
- Childhood and young adult years
- Living in a city and living in a small town

◆ PRACTICE 4.19

On a separate sheet of paper, write a comparison-and-contrast paragraph on the topic you chose in Practice 4.18. When you have finished, use the Self-Assessment Checklist on page 73 to help you revise your paragraph.

◆ PRACTICE 4.20

On a separate sheet of paper, write a final, edited draft of your comparison-and-contrast paragraph.

E Argument

Word Power

controversy a dispute between sides holding different views

controversial marked by controversy

So far, we have discussed paragraphs that are developed by means of *exemplification, narration, description,* and *comparison and contrast.* In these paragraphs, the main idea stated in the topic sentence is straightforward, not controversial or debatable. In an **argument paragraph**, however, the main idea *is* debatable: the topic sentence states a position on an issue, but reasonable people may disagree with this position. The rest of the paragraph supports the topic sentence with facts, examples, and reasons.

To write an effective argument paragraph, follow these guidelines.

- *Write a clear topic sentence that states your position.* Using *should, should not,* or *ought to* in your topic sentence will make your position on the issue clear to readers.

The city *ought to* lower the wage tax.

The school *should* change its drop/add policy.

- *Present convincing support.* Include facts, examples, and reasons that support your topic sentence. At first, your support will consist mainly of information from your own experience. Later, when you become a more experienced writer, you will support your points with information you get from research.
- *Address opposing arguments.* Try to anticipate possible opposing arguments and argue against them. By addressing these objections, you strengthen your position.

The following paragraph argues against animal experimentation.

Scientists should no longer ignore the suffering of animals. The work many scientists have already done on animal behavior suggests that animals feel, think, reason, and even communicate with each other. For example, work with dolphins and whales shows the intelligence of these animals. Not only can they be trained, but they can also think independently. It seems that the gap between us and the rest of the animal kingdom is getting smaller. This is making it more and more difficult to justify animal experiments. Of course, some people will say that animal experimentation is necessary to help save human lives. But the fact is that most experiments that are done on animals are not necessary, and even the few that are necessary could be done in ways that would cut down or even eliminate suffering and death. For this reason, it is hard not to feel uneasy about carrying out experiments on animals.

Agaja Reddy (student)

Writing Tip
Transitional words and phrases used in argument include *the first reason, the second reason, therefore, furthermore,* and *in conclusion.*

This paragraph begins with a topic sentence that states the writer's position on the issue and then presents facts, examples, and reasons to support the topic sentence. After the writer has presented her points, she addresses the opposing argument that animal experimentation is needed to save human lives. She ends with a sentence that sums up her position. Throughout the paragraph, transitional words and phrases—*for example, of course, the fact is,* and *for this reason*—lead readers through the argument.

✓ SELF-ASSESSMENT CHECKLIST: Writing an Argument Paragraph

- Does your topic sentence clearly state your position? Is your position debatable?
- Do you support your topic sentence with specific facts, examples, and reasons?
- Have you addressed possible opposing arguments?
- Have you used appropriate transitional words and phrases?

Writing Tip
Many everyday writing tasks require argument. For example, in a letter to your local newspaper, you might argue against a law banning drivers from using cell phones in moving vehicles.

◆ PRACTICE 4.21

Read this argument paragraph, and answer the questions that follow it.

Many American voters never cast a ballot, and voter turn-out is often below 50 percent even in presidential elections. It is tragic that people give up this hard-won right. It is in each person's best interest to vote. The most important reason to vote is that government affects every aspect of our lives. It is foolish not to have one's say about who makes the laws and regulations people have to live with. If a citizen does not vote, he or she loses control over what taxes one must pay, the educational system, health care, the environment, and even what roads will be built and which bridges repaired. Another reason to vote is to support a particular political party. If a person believes in that party's policies, it is important to vote to elect that party's candidates and keep them in power. Even if one's candidate does not win, one's vote isn't wasted. The voter has expressed his or her opinion by voting, and the government in power is affected by public opinion. Remember that to keep our democracy working and to participate in government, all citizens must exercise their right to vote.

1. Underline the topic sentence of the paragraph. Why do you think the writer places the topic sentence where he does?

____

____

____

2. What is the issue that the writer is dealing with?

____

____

____

What is the writer's position on the issue?

____

3. List some of the reasons the writer uses to support his position. The first reason has been listed for you.

The most important reason to vote is that government affects every aspect of our lives.

____

____

____

____

____

◆ PRACTICE 4.22

Following are four topic sentences for argument paragraphs. For each statement, list three points that could support the statement. For example, if you were arguing in favor of banning smoking in all public places, you could say that smoking is a nuisance, a health risk, and a fire hazard.

1. Employers should offer flexible time schedules to employees.

   ____

   ____

   ____

2. Women's college sports teams should be supported on an equal level with men's teams.

   ____

   ____

   ____

3. Driving under the influence of alcohol is a widespread problem among young people.

   ____

   ____

   ____

4. The space exploration program benefits everyone.

   ____

   ____

   ____

◆ PRACTICE 4.23

Choose one of the following topics (or one of your own choice) as the subject of an argument paragraph. Then, on a separate sheet of paper, state your position on the issue and list as much support (facts, examples, and reasons) as you can to back up your position. Use the invention strategies discussed in 2B to help you think of supporting points.

Why you would be a good president
Why stricter gun control is a good (bad) idea
Is college necessary for success?
Is our right to privacy being lost?
Why capital punishment is a good (bad) idea
A law that should be changed
Improvements needed in your town or neighborhood
Courses or requirements that your school should change or add
Why laws requiring motorcycle riders to wear helmets are a good (bad) idea

Why workplaces should offer facilities for childcare
An environmental policy or issue
A health-care issue
Safety on your campus
Financial aid policies at your school
Campus drug or alcohol policies

◆ PRACTICE 4.24

On a separate sheet of paper, write an argument paragraph on the topic you chose in Practice 4.23. When you have finished, use the Self-Assessment Checklist on page 77 to help you revise your paragraph.

◆ PRACTICE 4.25

On a separate sheet of paper, write a final, edited draft of your argument paragraph.

■ REVISING AND EDITING

Look back at your response to the Seeing and Writing exercise on page 61. First, determine which pattern of development your paragraph most closely matches. Then, consult the appropriate Self-Assessment Checklist (Exemplification—p. 62; Narration—p. 65; Description—p. 69; Comparison and Contrast—pp. 73–74; or Argument—p. 77). Next, referring to Chapter 3 if necessary, evaluate your paragraph for unity, development, and coherence. Finally, make any necessary revisions.

☑ REVIEW CHECKLIST: Patterns of Paragraph Development

- ☐ Exemplification paragraphs use specific examples to support the topic sentence. (See 4A.)
- ☐ Narrative paragraphs tell a story by presenting a series of events in time order. (See 4B.)
- ☐ Descriptive paragraphs use specific details to communicate a dominant impression. (See 4C.)
- ☐ Comparison-and-contrast paragraphs explain how two things are alike or how they are different. (See 4D.)
- ☐ Argument paragraphs support a position on a debatable issue. (See 4E.)

CHAPTER

5

Moving from Paragraph to Essay

PREVIEW

In this chapter, you will learn

- to understand essay structure (5A)
- to decide on a topic (5B)
- to use invention strategies (5C)
- to state your thesis (5D)
- to select and arrange ideas (5E)
- to draft your essay (5F)
- to revise and edit your essay (5G)

SEEING AND WRITING

Do you think there is too much violence in sports? Why or why not? Look at the picture above as you think about these questions. This chapter will take you through the process of writing an essay about the topic of violence in sports.

Word Power

brawl a noisy quarrel or fight

altercation a quarrel

A Understanding Essay Structure

In the previous chapters, we have been discussing paragraphs. Now, however, we will focus on essays. An **essay** is a group of paragraphs about one subject. In this chapter, you will see how the strategies you learned for writing paragraphs can also be helpful in writing essays.

For a discussion of how to write a paragraph, see Chapter 2.

In some ways, essays and paragraphs are similar. In a paragraph, the main idea is presented in a topic sentence, and the rest of the paragraph supports this main idea.

Paragraph

The **topic sentence** states the main idea of the paragraph.

Support develops the main idea with details, facts, and examples.

● **Writing Tip**

Many writing situations outside of school require you to write more than a paragraph. The skills you learn in this chapter can also be applied to these writing tasks.

In an essay, the main idea is presented in a **thesis statement**. The first paragraph—the **introduction**—presents the thesis statement. The main part of the essay consists of several **body paragraphs** that present support for the thesis statement. (Each of these body paragraphs contains a topic sentence that states the paragraph's main idea and shows how it relates to the thesis statement.) Finally, the essay ends with a **conclusion** that restates the thesis statement (in different words) and brings the essay to a close. This essay structure is called **thesis and support**.

Thesis-and-Support Essay

Opening remarks introduce the subject to be discussed.

The **thesis statement** presents the main idea of the essay in the last sentence of the first paragraph.

Introduction

Topic sentence (first point)

Support (details, facts, examples)

Topic sentence (second point)

Support (details, facts, examples)

Body paragraphs

Topic sentence (third point)

Support (details, facts, examples)

Body paragraphs

The **restatement of the thesis** summarizes the essay's main idea.

Closing remarks present the writer's last thoughts on the subject.

Conclusion

The rest of this chapter will introduce you to the process of writing a thesis-and-support essay.

B Deciding on a Topic

Most of the essays you write in college will be in response to assignments that your instructors give you. In your writing class, you may be given assignments such as the following ones.

- Discuss something your school could do to improve the lives of returning older students.
- Examine a decision you made that changed your life.
- Write about someone you admire.

Before you can respond to these general assignments, you will need to ask yourself some questions. Exactly what could the school do to improve the lives of older students? What decision did you make that changed your life? What person do you admire? By asking yourself questions like these, you can narrow these general assignments to **topics** that are specific enough to write about.

- Offering free day care for students
- The effects of giving up smoking
- My grandfather

◆ PRACTICE 5.1

The following topics are not narrow enough for an essay of four or five paragraphs. In the blank that follows each topic, narrow it further for a brief essay.

Example: Personal computers

How a personal computer changed my life

1. Stress

____

2. Ways people organize their time

____

3. Water pollution

____

4. Violent lyrics in popular music

____

5. Censorship

____

C Using Invention Strategies

For a discussion of these invention strategies, see 2B.

Before you begin writing about your topic, you need to find something to say about it. You do this by using invention strategies—*freewriting, brainstorming, clustering,* or *journal writing*—just as you do when you write a paragraph.

> **Student Voices**
>
> *Deciding what to say is the hardest part of the writing process.*
>
> *Shaun Berry*

◆ PRACTICE 5.2

Reread the Seeing and Writing exercise on page 81. Then, on a separate sheet of paper, use whatever invention strategies you like to help you generate material for an essay on violence in sports. If your instructor gives you permission, you can review your material with other students.

D Stating Your Thesis

> **Student Voices**
>
> *Once I figure out my thesis, the rest is easy.*
>
> *Carmen Johnson*

Once you have used one or more invention strategies to help you find information about your topic, you need to decide exactly what you want to say about it. You begin doing this by looking through your invention material to see what main idea it can support. You express this main idea in a single sentence called a **thesis statement**.

Topic	*Thesis Statement*
Offering free day care for students	Free day care would improve the lives of the many students who have children.

Topic	*Thesis Statement*
The effects of giving up smoking	Giving up smoking not only improved my self-image, it also gave me a great deal of self-respect.
My grandfather	My grandfather is my role model.

In order to be effective, a thesis statement must do two things.

- *An effective thesis statement must make a point or take a stand on your topic.* For this reason, it must do more than simply state a fact or announce the subject of your essay.

STATEMENT OF FACT	Free day care is not available on our campus.
ANNOUNCEMENT	In this essay, I will discuss free day care on campus.
EFFECTIVE THESIS STATEMENT	Free day-care facilities on campus would improve the lives of the many students who have children.

- *An effective thesis statement must be specific and clearly worded.*

VAGUE THESIS STATEMENT	Giving up smoking helped me a lot.
EFFECTIVE THESIS STATEMENT	Giving up smoking not only improved my self-image, it also gave me a great deal of self-respect.

FOCUS Stating Your Thesis

The thesis that you state at this stage of the writing process is not definite. In other words, it is *tentative*. As you write, you will probably change this tentative thesis several times.

◆ PRACTICE 5.3

In the space provided, indicate whether each of the following items is a fact (F), an announcement (A), a vague statement (VS), or an effective thesis (ET). If your instructor gives you permission, you can break into groups and do this exercise collaboratively.

Examples

I spend an hour each day, five days a week, working on college algebra. ___F___

College algebra is my favorite course. ___ET___

1. In this paper, I will discuss challenging and well-paying careers that are open to math majors. ____
2. The following strategies can help students improve their grades. ____
3. Domestic violence is a problem. ____
4. Several local programs can help victims of domestic violence. ____
5. Flexible work hours would have many advantages for both employers and employees. ____
6. Cliques in high school create hostility and unhappiness. ____
7. High school cliques are bad. ____
8. Many students must work while attending college. ____
9. The minimum wage is below $6 an hour in many states. ____
10. A raise in the minimum wage is necessary and long overdue. ____

◆ PRACTICE 5.4

Carefully review the material you have gathered about violence in sports. Then, write a tentative thesis statement for your essay on the following lines.

____

____

____

____

E Selecting and Arranging Ideas

After you have decided on a tentative thesis statement, your next step is to select and arrange the ideas you will use to support it. When you have identified the ideas you will discuss, list them in the order in which you intend to write about them—for example, from most general to most specific idea or from least important to most important idea. You can use this list of ideas as a rough outline for your essay.

◆ PRACTICE 5.5

Copy the tentative thesis statement you wrote in Practice 5.4 on the lines below.

____

____

Now, review the material you came up with in Practice 5.2, and decide which points you will use to support your thesis statement. List those points on the lines below.

____

____

____

____

____

Finally, arrange these points in the order in which you plan to write about them. Cross out any points that do not support your thesis statement.

1. ______________________________
2. ______________________________
3. ______________________________
4. ______________________________
5. ______________________________

F Drafting Your Essay

Once you have decided on a thesis and have arranged your ideas in the order in which you will present them, you are ready to draft your essay. Keep in mind that you are writing a rough draft, one that you will revise and edit later. Your goal at this point is simply to get your ideas down so you can react to them. Even so, your draft should have a thesis-and-support structure.

Here is the first draft of an essay by David Weaver, a student in an introductory writing class. Before he wrote his essay, David went through the process discussed in this chapter: he decided on a topic, brainstormed and wrote a journal entry, decided on a tentative thesis, and selected and arranged ideas.

Writing Tip

Put brackets around questions you think of as you write—[like this]. Later, when you revise your work, you can try to think of answers to the questions.

My Grandfather, My Role Model

My grandfather, Richard Weaver, is seventy years old and lives in Leola, a small town outside Lancaster, Pennsylvania. When I was eight, I lived with my grandparents for almost a year. During that time, my grandfather became my role model.

When I lived with my grandparents, there was never a dull moment. My grandfather always had interesting and unusual ideas. He showed me that you don't have to spend money or go places to have a good time. An afternoon in his workshop was more than enough to keep me entertained all day. Working next to my grandfather, I learned the value of patience and of doing a job right the first time.

If there ever is a problem, you can always count on my grandfather because he is a very caring and understanding person. He not only cares about his family, but he also cares about the whole community. He is known in the community as a caring and sharing person. Whenever anyone needs help, he is always there--whatever the cost or personal inconvenience.

One major thing that my grandfather taught me is always to be honest. He told me that in the long run, honesty will be its own reward. He taught me that if you find something that is not yours, you should make an effort to find the person who it belongs to so that the person will not suffer from the loss. This also shows how caring of other people my grandfather is.

These characteristics--doing a job right, caring, and honesty--describe my grandfather. Now that I have grown up, I have adopted these very special and important characteristics of his.

◆ PRACTICE 5.6

Reread David Weaver's first draft. What changes would you suggest he make? What might he add? What might he delete? Write your suggestions on the following lines. If your instructor gives you permission, you can break into groups and do this exercise collaboratively.

____

____

____

____

◆ PRACTICE 5.7

On a separate sheet of paper, write a draft of your essay about violence in sports. Be sure to include the thesis statement you drafted in Practice 5.4 as well as your list of ideas from the last part of Practice 5.5.

Writing Tip

Triple space your rough drafts. This will make revision easier.

G Revising and Editing Your Essay

When you **revise** your essay, you reconsider the choices you made when you wrote your first draft. As a result of this reevaluation, you rethink (and frequently rewrite) parts of your essay. Some of your changes will be major—

for example, deleting several sentences or even crossing out or adding whole paragraphs. Other changes will be minor—for example, crossing out a sentence or adding or deleting a word or phrase.

Before you begin to revise, put your essay aside for at least an hour or two. Time away from your essay will help you distance yourself from your writing so you can see it critically. When you do start to revise, keep in mind that revision is not a neat process. Don't be afraid to revise directly on your first draft, marking it up with lines, arrows, and cross-outs as well as writing between the lines and in the margins.

When you are finished revising, **edit** your essay, concentrating on grammar, punctuation, mechanics, and spelling.

In order to make your revision and editing more orderly and more efficient, you may want to use the following checklists.

Computer Tip

When you remove material from your draft, move it to the end of the draft or to a separate file. Do not delete it until you are sure you will not need it.

✓ SELF-ASSESSMENT CHECKLIST: Revising Your Essay

- Does your essay have an introduction, a body, and a conclusion?
- Does your essay have a clearly worded thesis statement?
- Does your thesis statement make a point about your topic?
- Does each body paragraph have a topic sentence?
- Does each body paragraph support the thesis statement?
- Are the body paragraphs unified, well developed, and coherent? (See Chapter 3.)
- Does your conclusion restate your thesis?

✓ SELF-ASSESSMENT CHECKLIST: Editing Your Essay

Editing for Common Sentence Problems

- Have you avoided run-ons and comma splices? (See Chapter 11.)
- Have you avoided sentence fragments? (See Chapter 12.)
- Do your subjects and verbs agree? (See Chapter 13.)
- Have you avoided illogical shifts? (See Chapter 14.)
- Have you avoided dangling and misplaced modifiers? (See Chapter 15.)

(continued on the following page)

(continued from the previous page)

Editing for Grammar

- Are your verb forms and verb tenses correct? (See Chapters 16 and 17.)
- Have you used nouns and pronouns correctly? (See Chapters 18 and 19.)
- Have you used adjectives and adverbs correctly? (See Chapter 20.)

Editing for Punctuation, Mechanics, and Spelling

- Have you used commas correctly? (See Chapter 22.)
- Have you used apostrophes correctly? (See Chapter 23.)
- Have you used capital letters where they are required? (See Chapter 24.)
- Have you used quotation marks correctly where they are needed? (See Chapter 24.)
- Have you spelled every word correctly? (See Chapter 25.)

Computer Tip

Use the Search function to find spelling errors that you commonly make (but that the spell checker won't catch)—using *there* instead of *their,* for example.

Writing Tip

Schedule an appointment with your instructor or with a writing lab tutor if you think you will need help with revising your essay.

When David Weaver revised his essay about his grandfather, he decided to change his tentative thesis statement so that it reflected what he had actually written. In addition, he added topic sentences to help readers see how his body paragraphs related to his thesis statement. In order to do this, he included transitional words and phrases (*one thing; another thing; the most important thing*). He also added examples to clarify several generalizations that he had made in his body paragraphs. (He took some of these examples from his journal.) Finally, he expanded his introduction and conclusion.

After he finished revising and editing his essay, David proofread it to make sure that he had not missed any errors. Then, he made sure his essay conformed to the following guidelines.

FOCUS Guidelines for Submitting Your Papers

Always follow the requirements that your instructor gives you for submitting papers.

- Use good-quality 8½-by-11-inch paper.
- Unless the instructor tells you otherwise, type or write your name, your instructor's name, the course name and number, and the date (day, month, and year) in the upper left-hand corner, one-half inch from the top.

(continued on the following page)

(continued from the previous page)

- Type or write on one side of each sheet of paper.
- Double-space if you type your work. (Many instructors also want handwritten papers to be double-spaced.)
- Leave one-inch margins on all sides of the page.
- Type or write your last name and the page number in the upper right-hand corner of each page (including the first).

Here is the final draft of David's essay.

Weaver 1

David Weaver
Professor Yanella
Composition 101
18 Oct. 2001

My Grandfather, My Role Model

My grandfather, Richard Weaver, is seventy years old and lives in Leola, a small town outside of Lancaster, Pennsylvania. He has lived there his entire life. As a young man, he apprenticed as a stone mason and eventually started his own business. He worked in this business until he got silicosis and was forced to retire. He now works part time for the local water department. When I was eight, my mother was very sick, and I lived with my grandparents for almost a year. During that time, my grandfather became not only my best friend, but also my role model.

One thing my grandfather taught me is that I did not have to spend money or go places to have a good time. An afternoon in his workshop was more than enough to keep me entertained all day. We spent many hours together working on small projects, such as building a wagon, and large projects, such as building a tree house. My grandfather even designed a pulley system that carried me from the roof of his house to the tree house. Working next to my grandfather, I also learned the value of patience and of hard work. He never cut corners or compromised. He taught me that it was easier to do the job right the first time than to do it twice.

Another thing that my grandfather taught me is the importance of helping others. Whenever anyone needs help, my grandfather is always there--whatever the cost or personal inconvenience. One afternoon a year ago, a friend called him from work and asked him to help fix a broken water pipe. My grandfather immediately canceled his plans and went to help. When he was a member of the

Opening remarks
Introduction
Thesis statement
Topic sentence
Support
First body paragraph
Topic sentence
Support
Second body paragraph

Weaver 2

volunteer fire department, my grandfather refused to quit even though my grandmother thought the job was too dangerous. His answer was typical of him: he said that because people depended on him, he could not let them down.

Third body paragraph — Topic sentence; Support

The most important thing my grandfather taught me is that honesty is its own reward. One day, when my grandfather and I were in a mall, I found a wallet. I grabbed it and proudly showed it to my grandfather. When I opened it up and saw the money inside, I couldn't believe it. I had wanted a mountain bike for the longest time, but every time I had asked my grandfather for one, he had told me to be thankful for what I already had. So, when I saw the money, I thought that my prayers had been answered. My grandfather, however, had other ideas. He told me that we would have to call the owner of the wallet and tell him that we had found it. Later that night, we called the owner (his name was on his driver's license inside the wallet), and he came over to pick up his money. As soon as I saw him, I knew that my grandfather was right. The owner really looked as if he needed the money. When he offered me a reward, I told him no. After he left, my grandfather told me how proud of me he was.

Conclusion — Restatement of thesis; Closing remarks

These characteristics--doing a job right, being caring, and being honest--make my grandfather my role model. Now that I have grown up, I have adopted these very special and important qualities of his. I only hope that someday I can pass them on to my own children, the way my grandfather has passed them on to me.

◆ PRACTICE 5.8

What material did David add to his draft? What did he delete? Why did he make these changes? Write your answers on the following lines.

____

____

____

____

____

____

____

◆ PRACTICE 5.9

Reread the final draft of David's essay. Do you think this draft is an improvement over the previous one? What other changes could David have made? Write your suggestions on the following lines.

REVISING AND EDITING

- Using the Self-Assessment Checklist for revising your essay on page 89 as a guide, evaluate the essay that you wrote in this chapter. Can you support your points more fully? What points can you delete? Can any ideas be stated more clearly? (You may want to get feedback by exchanging essays with another student.) On the following lines, describe any changes you think you should make to your draft.

- Revise and edit the draft of your essay, writing any new material between the lines or in the margins. Then, edit this revised draft, using the Self-Assessment Checklist for editing your essay on pages 89–90 to find errors in grammar, punctuation, mechanics, and spelling.

Computer Tip

Revise and edit by hand on a hard copy of your essay before you type in your changes.

CHAPTER REVIEW

◆ EDITING PRACTICE

After reading the following incomplete essay, write an appropriate thesis statement on the lines provided. (Make sure your thesis statement clearly communicates the essay's main idea.) Next, fill in the topic sentences for the second, third, and fourth paragraphs. Finally, restate the thesis (in different words) in your conclusion.

To Praise or Not to Praise

When I was growing up, praise was something children had to earn. It was not handed out lightly. Because I felt that more praise would have meant greater self-esteem in my growing years, I resolved to praise my own children every chance I got. However, ten years of experience as a parent has changed my views. I have come to realize that too much praise, given too easily, is not good. [Thesis statement:]

____

____

____

[Topic sentence for the second paragraph:] ____________________

____

____

Self-esteem is crucial to successful living. When children feel they are valued, they learn more easily and work harder when the going gets tough. Self-doubt makes children too fearful of failure to take risks and overcome obstacles. When my older son, Tim, was a preschooler, I gave him lots of praise in order to build his self-esteem. My strategy worked. He is now a confident fifth-grader who does well in school and has many friends. I did the same for Zachary, who is six, with the same good results.

[Topic sentence for the third paragraph:] ____________________

____

____

____

When you praise children, they know what is expected of them. They develop a set of inner rules, called a conscience, that with luck will last a lifetime. I believe that praise works better than criticism in molding a child's behavior. For example, when Tim was jealous of his newborn baby brother, my husband and I did not respond with criticism or threats. Instead, we encouraged Tim to help take care of the baby and praised him for doing so. He caught on, and his jealousy died down considerably. If we had criticized or threatened him, I am sure his natural jealousy of the baby would have gotten worse.

[Topic sentence for the fourth paragraph:] ______________________

____

____

One of the harmful effects of praising my children too much was that they did not continue working on anything once they were praised for it. If I told them a first draft of a report or a drawing or a kite they were making was good, they put it aside and stopped working on it. Then they would get angry if I tried to get them to improve their work. I finally learned not to praise things that needed more effort. I learned to say things like, "Tell me more about the topic of this report. It's interesting. What else do you know about it?" It took a while before I learned how to say things so that I was not criticizing the children but also was not overpraising them.

[Restatement of thesis in conclusion:] ______________________

____

____

____

My children seem to be less dependent on praise than they used to be, and they work harder at getting things right. I hope to use these new techniques in my future career as a preschool teacher and also teach them to other parents.

◆ COLLABORATIVE ACTIVITIES

1. Working with another student, find an article in a magazine or a newspaper about a controversial issue that interests both of you. Then, identify the thesis statement in the article and the main points used to develop that thesis. Underline topic sentences that state these points, and make a list of the details, facts, and examples that support each topic sentence. How does the article use the thesis-and-support structure to discuss the issue? How could the article be improved?
2. Working in a small group, develop thesis statements suitable for essays on two of the following topics.

   True friendship

   Professional athletes' salaries

   Gun control

   The value of volunteer work

   A course I will always remember

Improving the public schools

Soap operas

A community problem

3. Choose one of the thesis statements you wrote for activity 2. Working with another student, make a list of at least three points that could be used to support the thesis.

✓ REVIEW CHECKLIST: Moving from Paragraph to Essay

- Many essays have a thesis-and-support structure: the thesis statement presents the main idea, and the body paragraphs support the thesis. (See 5A.)
- When you write an essay, you begin by deciding on a topic. (See 5B.)
- Use one or more invention strategies to narrow your focus and find ideas to write about. (See 5C.)
- State your main idea in a thesis statement. (See 5D.)
- List the points that best support your thesis, and arrange them in the order in which you plan to discuss them. (See 5E.)
- As you write your first draft, make sure your essay has a thesis-and-support structure. (See 5F.)
- Revise your essay. (See 5F, G.)
- Edit the final draft of your essay. (See 5G.)

UNIT TWO

Writing Effective Sentences

CHAPTER

6

Writing Simple Sentences

SEEING AND WRITING

If you met a person who had never been to McDonald's, what would you tell him or her about this fast-food restaurant? Look at the picture above, and then write a paragraph that answers this question.

PREVIEW

In this chapter, you will learn

- to identify a sentence's subject (6A)
- to recognize singular and plural subjects (6B)
- to identify prepositions and prepositional phrases (6C)
- to distinguish a prepositional phrase from a subject (6C)
- to identify action verbs (6D)
- to identify linking verbs (6E)
- to identify main verbs and helping verbs (6F)

A **sentence** is a group of words that expresses a complete thought. A sentence includes a subject and a verb.

McDonald's is an American institution.

Word Power

institution a well-known person, place, or thing; something that has become associated with a particular place

A Identifying Subjects

The **subject** of a sentence tells who or what is being talked about in the sentence.

Marissa did research on the Internet.

Research was required for her paper.

It was due in March.

The subject of a sentence can be a noun or a pronoun. A **noun** names a person, place, or thing—*Marissa, research.* A **pronoun** takes the place of a noun—*I, you, he, she, it, we, they.*

FOCUS Simple and Complete Subjects

A sentence's **simple subject** is just a noun or a pronoun.

house witch she it they

A sentence's **complete subject** is the simple subject along with all the words that describe it.

our new house

the haunted house

a wicked witch

A two-word name, such as *Victor Frankenstein,* is a simple subject.

◆ PRACTICE 6.1

Underline the complete subject of each sentence in the following paragraph. (Be sure to underline not only the noun or pronoun that tells who or what the sentence is about, but also all the words that describe the subject.) Then, underline the simple subject twice.

Example: Reality shows are very popular with television viewers.

(1) One early television reality show was called *Candid Camera*." (2) On *Candid Camera,* hidden cameras recorded people in unusual situations. (3) Once, in a coffee shop, a man dunked his doughnut into strangers' coffee cups. (4) The strangers' reactions were shown on television. (5) They did not know about the cameras. (6) After a few minutes, the host would reveal the presence of *Candid Camera.* (7) Many viewers learned something about psychology from this show. (8) *Candid Camera*'s creator even won an award from the American Psychological Association. (9) The original show was on the air from 1960 to 1966. (10) During those years, many people in bizarre situations suspected *Candid Camera*'s presence.

◆ PRACTICE 6.2

Write in a simple subject that tells *who* or *what* is being talked about in the sentence.

Example: The ___wind___ howled.

1. ___The baby___ was terrified.
2. The ___firecracker___ was very loud.
3. ___Santa claus___ banged on the roof.
4. The ___dog___ barked in the distance.
5. The ___neighbor___ rapped on the window.
6. ___Tommy___ screamed and ran to the door.
7. Opening the door, ___the girl___ saw a frightening sight.
8. ___Mother___ closed the door immediately.
9. Outside, the ___smell___ grew stronger.
10. Finally, ___Mother___ and ___Tommy___ arrived.

◆ PRACTICE 6.3

The following sentences are not complete because they have no subjects. Complete each sentence by adding a subject, a word or words telling *who* or *what* is being talked about in the sentence.

Example: Runs a small business.

My sister runs a small business.

1. Crashed through the picture window.

   The Tree

2. Are my least favorite foods.

   vegetables and fruit

3. During halftime, gave the players a pep talk.

   the coach

4. Fell from the sky.

   The rain

5. Placed the glass slipper on Cinderella's foot.

   The coach driver

6. Always makes me cry.

   cutting onions

7. Disappeared into a black hole.

the gopher

8. Really meant a lot to me.

My Father

9. Ate five pounds of chocolate-covered cherries.

My daughter

10. Lived happily ever after in a cave.

the bears

B Recognizing Singular and Plural Subjects

Writing Tip

Sometimes an *-ing* word can be a singular subject: *Studying is important.*

For information on subject-verb agreement with compound subjects, see 13C.

The subject of a sentence can be *singular* or *plural.* A **singular subject** is one person, place, or thing (*Marissa, research, she*).

A **plural subject** is more than one person, place, or thing (*students, papers, they*).

Students often do research on the Internet.

A plural subject that joins two subjects with *and* is called a **compound subject.**

Marissa and Jason did research on the Internet.

PRACTICE 6.4

Each item listed here could be the subject of a sentence. Write *S* after each item that could be a singular subject and *P* after each item that could be a plural subject.

Examples

Joey Ramone S

The Ramones P

Joey and Johnny Ramone P

1. hot-fudge sundaes P
2. the USS *Enterprise* S
3. a blue-eyed baby girl S
4. the McCaughey septuplets P
5. my Web site S
6. three blind mice P
7. Betty and Barney Rubble P

8. her two children P

9. Texas S

10. Tommy Lee Jones S

◆ PRACTICE 6.5

First, underline the complete subject in each sentence. Then, label each singular subject *S*, and label each plural subject *P*. (Remember that a compound subject is plural.)

Example: The Vietnam Veterans Memorial opened to the public on November 11, 1982.

1. The memorial honors men and women killed or missing in the Vietnam War.
2. More than 58,000 names are carved into the black granite wall.
3. More than two and a half million people visit the Memorial each year.
4. People leave mementoes at the site.
5. Some visitors, for example, leave letters and photographs.
6. Combat boots, stuffed animals, rosaries, and dog tags have also been left there.
7. One man leaves a six-pack of beer each year.
8. Visitors also leave cigarettes, flowers, canned food, and clothing.
9. Spouses, children, parents, and friends leave offerings for men and women lost in the war.
10. A Persian Gulf War veteran left his medal for his father.

C Identifying Prepositional Phrases

As you have seen, every sentence needs a subject and a verb. As you try to identify sentence subjects, you may be confused by nouns or pronouns that cannot be subjects because they are part of prepositional phrases. If you learn to identify prepositional phrases, you will not have this problem.

A **prepositional phrase** is made up of a **preposition** (a word like *on, to, in,* or *with*) and its **object** (a noun or pronoun).

Preposition	+	*Object*	=	*Prepositional Phrase*
on		the roof		on the roof
to		Kobe's apartment		to Kobe's apartment
in		my Spanish class		in my Spanish class
with		her		with her

Writing Tip

A **phrase** is a group of words that is missing a subject or a verb or both. A phrase cannot stand alone as a sentence. (See 12B.)

Writing Tip

Prepositions are often combined with other words to form familiar expressions: *Debbie is addicted to chocolate.* (See 21L.)

Because the object of a preposition is a noun or a pronoun, it may look like the subject of a sentence. However, the object of a preposition can never be a subject. To identify a sentence's subject, cross out every prepositional phrase.

The price ~~of a new home~~ ~~in the San Francisco Bay area~~ is very high.

After you cross out the prepositional phrases, you will easily be able to identify the sentence's subject. Remember, every prepositional phrase is introduced by a preposition.

For more on prepositions, see 21K–21M.

Frequently Used Prepositions

about	behind	for	off	toward
above	below	from	on	under
across	beneath	in	onto	underneath
after	beside	including	out	until
against	between	inside	outside	up
along	beyond	into	over	upon
among	by	like	through	with
around	despite	near	throughout	within
at	during	of	to	without
before	except			

PRACTICE 6.6

Each of the sentences in the following paragraph includes at least one prepositional phrase. To identify a sentence's subject, first cross out each prepositional phrase. Then, underline the simple subject.

Example: Many people ~~in the United States~~ prefer telephones ~~without pictures~~.

(1) Telephone companies have been developing a picture telephone for almost seventy-five years. (2) AT&T demonstrated a picture phone in 1927. (3) The 1927 phone could only transmit a picture to the person on one end. (4) At the 1964 World's Fair, AT&T introduced the two-way Picturephone. (5) Only five hundred customers signed up for the Picturephone. (6) The biggest technical problem with visual telephones has been sending video signals over telephone lines. (7) The transmission of visual images became easier after the invention of high-speed DSL lines. (8) However, most buildings and homes will not have DSL lines for many years. (9) Some people like seeing the person on the other end of the line. (10) Others prefer talking without seeing images.

D Identifying Action Verbs

An **action verb** tells what the subject does, did, or will do.

Tiger Woods plays golf.

Columbus sailed across the ocean.

Andrea will go to Houston next month.

Action verbs can also show mental or emotional action.

Nirav often thinks about his future.

Wendy loves backpacking.

When the subject of a sentence performs more than one action, the sentence includes two or more action verbs joined to form a **compound verb**.

Lois left work, drove to Somerville, and met Carmen for dinner.

◆ PRACTICE 6.7

Underline all the action verbs in each of the following sentences.

Example: Many nineteenth-century Americans left their homes and journeyed to unfamiliar places.

(1) During the 1840s, thousands of Americans traveled west to places like Oregon, Nevada, and California. (2) Many travelers began their journey in Independence, Missouri. (3) In towns all around Missouri, travelers advertised in newspapers for strong young companions for the journey west. (4) Thousands of wagons eventually departed from Independence on the dangerous four-month trip to California. (5) Whole families packed their bags and joined wagon trains. (6) The wagons carried food, supplies, and weapons. (7) Some travelers wrote letters to friends and relatives back east. (8) Others wrote in journals. (9) From these letters and journals, we understand the travelers' fear and misery. (10) Traveling 2,500 miles west across plains, deserts, and mountains, many people suffered and died.

◆ PRACTICE 6.8

Insert an action verb in each space to show what action the subject is performing.

Example: I ___*drove*___ my car to the grocery store.

1. Good athletes sometimes __________ but often __________.
2. After opening the letter, Michele __________.
3. The little boat __________ and __________ on top of the waves.
4. Thousands of people __________ in the rain.
5. The computer __________, __________, and then died.
6. The hurricane __________ the residents and __________ the town.
7. Smoke __________ out of the windows.
8. The Doberman __________.
9. A voice __________ from the balcony.
10. Wanda __________ the door.

E Identifying Linking Verbs

A **linking verb** does not show action. Instead, it connects the subject to a word or words that describe or rename the subject.

Calculus is a difficult course.

In this sentence, the linking verb (*is*) links the subject (*calculus*) to the words that describe it (*a difficult course*).

Many linking verbs, like *is*, are forms of the verb *be*. Other linking verbs refer to the senses (*look, feel, seem,* and so on).

Tremaine looks very handsome today.

Time seemed to pass quickly.

Student Voices

I like to think of a linking verb as an equal sign (Tremaine = handsome).

Miriam Bravo

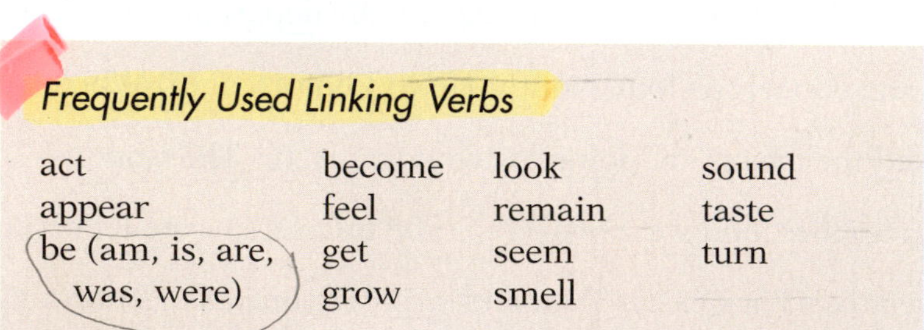

Frequently Used Linking Verbs

act	become	look	sound
appear	feel	remain	taste
be (am, is, are, was, were)	get	seem	turn
	grow	smell	

PRACTICE 6.9

Underline the verb in each of the following sentences. Then, in the blank, indicate whether the verb is an action verb (AV) or a linking verb (LV).

Example: Working mothers face difficult decisions. AV

1. Some women leave careers to raise their children. ______
2. My neighbor Jeanne was a graphic designer for twelve years. ______
3. She quit work to stay home with her baby. ______

4. Now, her son is six years old and in first grade. _____

5. Jeanne feels ready to return to an office job. _____

6. Twenty years ago, employers usually rejected applicants like Jeanne. _____

7. The employers were suspicious of gaps in an applicant's employment history. _____

8. However, two companies offered jobs to Jeanne last week. _____

9. They appreciate her skills and experience. _____

10. Today, taking time out to raise a family is not necessarily a career-ending decision. _____

◆ PRACTICE 6.10

Underline the linking verb in each of the following sentences. Then, circle the complete subject and any words or phrases that describe it.

Example: (The juice) tasted (sour.)

1. The night grew cold.
2. The song seems very familiar.
3. George W. Bush became the forty-third president of the United States.
4. College students feel pressured by their families, their instructors, and their peers.
5. Many people were outraged at the mayor's announcement.
6. The cheese smelled peculiar.
7. The fans appear exhausted by their team's defeat.
8. After the game, the crowd turned ugly.
9. Charlie got sick after eating six corn dogs at the fair.
10. A mother's love remains strong and true.

F Identifying Main Verbs and Helping Verbs

Many verbs are made up of more than one word. For example, the verb in the following sentence is made up of two words.

Andrew must make a choice.

In this sentence, *make* is the **main verb**, and *must* is a **helping verb**. A sentence's **complete verb** is made up of the main verb plus all the helping verbs that accompany it.

Helping verbs include forms of *be, have,* and *do* as well as the words *must, will, can, could, may, might, should,* and *would.*

- Some helping verbs, like forms of *be* and *have,* combine with main verbs to give information about when the action occurs.

  Ana has worked at the diner for two years.

- Forms of *do* combine with main verbs to form questions and negative statements.

  Does Ana still work at the diner?

  Ana does not work on Saturdays.

- Other helping verbs indicate ability (*can*), possibility (*may*), necessity (*should*), obligation (*must*), and so on.

  Ana can choose her own hours.

  Ana may work this Saturday.

  Ana should take a vacation this summer.

  Ana must work hard to earn money for college.

Writing Tip

Sometimes other words come between the parts of a complete verb: *Victoria can really succeed in life.*

Writing Tip

Some complete verbs include several helping verbs: *Brian should have called sooner.*

For information on past participles, see Chapter 17.

FOCUS Helping Verbs with Participles

Present participles, such as *thinking,* and many irregular **past participles**, such as *gone,* cannot stand alone as main verbs in a sentence. They need a helping verb to make them complete.

INCORRECT Samantha gone to the dentist.

CORRECT Samantha has gone to the dentist.

◆ PRACTICE 6.11

Each of these sentences includes one or more helping verbs as well as a main verb. Underline the complete verb (the main verb and all the helping verbs) in each sentence. Then, place a check mark above the main verb.

Example: Elizabeth II has been Queen of England since 1952.

1. Obese adolescents may risk serious health problems as adults.
2. The candidates will name their running mates within two weeks.
3. Henry has been thinking about his decision for a long time.
4. Do you want breakfast now?
5. I could have been a French major.
6. This must be the place.

7. I have often wondered about my family's history.
8. You should have remembered the mustard.
9. Jenelle has always loved animals.
10. Research really does take a long time.

◆ PRACTICE 6.12

Some verbs in the following sentences consist of only one word. Others consist of a main verb and one or more helping verbs. In each sentence, underline the complete verb once and the main verb twice.

Example: Dyed hair is becoming a trend at middle schools and high schools.

1. Once, no one wanted obviously dyed hair.
2. Hair dye was for covering gray hair.
3. Blond people were suspected of dyeing their hair.
4. Denying the use of hair dye, some blonds would even lie.
5. In the 1970s and 1980s, punk rockers often dyed their hair bright, unnatural colors.
6. Now, many high school students have dyed hair.
7. Twenty-five years ago, most men with dyed hair would have hidden that fact.
8. Today, more and more boys and young men are dyeing their hair.
9. Blond tips on dark hair can be seen on famous male athletes and musicians.
10. Popular colors can range from blond to pink, blue, and green.

■ REVISING AND EDITING

Look back at your response to the Seeing and Writing exercise on page 99. Reread it carefully, and then complete the following tasks.

- Underline the complete subject (the simple subject plus all the words that describe it) of every sentence once.
- Underline the complete verb (the main verb plus all the helping verbs) of every sentence twice.
- Circle all the helping verbs in each sentence, and put a check mark above the main verb.

CHAPTER REVIEW

◆ EDITING PRACTICE

Read the following essay. Underline the complete subject of each sentence once, and underline the complete verb of each sentence twice. If you have trouble locating the subject, try crossing out the prepositional phrases. The first sentence has been done for you.

The Triangle Shirtwaist Factory Fire

On March 25, 1911, a terrible event drew attention to unsafe conditions in garment factories across the United States. The Triangle Shirtwaist Company occupied the top floors of a ten-story building in New York City. The company employed more than five hundred people, mainly young immigrant women. The workers could not leave the building during working hours. Therefore, the owners locked most of the exit doors during the day.

The factory had always been overcrowded and cluttered with scraps of paper and cloth. On that March afternoon, some trash was ignited, perhaps by a cigarette or a spark from a sewing machine. The flames spread quickly through the building's wooden interior. Many of the workers were trapped at their sewing machines or behind the locked doors. Fire engine ladders could not reach the upper floors. The fire escapes collapsed under the weight of so many people. Fearing the fire more than the height, some people leaped to their deaths from the eighth and ninth floors of the burning building. By late afternoon, one hundred and forty-six people had died.

No one was ever officially blamed for the tragedy at the Triangle Shirtwaist Company. However, some things did change because of that disaster. For example, American labor unions grew stronger after the fire. Workers now have shorter work weeks and better working conditions. In addition, fire safety is taken seriously at most workplaces. Government agencies investigate on-the-job conditions. With these

safeguards, a nightmare like the Triangle Shirtwaist fire should never happen again.

◆ COLLABORATIVE ACTIVITIES

1. Working in a group of three or four people, write a subject on one slip of paper. On another slip, write a prepositional phrase; on a third, write a verb. Fold up the slips, keeping subjects, prepositional phrases, and verbs in separate piles. Choose one slip from each pile and use them to create a sentence, adding whatever other words are necessary.
2. Working in a group of three or four people, have one person write a noun on a blank sheet of paper and pass the paper to the next student, who should add a verb that makes sense with the noun. Then, have the second person pass the paper to the third person, who should do one of the following:

   - add words that describe the noun
   - add one or more helping verbs to the main verb
   - begin a new sentence with a new noun

   Keep passing the paper until your group has completed a story several sentences long.

COMPOSING ORIGINAL SENTENCES

3. Working in a group, create five simple sentences. Make sure each sentence contains a subject and a verb. When you have finished, check the sentences again to make sure each sentence begins with a capital letter and ends with a period.

☑ REVIEW CHECKLIST: Writing Simple Sentences

- ☐ The subject tells who or what is being talked about in the sentence. (See 6A.)
- ☐ A subject can be singular or plural. (See 6B.)
- ☐ The object of a preposition cannot be the subject of a sentence. (See 6C.)
- ☐ An action verb tells what the subject does, did, or will do. (See 6D.)
- ☐ A linking verb connects the subject to a word or words that describe or rename the subject. (See 6E.)
- ☐ Many verbs are made up of more than one word. The complete verb in a sentence includes the main verb plus all the helping verbs. (See 6F.)

CHAPTER

7

Writing Compound Sentences

PREVIEW

In this chapter, you will learn

- to form compound sentences with coordinating conjunctions (7A)
- to form compound sentences with semicolons (7B)
- to form compound sentences with conjunctive adverbs (7C)

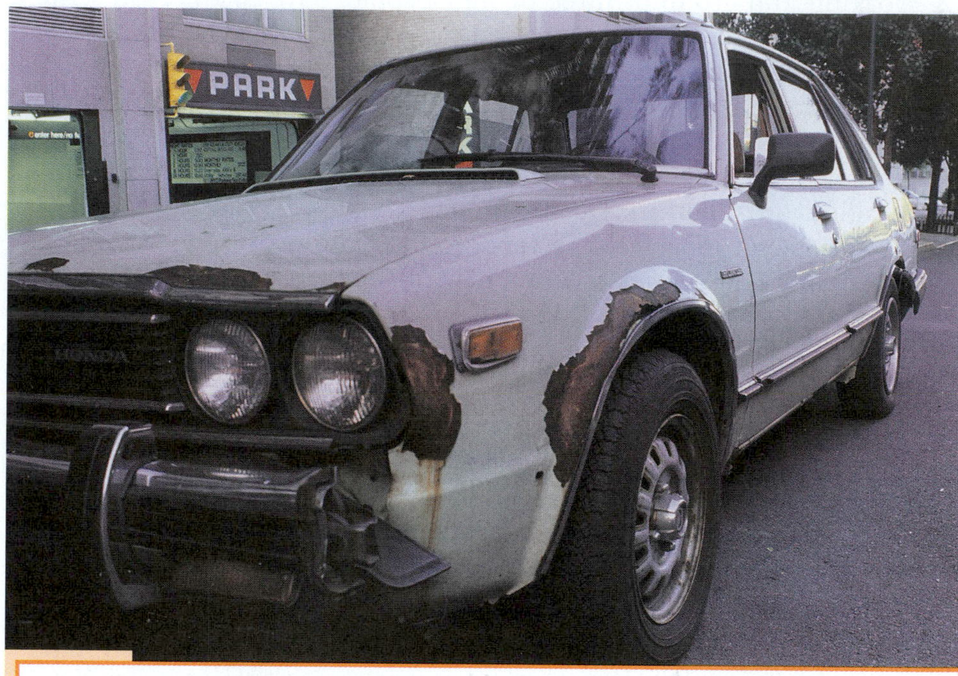

SEEING AND WRITING

Suppose you wanted to sell this car. Look at the picture above, and then describe the car in a way that would make someone want to buy it.

Word Power

classic something typical or traditional; something that has lasting importance or worth

A **compound sentence** is made up of two or more simple sentences joined by a coordinating conjunction, a semicolon, or a conjunctive adverb.

Writing Tip

A **clause** is a group of words that contains a subject and a verb. An **independent clause** can stand alone as a sentence; a **dependent clause** cannot. For more on dependent clauses, see Chapter 8.

A Forming Compound Sentences with Coordinating Conjunctions

A simple sentence is a single independent clause. It includes one subject and one verb.

Many college students major in psychology.

Many other students major in business.

A **compound sentence** is made up of two or more simple sentences. Two simple sentences can be joined into one compound sentence with a **coordinating conjunction**. Always place a comma before the coordinating conjunction.

Many college students major in psychology, but many other students major in business.

Coordinating Conjunctions

and	for	or
but	nor	so
		yet

Student Voices

To remember all the coordinating conjunctions, I use FANBOYS: for, and, nor, but, or, yet, so.

Melissa Donnell

PRACTICE 7.1

Each of the following compound sentences is made up of two short simple sentences joined by a coordinating conjunction. Underline the coordinating conjunction in each compound sentence. Then, bracket the two simple sentences. Remember that each simple sentence includes a subject and a verb.

Example: [I do not like unnecessary delays], nor [do I like lame excuses].

1. Speech is silver, but silence is golden.
2. I fought the law, and the law won.
3. The house was dark, so he didn't ring the doorbell.
4. He decided to sign a long-term contract, for he did not want to lose the job.
5. They will not surrender, and they will not agree to a cease-fire.
6. I could order the chicken fajitas, or I could have a vegetarian dish.
7. She had lived in California for years, yet she remembered her childhood in Kansas very clearly.
8. Professor Blakemore was interesting, but Professor Salazar was inspiring.
9. Melody dropped French, and then she added Italian.
10. Give me liberty, or give me death.

Coordinating conjunctions join ideas that are of equal importance.

Idea (Simple Sentence)	+	Coordinating Conjunction	+	Idea (Simple Sentence)	=	Compound Sentence
Brenda is a vegetarian	+	but	+	Larry eats everything	=	Brenda is a vegetarian, but Larry eats everything.

Coordinating conjunctions describe the relationship between two ideas, showing how and why the ideas are connected. Different coordinating conjunctions have different meanings.

- To indicate addition, use *and.*

  Edgar Allan Poe wrote horror fiction in the nineteenth century, and Stephen King writes horror fiction today.

- To indicate contrast or contradiction, use *but* or *yet.*

  Poe wrote short stories, but King writes both stories and novels.

  Poe died young, yet his stories live on.

- To indicate a cause-effect connection, use *so* or *for.*

  I liked *Carrie,* so I decided to read King's other novels.

  Poe's "The Tell-Tale Heart" is a chilling tale, for it is about a murder.

- To present alternatives, use *or.*

  I have to finish *Cujo,* or I won't be able to sleep.

- To eliminate alternatives, use *nor.*

  I have not read *The Green Mile,* nor have I seen the movie.

Writing Tip

Plus and *also* indicate addition, but they are not coordinating conjunctions. They cannot be used to join two simple sentences the way coordinating conjunctions can. (Incorrect: *I have a lot of homework, plus I'm exhausted.* Correct: *I have a lot of homework, and I'm exhausted.*)

Writing Tip

However indicates a contradiction, but it is not a coordinating conjunction. (See 7C.)

Writing Tip

Therefore indicates a cause-effect connection, but it is not a coordinating conjunction. (See 7C.)

Writing Tip

When you use *nor* to create a compound sentence, the verb comes before the subject in the second part of the sentence.

FOCUS Using Commas with Coordinating Conjunctions

When you use a coordinating conjunction to link two simple sentences into a compound sentence, always place a comma before the coordinating conjunction.

We can see a movie, or we can go to a club.

However, do not use a comma before a coordinating conjunction that does not link two complete sentences.

INCORRECT We can see a movie, or go to a club.

CORRECT We can see a movie or go to a club.

◆ PRACTICE 7.2

Fill in the coordinating conjunction—*and, but, for, nor, or, so,* or *yet*—that most logically links the two parts of each of the following compound sentences. Remember to insert a comma before each coordinating conjunction.

> **Example:** Many people travel abroad to adopt children, ___for___ adopting internationally is often easier than adopting an American child.

(1) Many people today desperately want children ________ they are unable to conceive a child. (2) For many of these people, adoption is the answer ________ a lot of them will choose international adoption. (3) Children adopted by Americans frequently come from orphanages in poor countries ________ starting a new life in the United States is not always easy for these children. (4) Loving parents and a stable home may seem like luxuries ________ the child is also leaving a familiar world behind. (5) Before the 1980s, adoption experts told adoptive parents to ignore their children's background ________ most children adopted internationally had no sense of their culture. (6) For example, either the Korean War orphans arriving in the United States in the 1950s were too young to remember Korea ________ they were urged to abandon any memories they had. (7) These Korean children were given American names ________ they often ended up living in towns where there were no other Asian children. (8) Today, adoptive parents usually try to find out all they can about their children's native country and language ________ teaching adopted children about their native culture is considered essential. (9) Adoptive parents often form support groups for adopted children from a particular country ________ in these groups, their children can meet others who have similar backgrounds. (10) Today's adoptive parents no longer ignore their children's cultural backgrounds ________ do they try to make their children conform to an "American" standard.

◆ PRACTICE 7.3

Using the coordinating conjunctions provided, complete each of the following pairs of sentences to create two different compound sentences. (Be sure you add a complete independent clause.) Remember that each coordinating conjunction establishes a different relationship between ideas. Be sure the idea you add includes a subject and a verb.

Example

They married at age eighteen, and *they had ten children*.

They married at age eighteen, so *they grew up together*.

1. Date rape is a complex and emotional issue, so ______________________.

   Date rape is a complex and emotional issue, but ______________________.

2. Drunk drivers should lose their licenses, for ______________________.

   Drunk drivers should lose their licenses, or ______________________.

3. A smoke-free environment has many advantages, and ______________________.

   A smoke-free environment has many advantages, but ______________________.

4. Female pilots have successfully flown combat missions, yet ______________________.

   Female pilots have successfully flown combat missions, so ______________________.

5. The death penalty can be abolished, or ______________________.

   The death penalty cannot be abolished, nor ______________________.

◆ PRACTICE 7.4

Add coordinating conjunctions to combine these sentences where necessary to relate one idea to another. Remember to put a comma before each coordinating conjunction you add.

Example: Drive-in movies were a popular form of entertainment in the 1950s*, but today,* ~~. Today,~~ only a few drive-ins remain.

(1) Americans love the freedom and independence of driving a car. (2) They also love movies. (3) Not surprisingly, therefore, the United States was the home of the very first drive-in movie theater. (4) The first drive-in opened in New Jersey in 1934. (5) The second one, Shankweiler's Drive-In in Orefield, Pennsylvania, opened in the same year. (6) Today, the very first drive-in no longer exists. (7) There is not a single drive-in theater remaining in the entire state of New Jersey. (8) However, Shankweiler's is still open for business. (9) Fans of drive-in theater history have something to celebrate. (10) Shankweiler's Drive-In still has the in-car speakers that moviegoers used to hang in their car windows. (11) They are rarely used. (12) Drive-in visitors simply turn on the car radio to hear the movie sound. (13) Shankweiler's was also the first drive-in to broadcast movie soundtracks on FM stereo. (14) Anyone with a car, a love of movies, and a sense of history should make a trip to Shankweiler's Drive-In.

◆ PRACTICE 7.5

Write an original compound sentence on each of the following topics. Use the specified coordinating conjunction, and remember to put a comma before the coordinating conjunction in each compound sentence.

Example: *Topic:* course requirements
Coordinating conjunction: but

Composition is a required course for all first-year students, but history is not required.

1. *Topic:* the high cost of textbooks
   Coordinating conjunction: so

2. *Topic:* interracial dating
   Coordinating conjunction: but

3. *Topic:* two things you hate to do
   Coordinating conjunction: and

   ____

   ____

4. *Topic:* why you made a certain decision
   Coordinating conjunction: for

   ____

   ____

5. *Topic:* something you regret
   Coordinating conjunction: yet

   ____

   ____

6. *Topic:* two possible career choices
   Coordinating conjunction: or

   ____

   ____

7. *Topic:* two chores you would rather not do
   Coordinating conjunction: nor

   ____

   ____

8. *Topic:* a reason why you came to college
   Coordinating conjunction: for

   ____

   ____

9. *Topic:* your favorite musician and musical group
   Coordinating conjunction: and

   ____

   ____

10. *Topic:* a first impression that turned out to be wrong
    Coordinating conjunction: but

    ____

    ____

B Forming Compound Sentences with Semicolons

Another way to create a compound sentence is by joining two simple sentences with a **semicolon**.

The Democrats held their convention in Los Angeles; the Republicans held their convention in Philadelphia.

A semicolon connects two ideas. Sometimes, you use a semicolon to show a close *connection* between two ideas; sometimes, you use a semicolon to show a strong *contrast* between two ideas.

The Democrats supported gun control; they also supported universal health insurance. (close connection between two ideas)

The Democrats supported gun control; the Republicans did not. (strong contrast between two ideas)

FOCUS Avoiding Sentence Fragments

Remember, a semicolon can only join two complete sentences. A semicolon cannot join a sentence and a fragment.

INCORRECT (FRAGMENT: Because the Philadelphia area had many hotel rooms) Because the Philadelphia area had many hotel rooms; it was a good choice for the convention.

CORRECT The Philadelphia area had many hotel rooms; it was a good choice for the convention.

For more on avoiding sentence fragments, see Chapter 12.

 **PRACTICE 7.6** 

Each of the following simple sentences can be linked with a semicolon to another simple sentence to form a compound sentence. In each case, add a semicolon; then, complete the compound sentence by adding a simple sentence.

Example: Some people love to watch sports on television *; others would rather play a game than watch one*.

1. Baseball is known as "America's pastime" ______________________.
2. The most-played sport in the United States is probably basketball ______________________.
3. Soccer has gained popularity in recent years ______________________.
4. American football requires size and strength ______________________.
5. Professional sports teams give their fans something to cheer about ______________________.

6. Individual athletes compete in sports such as track and field ______________________________.

7. The Olympic Games honor athletes from around the world ______________________________.

8. Some athletes are models of good sportsmanship ______________________________.

9. A good coach knows how to encourage an athlete ______________________________.

10. Many children admire sports heroes ______________________________.

C Forming Compound Sentences with Conjunctive Adverbs

Another way to join two simple sentences into a compound sentence is with a **conjunctive adverb**. Although you can use a semicolon alone to link similar or contrasting ideas, adding a conjunctive adverb shows the exact relationship between the ideas. When a conjunctive adverb joins two sentences, a semicolon always comes *before* the conjunctive adverb, and a comma always comes *after* it.

> Women's pro basketball games are often sold out; however, not many people watch the games on television.

Frequently Used Conjunctive Adverbs

also	instead	subsequently
besides	meanwhile	then
consequently	moreover	therefore
finally	nevertheless	thus
furthermore	otherwise	
however	still	

Writing Tip

Do not capitalize the word that follows a semicolon unless it is a proper noun. (See 24A for more on capitalization.)

Different conjunctive adverbs convey different meanings.

- Some conjunctive adverbs signal addition: *also, besides, furthermore, moreover.*

> Golf can be an expensive sport; besides, it can be hard to find a public golf course.

- Some conjunctive adverbs show a cause-effect connection: *therefore, consequently, thus.*

> Professional baseball players are bigger and stronger than ever before; therefore, home runs have become more common.

- Some conjunctive adverbs indicate contradiction or contrast: *nevertheless, however, still.*

  Some of the world's best athletes are track stars; nevertheless, few of their names are widely known.

- Some conjunctive adverbs present alternatives: *otherwise, instead.*

  Shawn got a football scholarship; otherwise, he could not have gone to college.

  He didn't make the first team; instead, he backed up other players.

- Some conjunctive adverbs indicate time relationships: *finally, meanwhile, subsequently, then.*

  The popularity of women's tennis has been growing; meanwhile, the popularity of men's tennis has been declining.

Writing Tip

When you use a conjunctive adverb or transitional expression to join two sentences, be sure to use a semicolon, too. If you leave out the semicolon, you create a run-on. (See 11B.)

FOCUS Transitional Expressions

Like conjunctive adverbs, **transitional expressions** can join two simple sentences into one compound sentence.

> Soccer has become very popular in the United States; in fact, more American children play soccer than any other sport.

Note that a semicolon comes *before* the transitional expression, and a comma comes *after* the transitional expression.

Frequently Used Transitional Expressions

after all	in contrast
as a result	in fact
at the same time	in other words
for example	of course
for instance	on the contrary
in addition	that is
in comparison	

◆ PRACTICE 7.7

Each item below consists of a simple sentence followed by a semicolon and a conjunctive adverb or transitional expression. For each item, add an independent clause to form a complete compound sentence.

Example: Shopping malls have spread throughout the country; in fact, *they have replaced many main streets*.

1. Nearly every community is near one or more shopping malls; as a result, ____.

2. Some malls include hundreds of stores; moreover, ____.

3. Malls include restaurants as well as stores; therefore, ____.

4. Some malls serve as social centers; in fact, ____.

5. Shopping at malls offers many advantages over traditional shopping; however, ____.

6. Malls offer many employment opportunities; for example, ____.

7. Malls provide a safe, attractive, climate-controlled atmosphere; nevertheless, ____.

8. Many stores seem to have similar merchandise; in addition, ____.

9. The Mall of America, in Minnesota, even includes an amusement park; therefore, ____.

10. Some people think malls are wonderful; still, ______________________________
____
____.

◆ PRACTICE 7.8

do odd

Add semicolons and commas to set off the conjunctive adverbs or transitional expressions that join the two independent clauses in each of the following sentences.

Example: Every political candidate talks about putting more computers in schools; however, some people believe that young children should not use computers.

1. Today, adults need computer skills to get good jobs consequently education experts want young people to learn how to use computers.
2. Every high school should have computers for students otherwise the students may feel unprepared for college and adult life.
3. Even some elementary schools have computer labs in fact some kindergarten children are learning to use computers.
4. Children pick up computer skills very quickly nevertheless they need to learn other skills first.
5. Some scientists think children need to play in addition they need to develop social skills.
6. Computer work is solitary however playing a game of tag involves other people.
7. Many adults now spend their free time online as a result they do not get enough exercise.
8. Meeting other people is important for both adults and children therefore spending too much time with computers can be harmful.
9. Young Americans need to understand technology still they need to understand other human beings as well.
10. Perhaps computer classes should not start until middle school then very young children would not be tempted to have a computer as a best friend.

◆ PRACTICE 7.9

Consulting the list of conjunctive adverbs on page 120 and the list of transitional expressions on page 121, choose a word or expression that logically connects each pair of sentences into one compound sentence. Be sure to punctuate appropriately.

> **Example:** Last winter was unusually warm. One year of record-breaking temperatures does not prove that the world is getting warmer.

1. Every year, unusual weather makes news somewhere in the United States. There may be droughts on the East Coast or floods in the Midwest.
2. People expect the summer to be hot in most of the country. Sometimes the temperature is even hotter than expected.
3. Winters are generally cold in this country. People plan for snow and ice.
4. In some years, the pattern changes. The El Niño winds may have kept the winter of 1998–1999 mild in most of the United States.
5. Weather is always changing. Big changes in weather patterns are hard to see.
6. Keeping records is the only way to track weather patterns. Years of records are needed to provide useful information.
7. Fortunately, most parts of the country have at least a century of weather records. Analysts can tell that the weather has gotten warmer in the last hundred years.
8. Experts still disagree about the causes of global warming. They disagree about the seriousness of the problem.
9. Some scientists say that the warming is insignificant. Others see a potential for disaster.
10. Nothing will solve global warming overnight. Overall weather patterns change too slowly to produce immediate results.

◆ PRACTICE 7.10

Using the specified topics and conjunctive adverbs or transitional expressions, create five compound sentences. Be sure to punctuate appropriately.

Example: *Topic:* popular music
Conjunctive adverb: nevertheless

Most popular singing groups today seem to have been put together by a committee; nevertheless, many of these groups sell millions of records.

1. *Topic:* finding a job
   Transitional expression: for example

   ____

   ____

2. *Topic:* gun control
   Conjunctive adverb: otherwise

   ____

   ____

3. *Topic:* teenage pregnancy
   Transitional expression: as a result

   ____

   ____

4. *Topic:* recycling
   Conjunctive adverb: still

   ____

   ____

5. *Topic*: watching television
   Transitional expression: however

   ____

   ____

■ REVISING AND EDITING

Look back at your response to the Seeing and Writing exercise on page 112. Underline every compound sentence. Have you used the coordinating conjunction, conjunctive adverb, or transitional

(continued on the following page)

(continued from the previous page)
expression that best communicates your meaning? Have you punctuated these sentences correctly? Make any necessary corrections.

Now, look for a pair of short simple sentences that you could combine into a compound sentence, and use one of the three methods discussed in this chapter to link them.

CHAPTER REVIEW

◆ EDITING PRACTICE

The following student essay contains many short, choppy, simple sentences. Revise it by linking pairs of sentences where appropriate with a coordinating conjunction, a semicolon, or a semicolon followed by either a conjunctive adverb or a transitional expression. (There are many different correct ways to revise the essay.) Remember to put commas before coordinating conjunctions and to use semicolons and commas correctly with conjunctive adverbs and transitional expressions. The first two sentences have been combined for you.

The State Fair

Like most Americans, I do not live on a farm; ~~In~~ in fact, I live in a medium-sized city. However, my parents both grew up on farms. My mother's parents had a family farm in Indiana. My father's parents raised wheat and sugar beets in Colorado. My parents decided not to farm. They knew enough about agriculture to understand how difficult and uncertain that life could be. My grandparents have all died. I do not have much contact with rural life. That is why I love to go to the state fair in late summer every year.

The fair has carnival rides and stands selling all kinds of junk food. My favorite part of the fair is the livestock pavilion. One barn contains beef cattle. Visitors admire the giant Black Angus bull from a safe distance. They walk past rows of white-faced Herefords. Another barn has dairy cattle of all kinds. There, Brown Swiss stand beside black-and-white Holsteins. If I arrive at the right time, I might see a milking demonstration. A butter sculpture may be on display in the milking barn. There may be fresh butter and milk shakes for sale.

Every animal has commercial possibilities. Otherwise, the farmers would not raise them. The dairy cows, for instance, are not the only milk producers at the fair. The goat barn has a dairy center where people can buy goat cheese. The sheep barn also has a cheese shop. Sheep farmers sell wool and handmade sweaters. They give sheep-shearing and yarn-spinning demonstrations. Some animals will end up as meat. The people who raise them cannot think of them as pets.

Plants are another feature of the fair. The gardening exhibit offers advice on gardening and landscape design. Unfortunately, I do not have a garden. I do not expect to have one in the near future. When I pass this area, I simply admire the work of other people. Another area shows prize-winning fruits and vegetables. Giant, glossy green peppers might take home the grand prize. The winner might be a basket of tart, firm apples.

After the fair, I sometimes wish I had a chance to live on a farm. I am glad that I don't have to live a farmer's life day in and day out. Still, I will keep going to the state fair every year. That way, I can see the sights and smell the smells without having to do the work.

◆ COLLABORATIVE ACTIVITIES

1. Working in a small group, pair each of the sentences in the left-hand column with a sentence in the right-hand column to create ten compound sentences. Use as many different coordinating conjunctions as you can to connect ideas. Be sure each coordinating conjunction you choose conveys a logical relationship between ideas, and remember to put a comma before each one. You may use some of the listed sentences more than once. *Note:* Many different combinations—some serious and factually accurate, some humorous—are possible.

Miniskirts get shorter every year.
Those shoes are an ugly color.
Berries usually ripen in the summer.
Wild mushrooms grow all over the world.
I bought seven pairs of earrings.
His pants are dragging on the ground.
Everyone at work has to wear a uniform.
The yard is full of dandelions.
Ostrich eggs are enormous.
Cherry tomatoes make excellent snacks.

Some come with a belt.
They are torn and dirty.
My mother hates them.
Some kinds are edible.
The silver ones are my favorites.
Only experts should pick them.
Digging them up is my job.
I will not try them on.
I love to throw them in salads.
Each one could make several omelettes.

2. Working in a group of three or four students, invent a new sport. First, write down one rule of the game in the form of a simple sentence. Then, pass the paper to the person on your right. That person should expand the rule into a compound sentence.

Example

ORIGINAL RULE The ball must not touch the ground.

CHANGED RULE The ball must not touch the ground; moreover, the players can only move it with their lips.

Keep going until you have five complete rules. Then, work together to write additional sentences describing the playing area, teams, uniforms, or anything else about the game that you like. Use compound sentences whenever possible.

COMPOSING ORIGINAL SENTENCES

3. Working in a group, create six compound sentences. Make sure that each compound sentence includes two simple sentences, each with its own subject and verb. Two sentences should join clauses with coordinating conjunctions, two with semicolons, and two with semicolons plus conjunctive adverbs or transitional expressions. When you have finished, check the sentences again to make sure you have punctuated them correctly.

✓ REVIEW CHECKLIST: Writing Compound Sentences

- Two simple sentences can be joined into one compound sentence with a coordinating conjunction—*and, but, for, nor, or,*

(continued on the following page)

(continued from the previous page)

so, or *yet*. A comma always comes before the coordinating conjunction. (See 7A.)

- A semicolon can join two simple sentences into one compound sentence. (See 7B.)
- A conjunctive adverb or transitional expression can also join two simple sentences into one compound sentence. When it joins two sentences, a conjunctive adverb or transitional expression is always preceded by a semicolon and followed by a comma. (See 7C.)

CHAPTER

8 Writing Complex Sentences

PREVIEW

In this chapter, you will learn

- to form complex sentences with subordinating conjunctions (8A)
- to punctuate dependent clauses introduced by subordinating conjunctions (8B)
- to form complex sentences with relative pronouns (8C)
- to punctuate dependent clauses introduced by relative pronouns (8D)

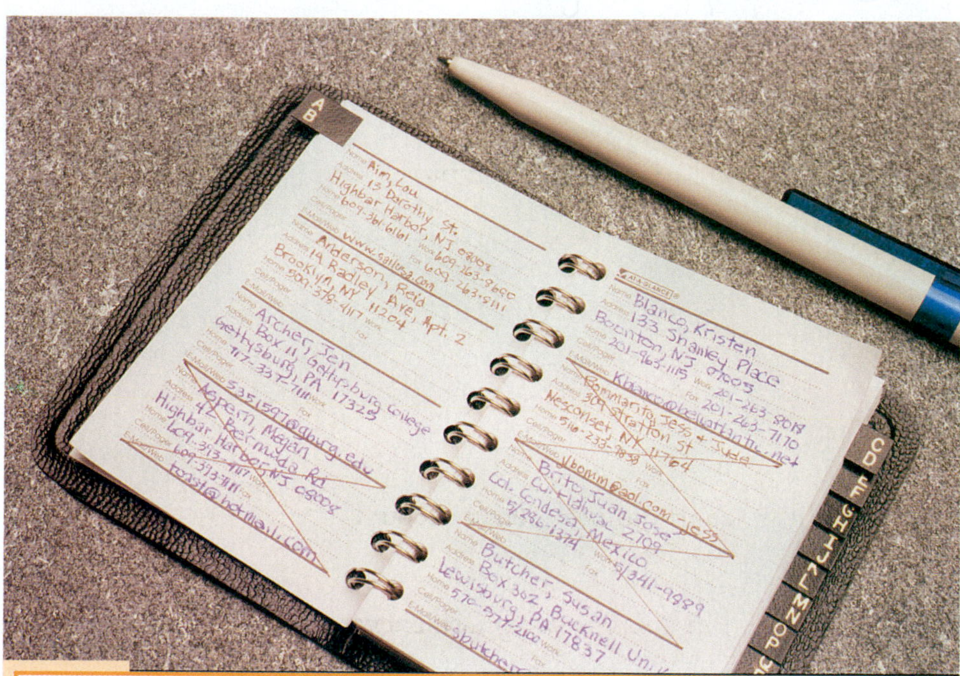

SEEING AND WRITING

What friends have you lost touch with? Why don't you see them anymore? Look at the picture above, and then write a paragraph that answers these questions.

Word Power

estranged separated from someone else by feelings of hostility or indifference

metamorphosis a change or transformation

dependent relying on another for support

independent free from the influence or control of others

A **complex sentence** is made up of one independent clause and one or more dependent clauses. A **clause** is a group of words that contains a subject and a verb. In this chapter, you will learn to combine dependent and independent clauses to create complex sentences.

An **independent clause** can stand alone as a sentence.

INDEPENDENT CLAUSE Tanya was sick yesterday.

A **dependent clause** cannot stand alone as a sentence. It needs other words to complete its meaning.

DEPENDENT CLAUSE Because Tanya was sick yesterday

What happened because Tanya was sick yesterday? To answer this question, you need to add an independent clause to complete the idea in the dependent clause. Combining these two clauses creates a **complex sentence.**

COMPLEX SENTENCE — Because Tanya was sick yesterday, I had to work a double shift. [DEPENDENT CLAUSE: Because Tanya was sick yesterday; INDEPENDENT CLAUSE: I had to work a double shift.]

> **Student Voices**
> *I used to write a lot of short sentences. Now, I try to combine them into longer sentences.*
> *Ben Stein*

A Forming Complex Sentences with Subordinating Conjunctions

One way to create a complex sentence is to join two simple sentences (independent clauses) with a **subordinating conjunction**—a word like *although* or *because.* Look at the following two sentences.

TWO SENTENCES — The election was close. The state supreme court did not order a recount.

What is the connection between the close election and the action of the court? Adding a subordinating conjunction makes the relationship between the two ideas clear.

COMPLEX SENTENCE — Although the election was close, the state supreme court did not order a recount.

Frequently Used Subordinating Conjunctions

after	even if	now that	though	whereas
although	even though	once	till	wherever
as	if	provided	unless	whether
as if	if only	rather than	until	while
as though	in order that	since	when	
because		so that	whenever	
before		than	where	

Different subordinating conjunctions express different relationships between dependent and independent clauses.

Relationship between Clauses	*Subordinating Conjunction*	*Example*
Time	after, before, since, until, when, whenever, while	Before the storm hit land, the people evacuated the town.
Reason or cause	as, because	The senator suggested raising the retirement age because the Social Security program was running out of money.

> **Writing Tip**
> A clause that begins with a subordinating conjunction does not express a complete thought. Used by itself, it is a sentence fragment. (See 12D.)

Result or effect	in order that, so that	We need to put computers in neighborhood community centers so that everyone can have access to the Internet.
Condition	even if, if, unless	The polar ice caps will melt unless we do something now.
Contrast	although, even though, though	Even though he dropped out of college, Bill Gates was able to start Microsoft.
Location	where, wherever	Where there's smoke, there's fire.

◆ PRACTICE 8.1

Write an appropriate subordinating conjunction in each blank. Consult the list of subordinating conjunctions on page 131 to make sure you choose a conjunction that establishes the proper relationship between ideas. (The required punctuation has been provided.)

Example: When people work together in a small space, they all need to mind their manners.

(1) ________ in the past every person working for a company might have had his or her own office, workers today are likely to share space with other people. (2) In fact, many companies provide small cubicles instead of large offices ________ office space is expensive. (3) ________ the company has plenty of space, many managers want employees to work in cubicles or simply to have desks in an open area. (4) These managers think sharing a space makes people work together ________ they feel like a team. (5) ________ workers share space, they may feel less isolated than they would in separate offices. (6) However, employees in a shared office space have to be considerate ________ they are spending so much time close to their coworkers. (7) For example, people should not cut fingernails, brush hair, shave, or apply makeup at their desks ________ no one else is nearby. (8) Also, ________ coworkers overhear personal telephone conversations, they should try to ignore what they hear. (9) ________ telephone technology is very advanced, people should remember to avoid shouting on the telephone. (10) Indeed, when sharing office space, people should behave ________ they would like others around them to behave.

◆ PRACTICE 8.2

Complete each of the following complex sentences by finishing the dependent clause on the line provided. Make sure you supply both a subject and a verb.

Example: Rachel did well on the test because *she understood the material*.

1. After finishing the Football season, Marco tried out for the basketball team.
2. Keisha organized a bake sale even though She knew nothing about baking.
3. Phil ran to the science building so that he could pick out the best seat.
4. Even if Joe will not step down from his position, Nils wants to become president of the student body.
5. Learning Latin has been Michiko's goal since he was transfered From Centeral High.
6. Tamara will major in mathematics unless her grades are not high enough.
7. Wherever he rides his bike or walks, Joe carries his violin.
8. When finished with his studies in medical school Ahmed began to apply to graduate schools.
9. Manwai found an English tutor before His grade dropped to low.
10. Since she is top in her class, Camille takes notes for disabled students.

B Punctuating with Subordinating Conjunctions

To punctuate a complex sentence that contains a subordinating conjunction, follow these rules.

- Place a comma after the dependent clause when it comes *before* the independent clause.

  Although they had no formal training as engineers, Orville and Wilbur Wright built the first airplane.

- Do not use a comma when the dependent clause comes *after* the independent clause.

  Orville and Wilbur Wright built the first airplane although they had no formal training as engineers.

◆ PRACTICE 8.3

Some of the following complex sentences are punctuated correctly, and some are not. Put a *C* next to every sentence that is correctly punctuated. If the punctuation is not correct, edit the sentence to correct it.

Example: After many people reported problems with the Firestone tires on their Ford Explorers, the tires were recalled. ____

1. More than six million Firestone tires were recalled in 2000, because the treads peeled off the surface of the tires. ____
2. When the treads come off a tire, the driver may have difficulty staying on the road. ____
3. A sport-utility vehicle (SUV) is likely to roll over if the treads come off its tires while it is being driven. ____
4. Since the recalled tires were sold on new Ford Explorers government safety experts have been investigating crashes involving those SUVs. ____
5. Although the government does not keep statistics on the brand of tire involved in a fatal accident, the Firestone company admitted making some faulty tires. ____
6. Firestone urged people to cut holes in the recalled tires, because some dealers were reselling them. ____
7. Some customers were buying the recalled tires, so that they could turn them in to Firestone and get brand-new replacements. ____
8. When tires wear out, they are sent to dumps and landfills. ____
9. If the tires catch fire they burn uncontrollably and pollute the air. ____
10. Manufacturers can create items like garden hoses, exercise mats, asphalt, and cement, after they get the unwanted tires back. ____

◆ PRACTICE 8.4

Combine each of the following pairs of sentences to form one complex sentence, using the subordinating conjunction that follows the pair. Make sure you include a comma where one is required.

Example: Although people ~~People~~ fear dreadful viruses such as Ebola, not ~~. Not~~ enough has been done to equip health-care workers in Africa with medical supplies. (although)

1. Many Westerners rarely think about problems in Africa. The lack of money for medical supplies should concern everyone. (although)
2. Contagious diseases in African countries often spread. Hospitals and medical personnel there do not have basic equipment. (because)
3. An outbreak of Ebola virus appeared in northern Uganda in 2000. Doctors and nurses caring for Ebola patients lacked disinfectants and latex gloves. (when)
4. Ebola spreads. Bodily fluids from an infected person come into contact with the skin of a healthy person. (whenever)
5. The Ebola virus makes a patient bleed profusely. Medical workers without gloves face grave danger. (because)
6. Health-care workers must take precautions in an Ebola outbreak. Their skin never touches the skin of their patients. (so that)
7. The virus is named for the Ebola River in Zaire. It first appeared in human beings. (where)
8. The Ugandan outbreak raged. Doctors and nurses did their best to contain it. (while)
9. A doctor and several nurses died of the Ebola virus. More than half of the patients survived. (even though)
10. Wealthier nations should help poor countries acquire basic medical supplies. Medical workers have a better chance of stopping these infections from spreading. (so that)

◆ PRACTICE 8.5

Use each of the subordinating conjunctions below in an original complex sentence. Make sure you punctuate the sentences correctly.

Example

subordinating conjunction: even though

My little sister finally agreed to go to kindergarten even though she was afraid.

1. *subordinating conjunction:* because

Tommy was not fond of brussel sprouts because of what they looked like

2. *subordinating conjunction:* after

After the movie, Tommy and Jill went to the malt shop

3. *subordinating conjunction:* even if

Jill wanted to go to the mall even if her friends did not want to

4. *subordinating conjunction:* until

Paul was told he could not go outside and play until his chores were done.

5. *subordinating conjunction:* whenever

Robin goes to the indoor playpark whenever it's rainy weather

C Forming Complex Sentences with Relative Pronouns

Another way to create a complex sentence is to join two simple sentences (independent clauses) with a **relative pronoun** (*who, which, that,* and so on). Consider the following pair of sentences.

TWO SENTENCES Tiger Woods had won every major golf tournament by the year 2000. He was only twenty-four years old at the time.

Adding a relative pronoun creates a dependent clause that describes a noun or a pronoun in the independent clause.

COMPLEX SENTENCE Tiger Woods, who was only twenty-four years old at the time, had won every major golf tournament by the year 2000.

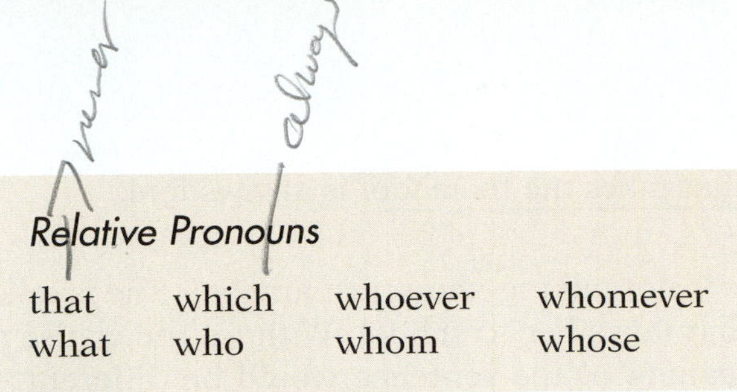

Relative Pronouns
that which whoever whomever
what who whom whose

◆ PRACTICE 8.6

In each of the following complex sentences, underline the dependent clause once, and underline the relative pronoun twice. Then, draw an arrow from the relative pronoun to the noun or pronoun it describes.

Example: People who want to become famous should think about the consequences.

1. Many people apparently agree with the idea that there is no such thing as bad publicity.
2. The man who shot John Lennon wanted to be a celebrity.
3. The people whom talk-show hosts humiliate are usually thrilled just to be on television.
4. Fame, which seems so appealing to many Americans, has drawbacks.
5. Famous people rarely get the privacy that they need to live a normal life.
6. Being in the spotlight twenty-four hours a day can make a person do strange things, which might include fighting with photographers.
7. The actor Sean Penn, who wanted to be alone, constantly got into fights with photographers.
8. Celebrity stalkers, who follow famous people, can be dangerously disturbed.
9. Money and fame, which many people think will make them happy, are rarely enough to make life worthwhile.
10. A culture that values celebrities more than ordinary people causes some people to do anything for fame.

D Punctuating with Relative Pronouns

Sometimes, a dependent clause introduced by a relative pronoun is set off with commas; sometimes, it is not. If the dependent clause is **restrictive**—that is, if it contains essential information—it should *not* be set off with commas.

RESTRICTIVE CLAUSE The bus that takes me to school is always late.

In this sentence, the writer is not talking about just any bus; she is talking about the particular bus that takes her to school. Without the clause *that takes me to school,* the meaning of the sentence would be different. Because the dependent clause is essential to the meaning of the sentence, it is not set off with commas.

However, if a dependent clause introduced by a relative pronoun is **nonrestrictive**—that is, if it does not contain information that is essential to the meaning of the sentence—it should be set off by commas.

NONRESTRICTIVE CLAUSE The *Titanic,* which sank in 1912, carried more than two thousand passengers.

In this sentence, the dependent clause *which sank in 1912* provides extra information, but the sentence communicates the same main idea without it (the *Titanic* carried more than two thousand passengers). Because the dependent clause is not essential to the meaning of the sentence, it is set off with commas.

Writing Tip

Who always refers to people; *that* and *which* refer to things.

FOCUS Introducing Restrictive and Nonrestrictive Clauses

Which always introduces a nonrestrictive clause. *That* always introduces a restrictive clause. *Who* can introduce either a restrictive or a nonrestrictive clause.

The concert, which took place in a football stadium, was very good. (Here, *which* introduces a nonrestrictive clause.)

The sneakers that I wear when I work out are white and green. (Here, *that* introduces a restrictive clause.)

Ernest Hemingway, who wrote *The Old Man and the Sea,* won the Nobel Prize in Literature in 1954. (Here, *who* introduces a nonrestrictive clause.)

The person who robbed the bank was captured almost immediately. (Here, *who* introduces a restrictive clause.)

◆ PRACTICE 8.7

Read the following sentences. If the dependent clause in the sentence is restrictive, write *R* in the blank; if the clause is nonrestrictive, write *N*. Then, if necessary, correct the punctuation of the sentence.

Example: Most Americans support the ideal of equality for women in the workplace, which is not yet a reality. N

1. Working women who have more career opportunities today than ever before are successful in many fields. _____
2. However, women may still encounter a "glass ceiling," which is a phenomenon that occurs when companies refuse to hire women for top positions. _____
3. After getting a position of power which almost always involves supervising other employees women may face additional problems. _____
4. Many workers whose bosses are female feel some resentment. _____
5. Workers admitted unhappiness with their female bosses on surveys, that questioned both male and female employees. _____
6. Female employees, who might be expected to sympathize with female bosses, resent them as much as the male employees do. _____
7. Employees are likely to consider criticism that comes from a female boss as unfair. _____
8. They accept criticism from male bosses which says a lot about the roles of men and women in our society. _____
9. People who admire a tough attitude in a man may not like the same attitude in a woman. _____
10. The news that younger workers do not seem to share these attitudes about female supervisors is encouraging. _____

◆ PRACTICE 8.8

Combine each of the following pairs of sentences into one complex sentence, using the relative pronoun that follows the pair. Be sure to punctuate correctly, using commas to set off only nonrestrictive clauses, not restrictive clauses.

Example: Whaling ^*, which inspired the great American novel Moby Dick,* was once a part of American culture. ~~Whale hunting inspired the great American novel *Moby Dick*.~~ (which)

1. In the nineteenth century, American whalers sailed around the world to hunt whales. Their jobs were very dangerous. (who)
2. Whale oil provided light in many American homes. It burns very brightly. (which)

3. Today, U.S. laws protect several species of whale. They are considered to be in danger of extinction. (that)
4. Most Americans approve of the U.S. ban on whaling. They no longer need whale oil or other whale products. (who)
5. Whale hunting is the focus of a disagreement between the United States and Japan. The two countries have different ideas about whaling. (which)
6. In 2000, Japanese whalers doubled the number of whales they killed. Japanese whalers have been killing some whales every year for research. (who)
7. Some of the whales killed in the Japanese hunt are considered by the U.S. government to be endangered. They include minke whales, Bryde's whales, and sperm whales. (which)
8. Whale meat is a special treat to some Japanese. They consider eating whale to be a part of Japanese culture. (who)
9. The U.S. government argues that the Japanese whale hunt is not for research, but for businesses. The businesses want whale meat to sell to restaurants. (that)
10. Many Japanese do not like the feeling that the United States is trying to tell them what to do. They may not think the Japanese whale hunt is a good idea. (who)

◆ PRACTICE 8.9

Complete the following complex sentences. Make sure that each clause of the complex sentence contains a subject and a verb, and be sure to punctuate correctly.

Example: A hamburger that *has been barbecued on a grill on a sunny summer day is one of my favorite things*.

1. When my mother ______________________________.
2. My best friend, who ______________________________.

3. If you ever ______________________________

______________________________.

4. Although most people ______________________________

______________________________.

5. My dream job, which ______________________________

______________________________.

REVISING AND EDITING

Look back at your response to the Seeing and Writing exercise on page 130. Underline every complex sentence, and circle the subordinating conjunction or relative pronoun. Then, check to make sure your punctuation is correct. Do you have any simple sentences that could be combined with a subordinating conjunction or a relative pronoun? Would combining sentences make the connection between them clearer? If so, revise the sentences to create a complex sentence.

CHAPTER REVIEW

EDITING PRACTICE

Read the following student essay, and then revise it by using subordinating conjunctions or relative pronouns to combine pairs of short sentences. Be sure to punctuate correctly. The first sentence has been revised for you.

Computer Tip

Using the word-processing function that shows the average length of sentences, compare your first and final drafts to see if your sentences have become more complex.

Daffodil

My first pet was a stray cat, ~~She~~ who wandered up to my brother and me and adopted us. I named her Daffodil. She didn't look much like a daffodil. She was gray and white with big green eyes. My mother has always liked cats. She told us we could keep Daffodil.

We got to know Daffodil better. We soon learned that she was a very independent cat. She liked to sleep on my bed. She did not like staying in the house all the time. She wanted to be around us, but only on her own terms. We were playing outside one day. Daffodil simply wandered away. She didn't come back all night, and she didn't come back the next night, either.

Several months had passed. I was in the yard one afternoon. Suddenly, I heard the sound of a cat. Daffodil strolled up to me as if she had been gone only a few minutes. She looked well-fed and happy. I opened the door to announce that Daffodil was back. She marched into the house as if she had owned the place. She went straight to my room, curled up on the bed, and fell asleep.

The years went by. This pattern repeated itself over and over. Daffodil disappeared for months at a time. We always wondered if we would ever see her again. She came back. We were always pleased to see her. We felt lucky that she had chosen us. My parents suspected that Daffodil had another part-time family. They were glad that she loved us enough to come back.

We wondered for years where Daffodil went. We never found out. The important thing for us was that she returned. Daffodil was our part-time pet. She now has a full-time place in my memories.

◆ COLLABORATIVE ACTIVITIES

1. Working in a group of four students, come up with a list of four well-known actors. Next, split into two pairs. In your pair, write a simple sentence about each actor on the list; follow the sentence with a subordinating conjunction or relative pronoun in parentheses. When both pairs have finished, trade papers; then, turn each simple sentence into a complex sentence by using the subordinating conjunction or relative pronoun suggested. Finally, get back together with your group and compare sentences.

   Example
   Samuel L. Jackson was unknown before *Pulp Fiction.* (although)

   Although Samuel L. Jackson was unknown before *Pulp Fiction,* he is now a very popular actor.

2. Go back to the list of actors your group generated in activity 1. Work together to create the plot of a film starring all the people on your list, explaining what part each actor plays. Use a subordinating conjunction or relative pronoun in each sentence you write.

3. Using simple sentences only, write one paragraph of a letter to a Hollywood studio explaining one reason why the film you made up in activity 2 should be made. Then, pass your paragraph to another member of your group, and ask him or her to create complex sentences from the simple sentences you wrote. When your group has finished with all four paragraphs, work together to turn the paragraph(s) with the best reason(s) into a letter arguing for the production of your film.

COMPOSING ORIGINAL SENTENCES

4. Working in a small group, write five complex sentences. Make sure that each one contains (1) a dependent clause with a subordinating conjunction, a subject, and a verb, and (2) an independent clause with a subject and a verb. When you have finished, check the sentences again to make sure you have punctuated them correctly.

☑ REVIEW CHECKLIST: Writing Complex Sentences

- A complex sentence consists of one independent clause and one or more dependent clauses. (See 8A.)
- Subordinating conjunctions—such as *after, although, because, when,* and *while*—can join two simple sentences into one complex sentence. (See 8A.)
- Always use a comma after a dependent clause when it comes before the independent clause in the sentence. Do not use a comma when the dependent clause follows the independent clause. (See 8B.)
- Relative pronouns can join two simple sentences into one complex sentence. Adding a relative pronoun creates a dependent clause that describes a noun or a pronoun in the independent clause. (See 8C.)
- If a dependent clause introduced by a relative pronoun is restrictive, it should not be set off by commas. If the dependent clause is nonrestrictive, it should be set off by commas. (See 8D.)

CHAPTER

9

Fine-Tuning Your Sentences

PREVIEW

In this chapter, you will learn

- to vary sentence openings (9A)
- to choose exact words (9B)
- to use concise language (9C)
- to avoid clichés (9D)

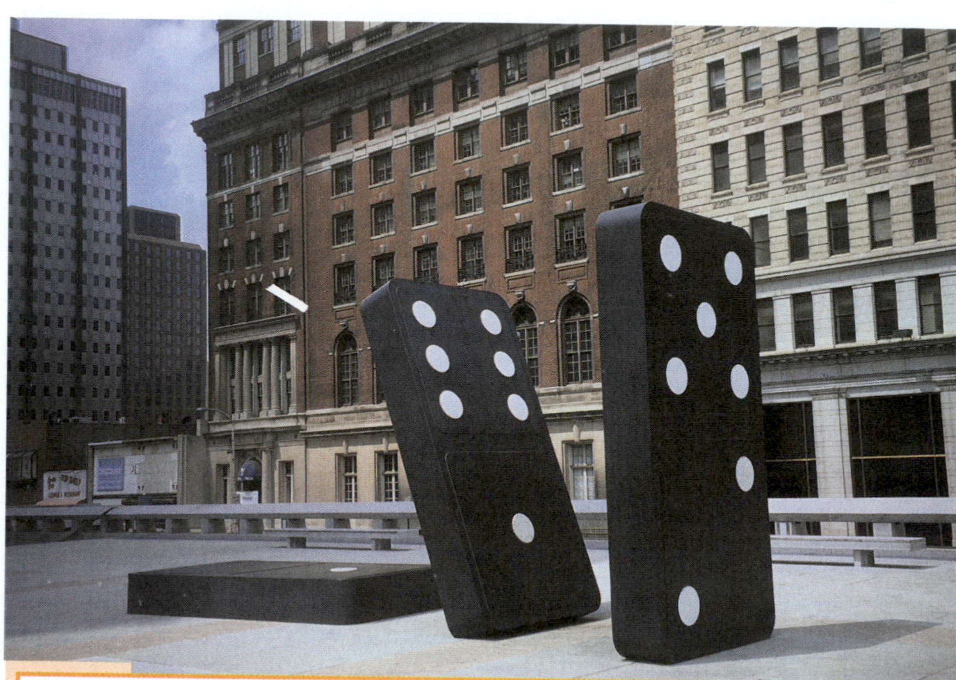

■ SEEING AND WRITING

Do you think publicly funded artworks like this one enrich our cities, or do you think the money they cost could be put to better use elsewhere? Look at the picture above, and then write a paragraph in which you explain your position.

Word Power

subsidize to give financial support to a project

priority important or urgent goal

commission to place an order for something

In Chapters 6 through 8, you learned to write simple, compound, and complex sentences. Now, you are ready to focus on fine-tuning your sentences.

Computer Tip

Use the Search or Find command to locate every use of *The, This,* and *It* at the beginning of a sentence. If necessary, revise your work to vary sentence openings.

A Varying Sentence Openings

When all the sentences in a paragraph begin in the same way, the paragraph may seem dull and repetitive. In the following paragraph, for example, every sentence begins with the subject.

The AIDS quilt contains thousands of panels. Each panel represents a death from AIDS. One panel is for a young college student. Another panel is for an eight-year-old boy. This panel displays his baseball cap. A third panel displays a large picture of a young man. This panel includes a quotation: "Blood saved his life, and it took it away."

The subject matter of this paragraph is interesting, but the style is not. Beginning every sentence with the subject makes the paragraph choppy and monotonous. You can make your paragraphs more interesting by varying your sentence openings.

Beginning with Adverbs

Instead of beginning every sentence with the subject, you can begin some sentences with **adverbs**.

> **Writing Tip**
> An adverb modifies a verb, an adjective, or another adverb. See 20A.

The AIDS quilt contains thousands of panels. Sadly, each panel represents a death from AIDS. One panel is for a young college student. Another panel is for an eight-year-old boy. This panel displays his baseball cap. Finally, a third panel displays a large picture of a young man. This panel includes a quotation: "Blood saved his life, and it took it away."

Adding the adverbs *sadly* and *finally* makes the paragraph's sentences flow more smoothly.

Beginning with Prepositional Phrases

You can also begin some sentences with **prepositional phrases**. A prepositional phrase is a preposition (*of, by, along,* and so on) and all the words that go along with it (for example, *of the people, by the curb, along the road*).

For a list of frequently used prepositions, see 6C.

The AIDS quilt contains thousands of panels. Sadly, each panel represents a death from AIDS. One panel is for a young college student. Another panel is for an eight-year-old boy. In the center, this panel displays his baseball cap. Finally, a third panel displays a large picture of a young man. Under the picture, this panel includes a quotation: "Blood saved his life, and it took it away."

> **Writing Tip**
> An adverb or prepositional phrase that opens a sentence is generally followed by a comma. However, if an introductory prepositional phrase has fewer than three words, the comma is optional. See 22B.

◆ PRACTICE 9.1

Several sentences in the following passage contain adverbs and prepositional phrases that could be moved to the beginnings of the sentences. Revise the passage to vary the sentence openings by moving adverbs to the beginnings of three sentences and moving prepositional phrases to the beginnings of three other sentences. Be sure to place a comma after these adverbs and prepositional phrases.

> **Computer Tip**
> Keep a list of possible sentence openings (adverbs and prepositional phrases, for example) in a separate file. Refer to this file to find different ways of beginning your sentences.

Example: In the late 1970s, heavy ~~Heavy~~ metal music was very popular. ~~in the late 1970s.~~

(1) The film *This Is Spinal Tap* became a cult favorite on its release in 1984. (2) Preview audiences before its release did not have good things to say about it. (3) They obviously did not understand the joke. (4) Spinal

Tap is not, in fact, a real band. (5) The members of this British heavy metal band are actually American actors. (6) They made up their own dialogue, wrote their own music, and played their own instruments for the film. (7) The actors toured with the band after the film began to play in theaters. (8) The fictional band somehow took on a life of its own and became real. (9) A longer version of the film returned to movie theaters in 2000. (10) New audiences are discovering Spinal Tap today. (11) The original viewers, meanwhile, can still recite all their favorite lines.

◆ PRACTICE 9.2

Listed below are three adverbs and three prepositional phrases. To vary sentence openings, add each of these words or phrases to the beginning of one sentence in the passage that follows. Be sure your additions connect ideas clearly and logically. Remember to add commas where they are needed.

Finally	In the wild
Fortunately	With their cuddly teddy-bear looks
Now	In addition

Example: ~~Breeding~~ Fortunately, breeding giant pandas in zoos may help prevent their extinction.

(1) Giant pandas are a favorite animal for people of all ages. (2) The fact that they are endangered concerns animal lovers around the world. (3) Saving the panda has been a priority for wildlife conservation experts for decades, but it is not an easy task. (4) A giant panda needs a huge area without many human beings in it, and each adult requires about ten tons of bamboo a year for food. (5) Wilderness areas are increasingly rare in China, the giant panda's home. (6) Poachers hunt giant pandas for their thick black-and-white fur coats.

(7) Some endangered wild animals have been saved by breeding programs in zoos, but panda-breeding programs have struggled. (8) One panda cub, born at the San Diego Zoo in August 1999, has managed to survive the difficult first weeks and thrive in captivity. (9) The cub, known as Hua Mei, is the first giant panda to be born outside of China.

(10) Hua Mei's mother, Bai Yun, has taken very good care of her tiny cub. (11) Wildlife conservationists hope that Hua Mei's success story will help them increase the numbers of giant pandas. (12) There may be a bright future for this popular animal after all.

B Choosing Exact Words

When you revise your writing, check to make sure you have used words that clearly express your ideas. Try to replace general words with more specific ones.

Specific words refer to particular people, places, and things. **General** words refer to entire classes of things. Sentences that contain specific words create a clearer, stronger picture for readers than sentences containing general ones. Consider the following sentences.

GENERAL The old car went down the street.

SPECIFIC The pink 1959 Cadillac convertible glided smoothly down Main Street.

GENERAL I would like to apply for the job you advertised.

SPECIFIC I would like to apply for the assistant manager's job you advertised in the Sunday *Inquirer.*

In each pair of sentences, the sentence that includes specific words is clearer and more interesting than the one that does not.

Student Voices

When I revise, I try to find general words that I can make more specific.

Krishna Mahajan

FOCUS Overused Words

Try to avoid overused, vague words like these.

good terrific bad
nice great interesting

◆ PRACTICE 9.3

In the following passage, underline the specific words that help you experience the scene the writer describes. The first sentence has been done for you.

(1) The School Day Parade was led by Uncle Sam, who was really a stiltwalker wearing red-and-white-striped pants that were ten feet long.

(2) He was followed by fez-wearing men on knee-high motorbikes that buzzed down Main Street. (3) The plump tuba player for Marion High School's marching band sweated in his red wool jacket. (4) Three seventh-grade boys armed with peashooters waited on the steps of the White Swan Cafe for the Park School sixth graders to march by waving their blue-and-white balloons. (5) At the end of the parade were the Millard sisters, four dark-haired look-alikes in identical satin cowgirl costumes—one red, one blue, one yellow, and one green—on their brown-and-white horses. (6) When the broom carriers walked past whisking piles of fresh horse manure neatly into the gutter, the parade was over.

◆ PRACTICE 9.4

Here are five general words. In the blank beside each, write a more specific word related to the general word. Then, use the more specific word in a sentence of your own.

Example

tool ___claw hammer___

Melanie pried the rusty nails out of each weather-beaten board with a claw hammer.

1. game ________________

____

____

2. house ________________

____

____

3. eat ________________

____

____

4. exercise ________________

____

____

5. like ______________________

____

____

◆ PRACTICE 9.5

The following paragraph is a vaguely worded job application letter. Rewrite the paragraph on a separate page, substituting specific words for the general words of the original and adding details where necessary. Start by making the first sentence, which identifies the applicant and the job, more specific. Then, add specific information about the applicant's background and qualifications, expanding the original paragraph into a three-paragraph letter.

> I am currently attending college and would like to apply for the position advertised. I have a strong interest in that field. My background includes high school and college coursework that relates to this position. I also have personal experience that would make me a good choice. I am qualified for this job, and I would appreciate the opportunity to be considered. Thank you for your consideration.

C Using Concise Language

Too many words can get in the way of good communication and make your point unclear. **Concise language** does just the opposite: it says what it has to say in as few words as possible. When you revise, cross out words that overload your sentences and add nothing to the meaning, substituting more concise language where necessary.

WORDY In spite of the fact that the British troops outnumbered them, the colonists fought on.

CONCISE Although the British troops outnumbered them, the colonists fought on.

WORDY There are many people who have serious allergies.

CONCISE Many people have serious allergies.

WORDY It is my opinion that everyone should have good health care.

CONCISE Everyone should have good health care.

WORDY During the period of the Great Depression, many people were out of work.

CONCISE During the Great Depression, many people were out of work.

WORDY In the newspaper article, it said the situation was serious.

CONCISE The newspaper article said the situation was serious.

▼ **Student Voices**

I used to have trouble with wordiness. It took me a long time to learn to spot it in my writing.

Vanessa Young

● **Writing Tip**

A short sentence is not necessarily concise. A sentence is concise when it contains only the words needed to convey its ideas.

● **Writing Tip**

Try to avoid flowery language and complicated sentences. In general, good writing is clear and concise.

FOCUS Using Concise Language

The following phrases add nothing to a sentence. You can usually delete them or substitute a more concise phrase with no loss of meaning.

Wordy	*Concise*
It is clear that	(delete)
It is a fact that	(delete)
The reason is that	Because
It is my opinion that	(delete)
Due to the fact that	Because
Despite the fact that	Although
At the present time	Today/Currently
At that time	Then
In most cases	Usually
In order to	To

Unnecessary repetition can also make your writing wordy.

WORDY Seeing the ocean for the first time was the most exciting and thrilling experience of my life.

WORDY Some people can't make their own decisions by themselves.

The repetition in the two sentences above adds nothing and for this reason should be deleted.

CONCISE Seeing the ocean for the first time was the most exciting experience of my life.

CONCISE Some people can't make their own decisions.

◆ PRACTICE 9.6

To make the following sentences more concise, cross out wordy expressions and unnecessary repetition, substituting more concise expressions where necessary.

Example: ~~It is a fact that the~~ The global economy makes many people feel powerless.

1. Protesters demonstrating at the World Trade Organization's meeting in Seattle in 1999 disrupted the meeting.
2. Before the occurrence of these protests, few Americans felt strongly about the World Trade Organization.

3. There were some violent incidents that happened in Seattle.
4. The protesters came from many different and varied backgrounds.
5. Some of the protesters were mainly interested in protecting the environment, which was their main cause.
6. Other people among the protesters were concerned about poverty in developing nations.
7. The Seattle protest was not an isolated event that happened only once.
8. Every year, the annual meetings of the World Trade Organization and the International Monetary Fund attract protests.
9. Many young people are getting involved in these protests due to the fact that they believe a global economy should help the poor as much as the wealthy.
10. There are many people who disagree strongly about the practices of international business organizations.

◆ PRACTICE 9.7

The following passage is wordy. Cross out unnecessary words, and make any revisions that may be needed.

Example: Soap and water can clean hands as well as antibacterial ~~germ-fighting~~ products.

(1) A few years ago, antibacterial cleaning products were introduced to the American market all across the country. (2) These products have been promoted in commercial advertisements. (3) The ads try to make people afraid and fearful of the germs in their homes. (4) Mothers of children are often the targets of these scary commercials. (5) When the ads appeared, frightened people immediately began buying antibacterial soap to kill off the invisible germs they could not see.

(6) It is a fact that ordinary soap does not kill every household germ. (7) But new research suggests that antibacterial products may kill good germs that are helpful to human beings. (8) These products may also strengthen dangerous bacteria due to the fact that the strongest germs will still survive. (9) Scientists have warned that children who grow up in

germ-free homes may get sick from normally harmless bacteria that do not usually hurt people. (10) In the final analysis, antibacterial products may do more harm than good.

D Avoiding Clichés

> **Computer Tip**
> Keep a file of overused expressions you encounter in your writing and reading. Refer to this file as you revise.

Clichés are phrases—like *big as a house* and *hard as a rock*—that have been used so often that people no longer pay attention to them. Clichés do nothing to improve writing; in fact, they get in the way of clear communication.

To make your point effectively, replace a cliché with a direct statement or a fresh expression.

CLICHÉ After a year of college, I learned that what goes around comes around.

REVISED After a year of college, I learned that if I don't study, I won't do well.

CLICHÉ With working and going to school, I feel as if I am on a treadmill.

REVISED With working and going to school, I feel as if I am constantly trying to walk up the down escalator.

◆ PRACTICE 9.8

Cross out any clichés in the following sentences. Then, either substitute a fresher expression, or restate the idea in more direct language.

Example: Many Americans hope that clean living will help them live ~~to a ripe old age.~~ *for many decades.*

(1) Americans take to health fads like ducks to water. (2) Today, gyms are a dime a dozen; corporations even provide free gyms for employees. (3) Weight training, which can make a person as strong as an ox, is now as common among students and homemakers as it is among athletes. (4) Exercise is not our only obsession; whenever Americans hear that certain foods are healthy, we eat them like there's no tomorrow. (5) Meanwhile, smokers have worn out their welcome in many office buildings. (6) In addition, many Americans now drink alcohol only once in a blue moon.

(7) Dr. Ruth Clifford Engs, a professor of applied health science, believes that once about every eighty years, Americans go off the deep end to be physically and morally healthy. (8) For a generation or so, people try to make their bodies and souls as clean as a whistle. (9) They exercise, eat foods they think are healthy, and avoid alcohol and cigarettes like the plague. (10) Usually, however, the next generation throws caution to the winds and stops exercising. Who knows what the U.S. population in 2020 will do for fun?

■ REVISING AND EDITING

Look back at your response to the Seeing and Writing exercise on page 144. Are your sentence openings varied? Revise them if necessary. Next, make sure that your language is as exact and concise as possible. Finally, make sure you have not used any clichés in your writing.

CHAPTER REVIEW

◆ EDITING PRACTICE

Read the following student essay, and then revise it by moving at least three adverbs and at least three prepositional phrases to the beginnings of sentences. Then, check to make sure that your revision uses exact words and concise language and that it avoids clichés. The first sentence has been revised for you.

Suburban Living

Parents want to raise their children in a ~~nice place.~~ *safe, quiet place with trees and grass nearby.* The suburbs are supposedly "family friendly," so many people move out of urban cities when they have children. Many areas that are in the suburbs are not planned with children in mind. There is nowhere that the kids have to gather and play. Some kids are bored out of their minds in the suburbs and turn to dangerous pastimes. Many parents may find in the long run that their children would have been just as happy as clams to grow up in the city.

Parents imagine that children in suburban homes ride bicycles or stroll along pretty streets. However, people take their lives in their hands if they bike down some suburban streets. It is also true that many suburbs have no sidewalks, so even pedestrians have to compete with cars. When suburban children visit a friend, their parents usually drive them in a car. The children don't spend enough time doing healthy things as a result.

Children may find the suburbs bad during their teenage years. Meeting the needs of teens is more challenging and difficult than keeping small children amused. Suburbs unfortunately offer few areas where teenagers can gather and get together. Boredom can make teenagers feel down in the dumps. A young person who is smart as a whip may do stupid things out of boredom.

In the final analysis, suburbs may seem so nice to city people, but they are not small towns. For children, cities with sidewalks, parks, museums, and public transportation may be more interesting than suburbs. Parents who are considering a move for the sake of the children should put on their thinking caps before making a decision.

◆ COLLABORATIVE ACTIVITIES

1. Working in a group of three or four students, make a list of every cliché you can think of. Then, working individually, write new, fresh expressions to replace the clichés on your list. Finally, discuss the new expressions with the rest of the group, and choose your favorites.
2. Working in the same group, write a paragraph containing two or three of the fresh expressions you wrote in activity 1. When you have finished, trade paragraphs with another group. Make any revisions in the paragraph that you think are necessary to vary sentence openings or to eliminate vague language or wordiness. Finally, discuss the changes in your paragraph and the other group's paragraph with the other group.
3. Bring in an article from a newspaper or magazine that you think contains wordy, vague, or clichéd language. Working in a group, look through the articles each person has contributed, and choose the one

paragraph that most needs revision. Then, revise the paragraph to eliminate the problems.

COMPOSING ORIGINAL SENTENCES

4. Working in a group, write five sentences. Be sure to vary your sentence openings, choose exact words, use concise language, and avoid clichés. When you have finished, check the sentences again to make sure you have corrected any errors in grammar, punctuation, or spelling.

✓ REVIEW CHECKLIST:
Fine-Tuning Your Sentences

- You can make your sentences more interesting by varying your sentence openings. (See 9A.)
- Try to replace general words with more specific ones. (See 9B.)
- Delete wordy expressions, substituting more concise language where necessary. (See 9C.)
- Avoid clichés (overused expressions). (See 9D.)

CHAPTER

10 Using Parallelism

PREVIEW

In this chapter, you will learn

- to recognize parallel structure (10A)
- to use parallel structure (10B)

SEEING AND WRITING

In what ways have you changed in the months (or years) since you graduated from high school? In what ways have you stayed the same? Look at the picture above, and then write a paragraph in which you answer these questions.

Word Power

mature full-grown

mellow to gain the wisdom and tolerance that are characteristic of maturity

A Recognizing Parallel Structure

In writing, using **parallelism** means repeating the same grammatical structure to express comparable or equivalent ideas.

> Paul Robeson was an actor and a singer. (two nouns)
>
> When my brother comes home from college, he eats, sleeps, and watches television. (three verbs)

Elephants are big, strong, and intelligent. (three adjectives)

Jan likes to run, to do aerobics, and to lift weights. (three phrases)

When different grammatical patterns are used to express similar ideas, sentences can seem awkward. Look at the following pairs of sentences, and see how parallelism can make them easier to read.

NOT PARALLEL I like composition, history, and taking math.

PARALLEL I like composition, history, and math. (All three items in the series are nouns.)

NOT PARALLEL All the wedding guests danced, ate, and were drinking toasts.

PARALLEL All the wedding guests danced, ate, and drank. (All three verbs are in the past tense.)

NOT PARALLEL The Manayunk bike race is long and climbs steeply and is difficult.

PARALLEL The Manayunk bike race is long, steep, and difficult. (All words in the series are adjectives.)

NOT PARALLEL We can go to the movies, or playing miniature golf is an option.

PARALLEL We can go to the movies, or we can play miniature golf. (Both independent clauses have the same structure.)

◆ PRACTICE 10.1

In each of the following sentences, underline the groups of words that are parallel.

Example: The pitcher threw a tantrum in the dugout, threatened his teammates in the locker room, and called a press conference to criticize the coaches.

1. The tornado was sudden, unexpected, and destructive.
2. Petra ordered an egg-white omelet, a green salad with no dressing, and two slices of cheesecake.
3. After the test, I wanted to lie down and take a nap.
4. Her friend had tattoos, a pierced nose, and perfect manners.
5. The store's new owners expanded the parking lot and added a deli counter.
6. The vandals broke the windows, painted graffiti on the walls, and threw garbage on the floor.
7. Before she goes to bed, my niece likes a bath, a bottle, and a lullaby.

8. The almanac predicted a long, cold, and snowy winter.
9. A beautiful voice and acting ability are important for an opera singer.
10. Maria bought a bicycle, Terence bought a bus pass, and Sheila bought a pair of hiking boots.

◆ PRACTICE 10.2

In each of the following sentences, decide whether the underlined words are parallel. If so, write *P* in the blank. If not, edit the sentence to make the words parallel.

Examples

The contestants argued, sunbathed, and ~~they~~ watched each other suspiciously. ____

A retired Navy SEAL, a river guide, and a corporate trainer were the last players on the island. P

1. Hundreds of people wanted to be on a game show that required them to live on an island, catch their own food, and they could not have contact with the outside world. ____
2. The contestants had to be resourceful and physically fit. ____
3. The last person on the island would win a car and a million dollars. ____
4. *Survivor* was modeled on a Swedish game show that had forty-eight contestants and a prize of about thirty thousand dollars. ____
5. The contestants held their breath underwater, rowed a canoe, and rats and caterpillars were eaten by them. ____
6. Many viewers decided that it was much more fun to watch *Survivor* than watching summer reruns. ____
7. Each week, the television audience saw one person win a contest and another person would get voted off the island. ____
8. The corporate trainer was manipulative, argumentative, and he often schemed. ____
9. Some viewers loved him, some viewers hated him, and all of them talked about his victory. ____

10. The show became so popular that the contestants came home to endorsements, acting roles, and becoming famous. ____

B Using Parallel Structure

Parallelism enables you to emphasize related ideas and make your sentences easier to read. Parallel structure is especially important when you present *paired items, comparisons,* or *items in a series.*

Writing Tip
Items listed in a résumé should be in parallel form: *designed ads; drew illustrations; created computer programs.*

Paired Items

Use parallel structure to present paired items connected by a **coordinating conjunction**—*and, but, for, nor, or, so,* or *yet.*

For more on coordinating conjunctions, see 7A.

Jemera takes Alex to day care *and* then goes to work.

You can register to vote now, *or* you can register next week.

You should also use parallel structure for paired items joined by **correlative conjunctions**.

Correlative Conjunctions

both . . . and	neither . . . nor	rather . . . than
either . . . or	not only . . . but also	

Computer Tip
Use the Search or Find function to look for correlative conjunctions in your writing. Make sure you have used parallel structure.

Darryl is good *both* in English *and* in math.

The movie was *not only* long *but also* boring.

I would *rather* take classes in the morning *than* wait until the afternoon.

Comparisons

Use parallel structure in comparisons formed with *than* or *as.*

It often costs less to rent a house *than* to buy one.

In basketball, natural talent is *as* important *as* hard work.

Items in a Series

Use parallel structure for items in a series.

Writing Tip
Use commas to separate three or more items in a series. See 22A.

Unemployment is low because of a healthy economy, low inflation, and high consumer demand.

In order to do well in school, you should attend class regularly, take careful notes, and set aside time to study.

Writing Tip

Elements in an outline should be presented in parallel terms.

I. Good habits
  A. Exercising
  B. Getting enough sleep
  C. Eating well

Use parallel structure for items in a numbered or bulleted list.

There are three reasons to go to college:

1. To learn
2. To increase self-esteem
3. To get a better job

◆ PRACTICE 10.3

In each of the following sentences, underline the parts of the sentence that should be parallel. Then, edit the sentence to make it parallel.

Example: The Internet is a great tool for ~~to get~~ getting information and finding long-lost friends.

1. I wanted to find the address of my old friend and also her telephone number.
2. She had moved to San Francisco, to Nebraska, and finally she had gone to Connecticut.
3. Her telephone numbers had been written and then I had crossed them out in my address book.
4. I tried calling her most recent number, telephoning directory assistance, and I even tried contacting her old boyfriend, but nothing worked.
5. Searching the Internet for her address was easier than to get the information any other way.
6. She had graduated from college, a baby had been born to her, and she had learned that her cousin had a rare disease.
7. She had used the Internet to find information on the disease and she wanted to learn if she was at risk.
8. Some Web sites were authoritative, informative, and they were a lot of help.
9. Other sites were developed by crackpots or people who knew little about the disease put the site together.
10. She was able to find information that would help her cousin and it would enable her to take action to prevent the disease.

◆ PRACTICE 10.4

In each of the following sentences, fill in the blanks with parallel words, phrases, or clauses of your own that make sense in context.

Example: When I have some free time, I love to *play music*, *sing to my baby sister*, and *make up new dances*.

1. If I could have any job in the world, I would want to be either a(n) __________ or a(n) __________.
2. I would enjoy this job because I could __________, __________, and __________.
3. In order to have this job, a person needs to be able to __________, __________, and __________.
4. College will [or will not] help me to prepare for this job because __________ and __________.
5. I will either __________ or __________ next semester.
6. When I graduate from college, I would rather __________ than __________.
7. Both __________ and __________ are very important to me.
8. My hero is [fill in name here] because __________, __________, and __________.
9. [He/she] __________, but other people __________.
10. I am a little bit like [him/her] because I am __________, __________, and __________.

◆ PRACTICE 10.5

Rewrite the following sentences to achieve parallel structure.

Example: Teenaged readers fifty years ago liked stories about detectives who were clever, attractive, and they were also young.

Teenaged readers fifty years ago liked stories about detectives who were clever, attractive, and young.

1. Young people in the 1930s, 1940s, and 1950s read about the adventures of Nancy Drew, and they also liked the Hardy Boys.

2. These characters not only solved crimes, but also they behaved like normal teenagers of their time.

3. The Hardy Boys' father was a former policeman, a good father, and he had become famous doing detective work.

4. Their Aunt Gertrude tried to keep them from sleuthing, scolded them constantly, and she always meddled in their lives.

5. Frank and Joe Hardy found smugglers, thieves, and counterfeiting all over their town, but it also seemed like a nice place to live.

6. Apparently, the Hardy Boys needed neither money nor did they have to get an education.

7. Nancy Drew was blond, attractive, and she had a lot of money.

8. Nancy Drew knew how to fix a car, cook a gourmet meal, and she could fly an airplane.

9. Nancy was both a sleuth and she was a loyal friend to Bess and George.

____

____

10. To Nancy Drew and the Hardy Boys, working for justice was more important than a reward.

____

____

REVISING AND EDITING

Look back at your response to the Seeing and Writing exercise on page 156. First, underline every pair or series of words or phrases. Then, revise your work to make sure you have used parallel words where necessary.

CHAPTER REVIEW

EDITING PRACTICE

Read the following essay, which contains examples of faulty parallelism. Then, identify the sentences you think need to be corrected, and make the changes necessary to achieve parallelism. The first sentence has been edited for you.

The Strangest Instrument

Many people think that electronic musical instruments are a recent invention and ~~produced by~~ *a product of* modern technology. In some cases, modern computers have changed the recording, playing, and the way music is composed, but the first electronic instrument was created just after World War I. In 1919, a Russian electronics genius named Leon Theremin created an instrument that looked strange and was equally strange sounding. Today, this instrument, which is called a theremin, has a small group of fans but they are very devoted.

A theremin looks like a metal box with two antennae; one antenna controls volume, and pitch is controlled by the other. The theremin player touches neither the box nor does he or she come in contact with the antennae. Instead, the player's hands become a part of an electrical circuit that creates sound. A theremin player moves his or her hands over the antennae to change the pitch or for adding vibrato.

Playing the theremin is difficult. Only a handful of professional theremin players are able to make the instrument play the right note and also play it at the right time. Because of its weird, outer-space sound, the theremin has been used to create background music in science fiction movies and films that are horror movies.

Today, theremin collectors buy expensive early theremins, purchase new theremins, and kits to build theremins. Most collectors would rather have a theremin that they will never learn to play well than not to have one at all. The eerie sound of the theremin, the "magical" way it produces sound, and having an interesting history are reward enough.

◆ COLLABORATIVE ACTIVITIES

1. Working on your own, write a sentence that contains no parallel nouns, verbs, adjectives, phrases, or clauses. Then, working in a group of three students, pass the paper to another person in the group who should add a parallel noun, verb, adjective, phrase, or clause to the sentence. Next, pass the paper to the third person in the group to check for correct parallelism. Finally, as a group, compare the finished sentences to the originals and discuss the changes.
2. Working on your own, make a list of at least three points to support one of these topics:

   Why I like a particular recording artist

   Why I chose this college

   The worst problems in my hometown

   Next, write a sentence that includes all the items on your list. Then, working in a group, read aloud the sentence you wrote. Finally, discuss the parallelism in the finished sentence.
3. Working in a group, decide on a topic for a paragraph. Next, have each student write a sentence containing parallel words, phrases, or clauses. Then, as a group, choose the sentence you like best and write a para-

graph that includes that sentence. Be sure that the finished paragraph includes at least three sentences containing parallel items. Be sure to vary the sentences—for example, write one with parallel nouns, one with parallel adjectives, and one with parallel phrases.

COMPOSING ORIGINAL SENTENCES

4. Working in a group, collaborate to create five sentences illustrating effective parallelism. When you have finished, check the sentences to make sure you have corrected any errors in grammar, punctuation, or spelling.

✓ REVIEW CHECKLIST: Using Parallelism

- Repeat the same grammatical structure to express comparable or equivalent ideas. (See 10A.)
- Use parallel structure with paired items. (See 10B.)
- Use parallel structure in comparisons formed with *than* or *as*. (See 10B.)
- Use parallel structure for items in a series or in a numbered or bulleted list. (See 10B.)

UNIT THREE

Solving Common Sentence Problems

CHAPTER

11

Run-Ons and Comma Splices

PREVIEW

In this chapter, you will learn

- to recognize run-ons and comma splices (11A)
- to correct run-ons and comma splices in five different ways (11B)

■ SEEING AND WRITING

Do you think Barbie is a positive role model for young girls? Why or why not? Look at the picture above, and then write a paragraph in which you answer these questions.

Word Power

role model a person who serves as a model of behavior for someone else to imitate

A Recognizing Run-Ons and Comma Splices

A **run-on** is an error that occurs when two sentences are joined without punctuation.

RUN-ON Unemployment is at an all-time low many people still do not have jobs.

A **comma splice** is an error that occurs when two sentences are joined with just a comma.

COMMA SPLICE Unemployment is at an all-time low, many people still do not have jobs.

> **Writing Tip**
>
> A comma can join sentences only when it is followed by a coordinating conjunction. (See 7A.)

PRACTICE 11.1

Some of the sentences in the following passage are correct, but others are run-ons or comma splices. In the blank after each sentence, write *C* if the sentence is correct, *RO* if it is a run-on, and *CS* if it is a comma splice.

Example: Old U.S. currency was too easy to copy, the U.S. Treasury changed the designs of the bills. CS

(1) Making counterfeit American dollars is a huge business in Colombia. ______ (2) U.S. money has been redesigned to stop counterfeiters, the Colombians have found ways to get around most of the new difficulties. ______ (3) The dollar is printed on special paper it has a distinctive look and feel. ______ (4) Counterfeiters solve this problem by using the same paper they simply remove the ink from genuine one-dollar bills. ______ (5) Another part of the new design is an off-center portrait, the counterfeiters engrave metal plates using photographs to match the new bills. ______ (6) One of the most challenging protective devices is a strip inside each genuine bill, the strip is visible when the bill is held up to the light. ______ (7) This strip includes the denomination and the letters *USA*. ______ (8) Some counterfeiters in Colombia are very talented, they actually insert an imitation strip into the genuine currency paper of each bill. ______ (9) The counterfeiters sell the bills in the United States some can cost up to half of their face value. ______ (10) Counterfeiters realize that U.S. dollars used to be much easier to copy, these criminals rely on the fact that most Americans do not look closely at their money. ______

> **Computer Tip**
>
> Grammar checkers sometimes identify a sentence as a run-on or a comma splice simply because it is long, but sometimes a long sentence can be correct. Before you make changes, be sure you actually have an error (two sentences joined together without punctuation or joined with just a comma).

B Correcting Run-Ons and Comma Splices

You can correct run-ons and comma splices in five different ways.

- *Create two separate sentences.*

> **Student Voices**
>
> *I used to think run-ons were just very long sentences, so I was never sure where to break them. Now, I know to break them into simple sentences.*
>
> *Iris Colon*

INCORRECT Frances Perkins was the first female cabinet member she was President Franklin D. Roosevelt's secretary of labor. (run-on)

INCORRECT Frances Perkins was the first female cabinet member, she was President Franklin D. Roosevelt's secretary of labor. (comma splice)

CORRECT Frances Perkins was the first female cabinet member. She was President Franklin D. Roosevelt's secretary of labor. (two separate sentences)

- *Connect ideas with a coordinating conjunction.* If you want to indicate a particular relationship between ideas—for example, a cause-effect link or a contrast—use a coordinating conjunction (*and, but, for, nor, or, so,* or *yet*) to connect the ideas. Always place a comma before the coordinating conjunction.

For more on connecting ideas with coordinating conjunctions, see 7A.

INCORRECT "Strange Fruit" is best known as a song performed by Billie Holiday it was originally a poem. (run-on)

INCORRECT "Strange Fruit" is best known as a song performed by Billie Holiday, it was originally a poem. (comma splice)

CORRECT "Strange Fruit" is best known as a song performed by Billie Holiday, but it was originally a poem. (ideas are connected with the coordinating conjunction *but*)

- *Connect ideas with a semicolon.* If you want to indicate a close connection—or a strong contrast—between two ideas, use a semicolon.

INCORRECT Jhumpa Lahiri is the daughter of immigrants from Calcutta she won the Pulitzer Prize for her first book. (run-on)

INCORRECT Jhumpa Lahiri is the daughter of immigrants from Calcutta, she won the Pulitzer Prize for her first book. (comma splice)

CORRECT Jhumpa Lahiri is the daughter of immigrants from Calcutta; she won the Pulitzer Prize for her first book. (ideas are connected with a semicolon)

- *Connect ideas with a semicolon and a conjunctive adverb or transitional expression.* To show a specific relationship between two closely related ideas, add a conjunctive adverb or transitional expression after the semicolon.

INCORRECT The human genome project is very important it may be the most important scientific research of the last hundred years. (run-on)

INCORRECT The human genome project is very important, it may be the most important scientific research of the last hundred years. (comma splice)

CORRECT The human genome project is very important; in fact, it may be the most important scientific research of the last hundred years. (ideas are connected with a semicolon and the transitional expression *in fact*)

Writing Tip

Conjunctive adverbs include words such as *however* and *therefore;* transitional expressions include *in fact, as a result,* and *for example.* (See 7C.)

Word Power

genome a complete set of chromosomes and its associated genes; DNA

FOCUS Using Semicolons

A run-on or comma splice often occurs when you use a conjunctive adverb or transitional expression to join two sentences but do not use the required punctuation.

INCORRECT It is easy to download information from the Internet however it is not always easy to evaluate the information. (run-on)

INCORRECT It is easy to download information from the Internet, however it is not always easy to evaluate the information. (comma splice)

To correct this kind of run-on or comma splice, insert a semicolon before the conjunctive adverb or transitional expression, and a comma after it.

CORRECT It is easy to download information from the Internet; however, it is not always easy to evaluate the information.

Student Voices

I always write comma splices when I use however *or* therefore, *so I check my sentences carefully when I use these words.*

Courtney Abbott

Writing Tip

Remember, a comma is *required* after the conjunctive adverb or transitional expression that links two independent clauses.

For more on connecting ideas with subordinating conjunctions and relative pronouns (and complete lists of these words), see Chapter 8.

- *Connect ideas with a subordinating conjunction or relative pronoun.* When one idea is dependent on another, you can turn the dependent idea into a dependent clause by adding a subordinating conjunction (such as *although, because,* or *when*) or a relative pronoun (such as *who, which,* or *that*).

INCORRECT J. K. Rowling is now the bestselling author of the Harry Potter books not long ago she was an unemployed single mother. (run-on)

INCORRECT J. K. Rowling is now the bestselling author of the Harry Potter books, not long ago she was an unemployed single mother. (comma splice)

CORRECT Although J. K. Rowling is now the bestselling author of the Harry Potter books, not long ago she was an unemployed single mother. (ideas are connected with the subordinating conjunction *although*)

INCORRECT Harry Potter is an orphan he is also a wizard with magical powers. (run-on)

INCORRECT Harry Potter is an orphan, he is also a wizard with magical powers. (comma splice)

CORRECT Harry Potter, who is an orphan, is also a wizard with magical powers. (ideas are connected with the relative pronoun *who*)

Writing Tip

When you use a relative pronoun to correct a run-on or comma splice, the relative pronoun takes the place of a noun or pronoun in the sentence. (For example, in the sentence to the right, *who* takes the place of *he*.)

◆ PRACTICE 11.2

Correct each of the run-ons and comma splices below in one of the following ways: by creating two separate sentences, by connecting ideas with a comma followed by a coordinating conjunction, by connecting ideas with a semicolon, or by connecting ideas with a semicolon and a conjunctive adverb or transitional expression. Be sure the punctuation is correct. Remember to put a semicolon before, and a comma after, each conjunctive adverb or transitional expression.

Example: All over the world, people eat flatbreads, ^and different countries have different kinds.

1. Flatbread is bread that is flat usually it does not contain yeast.
2. An example of a flatbread in the United States is the pancake, many Americans eat pancakes with maple syrup.
3. The tortilla is a Mexican flatbread tortillas are made of corn or wheat.
4. A favorite flatbread in the Middle East is the pita, it may have a pocket that can be filled with vegetables or meat.
5. Italians eat focaccia, when they put cheese on a focaccia, it becomes a pizza.
6. Crackers are another kind of flatbread the dough is baked until it is crisp.
7. Indian cooking has several kinds of flatbreads, all of them are delicious.
8. Matzoh resembles a large, square cracker, it is a traditional food for the Jewish holiday of Passover.
9. Fifty years ago, most people ate only the flatbreads from their native land, today flatbreads are becoming internationally popular.
10. Many American grocery stores sell tortillas, pita bread, and other flatbreads most of their customers love flatbread sandwiches.

◆ PRACTICE 11.3

Use the list of subordinating conjunctions on page 131 and the relative pronouns *who, which,* or *that* to help you correct the following run-ons and comma splices. Be sure to add punctuation where necessary.

Examples

Teenagers should not take illegal drugs, ^which ~~they~~ can be very harmful.

Taking drugs for recreation is not safe ^because they can have unexpected effects.

1. Some Americans have serious drug problems, these problems can be difficult to treat.
2. During the Vietnam War, many American soldiers became addicted to heroin it was cheap and widely available in Southeast Asia.
3. Richard Nixon was president of the United States at the time he realized that drug-addicted soldiers were a problem.
4. Nixon was generally tough on crime, he encouraged Congress to fund treatment programs for drug users.
5. Drugs such as marijuana and cocaine were illegal during the 1960s and 1970s, drug use was ignored or tolerated by many Americans.
6. The "War on Drugs" came about in the 1980s parent groups were concerned.
7. Laws against illegal drugs became stricter, possession of small amounts of many drugs was enough to send a young person to jail.
8. The "War on Drugs" was treated as a real war, government money was spent on police rather than on drug treatment.
9. The "Just Say No" drug policy was widespread in the 1980s, it tried to convince young people to avoid drugs.
10. Unfortunately, the "Just Say No" policy was not successful it offered no real solutions to the drug problem.

◆ PRACTICE 11.4

Review the five strategies for correcting run-ons and comma splices. Then, correct each run-on and comma splice in the following passage in the way that best indicates the relationship between ideas. Be sure the punctuation is appropriate.

Example: Rapping is a kind of spoken poetry, ^so why shouldn't teenagers study it?

(1) Older generations may not approve of rap however it appears to be here to stay. (2) Rap is now part of mainstream music, young people of all races and backgrounds listen to it. (3) However, this music still has critics many feel that rap lyrics are too violent. (4) Other people worry about rap's attitude toward women. (5) Another issue is the crude language, many rap artists use it. (6) Now, some schools are trying to use rap as a teaching tool, rap may inspire an interest in more traditional poetry or music. (7) Rappers use crude language to discuss unpleasant topics, students can talk about this strategy. (8) Rap does not always use perfect grammar students should understand the difference between spoken and written language. (9) Rap cannot reach every student, some people do not relate to Shakespeare, either. (10) Using popular music in the classroom probably will not hurt students it just might help.

REVISING AND EDITING

Look back at your response to the Seeing and Writing exercise on page 169. Can you spot any run-ons or comma splices? Correct each run-on and comma splice you find. If you do not find any run-ons or comma splices in your own writing, work with a classmate to correct his or her writing, or edit the work you did for another assignment.

CHAPTER REVIEW

EDITING PRACTICE

Read the following essay. Now, revise it by eliminating run-ons and comma splices and carefully correcting them to indicate the relationships between the ideas. Be sure that the punctuation is correct. The first error has been corrected for you.

Stripes

Prison inmates in old movies always wear striped uniforms, but most prisons today do not make prisoners wear stripes. Instead, prisoners usually wear brightly colored jumpsuits they even wear street clothes in some prisons. Old-fashioned ideas about prison life are becoming popular again the striped prison uniform is making a comeback.

Most American prisons stopped having prisoners wear stripes at least fifty years ago, at the time, many people felt that wearing stripes was humiliating. However, there is a reason for bringing back striped uniforms these uniforms help people identify escaped prisoners. Most people outside of prisons do not wear jumpsuits with horizontal stripes other popular prison clothing resembles everyday clothing. Denim is a popular uniform material in prisons, denim blends in too well with clothing worn by people on the street. Orange jumpsuits may be noticeable, they also may look too much like the uniforms worn by sanitation workers. Escaped prisoners in striped suits are easy to spot, even at night, the stripes are highly visible.

Some people still dislike striped uniforms they argue that wearing these uniforms is a form of humiliation. However, in states that have brought back the old uniforms, the stripes are very popular with voters. Many Americans think prison life is too easy they want prisoners to be treated more harshly. Some states make prisoners work on chain gangs striped uniforms are part of the same trend toward strict treatment of prisoners.

Movies from the 1930s showed prisoners in black-and-white uniforms, the uniforms instantly identified them as prisoners. Soon, people may begin to think of the striped uniforms as a part of the present instead of the past. Americans may eventually think this a good idea, that depends on how they feel about prisoners and prison life in this country.

◆ COLLABORATIVE ACTIVITIES

1. Find two examples of run-ons or comma splices (or one of each). You can look for these errors in papers you have written, in your school newspaper, or online; sometimes, errors like these also appear in national magazines or newspapers. Bring the two examples to class.

Then, working with another student, exchange examples and make corrections to the run-ons or comma splices your classmate found. Finally, discuss your corrections with each other.

2. Transcribe (write down) four sentences from a television or radio news program and bring your sentences to class. Then, working in a group of three or four students, pass your sentences to another person in the group. Make sure that the sentences you receive contain no run-ons or comma splices.
3. Working in a group, rewrite the sentences transcribed for activity 2, turning them into run-ons or comma splices. Then, exchange incorrect sentences with another group and correct their sentences. Finally, compare the original sentences with your corrected sentences and discuss the differences with the other group.

COMPOSING ORIGINAL SENTENCES

4. Working in a group, collaborate to write five sentences on a topic of the group's choice that contain no run-ons or comma splices. When you have finished, check the sentences again to make sure you have corrected any errors in grammar, punctuation, or spelling.

✓ REVIEW CHECKLIST: Run-Ons and Comma Splices

- A run-on is an error that occurs when two sentences are joined without punctuation. (See 11A.)
- A comma splice is an error that occurs when two sentences are joined with just a comma. (See 11A.)
- You can correct a run-on or comma splice in one of five ways:
  - by creating two separate sentences;
  - by connecting ideas with a comma followed by a coordinating conjunction;
  - by connecting ideas with a semicolon;
  - by connecting ideas with a semicolon and a conjunctive adverb or transitional expression; or
  - by connecting ideas with a subordinating conjunction or relative pronoun. (See 11B.)

CHAPTER

12 Sentence Fragments

PREVIEW

In this chapter, you will learn

- to recognize sentence fragments (12A)
- to correct sentence fragments created when phrases are punctuated as sentences (12B)
- to correct sentence fragments created when verbs are incomplete (12C)
- to correct sentence fragments created when dependent clauses are punctuated as sentences (12D)

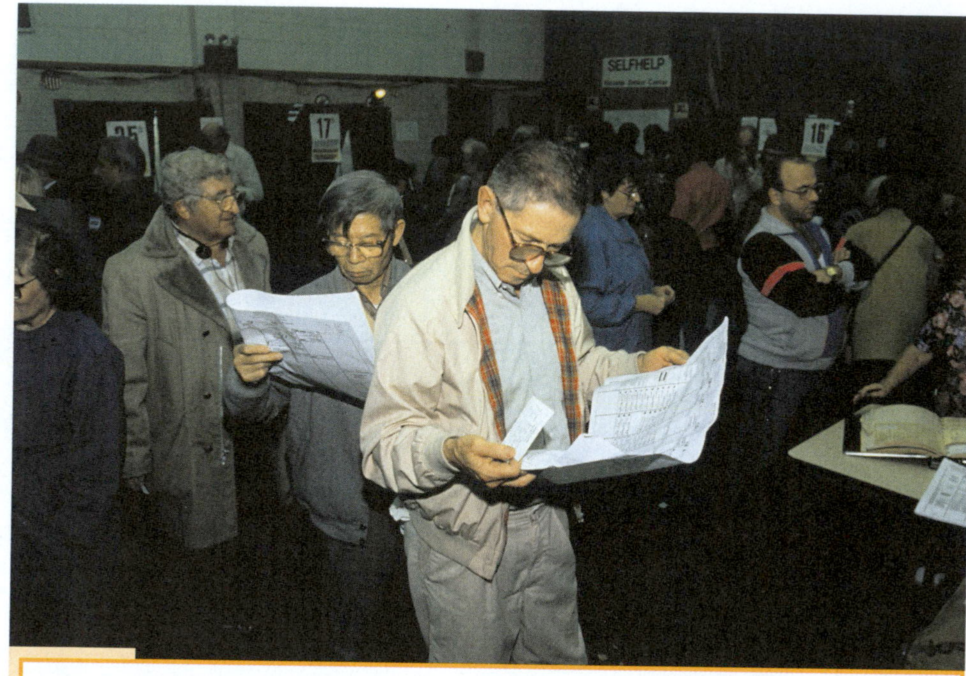

SEEING AND WRITING

Why do you think so many young people don't vote? Look at the picture above, and then write a paragraph explaining why you think this problem exists.

Word Power

apathy lack of interest

apathetic feeling or showing a lack of interest

alienated emotionally withdrawn or unresponsive

Writing Tip

You may see sentence fragments in advertisements ("A full head of hair in just 30 minutes!"), but fragments are not acceptable in college writing.

A Recognizing Sentence Fragments

A **sentence fragment** is an incomplete sentence. Every sentence must include at least one subject and one verb, and every sentence must express a complete thought. If a group of words does not do *all* these things, it is a fragment and not a sentence—even if it begins with a capital letter and ends with a period.

SENTENCE A new U.S. president was elected. (includes both a subject and a verb and expresses a complete thought)

FRAGMENT A new U.S. president. (verb is missing)

FRAGMENT Was elected. (subject is missing)

The first group of words, *A new U.S. president,* has no verb: What is being said about the new president? The second group of words, *Was elected,* has no subject: Who was elected? A sentence must have both a subject and a verb and express a complete thought. These two groups of words are fragments, not sentences.

◆ PRACTICE 12.1

Each of the following items is a fragment because it lacks a subject, a verb, or both. Add any words needed to turn the fragment into a complete sentence.

Example: The sparkling water on the lake.

The sparkling water on the lake invited us in for a swim.

____

1. Eats sunflower seeds for breakfast.

____

____

2. A terrible scream.

____

____

3. Ran and jumped, hoping to win.

____

____

4. Answered the question.

____

____

5. Wore a purple and pink tutu and waved a magic wand.

____

____

6. Harold and Sally, the king and queen of the prom.

____

____

7. The mansion on the hill, dark and empty.

____

____

8. The last two pieces of dental floss.

____

____

9. Skidded off the road into a ditch.

____

____

10. The leaves in their fall colors.

____

____

FOCUS Identifying Sentence Fragments

In paragraphs and longer pieces of writing, sentence fragments sometimes appear next to complete sentences. You can often correct a sentence fragment by attaching it to a nearby sentence that includes the missing subject or verb. Here, a fragment appears right after a complete sentence.

COMPLETE SENTENCE — FRAGMENT

Okera majored in two subjects. English and philosophy.

To correct the fragment, simply attach it to the complete sentence that contains the missing subject (*Okera*) and verb (*majored*).

Okera majored in two subjects, English and philosophy.

◆ PRACTICE 12.2

In the following passage, some of the numbered groups of words are missing a subject, a verb, or both. First, identify each fragment by labeling it *F.* Next, decide how each fragment could be attached to a nearby word group to create a complete new sentence. Finally, rewrite the entire passage, using complete sentences, on the lines provided.

Example: Some people use lip balm. _____ To keep their lips from drying out. F

Rewrite: Some people use lip balm to keep their lips from drying out.

(1) According to some people. _____ (2) Who frequently use lip balm. _____ (3) This product is addictive. _____ (4) The purpose of lip balm. _____ (5) Is to keep the lips. _____ (6) From getting chapped. _____ (7) Can people become dependent on lip balm? _____ (8) Some users say yes. _____ (9) However, the makers of lip balm. _____ (10) Deny the possibility of addiction. _____

Rewrite:

____

____

____

____

____

____

◆ PRACTICE 12.3

In the following passage, some of the numbered groups of words are missing a subject, a verb, or both. First, underline each fragment. Then, decide how each fragment could be attached to a nearby word group to create a complete new sentence. Finally, rewrite the entire passage, using complete sentences, on the lines provided.

Example: When they feel threatened, bears can be dangerous. And unpredictable.

Rewrite: *When they feel threatened, bears can be dangerous and unpredictable.*

(1) Hikers often wear bells. (2) To make noise on the trail. (3) Especially areas populated by bears. (4) Bears can hear very well. (5) But cannot see long distances. (6) Sometimes, bears can be frightened by humans. (7) And attack them. (8) However, a bear may hear a person coming. (9) And then is very likely to avoid the person. (10) This is why experienced hikers never go hiking without bells.

Rewrite:

____

____

B Correcting Phrase Fragments

A **phrase** is a group of words that is missing a subject or a verb or both. When you punctuate a phrase as if it is a sentence, you create a fragment.

Two kinds of phrases that are often written as sentence fragments are *appositives* and *prepositional phrases.*

Appositive Fragments

For information on using commas with appositives, see 22D.

An **appositive** is a group of words that identifies or renames a noun or a pronoun. An appositive cannot stand alone as a sentence. To correct an appositive fragment, add the words needed to make it a complete sentence: the nouns or pronouns that the appositive identifies. (You will often find these words in a nearby sentence.)

INCORRECT The *Lethal Weapon* movies have two stars. Mel Gibson and Danny Glover. [APPOSITIVE FRAGMENT: Mel Gibson and Danny Glover.]

CORRECT The *Lethal Weapon* movies have two stars, Mel Gibson and Danny Glover.

Sometimes an expression like *such as* introduces an appositive. Even if an appositive is introduced by *such as,* it still cannot stand alone as a sentence.

INCORRECT Sequels have been made for many popular action movies. Such as *Lethal Weapon, Die Hard, Alien,* and *Terminator.* [APPOSITIVE FRAGMENT: Such as *Lethal Weapon, Die Hard, Alien,* and *Terminator.*]

CORRECT Sequels have been made for many popular action movies, such as *Lethal Weapon, Die Hard, Alien,* and *Terminator.*

Prepositional Phrase Fragments

For more on prepositional phrases, see 6C.

A **prepositional phrase** consists of a preposition and its object. A prepositional phrase cannot stand alone as a sentence. To correct a prepositional phrase fragment, add the words needed to make it a complete sentence. (You will often find these words in a nearby sentence.)

INCORRECT The horse jumped. Over the fence. [PREPOSITIONAL PHRASE FRAGMENT: Over the fence.]

CORRECT The horse jumped over the fence.

◆ PRACTICE 12.4

Each of the following phrases is a fragment because it lacks a subject, a verb, or both. Correct each fragment by adding any words needed to turn the fragment into a complete sentence.

Example: With a loud crash.

The bookcase fell to the floor with a loud crash.

1. A high-rise apartment building.

2. On the ledge outside the window.

3. After the race.

4. At the beginning of football season.

5. The excited contestants.

6. During the announcement.

7. Such as a brand-new washing machine.

8. The wealthiest people in town.

9. Before the first flash of lightning.

____

____

10. A gray mist creeping slowly over the grass.

____

____

◆ PRACTICE 12.5

In the following passage, some of the numbered groups of words are appositive fragments or prepositional phrase fragments. First, identify each fragment by labeling it *F.* Then, decide how each fragment could be attached to a nearby word group to create a complete new sentence. Finally, rewrite the entire passage, using complete sentences, on the lines provided.

Example: People around the world will miss the Kahiki. ____ A Polynesian restaurant in Columbus, Ohio. __*F*__

Rewrite: *People around the world will miss the Kahiki, a Polynesian restaurant in Columbus, Ohio.*

(1) In August 2000. ____ (2) The Kahiki closed its doors forever. ____ (3) This Columbus landmark was famous. ____ (4) For its tropical drinks, grass huts, giant Tiki gods, and indoor rainstorms. ____ (5) The restaurant was built in a more innocent time. ____ (6) The 1950s. ____ (7) The outside of the building was impressive. ____ (8) With its wooden idols and canoe-shaped roof. ____ (9) The Kahiki had recently been added. ____ (10) To the National Register of Historic Places. ____ (11) Now, the building will be replaced by something more modern. ____ (12) A drugstore. ____

Rewrite:

____

____

____

____

____

____

◆ PRACTICE 12.6

In the following passage, some of the numbered groups of words are appositive fragments or prepositional phrase fragments. First, underline each fragment. Then, decide how each fragment could be attached to a nearby word group to create a complete new sentence. Finally, rewrite the entire passage, using complete sentences, on the lines provided.

Example: In the primary elections in 2000. Kansas citizens voted in a new board of education.

Rewrite: *In the primary elections in 2000, Kansas citizens voted in a new board of education.*

(1) In 1999. (2) The Kansas State Board of Education voted to change the standards. (3) For science education in the state's public schools. (4) The board members voted. (5) To stop teaching students about evolution. (6) This decision horrified science teachers across the country. (7) And had economic consequences. (8) Some technology companies decided not to move. (9) To Kansas. (10) A place where future workers might not have a good science background.

Rewrite:

____

____

____

____

____

____

____

____

C Correcting Incomplete Verbs

Every sentence must include a **complete verb**. Present participles and past participles are not complete verbs. They need **helping verbs** to complete them.

A **present participle**, such as *rising,* is not a complete verb because it cannot stand alone in a sentence without a helping verb.

Writing Tip

A complete verb consists of the **main verb** and any **helping verbs**. For more on main verbs and helping verbs, see 6F.

FOCUS Using Helping Verbs with Present Participles

To serve as the main verb of a sentence, a present participle must be completed by a form of the verb *be*.

Helping Verb	+	*Present Participle*	=	*Complete Verb*
am		rising		am rising
is		rising		is rising
are		rising		are rising
was		rising		was rising
were		rising		were rising
has been		rising		has been rising
have been		rising		have been rising
had been		rising		had been rising

Writing Tip

Be careful not to create dangling modifiers with participles such as *rising*. (See 15C.)

When you use a present participle without a helping verb, you create a fragment.

FRAGMENT The moon rising over the ocean.

To correct the fragment, add a helping verb.

SENTENCE The moon was rising over the ocean.

For a list of irregular past participles, see 17B.

An irregular **past participle** is not a complete verb because it cannot stand alone in a sentence without a helping verb.

FOCUS Using Helping Verbs with Past Participles

To serve as the main verb of a sentence, a past participle must be completed by a form of the verb *be* or *have*.

Helping Verb(s)	+	*Past Participle*	=	*Complete Verb*
am		hidden		am hidden
is		hidden		is hidden
are		hidden		are hidden
was		hidden		was hidden
were		hidden		were hidden
has		hidden		has hidden
have		hidden		have hidden
had		hidden		had hidden
has been		hidden		has been hidden
have been		hidden		have been hidden
had been		hidden		had been hidden

When you use an irregular past participle without a helping verb, you create a fragment.

FRAGMENT The sun hidden behind a cloud.

To correct the fragment, add a helping verb.

SENTENCE The sun was hidden behind a cloud.

◆ PRACTICE 12.7

Each of the following is a fragment because it does not have a complete verb. Correct each fragment by completing the verb.

Example: She is sending an e-mail to her brother in California.

1. My sister forgotten the house where we used to live.
2. Now, the nights getting colder.
3. The baby been crying ever since you left.
4. Lately I been too tired to do my homework.
5. Vivian and her daughters gone to the supermarket to pick up some groceries for dinner.
6. They never eaten beef before they moved to this country.
7. Until yesterday, the choir never sung a hymn that featured two soloists.
8. Reverend Martin given beautiful sermons this month.
9. More and more airplanes flying over this neighborhood every day.
10. He swum across this river at least once a week for twenty years.

D Correcting Dependent Clause Fragments

Every sentence must include a subject and a verb and express a complete thought. A **dependent clause** is a group of words that includes a subject and a verb but does not express a complete thought. A dependent clause cannot stand alone as a sentence.

The following dependent clause is punctuated as if it were a sentence.

FRAGMENT After Jeanette got a full-time job.

This sentence fragment includes a subject (*Jeanette*) and a complete verb (*got*), but it does not express a complete thought. Readers expect the thought to continue, but it stops short. What happened after Jeanette got a full-time job? Was the result positive or negative? To turn this fragment into a sentence, you need to complete the thought.

SENTENCE After Jeanette got a full-time job, she was able to begin paying off her loans.

Dependent Clauses Introduced by Subordinating Conjunctions

For more on subordinating conjunctions, see 8A.

Some dependent clauses are introduced by **subordinating conjunctions** (*although, because, if,* and so on).

The following dependent clause is punctuated as if it were a sentence.

FRAGMENT Although many students study French in high school.

This sentence fragment includes a subject (*many students*) and a complete verb (*study*), but it does not express a complete thought.

One way to correct this fragment is to add an **independent clause** (a complete sentence) to complete the idea and finish the sentence.

SENTENCE Although many students study French in high school, Spanish is more popular.

Another way to correct the fragment is to leave out the subordinating conjunction *although,* the word that makes the idea incomplete.

SENTENCE Many students study French in high school.

Student Voices

Whenever I write a sentence that begins with although *or* because, *I double-check to make sure my idea is complete.*

Alana Krakov

For information on punctuation with subordinating conjunctions, see 8B.

Computer Tip

Use the Search or Find function to look for subordinating conjunctions in your writing. (For a list of subordinating conjunctions, see 8A.)

Dependent Clauses Introduced by Relative Pronouns

For more on relative pronouns, see 8C.

Other dependent clauses are introduced by **relative pronouns** (*who, which, that,* and so on).

The following dependent clauses are punctuated as if they were sentences.

FRAGMENT Marc Anthony, who is Puerto Rican.

FRAGMENT Zimbabwe, which was called Rhodesia at one time.

FRAGMENT One habit that has been observed in many overweight children.

Each of these three sentence fragments includes a subject (*Marc Anthony, Zimbabwe, One habit*) and a complete verb (*is, was called, has been observed*). However, they are not sentences because they do not express complete thoughts.

One way to correct each of these fragments is to add the words needed to complete the idea.

For information on punctuation with relative pronouns, see 8D.

SENTENCE Marc Anthony, who is Puerto Rican, records in both English and Spanish.

SENTENCE Zimbabwe, which was called Rhodesia at one time, is a country in Africa.

SENTENCE One habit that has been observed in many overweight children is excessive television viewing.

Another way to correct the fragments is to leave out the relative pronouns that make the ideas incomplete.

SENTENCE Marc Anthony is Puerto Rican.

SENTENCE Zimbabwe was once called Rhodesia.

SENTENCE One habit has been observed in many overweight children.

◆ PRACTICE 12.8

Correct each of the following dependent clause fragments in two ways. First, make the fragment a complete sentence by adding a group of words that completes the idea. Second, make the fragment a complete sentence by deleting the subordinating conjunction or relative pronoun that makes the idea incomplete.

Example: Because he wanted to get married.

Revised: *He needed to find a job because he wanted to get married.*

Revised: *He wanted to get married.*

1. This young man, who has a very promising future.

   Revised: ______________________________

   Revised: ______________________________

2. After the music and dancing had stopped.

   Revised: ______________________________

   Revised: ______________________________

3. A box turtle that was trying to find water.

   Revised: ______________________________

   Revised: ______________________________

4. Even though hang gliding is a dangerous sport.

Revised: ______________________________

____

Revised: ______________________________

____

5. Although most people think of themselves as good drivers.

Revised: ______________________________

____

Revised: ______________________________

____

6. Parents who do not set limits for their children.

Revised: ______________________________

____

Revised: ______________________________

____

7. Frequent-flier miles, which can sometimes be traded for products as well as for airline tickets.

Revised: ______________________________

____

Revised: ______________________________

____

8. Whenever Margaret got up late.

Revised: ______________________________

____

Revised: ______________________________

____

9. While she searched the crowd frantically.

Revised: ______________________________

____

Revised: ______________________________

____

10. A politician, who has to raise huge amounts of money to run for office.

Revised: ______________________________

____

Revised: ______________________________

____

◆ PRACTICE 12.9

All of the following are fragments. Make each fragment a complete sentence, and write the revised sentence on the line below the fragment. Whenever possible, try creating two different revisions.

Example: When a huge bat flew out of the closet.

Revised: *I was just climbing into bed when a huge bat flew out of the closet.*

Revised: *When a huge bat flew out of the closet, I decided to check out of the hotel.*

1. Finding a twenty-dollar bill on the sidewalk.

Revised: ______________________________

____

Revised: ______________________________

____

2. To make matters worse.

Revised: ______________________________

____

Revised: ______________________________

____

3. The tiny plastic ballerina spinning inside the music box.

Revised: ______________________________

____

Revised: ______________________________

____

4. Anyone who has ever worked for tips.

Revised: ______________________________

____

Revised: ______________________________

____

5. The basket, which was filled with exotic tropical fruits.

Revised: ______________________________

____

Revised: ______________________________

____

6. Banned from the sport for life.

Revised: ______________________________

____

Revised: ______________________________

____

7. Without a hat or coat.

Revised: ______________________________

____

Revised: ______________________________

____

8. Continuing to play with her toys.

Revised: ______________________________

____

Revised: ______________________________

____

9. Returning to the scene of the crime.

Revised: ______________________________

____

Revised: ______________________________

____

10. Below the surface of the muddy brown river.

Revised: ______________________________

____

Revised: ______________________________

____

■ REVISING AND EDITING

Look back at your response to the Seeing and Writing exercise on page 178. Is every sentence complete? Check every sentence to be sure that it has a subject and a verb, that the verb is complete, and that the sentence expresses a complete thought. If you spot a fragment, revise it by adding the words needed to make it a complete sentence. (Remember, you may be able to correct a fragment simply by attaching it to a nearby sentence or by crossing out a subordinating conjunction or relative pronoun.) If you do not find any fragments in your own writing, work with a classmate to correct his or her writing, or edit the work that you did for another assignment.

CHAPTER REVIEW

◆ EDITING PRACTICE

Read the following essay, and underline each fragment. Then, correct it by adding the words necessary to complete it or by attaching it to a nearby sentence that completes the idea. The first fragment has been underlined and corrected for you.

High Anxiety

Everyone feels anxious, ~~From~~ from time to time. It is normal to worry about stressful events in life. Such as an upcoming test or a job interview. Sometimes, however, anxiety can be a real problem. If a person fears everyday activities like driving, talking to strangers, or riding in an elevator. That fear can prevent him or her from leading a normal life. Other anxious people develop obsessive-compulsive disorders. Forcing themselves to repeat tasks. Such as washing their hands. Some people who feel that anxiety is too much a part of their lives. They may have an anxiety disorder.

Anxiety disorders are becoming more common. Because modern life is extremely stressful. Technology, which changes the way people live much faster than the human brain can change. When something strange happens. People feel fear or anxiety. Whether there is a real danger or not. As for the question of why some people are affected more strongly than others. No one seems to know the answer.

More than twenty million Americans are struggling. With some kind of anxiety disorder. Some are phobics who are terrified at the thought of getting on an airplane. Other people suffer from post-traumatic stress syndrome. After they have experienced combat or a horrible crime. Some people repeat actions. That they cannot seem to stop. They are victims of obsessive-compulsive disorder. For still other anxious Americans. Panic attacks occur more and more frequently.

Fortunately, there is help for anxiety sufferers. If they look for it. Therapists today are trained. To treat anxiety disorders. New drugs can make a difference, too. With so much expert help available. No one should have to face anxiety alone.

◆ COLLABORATIVE ACTIVITIES

1. Copy three fragments that you find in magazine or newspaper advertisements, and bring them to class. Then, trade your fragments with another student. Correct the fragments you receive, either by adding words or by connecting them to other sentences in the advertisement. Finally, discuss your corrections with your classmate.
2. Bring a newspaper to class. Working in a group of three or four students, find three headlines that are fragments. Then, working on your own, turn the fragments into complete sentences. Finally, compare your sentences with those written by other students in your group, and choose the best one for each headline.
3. Discuss some of the fragments you worked on in activities 1 and 2. Why were fragments used in the advertisements and the headlines? How are these fragments different from the complete sentences you wrote? Which work more effectively? Why?

COMPOSING ORIGINAL SENTENCES

4. Working in a group, collaborate to produce five sentences that contain no fragments. Make sure at least one sentence contains a prepositional phrase, at least one contains an appositive, at least one contains a present participle, and at least one contains a past participle. When you have finished, check the sentences to make sure you have corrected any errors in grammar, punctuation, or spelling.

✓ REVIEW CHECKLIST: Sentence Fragments

- A sentence fragment is an incomplete sentence. Every sentence must include a subject and a verb and express a complete thought. (See 12A.)
- Phrases cannot stand alone as sentences. (See 12B.)
- Every sentence must include a complete verb. (See 12C.)
- Dependent clauses cannot stand alone as sentences. (See 12D.)

CHAPTER

13

Subject-Verb Agreement

PREVIEW

In this chapter, you will learn

- to understand subject-verb agreement (13A)
- to avoid agreement problems with *be, have,* and *do* (13B)
- to avoid agreement problems with compound subjects (13C)
- to avoid agreement problems when a prepositional phrase comes between the subject and the verb (13D)
- to avoid agreement problems with indefinite pronouns as subjects (13E)
- to avoid agreement problems when the subject comes after the verb (13F)
- to avoid agreement problems with the relative pronouns *who, which,* and *that* (13G)

SEEING AND WRITING

Look at the picture above. Then, using present tense verbs, write a paragraph describing what you see.

Word Power

monument a structure built as a memorial

symbol something that represents something else

A Understanding Subject-Verb Agreement

A sentence's subject (a noun or a pronoun) and verb must **agree**: singular subjects take singular verbs, and plural subjects take plural verbs.

I walk to work. (The first-person singular pronoun *I* takes the singular verb *walk.*)

You walk to work. (The second-person singular pronoun *you* takes the singular verb *walk.*)

Alex walks to work. (The third-person singular noun *Alex* takes the singular verb *walks.*)

For more on person, see 14B.

Alex and I walk to work. (The compound subject *Alex and I* takes the plural verb *walk.*)

You all walk to work. (The second-person plural pronoun *you* takes the plural verb *walk.*)

They walk to work. (The third-person plural pronoun *they* takes the plural verb *walk.*)

For more on compound subjects, see 13C.

Most subject-verb agreement problems occur in the present tense, where the third-person singular subjects require special verb forms. Regular verbs in the present tense form the third-person singular by adding *-s* or *-es* to the third-person singular form of the verb. In all other tenses, the same form of the verb is used with every subject: *I walked, he walked, they walked; I will walk, she will walk, they will walk.*

Subject-Verb Agreement

	Singular	**Plural**
1st person	I walk	Alex and I/we walk
2nd person	you walk	you walk
3rd person	he/she/it walks	they walk
	the woman walks	the women walk
	Alex walks	Alex and Sam walk

Writing Tip
Subject-verb agreement presents special problems with the irregular verb *be*. (See 13B.)

PRACTICE 13.1

Underline the correct form of the verb in each of the following sentences. Make sure the verb agrees with the subject.

Example: Exercise (takes/take) a lot of time.

(1) Office workers (sits/sit) behind a desk all day. (2) Commuters (drives/drive) long distances to work. (3) The body (needs/need) a workout, but many people cannot find the time to exercise. (4) Others (thinks/think) most exercise is difficult or boring. (5) Jogging is hard work, and it (requires/require) strong knees. (6) It (leaves/leave) a person out of breath. (7) Many people (enjoys/enjoy) swimming, but they do not have access to a pool. (8) However, one exercise (brings/bring) back the feeling of being a child again. (9) Skipping is fun and (works/work) many muscles.

(10) A child (skips/skip) when he or she is feeling happy. (11) However, teenagers (stops/stop) skipping because they are afraid of looking silly. (12) Adults (skips/skip) very rarely. (13) But physical therapists (thinks/think) skipping is an excellent exercise. (14) Skipping clubs

(meets/meet) in some cities to remind adults how much fun skipping can be. (15) The next time you (sees/see) a group of adults skipping, don't be surprised.

◆ PRACTICE 13.2

Fill in the blank with the correct present tense form of the verb in parentheses.

Example: During the summer, huge storm clouds ___form___ (form) over the western Great Plains.

(1) Every summer, cool air ______________ (blow) east from the Rocky Mountains. (2) Near Goodland, Kansas, this air ______________ (meet) warmer air heated on the plains. (3) Storm clouds called thunderheads form there, and sometimes they ______________ (reach) great heights. (4) These thunderheads ______________ (produce) heavy rain and electrical storms. (5) Tornadoes also ______________ (come) from thunderheads. (6) Goodland ______________ (experience) some of the most dramatic storms in the United States. (7) In fact, Goodland is part of "Tornado Alley," and dangerous windstorms ______________ (cause) damage in the area quite often. (8) For this reason, weather researchers ______________ (spend) a lot of time in Goodland. (9) They ______________ (want) to learn how storms form. (10) This information ______________ (help) researchers develop better warning systems.

B Avoiding Agreement Problems with *Be, Have,* and *Do*

The verbs *be, have,* and *do* are irregular in the present tense. The best way to avoid problems with these verbs is to memorize their forms.

The past tense forms of be *are shown in 16C.*

Subject-Verb Agreement with Be

	Singular	**Plural**
1st person	I am	we are
2nd person	you are	you are
3rd person	he/she/it is	they are
	Tran is	Tran and Ryan are
	the boy is	the boys are

Subject-Verb Agreement with Have

	Singular	**Plural**
1st person	I have	we have
2nd person	you have	you have
3rd person	he/she/it has	they have
	Shana has	Shana and Robert have
	the student has	the students have

Writing Tip

For information on forming contractions with *be, have,* and *do,* see 23A.

Subject-Verb Agreement with Do

	Singular	**Plural**
1st person	I do	we do
2nd person	you do	you do
3rd person	he/she/it does	they do
	Ken does	Ken and Mia do
	the book does	the books do

◆ PRACTICE 13.3

Fill in the blank with the correct present tense form of the verb *be*.

Example: Cell phones ____*are*____ a useful tool.

1. Mark __________ very happy with his new cell phone.
2. His wife __________ angry because he uses the phone in restaurants and in the car.
3. I __________ not sure if I need a cell phone.
4. My family and I __________ far apart, so long-distance calls can be expensive.
5. Working pay phones __________ sometimes hard to find.
6. A cell phone __________ wonderful to have in an emergency.
7. Some people believe that a cell phone's radiation __________ harmful to human beings.
8. A cell phone __________ not very expensive.
9. However, cellular calling plans __________ often full of hidden charges.
10. Even if you __________ certain that you need a cell phone, you should do plenty of research before you buy one.

PRACTICE 13.4

Fill in the blank with the correct present tense form of the verb *have*.

Example: Lizzie ___has___ a teddy bear.

1. Some children __________ imaginary friends.
2. My daughter __________ a friend named Mr. Bibble.
3. She says that he __________ fuzzy red hair.
4. I __________ no idea how she invented Mr. Bibble.
5. Our neighbors __________ two little girls.
6. The older one, Sharon, __________ a doll that she takes everywhere.
7. The doll, Lucille, __________ a mind of her own, according to Sharon.
8. Lucille and Mr. Bibble __________ tea parties.
9. Sharon's mother and I __________ lunch while the children play games.
10. We wonder what Lucille and Mr. Bibble __________ in common.

PRACTICE 13.5

Fill in the blank with the correct present tense form of the verb *do*.

Example: She ___does___ errands every Saturday.

1. Tino __________ his homework before he goes to sleep.
2. My father __________ the dishes after dinner.
3. I __________ all the cleaning around here.
4. Tyler __________ the laundry every week.
5. Sandra __________ research all day in the laboratory where she works.
6. Her paycheck __________ a lot to help us make ends meet.
7. You __________ nothing except watch television while we work.
8. You always __________ the crossword puzzle before I even see the newspaper.
9. We __________ our fair share to help out around the house.
10. We have asked you to help, but asking __________ no good.

◆ PRACTICE 13.6

Fill in the blank with the correct present tense form of *be, have,* or *do.*

Example: Soccer ___is___ (be) better known outside the United States than in this country.

(1) All over the world, soccer ______________ (be) a popular sport. (2) The game ______________ (be) usually known as football. (3) In the United States, however, football ______________ (have) a different meaning. (4) Although American football ______________ (have) many fans, most of them ______________ (be) in this country. (5) Soccer ______________ (have) a larger audience worldwide than the game Americans call football.

(6) The World Cup ______________ (be) the championship series in soccer. (7) World Cup matches ______________ (be) really contests between countries. (8) Some countries ______________ (have) world-famous soccer teams. (9) A famous team ______________ (do) anything to win, and if its players lose, they may feel that they have let their country down.

(10) The United States ______________ (have) its own men's soccer team that plays in the World Cup. (11) We also ______________ (have) a women's team that usually ______________ (do) very well during its season. (12) Some women on the U.S. team ______________ (have) many fans. (13) For example, Brandi Chastain and Mia Hamm ______________ (be) role models for many young soccer players. (14) These women ______________ (do) feats that young children cannot imitate, but soccer ______________ (be) still a game that most children can play. (15) Even a small child ______________ (be) able to run and kick; those ______________ (be) two important skills for playing soccer.

(16) American football ______________ (do) a good job of attracting a television audience in the United States. (17) But some older football fans ______________ (be) not interested in soccer. (18) However, because so many young Americans play soccer, the sport ______________

(have) a great future in this country. Perhaps someday soccer will be the sport Americans think of when they hear the word *football.*

C Avoiding Agreement Problems with Compound Subjects

The subject of a sentence is not always a single word. Sometimes, a sentence has a **compound subject**, one that consists of two or more words. To avoid agreement problems with compound subjects, follow these rules.

- If the parts of a compound subject are connected by *and,* use a plural verb.

  Every day, Sarah and Tom drive to school.

- If the parts of a compound subject are connected by *or* and both parts are singular, use a singular verb.

  Every day, Sarah or Tom drives to school.

- If the parts of a compound subject are connected by *or* and both parts are plural, use a plural verb.

  Every day, Sarah's parents or Tom's parents drive to school.

- If the parts of a compound subject are connected by *or* and one part is singular and the other part is plural, the verb agrees with the part of the compound subject that is nearer to it.

  Every day, Sarah or her friends drive to school.
  Every day, her friends or Sarah drives to school.

◆ PRACTICE 13.7

Underline the correct verb in each of the following sentences.

Example: Katie and David (is/are) expecting a baby in June.

1. Toast or pancakes (is/are) my usual breakfast.
2. The teachers and the students (dresses/dress) differently.
3. Her father and mother (works/work) in the suburbs.
4. Diamonds or pearls (costs/cost) more than costume jewelry.
5. The album and the CD (shares/share) the same cover art, but the CD has more songs.
6. Thunder and rain or too much heat (spoils/spoil) the fun of hiking in the woods.

7. Winter squash and pumpkins (makes/make) delicious pies.
8. Several tadpoles and a frog (swims/swim) in the pond.
9. Take-out food and restaurants (saves/save) time, but both are more expensive than cooking at home.
10. Dental floss and a toothbrush (protects/protect) your teeth if you use them often.

◆ PRACTICE 13.8

Circle the correct verb in each of the following sentences.

Example: The roof and plumbing (needs/need) immediate repair.

1. Cornmeal or whole wheat flour (is/are) a possible substitute for white flour in that recipe.
2. In wet weather, a raincoat and boots (keeps/keep) me from getting soaked.
3. All U.S. senators and representatives (has/have) Web sites now.
4. A woodchuck or raccoons (eats/eat) all the ripe strawberries in my garden every night.
5. These photograph albums or this envelope (contains/contain) the pictures from our vacation.
6. My futon and easy chair (fills/fill) the whole apartment.
7. I don't remember whether blue or green (is/are) my father's favorite color.
8. Water and iced tea (quenches/quench) thirst better than cola.
9. Riding a bus or taking the subway (costs/cost) the same.
10. Styrofoam cups and yellowed newspapers (litters/litter) the floor of the waiting room.

D Avoiding Agreement Problems When a Prepositional Phrase Comes between the Subject and the Verb

Do not be confused by a prepositional phrase that comes between the subject and the verb. Keep in mind that prepositional phrases (phrases that begin with *of, in, between,* and so on) cannot contain the subject of the sentence.

For more on prepositional phrases and for a list of prepositions, see 6C.

A box of chocolates makes a very good gift.

High levels of radon occur in some houses.

Volunteers, including my brother, help clean up the community.

An easy way to identify the subject of a sentence that contains a prepositional phrase is to cross out the prepositional phrase.

A box ~~of chocolates~~ makes a very good gift.

High levels ~~of radon~~ occur in some houses.

Volunteers, ~~including my brother~~, help clean up the community.

◆ PRACTICE 13.9

In each of the following sentences, cross out the prepositional phrase that separates the subject and the verb. Then, underline the simple subject of the sentence once and the verb that agrees with the subject twice.

Example: Some people ~~in China~~ (travels/travel) by bicycle.

1. A resident of one of China's cities (goes/go) a long distance to work.
2. Westerners in China (expects/expect) to see many bicycles.
3. A black bicycle with a huge, heavy frame (has/have) been a common sight in China for many years.
4. The streets in Beijing and other large cities (has/have) bicycle lanes.
5. Today, the economy of China (is/are) booming.
6. Chinese citizens with high-paying jobs (is/are) not likely to commute by bicycle.
7. A worker with a long commute (does/do) not want to spend hours bicycling to work.
8. A bus or a private car, although convenient, (pollutes/pollute) the air.
9. Many Chinese people under age thirty (does/do) not even know how to ride a bicycle.
10. A Chinese store with a stock of bicycles (rents/rent) the old-fashioned black ones, mainly to tourists.

◆ PRACTICE 13.10

In each of the following sentences, cross out the prepositional phrase that separates the subject and the verb. Then, underline the simple subject of the sentence once and the verb that agrees with the subject twice.

Example: My memory ~~of those ten days~~ (remains/remain) clear.

1. The roots of these plants (goes/go) deep into the soil.
2. Some chess players in the park (meets/meet) every morning.
3. Firefighters on the night shift (takes/take) turns cooking dinner for the crew.
4. The woman across the street (sings/sing) opera while doing her laundry.
5. A wedding with a hundred guests (costs/cost) a small fortune.
6. The lights of Las Vegas (appears/appear) suddenly to travelers in the desert.
7. That book about chimpanzees (was/were) due back at the library last week.
8. Even a movie with expensive special effects (needs/need) an interesting plot.
9. Tickets to this week's performances (is/are) already sold out.
10. The sandy banks along the river (disappears/disappear) during spring floods.

E Avoiding Agreement Problems with Indefinite Pronouns as Subjects

Most indefinite pronouns—*anybody, everyone,* and so on—are singular. Singular indefinite pronouns are used with singular verbs.

> **Writing Tip**
> Many indefinite pronouns end in *-one, -body,* or *-thing.* These pronouns are always singular.

Everyone likes ice cream.
Each of the boys carries a beeper.
Neither of the boys misses class.
Nobody wants to see the team lose.

Singular Indefinite Pronouns

anybody	either	neither	one
anyone	everybody	nobody	somebody
anything	everyone	no one	someone
each	everything	nothing	something

For more on indefinite pronouns, see 19C.

Some indefinite pronouns are plural—*many, several, few, both, others.* Plural indefinite pronouns are used with plural verbs.

Many watch the nightly news on television.

Few get their news from the Internet.

◆ PRACTICE 13.11

Underline the correct verb in each of the following sentences.

Example: Everyone in my family (has/have) helped to create our dollhouse.

(1) My sister and I have a dollhouse, and neither of us (wants/want) to stop playing with it even though we are now adults. (2) Everything in it (reminds/remind) us of our past. (3) One of the chairs (looks/look) like a piece of furniture our parents had when we were young. (4) In the kitchen, one of the items (is/are) an icebox like the one my grandmother had. (5) Everybody in my family (remembers/remember) the kitchen at her old house, so the dollhouse brings back happy memories. (6) Each of the beds in the little bedrooms (has/have) a quilt that my mother made. (7) Nobody (knows/know) how she was able to make such tiny stitches. (8) Now and then, someone (tells/tell) us about a new miniature furniture store, and we add new pieces to the dollhouse. (9) We hope to find a little painting like the one in our parents' living room, but no one (seems/seem) to sell those. (10) Still, something about our dollhouse (gives/give) my sister and me a lot of satisfaction.

F Avoiding Agreement Problems When the Subject Comes after the Verb

A verb agrees with its subject even if the subject comes after the verb. In questions, the subject usually follows the verb.

V S
Where is the ATM?

Where are Zack and Angela?

Why are they running?

If you have trouble identifying the subject, answer the question with a statement.

Where is the ATM? The ATM is inside the bank.

FOCUS ***There is* and *There are***

Even if a sentence begins with *there is* or *there are,* the word *there* cannot be the subject of the sentence. The true subject comes after the form of the verb *be.*

There is still one ticket available for the playoffs.

There are still ten tickets available for the playoffs.

Writing Tip

Try to avoid beginning a sentence with *there is* or *there are.* If possible, write more directly: *One ticket is still available for the playoffs. Ten tickets are still available for the playoffs.*

◆ PRACTICE 13.12

First, underline the simple subject of each sentence. Then, circle the correct form of the verb.

Example: What (is/are) your reasons for applying to this college?

1. There (is/are) an excellent nursing program here.
2. Where (is/are) you planning to live during the semester?
3. There (is/are) an inexpensive dormitory on Third Avenue.
4. What (does/do) the students here usually like best about the school?
5. How difficult (is/are) the placement tests?
6. What (has/have) been the most popular major in the last five years?
7. There (is/are) more people taking business courses today than there were twenty years ago.
8. There (has/have) been few nursing jobs available lately.

9. How many years (does/do) an average student take to graduate?
10. There (is/are) no simple answer to that question.

◆ PRACTICE 13.13

Circle the correct form of the verb *be* in each of the following sentences.

Example: There (is/are) several ways to write a good résumé.

1. There (is/are) a potato in her garden that resembles Richard Nixon.
2. There (is/are) furniture designed by Frank Lloyd Wright in our local museum.
3. There (is/are) three cellists in the high school orchestra.
4. There (is/are) sand in my shoes.
5. There (is/are) stories I've heard that would make your hair stand on end.
6. There (is/are) trains to the shore six or seven times a day.
7. There (is/are) other fish in the sea.
8. There (is/are) a list of names engraved on the side of the monument.
9. There (is/are) nothing on television tonight.
10. There (is/are) many people who deserve this award more than I do.

G Avoiding Agreement Problems with the Relative Pronouns *Who, Which,* and *That*

For more on who, which, that, *and other relative pronouns, see 8C and 8D.*

The relative pronouns *who, which,* and *that* are singular when they refer to a singular word and plural when they refer to a plural word. The verb in the dependent clause introduced by the relative pronoun must agree with the word to which the relative pronoun refers.

> Workers who have health insurance are lucky. (The verb *have* is plural because the relative pronoun *who* refers to *workers,* which is plural.)

> Anyone who has health insurance is lucky. (The verb *has* is singular because the relative pronoun *who* refers to *anyone,* which is singular.)

The house, which stands at the corner of Fifth and Spring Garden, is open to tourists. (The verb *stands* is singular because the relative pronoun *which* refers to *house,* which is singular.)

Books that have large print are easy to read. (The verb *have* is plural because the relative pronoun *that* refers to *books,* which is plural.)

◆ PRACTICE 13.14

In the blank, write the word that *who, which,* or *that* refers to. Then, circle the correct form of the verb.

Example: ___toys___ I found an attic full of toys that (sells/sell) for high prices at antique shows.

_______ 1. Her mother, who (watches/watch) at least two movies a day, is working on a film encyclopedia.

_______ 2. In Hawaii, he saw the whales that (migrates/migrate) through the islands.

_______ 3. Newscasters who constantly (smiles/smile) make me nervous.

_______ 4. She owns the city's first Ethiopian restaurant, which (serves/serve) a young, enthusiastic crowd on weekend nights.

_______ 5. Some countries provide free medical care to all citizens who (needs/need) it.

_______ 6. The two horses that (lives/live) in my neighbor's pasture love to eat sugar cubes.

_______ 7. The baby is going to spill her grape juice, which (leaves/leave) permanent stains.

_______ 8. My brother bought a coffeemaker that (makes/make) very strong coffee.

_______ 9. Their hot water is heated by solar panels, which (charges/charge) a battery for use on cloudy days.

_________ 10. According to the courts, video cameras can film anyone who (appears/appear) in a public place.

◆ PRACTICE 13.15

First, draw an arrow from *who, which,* or *that* to the word it refers to. Then, circle the correct form of the verb.

Example: Young people who (plays/play) violent video games may become aggressive.

(1) Researchers who (studies/study) violence disagree about the effects of violent television shows, movies, and video games. (2) Teenagers who (sees/see) this kind of violence may become less concerned about violence. (3) A cartoon that (shows/show) violent characters may cause children to imitate it. (4) Young people who (enjoys/enjoy) violent video games seem amused by the bloody killings. (5) After several school shootings in the 1990s, which (was/were) very shocking to most Americans, many adults worried about exposing children to violence. (6) Today, every company that (makes/make) video games rates each new game. (7) Movie theaters that (shows/show) R-rated films ask teenagers for proof that they are at least seventeen years old. (8) However, some research, which (has/have) many supporters, suggests that movie, television, and video violence does not affect most teenagers. (9) Teenagers who (is/are) not mentally ill can tell the difference between real and imaginary violence. (10) Any parent who (worries/worry) about children's television and movie watching habits must wonder what to believe.

■ REVISING AND EDITING

Look back at your response to the Seeing and Writing exercise on page 196. Make sure every verb agrees with its subject. (Remember to check for the situations discussed in sections B through G of this chapter.) If you find any incorrect verb forms, cross them out and write the correct forms above them.

CHAPTER REVIEW

EDITING PRACTICE

Read the following student essay. Decide whether each of the underlined verbs agrees with its subject. If it does not, cross out the verb and write in the correct form. If it does, write *C* above the verb. The first sentence has been done for you.

Balanced Budgets?

Everyone knows (C) that officials in the government ~~has~~ have been arguing about balancing the federal budget. One argument that is made over and over again compare the government's budget to a family's budget. Politicians in Washington likes to say, "Nobody in the United States has money to spend when the paycheck is gone." How true is this statement? There is a lot of people in this country who sticks to a budget, but there is many others who are deeply in debt.

If someone claim that people in a family cannot spend more than they earn, that person has forgotten something. There is such things as credit cards. I, for example, has used credit cards to pay my tuition. Why does I spend more than I have? My income do not cover my college expenses. If I want to continue my education, I has little choice. I be not the only person who thinks this way. Many of my friends also borrows with credit cards.

There are nothing wrong with asking the government to be responsible. After all, officials in Washington is spending your money and mine. But every senator and representative should realize that American families, too, often spends more than they earn. Perhaps if the federal government balances its checkbook, the rest of us will learn to do the same.

COLLABORATIVE ACTIVITIES

1. Working on your own, write five subjects (people, places, or things) on a sheet of paper. The subjects can be singular or plural. Then, working in a group of three students, pass the paper to another member of the

group. On the paper you receive, write a dependent clause beginning with *who, which,* or *that* for each of the five subjects. Then, pass the paper again, and finish the sentences on the paper you receive.

Example

First Person	*Second Person*	*Third Person*
The pizza	*that has a burned crust*	*tastes funny.*

Finally, review the paper you started with, and correct any subject-verb agreement errors in the sentences that have been created from your subjects.

2. Each person in the group should write the same five subjects from activity 1 on another sheet of paper. Next, each person should pass his or her paper to another member of the group, who will add a prepositional phrase to follow each subject. Then, the third member of the group will complete the sentences. When you get your paper back, check subject-verb agreement.
3. Working in the same group, choose one sentence from activity 1 and one sentence from activity 2. As a group, write a paragraph that contains both sentences. Make sure that at least one additional sentence contains an indefinite pronoun used as a subject. Check the paragraph to be sure there are no errors in subject-verb agreement. When your group is satisfied with its paragraph, have one member read it to the class.

COMPOSING ORIGINAL SENTENCES

4. Working in a group of three students, write five sentences in the present tense. Make sure that one has a compound subject, one has a prepositional phrase between the subject and the verb, one has an indefinite pronoun as a subject, and one has a subject that comes after the verb. Make sure none of the sentences contains errors in subject-verb agreement.

✓ REVIEW CHECKLIST: Subject-Verb Agreement

- Singular subjects (nouns and pronouns) take singular verbs, and plural subjects take plural verbs. (See 13A.)
- The irregular verbs *be, have,* and *do* often present problems with subject-verb agreement in the present tense. (See 13B.)
- Compound subjects can cause problems in agreement. (See 13C.)
- A prepositional phrase that comes between the subject and the verb does not affect subject-verb agreement. (See 13D.)

(continued on the following page)

(continued from the previous page)

- Most indefinite pronouns, such as *no one* and *everyone,* are singular and take a singular verb when they serve as the subject of the sentence. (See 13E.)
- A verb agrees with its subject even if the subject comes after the verb. (See 13F.)
- The relative pronouns *who, which,* and *that* are singular when they refer to a singular word and plural when they refer to a plural word. (See 13G.)

CHAPTER

14 Illogical Shifts

PREVIEW

In this chapter, you will learn

- to avoid illogical shifts in tense (14A)
- to avoid illogical shifts in person (14B)
- to avoid illogical shifts in voice (14C)

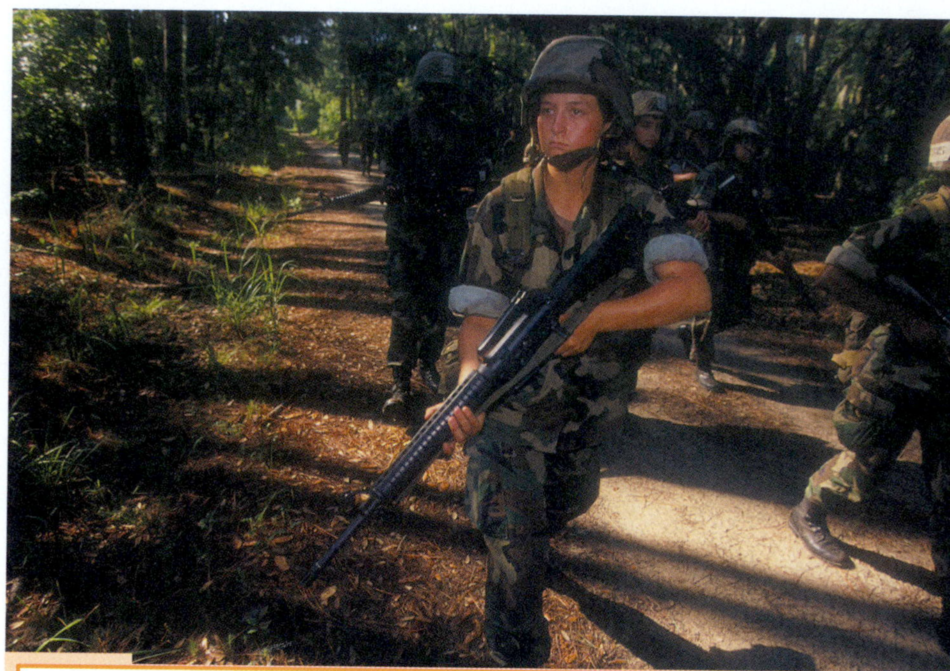

SEEING AND WRITING

Do you think women should be allowed to serve in combat? Why or why not? Look at the picture above, and then write a paragraph in which you answer these questions.

Word Power

gender a person's sex

rigor hardship or difficulty

parity equality in power or value

A **shift** occurs whenever a writer changes *tense, person,* or *voice* in a sentence or a paragraph. As you write and revise, make sure that any shifts you make are logical—that is, they occur for a reason.

A Avoiding Illogical Shifts in Tense

For more on tense, see Chapters 16 and 17.

Tense is the form a verb takes to show when an action took place or a situation occurred. An **illogical shift in tense** occurs when a writer shifts from one tense to another for no apparent reason.

ILLOGICAL SHIFT We sat at the table for more than an hour before a server comes and takes our order. (shift from past tense to present tense)

REVISED We sat at the table for more than an hour before a server came and took our order. (consistent use of past tense)

Of course, a shift in tense is sometimes necessary. In the following sentence, for example, a shift from past to present tense shows a change in the writer's attitude between one period and another.

LOGICAL SHIFT In high school, I just wanted to have fun, but now I want to become a graphic artist.

◆ PRACTICE 14.1

Underline the verbs in the following sentences. Then, correct any illogical shifts by writing the correct verb tense above the line. If a sentence is correct, write *C* in the blank after the sentence.

Examples

Thomas ate meat until he married Meena, but now he is a vegetarian. C

As I drove through the woods, a deer suddenly ~~runs~~ ran across the road. ____

1. I ordered a CD online, but it takes more than a week to arrive. ____
2. Although the zookeeper warned us about feeding the animals, one couple ignores him. ____
3. Last night, he felt sad; this morning, he is much more cheerful. ____
4. The noon whistle blew, and immediately everyone stop working. ____
5. The baby makes a terrible mess every time he eats. ____
6. The movie was out of focus, so we complain to the manager. ____
7. She offered us free tickets and tells us to use them anytime. ____
8. She sang the blues in Mississippi before she arrives in Detroit. ____
9. Even though the landlord agreed to allow pets, now he wants me to get rid of my dog. ____
10. The deejay played great dance music until the sun comes up. ____

◆ PRACTICE 14.2

Edit the following sentences for illogical shifts in tense. If a sentence is correct, write *C* in the blank.

Example: The New York City Draft Riots occurred in 1863 when President Lincoln ~~announces~~ announced a draft for the Civil War. ____

(1) The Civil War began in 1861, and by 1863, both sides needed more soldiers. ____ (2) Abraham Lincoln was president of the United States at that time, and on March 3, 1863, he begins drafting men in the North to fight in the war. ____ (3) Lincoln needs 300,000 more men. ____ (4) Everyone agreed that the draft is not fair. ____ (5) For example, a rich man could pay a "commutation fee" that allows him to pay someone else to fight so that he could stay home. ____ (6) Most people in the North are tired of the war, and not all of them supported the cause of freeing the slaves in the South. ____ (7) On June 12, 1863, the first draftees were named, and soon mobs begin to form. ____ (8) There are eventually about fifty thousand people rioting in New York City, and many of the rioters targeted blacks. ____ (9) The mob looted dozens of stores and killed about a hundred people. ____ (10) Federal troops had to end the rioting after three days; the troops remained in New York for several weeks. ____

B Avoiding Illogical Shifts in Person

Person is the form a pronoun takes to indicate who is speaking, spoken about, or spoken to.

Person

	Singular	**Plural**
First person	I	we
Second person	you	you
Third person	he, she, it	they

An **illogical shift in person** occurs when a writer shifts from one person to another for no apparent reason.

ILLOGICAL SHIFT Before a person gets a job in the computer industry, you have to take a lot of courses. (shift from third person to second person)

REVISED Before a person gets a job in the computer industry, he or she has to take a lot of courses. (consistent use of third person)

ILLOGICAL SHIFT The students were told that you have to attend a conference each week. (shift from third person to second person)

REVISED The students were told that they had to attend a conference each week. (consistent use of third person plural)

Writing Tip

Be careful not to use the pronoun *he* to refer to a noun that could be either masculine or feminine.

For more on subject-verb agreement, see Chapter 13.

◆ PRACTICE 14.3

Correct any illogical shifts in person in the following sentences. If necessary, change any verbs that do not agree with the new subjects. If a sentence is correct, write *C* in the blank.

Example: The guide told us that ~~you~~ we had to learn certain skills to survive in the wilderness. ____

1. The students learned that you needed to use proper lab technique. ____
2. A salesman can successfully sell products door-to-door; you just have to be persistent. ____
3. I worked on an assembly line where you could not spend more than thirty seconds on each task. ____
4. The manager told me that I should improve my attitude. ____
5. His boss told him that you have to be on time for work every day. ____
6. Maria discovered that you cannot buy friends. ____
7. The officer who stopped us claimed that we had disturbed a crime scene. ____
8. You must respect your coworkers if you want to get along in the office. ____

9. His brother said that you could find almost anything on the Internet. _____

10. The boss's daughter found out that you could use family connections to get a job but that you needed talent to keep it. _____

◆ PRACTICE 14.4

The following paragraph contains illogical shifts in person. Edit it so that pronouns are used consistently. Be sure to change the verb if necessary to make it agree with the new subject.

Example: We all realized that ~~you~~ we would not be able to get the tickets in time.

(1) My brother found out that you had to get tickets for the high school graduation so that your family could attend. (2) Unfortunately, you were allowed only two tickets. (3) If more than two family members wanted to come to the graduation, they had to sit in the gym, where you could hear the speeches but not see anything. (4) My brother heard that it might be possible to get extra tickets if you looked in the right place. (5) One of his friends, who had graduated the year before, said that you should check the bulletin boards. (6) You could also ask students who might not need both tickets. (7) My brother did not understand how you could walk up to another student and say, "Is it true that only one person wants to come to your graduation?" (8) By checking the bulletin boards, he found someone with extra tickets, but you would have to pay thirty dollars each for them. (9) He could not believe that you had to deal with ticket scalpers for a high school graduation. (10) In the end, my parents watched the graduation, and my sister and I sat in the gym, where you yelled and cheered loudly for every graduate.

▼ **Student Voices**

I tend to write in the passive voice. I guess what they taught me in high school didn't stick.

Jessi Allender

C Avoiding Illogical Shifts in Voice

When a sentence is in the **active voice**, the subject *performs* the action. When a sentence is in the **passive voice**, the subject *receives* the action.

ACTIVE VOICE Pablo Neruda won the Nobel Prize in literature in 1971. (Subject *Pablo Neruda* performs the action.)

PASSIVE VOICE The Nobel Prize in literature was won by Pablo Neruda in 1971. (Subject *The Nobel Prize in literature* receives the action.)

An **illogical shift in voice** occurs when a writer shifts from active to passive voice or from passive to active voice for no apparent reason.

ILLOGICAL SHIFT The jazz musician John Coltrane played the saxophone, and the clarinet was also played by him. (active to passive)

REVISED The jazz musician John Coltrane played the saxophone, and he also played the clarinet. (consistent use of active voice)

ILLOGICAL SHIFT *Fences* was written by August Wilson, and he also wrote *The Piano Lesson*. (passive to active)

REVISED August Wilson wrote *Fences*, and he also wrote *The Piano Lesson*. (consistent use of active voice)

FOCUS Changing from Passive to Active Voice

In your college writing, you should use the active voice in most cases because it is stronger and more direct than the passive voice. To change a sentence from passive to active voice, determine who or what performs the action, and make this noun the subject of your sentence.

PASSIVE VOICE Three world records in track were set by Jesse Owens in a single day. (Jesse Owens performs the action.)

ACTIVE VOICE Jesse Owens set three world records in track in a single day.

Computer Tip

To see if you overuse the passive voice in your writing, use the Search or Find command to look for *is, are, was,* and *were,* which often appear as part of passive-voice verbs.

◆ PRACTICE 14.5

Correct any illogical shifts in voice in the following sentences, using active voice wherever possible. If necessary, change any verbs that do not agree with the new subjects. If a sentence is correct, write *C* in the blank.

Example: Michael washed his car, but ~~it was not waxed by him~~. he did not wax it.

____

1. A settlement was discussed by the lawyers, but the defendant refused it. ____

2. A good crop was harvested by the farmers, and the farmers' market attracted big crowds. _____

3. Roberto signed up for calculus, so a new calculator was bought by him. _____

4. Lightning struck the chimney, and two bricks fell to the sidewalk below. _____

5. As the waves battered the beach, a surfboard was clutched by a gasping young man. _____

6. A hymn was sung by the choir while the congregation passed the collection plate. _____

7. When Brandon met Jane, she was asked by him for a date. _____

8. The children watched television, and dinner was cooked by their parents. _____

9. Kathy mowed her grandfather's lawn, and his yardwork was also done by her. _____

10. When my father lost his job, my mother worked longer hours. _____

◆ PRACTICE 14.6

The following sentences contain illogical shifts in voice. Revise each sentence by changing the underlined passive-voice verb to the active voice.

Example: I had a little book of poetry when I was a child, and even today it is treasured by me.

I had a little book of poetry when I was a child, and even today I treasure it.

1. This book was kept beside my bed, and I read it every night before I went to sleep.

_____

_____

2. Some nights, I just read one poem; other nights, several poems were read.

_____

_____

3. I loved Poe's "Annabel Lee," and his poem "The Bells" was also enjoyed by me.

____

____

4. Now, many other poems have been read by me, but I still reread the poems in my childhood book.

____

____

5. Maybe that book explains why reading poetry is liked by me and why I like writing my own poems.

____

____

REVISING AND EDITING

Look back at your response to the Seeing and Writing exercise on page 214. Revise any illogical shifts in tense, person, or voice.

CHAPTER REVIEW

EDITING PRACTICE

Read the following essay, which contains illogical shifts in tense, person, and voice. Then, edit the essay to correct the illogical shifts, making sure subjects and verbs agree. The first sentence has been edited for you.

A Great Olympic Moment

When swimming fans saw Eric Moussambani, a swimmer from Equatorial Guinea, arrive at the 2000 Olympic Games in Sydney, Australia, ~~you~~ *they* knew that this athlete ~~has~~ *had* no chance to win a medal. Fans expected famous athletes and record-holders to win gold medals, and Moussambani's name was not known by them; besides, his qualifying times are much slower than those of other swimmers. The organizers of the games invited Moussambani only because of an Olympic rule allowing athletes to compete without qualifying if you came from a developing country.

Many obstacles were faced by Eric Moussambani, and this explained his poor qualifying time. He had no coach, his country had no swim team, and he trains in the ocean instead of in a pool. In Sydney, Moussambani saw his first Olympic-size pool. As he prepared to swim in his qualifying heat for the 100-meter freestyle race, he hopes just to be able to finish the two laps.

Moussambani's qualifying heat begins early in the morning as he stood at the side of the pool with two other "wild card" swimmers. Before the starting signal was heard by them, the other two swimmers leaped into the pool. Olympic officials disqualified them, and Moussambani had to swim his laps alone.

At first, the crowd pays little attention to the events in the pool because you knew that the qualifying heat would not affect the final outcome of the race. Soon, the spectators noticed the lone swimmer from Equatorial Guinea, struggling to swim two lengths of the long pool. Moussambani looks exhausted when he reaches the end of his first lap. He was cheered on by the crowd as he splashed slowly toward the finish line because you saw his Olympic spirit. Moussambani was clearly not swimming fast enough to qualify for the finals, but he was trying hard.

Although he did not win, the race was finished by Eric Moussambani. That night, television viewers around the world watched his heroic swim, and their hearts were won by the athlete from Equatorial Guinea. When he tells interviewers that he hoped to find a coach, train hard, and win a medal in the 2004 Olympic Games, television viewers around the world understood, and you hoped that his dream would come true.

◆ COLLABORATIVE ACTIVITIES

1. Working in a group of four students, choose a subject to write sentences about. Each pair of students should write two simple sentences, one using the subject with a present tense verb and the other using the

same subject with a past tense verb. Then, work with your partner to combine the two sentences into a single sentence containing an illogical shift. Finally, exchange sentences with the other pair in your group, and correct the shifts in the other pair's sentence.

Example

SUBJECT	*Three blind mice*
PRESENT TENSE SENTENCE	*Three blind mice hide from the cat.*
PAST TENSE SENTENCE	*Three blind mice ran after the farmer's wife.*
SENTENCE WITH ILLOGICAL SHIFT	*Three blind mice hide from the cat and ran after the farmer's wife.*
CORRECTED SENTENCE	*Three blind mice hid from the cat and ran after the farmer's wife.*

2. Working in a group of three or four students, write a paragraph explaining how to do a simple task. Use *you* as the subject throughout the paragraph. When you have finished, go back and change every other sentence so that the subject is *a person, someone, people, students,* or some other third-person word or phrase. Then, exchange your paragraph with another group. Correct the illogical shifts in person so that the whole paragraph uses the third person.
3. Bring to class three sentences from newspapers, magazines, or textbooks that use the passive voice. Then, work in a group of three students to revise these sentences. Begin by changing your own sentences to active voice, if possible; then, give your original sentences to another member of the group and ask him or her to do the same thing. As a group, discuss the answers you came up with. If a sentence is awkward in the active voice, or if you cannot change it to the active voice, discuss the reasons why this is so.

COMPOSING ORIGINAL SENTENCES

4. Working in a group of three students, write five sentences in the active voice. When you have finished, check the sentences again to make sure you have corrected any errors in grammar, punctuation, or spelling.

☑ REVIEW CHECKLIST: Illogical Shifts

- An illogical shift in tense occurs when a writer shifts from one verb tense to another for no apparent reason. (See 14A.)
- An illogical shift in person occurs when a writer shifts from one person to another for no apparent reason. (See 14B.)
- An illogical shift in voice occurs when a writer shifts from active to passive voice or from passive to active voice for no apparent reason. (See 14C.)

CHAPTER

15 Dangling and Misplaced Modifiers

PREVIEW

In this chapter, you will learn

- to identify present participle modifiers (15A)
- to identify past participle modifiers (15B)
- to recognize and correct dangling modifiers (15C)
- to recognize and correct misplaced modifiers (15D)

SEEING AND WRITING

Look at the picture above, and then write a paragraph in which you tell a story from your family's history. If possible, discuss the significance this story has for your family.

Word Power

generation a group of individuals born and living at about the same time

heritage something passed down from previous generations

migrate to move from one area or region to another

Writing Tip

A modifier can function as an adjective or as an adverb. An **adjective** modifies a noun or a pronoun. An **adverb** modifies a verb, an adjective, or another adverb. (See Chapter 20.)

A **modifier** is a word or word group that **modifies** (provides information about) another word or word group in a sentence—for example, *a wonderful day* or *a surprisingly successful mission.* Many word groups that act as modifiers are introduced by present participles (*the column supporting the roof*) or past participles (*an afternoon warmed by the sun*). In order to communicate its meaning, a modifier must clearly refer to the word or group of words it modifies.

A Identifying Present Participle Modifiers

A **present participle modifier** consists of the *-ing* form of the verb along with the words it introduces. The modifier provides information about a noun or a pronoun that appears next to it in a sentence.

PRESENT PARTICIPLE MODIFIER

Remembering what he had come to do, Robert reached in his pocket for the ring.

PRESENT PARTICIPLE MODIFIER

Dancing to the music of Frank Sinatra, Madeline knew she was in love.

FOCUS Placing Present Participle Modifiers

A present participle modifier can come at the beginning, in the middle, or at the end of a sentence.

Returning to the streets they had left, many early rock singers were soon forgotten.

Many early rock singers, returning to the streets they had left, were soon forgotten.

Many early rock singers were soon forgotten, returning to the streets they had left.

◆ PRACTICE 15.1

In each of the following sentences, underline the present participle modifier, and then draw an arrow from the modifier to the word or word group it modifies.

Example: Singing in the rain, Gene made a splash.

1. The young soldier, fearing for his life, tried to steady his shaky hands.
2. Sailing out into the open ocean, the fishing boat looked very small.
3. The pageant winner clutched her bouquet, smiling professionally.
4. Dropping a book on his desk, the professor cried, "Time's up!"
5. Standing in the barbershop doorway, the two young men asked me for help.

6. Sipping his coffee, Mark prepared to pull the big rig out of the parking lot.
7. The telephone woke me up again, ringing loudly at 2 a.m.
8. Emilia, drawing on her last bit of strength, crossed the finish line first.
9. The foreman irritated me, blowing his whistle loudly in my ear.
10. Roaring toward the waterfall, the river took control of my canoe.

◆ PRACTICE 15.2

In each of the following sentences, underline the present participle modifier, and then draw an arrow from the modifier to the word or word group it modifies.

Example: Having yellow and black markings, yellow jackets are small stinging wasps.

1. Appearing at picnics and other outdoor gatherings, yellow jackets can be a nuisance.
2. These insects can also be dangerous, stinging when disturbed.
3. Yellow jacket stings, causing allergic reactions in many people, kill about fifty Americans every year.
4. Female yellow jackets, reaching the end of their lives, often sting in the fall.
5. Looking for food, the females usually go where people are.
6. Having a taste for sugar, yellow jackets find soft drinks appealing.
7. A garbage can, overflowing with trash, is a feast for yellow jackets.
8. Fruit trees, dropping overripe apples and pears on the ground, provide additional meals for these insects.
9. Pollinating flowers and eating other harmful insects, yellow jackets have some good qualities.
10. Taking steps to keep yellow jackets away, people wear light-colored clothing and keep sweet food and drinks covered.

◆ PRACTICE 15.3

Write five sentences that contain present participle modifiers. Then, underline each modifier, and draw an arrow from the modifier to the word or word group it modifies.

Example: *Wearing her new dress, my sister went to Sunday school.*

1. ______________________________

____

2. ______________________________

____

3. ______________________________

____

4. ______________________________

____

5. ______________________________

____

B Identifying Past Participle Modifiers

A **past participle modifier** consists of the past participle form of the verb (usually ending in *-d* or *-ed*) along with the words it introduces. Like a present participle modifier, a past participle modifier provides information about a noun or a pronoun that appears next to it in a sentence.

For more on past participles, see 17A.

Submitted to the Continental Congress on June 7, 1776, the Declaration of Independence was approved on July 4.

Invited to the White House, Sojourner Truth met President Abraham Lincoln.

Writing Tip

Not all past participles end in *-d* or *-ed.* Irregular participles—*cut* and *written,* for example—may have different forms.

FOCUS Placing Past Participle Modifiers

A past participle modifier can come at the beginning, in the middle, or at the end of a sentence.

Shocked by the ruling, the defendant said she would appeal.

The defendant, shocked by the ruling, said she would appeal.

"I will appeal," said the defendant, shocked by the ruling.

For a list of irregular past participles, see 17B.

◆ PRACTICE 15.4

In each of the following sentences, underline the past participle modifier, and then draw an arrow from the modifier to the word or word group it modifies.

Example: Planted in rich soil, the sapling soon grew taller than me.

1. Plastered with bumper stickers, her old car rattled down the dirt road.
2. Bored to tears with my job, I sent out a new résumé.
3. Sarah scratched her legs, covered with mosquito bites.
4. Waxed and polished, the marble steps gleamed at the entrance to the banquet hall.
5. The roof, buried under two feet of snow, sagged dangerously.
6. Dulled from years of use, the knife could not slice through the lemon peel.
7. Shattered in its fall from the mantle, the vase lay in pieces on the floor.
8. The cyclists, exhausted after the steep hills, agreed to stop at the nearest motel.
9. Her book, rejected by six publishers, eventually became a best-seller.
10. The test, written too quickly, had several confusing questions.

◆ PRACTICE 15.5

In each of the following sentences, underline the past participle modifier, and then draw an arrow from the modifier to the word or word group it modifies.

Example: Unsolved to this day, the murders of Andrew and Abby Borden occurred in 1892.

(1) The shocking crime, committed in Fall River, Massachusetts, left a wealthy man named Andrew Borden and his wife dead in their home. (2) Attacked with a hatchet, Mr. and Mrs. Borden were both killed on a hot August morning. (3) Horrified at the news of this murder, the people of Fall River were even more astonished when a suspect appeared. (4) The suspect was Mr. Borden's 32-year-old daughter Lizzie, tried for killing her father and stepmother. (5) Lizzie Borden's story, changed repeatedly,

made many people suspicious. (6) Asked where she had been at the time of the murders, Lizzie gave several different answers. (7) A possible motive for the killings, discussed in every home in town, was an enormous inheritance. (8) However, no evidence gathered at the house connected Lizzie to the crime. (9) The jury, faced with a circumstantial case, found her not guilty. (10) A children's rhyme, well known more than a century later, judged Lizzie more harshly: "Lizzie Borden took an axe, gave her mother forty whacks."

◆ PRACTICE 15.6

Write five sentences that contain past participle modifiers. Then, underline the modifier, and draw an arrow from the modifier to the word or word group it modifies.

Example: Frightened by the thunder, the cat hid under the couch.

1. ______________________________

____

2. ______________________________

____

3. ______________________________

____

4. ______________________________

____

5. ______________________________

____

C Correcting Dangling Modifiers

A **dangling modifier** "dangles" because the word or word group it is supposed to modify is not present in the sentence. Often, a dangling modifier comes at the beginning of a sentence and appears to modify the word that follows it.

DANGLING MODIFIER Working overtime, my salary almost doubled.

In the preceding sentence, the present participle *working overtime* seems to be describing *my salary.* But, of course, this makes no sense. How can salary work overtime? The word the present participle modifier should logically modify is missing. To correct this sentence, you need to supply the missing word.

REVISED Working overtime, I almost doubled my salary.

As the example above illustrates, the easiest way to correct a dangling modifier is to supply the word or word group the dangling modifier should actually modify.

DANGLING MODIFIER Living in England, his first collection of poems was published. (Did the poetry collection live in England?)

REVISED Living in England, Robert Frost published his first collection of poems.

DANGLING MODIFIER Distracted by my cell phone, my car almost drove off the road. (Did the phone distract the car?)

REVISED Distracted by my cell phone, I almost drove my car off the road.

◆ PRACTICE 15.7

Rewrite the following sentences, which contain dangling modifiers. You will have to supply a word or word group to which each modifier can logically refer.

Example: Dreaming of easy money, the game show was very appealing.

Dreaming of easy money, he thought the game show sounded very appealing.

1. Hanging by one hand from the edge of the roof, the fire escape could not be reached.

____

____

2. Signing a one-year contract, burglars would be discouraged by the new alarm system.

____

____

3. Frightened by the alligator, my canoe almost turned over.

____

4. Getting to the station late, the train was seen leaving.

____

5. Sitting on the dock in the bay, many fish were caught.

____

6. Sitting in the back of the auditorium, the announcement could hardly be heard.

7. Given a second chance, her luck ran out.

8. Forced to make a decision in the voting booth, the wrong lever was pulled.

9. Feeling sick to her stomach, the bathroom was too far away to reach in time.

10. Prepared for an afternoon at the baseball game, the rain was unexpected.

◆ PRACTICE 15.8

On the lines below, supply a word to which each modifier can logically refer. Then, complete the sentence.

Example: Startled out of a sound sleep, *I jumped out of bed and ran to the window*.

1. Expecting a package, ______.
2. Dreaded by every student in the class, ______.
3. Wondering why I had decided to go on the trip, ______.
4. Seated in the stadium, ______.
5. Left at the side of the road, ______.

6. Told to remember her manners, ______________________________
______________________________.

7. Sipping coffee, ______________________________
______________________________.

8. Trying to hit a home run, ______________________________
______________________________.

9. Wearing his oldest clothes, ______________________________
______________________________.

10. Attracted by the smell of baking bread, ______________________________
______________________________.

D Correcting Misplaced Modifiers

A modifier should be placed as close as possible to the word it modifies. Ideally, it should come right before or right after it. A **misplaced modifier** appears to modify the wrong word because it is placed incorrectly in the sentence. To correct this problem, move the modifier so that it is as close as possible to the word it is supposed to modify.

MISPLACED MODIFIER I ran to the window wearing my bathrobe. (Was the window wearing the bathrobe?)

REVISED Wearing my bathrobe, I ran to the window.

MISPLACED MODIFIER The dog ran down the street frightened by the noise. (Was the street frightened by the noise?)

REVISED Frightened by the noise, the dog ran down the street.

FOCUS Misplaced Modifiers

Not all misplaced modifiers are participles. Prepositional phrases can also be misplaced in a sentence.

MISPLACED MODIFIER My sister served cookies to her friends on tiny plates. (Were the friends sitting on tiny plates?)

REVISED My sister served cookies on tiny plates to her friends.

◆ PRACTICE 15.9

Rewrite the following sentences, which contain misplaced modifiers, so that each modifier clearly refers to the word or word group it logically modifies.

Example: Wallowing in a cool mud bath, Mr. Phelps scratched the back of the prize pig.

Mr. Phelps scratched the back of the prize pig wallowing in a cool mud bath.

1. The angry bull threw every rodeo rider with a ring in its nose.

2. The trick-or-treaters rang every doorbell carrying enormous bags of candy.

3. Blushing furiously, the bathroom door was quickly closed by Henry.

4. Attracted to the bright light, the candles were surrounded by moths.

5. A car is not likely to be damaged by rust kept in a garage.

6. A group of homeless men camped at the edge of the city under a highway overpass.

7. A bartender served strong drinks with long hair.

8. Decorated with a skull and crossbones, she carefully read the warning label.

9. Blowing kisses, a white limousine waited as the director emerged from the restaurant.

10. Accidentally tying her shoelaces together, nursery school was a struggle for Amy that morning.

Computer Tip

By entering *-ing* or *-ed*, you can use the Search or Find function to find present participles and past participles in your writing. Then, you can check to make sure you have no dangling or misplaced modifiers.

REVISING AND EDITING

Look back at your response to the Seeing and Writing exercise on page 224. First, underline any present or past participle modifiers you find. Then, revise any dangling or misplaced modifiers. Make sure each modifier refers to a word or word group that it can logically describe.

CHAPTER REVIEW

EDITING PRACTICE

Read the following essay. Then, rewrite the sentences to correct dangling and misplaced modifiers. In some cases, you may have to supply a word or word group to which the modifier can logically refer. The first sentence has been corrected for you.

The Popcorn Story

~~Usually eaten in a movie theater, most~~ *Most* Americans do not think much about popcorn*, usually eaten in a movie theater.* However, popcorn has a long and interesting history.

Respected in the past as a food of the gods, Americans need to learn more about popcorn.

Popcorn is truly an American food. Exploring a cave in New Mexico, ears of popping corn more than five thousand years old were found. Arriving from Europe, native peoples offered to sell popcorn to Columbus and his crew. Popcorn was also an important food for the Aztecs in Mexico. Honoring their gods, idols were decorated with strings of popcorn. Writing about a religious ceremony, the fact that popcorn was scattered in front of a god's statue was recorded by a Spanish priest.

Brought by the native Americans, the Pilgrims ate popcorn at the first Thanksgiving. Liking this local food, popcorn was eaten as a breakfast food by early American colonists. By the nineteenth century, street vendors sold popcorn from pushcarts. Sold in movie theaters, films were soon associated with popcorn. The popularity of the fluffy white snack continued through the Great Depression.

Arriving in the 1940s, the movie business was hurt by television, and as a result people ate less popcorn. However, things soon changed. Invented in the 1940s, popcorn was the first food cooked in the microwave oven. Preparing their favorite movie food at home, popcorn was made popular again. In the 1950s, people made popcorn in pots on the stove. In the 1960s, people bought popcorn in pre-packaged foil pans that puffed out as the popcorn popped. Later, in the diet-conscious 1980s and 1990s, popcorn was made with electric poppers that used hot air instead of oil.

Popped in a microwave, in an electric popper, or on the stove, American families enjoy popcorn when they watch their favorite television shows or videos. Sold in theaters, a trip to the local multiplex is made a more enjoyable experience. Most Americans are unaware of the long history of their favorite snack.

◆ COLLABORATIVE ACTIVITIES

1. Work in a group of four or five students. On a sheet of paper, one student should write a present or past participle modifier. The next student should then complete the sentence and pass the sheet to a third student, who should write another modifier to continue the thought begun in the first sentence. Keep passing the paper from student to student until the group has written at least six sentences.
2. Look over the sentences your group wrote in activity 1. Then, discuss the ways you decided to complete the sentences. Check to be sure that no modifiers are dangling or misplaced.
3. Working in a group, write five present or past participle modifiers. Then, trade lists with another group. Work together to complete the sentences, making sure that at least two sentences contain dangling or misplaced modifiers (the funnier, the better). Finally, pass the sentences back to the group that wrote the modifiers, and have them correct the sentences.

COMPOSING ORIGINAL SENTENCES

4. Working together, write five sentences that contain present or past participle modifiers. Make sure that none of the sentences contain a dangling or misplaced modifier. When you have finished, check the sentences again to make sure you have corrected any errors in grammar or punctuation.

✓ REVIEW CHECKLIST: Dangling and Misplaced Modifiers

- A present participle modifier consists of the present participle (the *-ing* form of the verb) along with the words it introduces. (See 15A.)
- A past participle modifier consists of the past participle (usually ending in *-d* or *-ed*) along with the words it introduces. (See 15B.)
- Correct a dangling modifier by supplying a word or word group to which the dangling modifier can logically refer. (See 15C.)
- Avoid misplaced modifiers by placing modifiers as close as possible to the word or word group they modify. (See 15D.)

UNIT FOUR

Understanding Basic Grammar

CHAPTER

16

Verbs: Past Tense

PREVIEW

In this chapter, you will learn

- to understand regular verbs in the past tense (16A)
- to understand irregular verbs in the past tense (16B)
- to deal with problem verbs in the past tense (16C and 16D)

SEEING AND WRITING

Look at the picture above. Then, select a newsworthy event in your life, and write a one-paragraph news story about it. Include a headline, and be sure to use the past tense.

Word Power

newsworthy interesting enough to be worth reporting in the news

unique one of a kind

Verb tense indicates when an action or situation took place.

A Understanding Regular Verbs in the Past Tense

The **past tense** indicates that an action or situation has already happened. **Regular verbs** form the past tense by adding *-d* or *-ed* to the **base form** of the verb (the present tense form of the verb that is used with *I*).

FOCUS Regular Verbs in the Past Tense

- Most regular verbs form the past tense by adding *-ed* to the base form of the verb.

  I edited my paper.

  Tia handed in her paper yesterday.

- Regular verbs that end in *-e* form the past tense by adding *-d*.

  He refused to take no for an answer.

  Last summer they biked through northern California.

- Regular verbs that end in *-y* form the past tense by changing the *y* to *i* and adding *-ed*.

  try tried
  vary varied

Writing Tip
All regular verbs use the same form for singular and plural in the past tense: *I cheered, They cheered.*

PRACTICE 16.1

Some of the verbs in the following sentences are in the present tense, and some are in the past tense. First, underline the verb in each sentence. Then, on the line after each sentence, write *present* if the verb is present tense and *past* if the verb is past tense.

Examples

James chopped the log into firewood. *past*

She donates money to UNICEF every year. *present*

1. Marguerite sings in the choir. ________
2. The audience members hand their tickets to the usher. ________
3. The coach protested the referee's decision. ________
4. One passenger talked loudly on a cell phone. ________
5. The children cried during the scary parts of the movie. ________
6. We sometimes fail to agree. ________
7. The water gurgled down the drain. ________
8. Many people drink coffee at work. ________
9. The waiters pool their tips. ________
10. My teacher confused everyone with his explanation of grammar. ________

◆ PRACTICE 16.2

Change the present tense verbs in the following passage to past tense. Cross out the present tense form of each underlined verb, and write the past tense form above it.

Example: Anne ~~watches~~ watched her dog carefully as they ~~cross~~ crossed the street.

(1) My neighbor, Anne, walks Muffin, her Rottweiler, every morning. (2) She and Muffin stroll up the street toward the park. (3) On the way, Muffin smells the flowers in my yard. (4) Muffin likes to sniff at the petunias, but she loves the smell of roses. (5) After a while, Anne pulls her dog along. (6) Muffin barks at the passing cars. (7) Then, Anne and her dog follow a footpath through the park. (8) Muffin wants to swim in the lily pond, but Anne refuses to allow it. (9) So, the dog chases butterflies in the meadow and jumps in the air. (10) Anne and Muffin enjoy their daily trip to the park.

B Understanding Irregular Verbs in the Past Tense

Many **irregular verbs** do not form the past tense by adding *-d* or *-ed*. In fact, their past tense forms may look very different from their present tense forms.

The chart on page 242 lists the base form and the past tense form of the most common irregular verbs. If you do not find a verb on this chart, look it up in a dictionary. If the verb is irregular, the dictionary will list its forms after the base form: for example, *get/got/gotten/getting*. (*Get* is the base form, *got* is the past tense form, *gotten* is the past participle, and *getting* is the present participle.)

▼ Student Voices

Sometimes I have trouble with verb tenses.

Thui Trong

Computer Tip

Use the Search or Find command to find in your writing the irregular verbs that give you the most trouble.

◆ PRACTICE 16.3

Use the list of irregular verbs on page 242 to find the correct past tense form of the irregular verb in parentheses. Then, write the correct form in the space provided.

Example: The defendant swore (swear) that he had never entered the store.

1. After staying up all night to finish his paper, Nick ________ (sleep) too late to get to class on time.
2. The cat ________ (drink) some spilled champagne on New Year's Eve.

Irregular Verbs in the Past Tense

Base Form	Past Tense	Base Form	Past Tense
awake	awoke	let	let
be	was, were	lie (to recline)	lay
become	became	light	lit
begin	began	lose	lost
bet	bet	make	made
bite	bit	meet	met
blow	blew	pay	paid
break	broke	quit	quit
bring	brought	read	read
build	built	ride	rode
buy	bought	ring	rang
catch	caught	rise	rose
choose	chose	run	ran
come	came	say	said
cost	cost	see	saw
cut	cut	sell	sold
dive	dove, dived	send	sent
do	did	set	set
draw	drew	shake	shook
drink	drank	shine	shone, shined
drive	drove	sing	sang
eat	ate	sit	sat
fall	fell	sleep	slept
feed	fed	speak	spoke
feel	felt	spend	spent
fight	fought	spring	sprang
find	found	stand	stood
fly	flew	steal	stole
forgive	forgave	stick	stuck
freeze	froze	sting	stung
get	got	swear	swore
give	gave	swim	swam
go	went	take	took
grow	grew	teach	taught
have	had	tear	tore
hear	heard	tell	told
hide	hid	think	thought
hold	held	throw	threw
hurt	hurt	understand	understood
keep	kept	wake	woke, waked
know	knew	wear	wore
lay (to place)	laid	win	won
lead	led	write	wrote
leave	left		

3. The doctor __________ (give) me a flu shot, but I still got sick.

4. Carla __________ (quit) her job when she __________ (win) the lottery.

5. A red balloon __________ (rise) slowly past my office window.

6. Tiger Woods __________ (choose) a club for a short putt.

7. Sharon __________ (tear) down her opponent's campaign posters.

8. Donald Trump __________ (build) a skyscraper that blocked my view.

9. Angel __________ (hurt) Teresa's feelings by criticizing her mother.

10. Jim __________ (feed) his brother's fish too much, so they all died.

◆ PRACTICE 16.4

In the following passage, fill in the correct past tense form of the irregular verb in parentheses. Refer to the list of irregular verbs on page 242.

Example: The salesman was untrustworthy, so he ___lost___ (lose) my business.

(1) I recently __________ (buy) a car for the first time. (2) I __________ (find) the experience a little scary. (3) I __________ (take) one car for a test drive, and it seemed to handle well. (4) The salesman at the dealership __________ (know) I was interested in that car, so he tried very hard to sell it to me. (5) Although my father once __________ (tell) me that buying a car involved bargaining, I was unprepared for that part of the process. (6) I asked how much the car __________ (cost), and the salesman hesitated. (7) He finally __________ (make) an offer that seemed reasonable, but he refused to put the price in writing. (8) At this point, I __________ (become) suspicious. (9) Realizing that I was about to be cheated, I __________ (leave). (10) A few weeks later, my sister __________ (sell) me her old car.

C Problem Verbs in the Past Tense: *Be*

The irregular verb *be* can cause problems for writers because it has two different past tense forms—a singular form and a plural form.

Writing Tip

Be is the only verb in English with more than one past tense form. For information about subject-verb agreement with *be*, see 13B.

Past Tense Forms of the Verb Be

	Singular	**Plural**
1st person	I was tired.	We were tired.
2nd person	You were tired.	You were tired.
3rd person	He was tired.	
	She was tired.	They were tired.
	It was tired.	

◆ PRACTICE 16.5

In each of the following sentences, circle the correct form of the verb *be*.

Example: The toy chicken (was/were) surprisingly loud.

1. Two lighthouses (was/were) visible from the ship.
2. A kitten (was/were) asleep on her lap.
3. After the show, our parents (was/were) ready to go home.
4. With its old, frayed wires, the lamp (was/were) dangerous.
5. From the moment I bought it, the goldfish (was/were) doomed.
6. The children (was/were) hardly able to keep their eyes open after sledding all day.
7. We (was/were) out of the country last summer.
8. The barbarians (was/were) just outside the walls of the city.
9. The potato salad (was/were) the best thing about that meal.
10. A little girl in a witch costume (was/were) the first person to ring my doorbell last Halloween.

◆ PRACTICE 16.6

Edit the following passage for errors in the use of the verb *be*. Cross out any underlined verbs that are incorrect, and write the correct forms above them. If a verb form is correct, label it *C*.

Example: The two computers were different from each other. *C*

(1) In Stanley Kubrick's film *2001,* the spaceship were controlled by a computer named Hal, which had a man's voice. (2) There was some problems with Hal, and the computer nearly destroyed the ship. (3) On

the original *Star Trek* television show, the voice of the computer were female. (4) Its tone was nasal, and the pitch never changed; the computer sounded like a machine. (5) Unlike Hal, the *Star Trek* computer never caused serious problems on the *Enterprise;* the people on board was usually able to rely on their computer.

(6) Recently, volunteers in an experiment were asked to say whether "male" or "female" computerized voices had more authority. (7) Several of the voices, which were created entirely by computer chips, was made to sound female, like the *Star Trek* computer, whereas others sounded male. (8) The researchers was surprised to learn that the volunteers preferred the "male" voices in most situations. (9) The computerized voices in the study were all saying the same words, but people found the information more believable when they thought that a man was speaking. (10) Of course, these people was really listening to a human being.

D Problem Verbs in the Past Tense: *Can/Could* and *Will/Would*

The helping verbs *can/could* and *will/would* can cause problems for writers because their past tense forms are sometimes confused with their present tense forms.

For more on helping verbs, see 6F.

Can/Could

Can, a present tense verb, means "is able to" or "are able to." *Could,* the past tense of *can,* means "was able to" or "were able to."

Students can use the copy machines in the library.

Columbus told the queen he could find a short route to India.

Could is also used to express a possibility or a wish.

The president wishes he could balance the budget.

Will/Would

Will, a present tense verb, talks about the future from the perspective of the present. *Would,* the past tense of *will,* talks about the future from the perspective of the past.

I will finish writing the report tomorrow.

Last week, I told my boss that I would work an extra shift today.

Would is also used to express a possibility or a wish.

Felicia would like to buy a new car.

FOCUS ***Can/Could* and *Will/Would***

Can/could and *will/would* never change form, no matter what the subject is.

I can/he can/they can

I could/he could/they could

I will/he will/they will

I would/he would/they would

◆ PRACTICE 16.7

In each of the following sentences, circle the correct form of the helping verb.

Example: When I was a child, I (can/could) play for hours without getting tired.

1. My boss promised that she (will/would) get me tickets for the World Series.
2. Anyone who works hard (can/could) learn to speak a second language.
3. If he liked the book, he (will/would) buy it.
4. Sheila (will/would) have to go to the post office tomorrow.
5. Before she was injured, she (can/could) walk without a cane.
6. I hope that the apples (will/would) be ripe before the first frost.
7. The kindergarten teacher is pleased that all the children in the class (can/could) tie their shoes.
8. The guide said that we (will/would) see whales from the boat.
9. The parade (can/could) be rained out, but the forecast calls for sunny skies.
10. Don bragged that he (can/could) outscore any of us on the basketball court.

◆ PRACTICE 16.8

In the following passage, circle the correct form of the helping verb from the choices in parentheses.

Example: In the 1970s, my father decided that his next car (will/would) get good gas mileage.

(1) Although everyone complains about the high cost of energy, people (can/could) do something about their energy use. (2) As the price of gasoline rises, drivers (will/would) pay more to fill up their vehicles. (3) If car owners switched from gas-guzzling SUVs to smaller cars, they (will/would) save money and do something good for the environment. (4) Heating oil (can/could) also be a major expense during the winter. (5) Although no one (can/could) do anything about the weather, homeowners (can/could) lower their heating bills if they kept the thermostat turned down and wore sweaters around the house. (6) During the energy crisis of the 1970s, people realized that they (will/would) save energy this way. (7) Keeping a house cooler in winter and warmer in summer helps; if every household took this step, the United States (will/would) dramatically lower its dependence on foreign oil. (8) Even changing a light bulb (can/could) make a difference in energy use. (9) A person who replaces a single light bulb with an energy-efficient compact fluorescent bulb (will/would) not see a huge difference in the electric bill, but if everyone made this change, the United States (will/would) save a noticeable amount of electricity. (10) People in previous decades were able to make sacrifices to save energy, and Americans today (can/could) lower their energy use, too.

■ REVISING AND EDITING

Look back at your response to the Seeing and Writing exercise on page 239. Underline every past tense verb you have used, and check to make sure you used the correct past tense form in each case. Then, cross out any incorrect forms, and write the correct past tense form of the verb above the line.

CHAPTER REVIEW

EDITING PRACTICE

Read the following essay, which contains errors in past tense verb forms, and decide whether each of the underlined past tense verbs is correct. If the verb is correct, write *C* above it. If it is not, cross out the verb and write in the correct past tense form. The first sentence has been corrected for you. (If necessary, consult the list of irregular verbs on p. 242.)

Outsmarting the Squirrels

When my family ~~move~~ moved to a rural part of our state, I decided to start feeding wild birds. I buyed a book on birds so that I could learn to identify different species. I ask the clerk at a local pet supply store about the types of birdfeeders for sale there. There was only one thing I forget to do: learn how to outsmart the squirrels.

The first birdfeeder I choosed was a little wooden house. I pour sunflower seeds in the feeder because the pet supply store telled me that most of the local birds preferred those seeds. I hanged the feeder outside the living room window so that the whole family can enjoy the bird activity, and I sat back to watch dozens of happy birds in my yard.

The birds come to the feeder at first, but before long, the squirrels finded it, too. Because they was larger and greedier than any bird in our area, the squirrels taked control of the feeder. They sitted there, stuffing their little squirrel faces with my premium birdseed while the poor birds watched miserably from a nearby tree. The feeder was empty by evening, and I had put five pounds of seed in it that morning.

I talk to some more experts and ended up with a new birdfeeder. This one were surrounded by a little wire cage that protect the seed from hungry squirrels. The birds can fit their beaks through the wire, but a squirrel's fat little face will get stuck. That was the idea, anyway. For a couple of days, the feeder work very well; on the third day, however, one clever squirrel figure out how to hang upside down and reach into the feeder with his paws. Once again, the birds stayed away, and the squirrel clean out my feeder.

I return to the pet supply store and said that I was defeated. The sales clerk offer me a seventy-five-dollar "squirrel-proof" feeder. The seed openings will slam shut if a heavy object—a squirrel—sat on the feeder. The little rodents can get to the feeder, but they would not be able to eat the birdseed. I thought about this for a while but decided not to buy the new feeder. Instead, I leaved the store with a large bag of birdseed. When I got home, I placed my new purchase in the yard a short distance from the birdfeeder.

For the rest of the winter, our family spended many enjoyable hours by the window. The birds flied around and eat the seed at their feeder, brightening the yard with their color and sound. The yard was still full of squirrels, but now they have their own feeder.

◆ COLLABORATIVE ACTIVITIES

1. List ten verbs in the present tense. Then, exchange papers with another student and write the past tense form of each verb beside the present tense form. Exchange papers again, and check the other student's work.
2. Work in a group of three or four students to choose ten verbs from the lists you made for activity 1. Work together to write a sentence for each of the verbs in the present tense. Then, exchange the sentences with another group, and ask them to rewrite the sentences in the past tense. When you have finished, check each other's work.
3. Working in a group, collaborate on a paragraph about an event that occurred in the past. First, write the paragraph in the present tense, as if the event were happening as you write. Then, exchange paragraphs with another group, and rewrite their paragraph by putting the verbs in the past tense wherever appropriate. When you get your group's paragraph back, check to make sure that all the past tense forms are correct.

COMPOSING ORIGINAL SENTENCES

4. Working in a group, compose five sentences with past tense verbs. Make sure that the verb forms are correct. When you have finished, check the sentences again to make sure you have corrected any errors in grammar, punctuation, or spelling.

☑ REVIEW CHECKLIST:
Verbs: Past Tense

- The past tense of a verb indicates that an action or situation has already happened. (See 16A.)
- Regular verbs form the past tense by adding either *-d* or *-ed* to the base form of the verb. (See 16A.)
- Irregular verbs have irregular forms in the past tense. (See 16B.)
- *Be* is the only verb in English that has two different forms in the past tense—one for singular and one for plural. (See 16C.)
- *Could* is the past tense of *can*. *Would* is the past tense of *will*. (See 16D.)

CHAPTER

17

Verbs: Past Participles

PREVIEW

In this chapter, you will learn

- to identify regular past participles (17A)
- to identify irregular past participles (17B)
- to use the present perfect tense (17C)
- to use the past perfect tense (17D)
- to use past participles as adjectives (17E)

SEEING AND WRITING

Look at the picture above, and then write a paragraph about something you really wanted and finally got. Tell how the thing you got has (or has not) lived up to your expectations.

Word Power

envision to imagine

anticipate to look forward to

A Identifying Regular Past Participles

Every verb has a form that is a **past participle**. The past participle form of a regular verb adds *-d* or *-ed* to the base form of the verb (just as the past tense form does).

Writing Tip

The **base form** is the present tense form of the verb used with *I*.

PRESENT TENSE She repairs her own car whenever it breaks down.

PAST TENSE She repaired her own car before the trip.

PAST PARTICIPLE She has repaired her own car for years.

PAST PARTICIPLE He was surprised to learn that she had repaired her own car.

Note that the helping verb changes its form to agree with its subject, but the past participle always has the same form: *I have repaired/She has repaired.*

◆ PRACTICE 17.1

Below are the base forms of ten regular verbs. In the spaces after each verb, write the appropriate present tense form, past tense form, and past participle form.

Example
shout

present: She ___shouts___ every day.

past: They ___shouted___ yesterday.

past participle: I have always ___shouted___ too much.

1. agree

   present: He always __________.

   past: We __________ yesterday.

   past participle: You had __________ before the summit meeting.

2. love

   present: She __________ them.

   past: You __________ them last week.

   past participle: He has __________ her for years.

3. drop

   present: He always __________ the ball.

   past: I __________ that course last semester.

   past participle: She has always __________ the children off at day care before work.

4. cry

   present: The baby __________ every night.

   past: He __________ when she left.

   past participle: She had __________ the night before.

5. work

   present: It __________ every time.

past: I __________ the late shift last year.

past participle: You have __________ since you were fourteen years old.

6. dance

present: Marilyn __________ the tango professionally.

past: They __________ all night at their wedding.

past participle: We have __________ together for years.

7. gargle

present: He __________ every morning.

past: I __________ before work yesterday.

past participle: They had always __________ before the mouthwash ran out.

8. hesitate

present: She __________ before she speaks.

past: We __________ to buy it last week.

past participle: I have __________ many times.

9. confuse

present: My teacher __________ me every day.

past: He __________ us last night.

past participle: You have __________ us all repeatedly.

10. organize

present: The collector __________ his records all the time.

past: I __________ a luncheon in his honor last March.

past participle: They have __________ all the meetings so far.

◆ PRACTICE 17.2

Fill in the correct past participle form of each verb in parentheses.

Example: Many parents have ___*discovered*___ (discover) that their children love to watch television.

(1) Psychologists have ______________ (fear) for many years that children spend too much time watching television. (2) For several

generations, many parents have ______________ (allow) their children to watch hours of television each day. (3) The average child has ______________ (watch) hundreds of acts of violence on television before reaching high school. (4) No one knows for certain how this violence has ______________ (affect) American children. (5) Recently, some child psychologists have also ______________ (attack) nonviolent programs. (6) These critics believe that television viewing has ______________ (influence) children's health. (7) Indeed, many American children have ______________ (gain) so much weight that they are considered obese. (8) The psychologists believe that the "couch potato" lifestyle has ______________ (cause) these children to eat too much and exercise too little. (9) Some researchers even argue that television has ______________ (prevent) children from developing the ability to concentrate. (10) The American Academy of Pediatrics has ______________ (recommend) that parents keep children under age two from watching any television at all.

B Identifying Irregular Past Participles

Student Voices

I proofread my papers twice: once for verb tenses and once for other types of errors.

Lisa Wu

Unlike regular verbs, irregular verbs almost always have different past tense and past participle forms.

PRESENT TENSE He chooses.
PAST TENSE He chose.
PAST PARTICIPLE He had chosen. (past perfect tense)

PRESENT TENSE They sing.
PAST TENSE They sang.
PAST PARTICIPLE They had sung. (past perfect tense)

The following chart lists the base form, the past tense form, and the past participle of the most common irregular verbs. If you do not find a verb on this chart, look it up in a dictionary. If the verb is irregular, the dictionary will list its forms after the base form: for example, *get/got/gotten/getting*. (*Get* is the base form, *got* is the past tense form, *gotten* is the past participle, and *getting* is the present participle.)

Irregular Past Participles

Base Form	Past Tense	Past Participle
awake	awoke	awoken
be (am, are)	was, were	been
beat	beat	beaten
become	became	become
begin	began	begun
bet	bet	bet
bite	bit	bitten
blow	blew	blown
break	broke	broken
bring	brought	brought
build	built	built
buy	bought	bought
catch	caught	caught
choose	chose	chosen
come	came	come
cost	cost	cost
cut	cut	cut
dive	dove, dived	dived
do	did	done
draw	drew	drawn
drink	drank	drunk
drive	drove	driven
eat	ate	eaten
fall	fell	fallen
feed	fed	fed
feel	felt	felt
fight	fought	fought
find	found	found
fly	flew	flown
forgive	forgave	forgiven
freeze	froze	frozen
get	got	got, gotten
give	gave	given
go	went	gone
grow	grew	grown
have	had	had
hear	heard	heard
hide	hid	hidden
hold	held	held
hurt	hurt	hurt
keep	kept	kept
know	knew	known
lay (to place)	laid	laid
lead	led	led

(continued on the following page)

(continued from the previous page)

Base Form	Past Tense	Past Participle
leave	left	left
let	let	let
lie (to recline)	lay	lain
light	lit	lit
lose	lost	lost
make	made	made
meet	met	met
pay	paid	paid
put	put	put
quit	quit	quit
read	read	read
ride	rode	ridden
ring	rang	rung
rise	rose	risen
run	ran	run
say	said	said
see	saw	seen
sell	sold	sold
send	sent	sent
set	set	set
shake	shook	shaken
shine	shone, shined	shone, shined
sing	sang	sung
sit	sat	sat
sleep	slept	slept
speak	spoke	spoken
spend	spent	spent
spring	sprang	sprung
stand	stood	stood
steal	stole	stolen
stick	stuck	stuck
sting	stung	stung
swear	swore	sworn
swim	swam	swum
take	took	taken
teach	taught	taught
tear	tore	torn
tell	told	told
think	thought	thought
throw	threw	thrown
understand	understood	understood
wake	woke, waked	woken, waked
wear	wore	worn
win	won	won
write	wrote	written

◆ PRACTICE 17.3

Below are the base forms of ten irregular verbs. In the spaces after each verb, write the appropriate present tense form, past tense form, and past participle form.

Example
begin

present: The show ___begins___ at 8 p.m. every night.

past: I ___began___ a new book this morning.

past participle: We have ___begun___ to understand.

1. go

   present: The summer vacation always ______________ too quickly.

   past: He ______________ home an hour ago.

   past participle: They have ______________ to Maine every August for twenty years.

2. think

   present: She ______________ carefully about each question.

   past: We ______________ you wanted a job.

   past participle: I have ______________ a lot about that subject.

3. drink

   present: He ______________ only bottled water.

   past: We ______________ six bottles of water after the race.

   past participle: You have just ______________ the last cold soda.

4. win

   present: Every year, his chili ______________ a blue ribbon at the fair.

   past: They ______________ a bowling trophy last night.

   past participle: We have never ______________ anything.

5. feel

   present: It ______________ very warm in here.

   past: He ______________ sick after lunch.

   past participle: They had ______________ exhausted even before the hike.

6. become

present: He _______________ unpleasant when he is under stress.

past: The argument eventually _______________ difficult to ignore.

past participle: Her shoelaces had _______________ loose before she fell.

7. keep

present: It just _______________ raining.

past: We _______________ the doors locked when we went out.

past participle: Simone has always _______________ secrets very well.

8. lie

present: She _______________ on the couch every night after work.

past: The dog _______________ on the rug while we ate.

past participle: You have _______________ there for more than an hour.

9. understand

present: He _______________ more English than he speaks.

past: You _______________ what the teacher wanted.

past participle: My father has never _______________ rap music.

10. write

present: She _______________ long e-mails.

past: I _______________ to Jack when he was in the navy.

past participle: My little brother has never _______________ a paper without using his computer.

◆ PRACTICE 17.4

Fill in the correct past participle form of each verb in parentheses. Refer to the chart on pages 255–56 as needed.

Example: Bowhead whales have always ___swum___ (swim) past the Aleutian Islands as they migrate.

(1) Biologists have recently _______________ (make) a surprising discovery in the Arctic Ocean. (2) Bowhead whales, which have _______________ (spend) their winters in the Bering Sea near Alaska for

centuries, may be the world's longest-lived mammals. (3) Members of Alaska's Inupiat tribe have _______________ (keep) up their ancestors' tradition of hunting the bowheads. (4) They have _______________ (catch) several whales each year for generations. (5) Since 1981, Inupiats have _______________ (find) six stone or ivory spear points in the captured whales. (6) No one in today's Inupiat tribe had _______________ (see) a stone or ivory harpoon before these finds. (7) These harpoons had not _______________ (be) popular among the Inupiats for at least a century. (8) The Inupiats had _______________ (know) for years that whales could live for sixty or more years, but no one had suspected they could live for over a century. (9) Biologists who had _______________ (hear) about the unusual situation analyzed the whales' flesh. (10) They have not _______________ (come) to a conclusion, but the early results suggest that some bowhead whales may live more than two hundred years.

◆ PRACTICE 17.5

The following passage contains errors in irregular past participles. Cross out any underlined past participles that are incorrect, and write the correct form above them. If the verb form is correct, label it *C*.

Example: The workers at Homeboy Industries have ~~took~~ *taken* on a big responsibility.

(1) In East Los Angeles, Homeboy Industries has gotten a city contract to clean up graffiti. (2) Homeboy was founded by a Jesuit priest who has taught job skills to young men in the neighborhood. (3) Most of the young men who work for Homeboy Industries have spend time in gangs. (4) Now, however, they have lefted gang life. (5) Instead, they have began working to cover up the gangs' graffiti. (6) Removing the graffiti has sometimes be dangerous for the Homeboy crew. (7) After all, current gang members are not pleased when someone paints over the tags that they have wrote. (8) The gangs have often made their marks to show the boundaries of their turf or to honor a dead gang member, so the tags are

important to them. (9) On most days, the Homeboy workers have already went out with their paintbrushes at 5 a.m., when most gang members are asleep. (10) Homeboy Industries has not beat gangs or graffiti yet. (11) However, it has gave its young employees skills and a new start in life.

C Using the Present Perfect Tense

For more on helping verbs, see 6F.

The **present perfect tense** consists of the present tense of the helping verb *have* plus the past participle.

The Present Perfect Tense (have or has + past participle)

Singular	**Plural**
I have gained.	We have gained.
You have gained.	You have gained.
He has gained.	They have gained.
She has gained.	
It has gained.	

Computer Tip

Use the Find or Search command to find all uses of *have, has,* and *had* in your writing. See if the correct past participle form follows each helping verb.

For more on the past tense, see 16A.

As you have already learned, the past tense indicates that an action or situation has already happened. The present perfect tense has two uses.

Use the present perfect tense to indicate that an action or activity began in the past and continues into the present.

PRESENT PERFECT TENSE The Gallup poll has predicted elections since the 1930s. (The predicting began in the past and continues into the present.)

Also, use the present perfect tense to indicate that an action has just occurred.

PRESENT PERFECT TENSE I have just voted. (The voting has just occurred.)

Writing Tip

Use the words *just, now, already,* and *recently* to show that an action has just occurred.

◆ PRACTICE 17.6

In each of the following sentences, fill in the correct form of *have* and the correct past participle form of the verb in parentheses.

Example: Some people ___have___ ___lit___ (light) up every corner of their house and yard.

(1) Every December for the past twenty years, my neighborhood ________ ________ (put) on a holiday light show.

(2) By the second week of December, many households ______________ ______________ (put) up strings of lights. (3) Each year, it seems, the light displays ______________ ______________ (get) larger. (4) Even people who do not celebrate the holidays ______________ ______________ (catch) the light-show fever. (5) In some cases, the displays ______________ ______________ (become) a little ridiculous. (6) Until two years ago, one of my neighbors ______________ always ______________ (choose) to put up a simple string of lights. (7) Before we knew what was going on, his son ______________ ______________ (draw) him into a serious competition with the man next door. (8) For the past two winters we ______________ ______________ (have) to watch as the two households put up increasingly elaborate lights, yard decorations, and rooftop displays. (9) After I saw six plastic sleighs perched on those two roofs, I realized that I ______________ ______________ (become) tired of the light shows. (10) At that point, I would ______________ ______________ (give) anything to return to the little displays that used to light up the winter nights.

◆ PRACTICE 17.7

Circle the appropriate verb tense (past or present perfect) from the choices in parentheses.

Example: Don Larsen (threw/has thrown) the ceremonial first pitch in game one of the 2000 World Series.

(1) Baseball fans (enjoyed/have enjoyed) talking about their favorite games for more than a century. (2) One of the most famous games ever played (was/has been) the fifth game of the 1956 World Series. (3) The New York Yankees (played/have played) the Brooklyn Dodgers in the World Series that year. (4) In game five, the Yankees' Don Larsen (pitched/has pitched) a perfect game, allowing no hits and no runs. (5) People who (saw/has seen) that game agree that they (never saw/have never seen) anything like it since. (6) Perfect games (were always/have always been) extremely rare. (7) Only a few pitchers (ever had/have ever had) a

perfect game, and so far, no one other than Larsen (ever threw/has ever thrown) a perfect game in the World Series. (8) The Yankees (won/have won) the 1956 World Series in seven games. (9) In 1957, the Brooklyn Dodgers (moved/have moved) to Los Angeles. (10) The 1956 World Series (was/has been) the last all–New York series until 2000, when the Mets (played/have played) the Yankees.

◆ PRACTICE 17.8

Fill in the appropriate tense (past or present perfect) of the verb in parentheses.

Example: Twenty years ago, children around the country ___rang___ (ring) doorbells on the night of October 31.

(1) When I ______________ (be) young, children ______________ (go) trick-or-treating on Halloween. (2) We ______________ (have) fun dressing up as witches, ghosts, and princesses. (3) People who couldn't be at home usually ______________ (leave) treats on the porch for us. (4) No one ______________ (worry) about anything more dangerous than finding toilet paper hanging from every tree in the yard. (5) Today, however, many parents feel that trick-or-treating ______________ (become) too dangerous for young children. (6) In the past twenty years, I ______________ (hear) many stories about people putting razor blades, poison, or drugs in candy and apples for trick-or-treaters. (7) Recently, experts ______________ (claim) that some of these stories are not true, but the damage ______________ (be) done. (8) Of course, even if no one ______________ (do) any of these horrible things, everyone today believes that such acts are possible. (9) I ______________ (love) Halloween as a child, but since I ______________ (become) a parent, I ______________ (find) it positively scary. (10) In my neighborhood, mothers and fathers ______________ (begin) taking the children trick-or-treating in the daytime—and only to the homes of people they know.

D Using the Past Perfect Tense

The **past perfect tense** consists of the past tense of the helping verb *have* plus the past participle.

The Past Perfect Tense
(had + past participle)

Singular	**Plural**
I had returned.	We had returned.
You had returned.	You had returned.
He had returned.	They had returned.
She had returned.	
It had returned.	

Use the past perfect tense to indicate that one past action occurred before another past action.

PAST PERFECT TENSE The job applicant told (PAST) the receptionist that he had arrived (PAST PERFECT).

This sentence discusses two actions that happened in the past. The verb in the first part of the sentence (*told*) is in the past tense. The verb in the second part of the sentence (*had arrived*) is in the past perfect tense. The use of the past perfect tense indicates that the job applicant arrived at the interview *before* he talked to the receptionist.

◆ PRACTICE 17.9

Circle the appropriate verb tense (present perfect or past perfect) from the choices in parentheses.

Example: Computers (have made/had made) our lives easier in many ways.

1. Some businesses today (have invested/had invested) in "detective" software.
2. Before they bought the software, some of these companies (have become/had become) convinced that their employees were not always working when they were online.
3. The manufacturers of "detective" software (have allowed/had allowed) companies to track the Web sites their workers visit.
4. Previously, if an employee (has visited/had visited) pornographic sites, the company had no way of knowing about it.

5. Now, however, any worker who (has made/had made) visits to such sites on company time can expect the company to find out.
6. The manufacturers (have expected/had expected) businesses to be interested in their software, but they were surprised at the amount of consumer interest.
7. Apparently, many people (have wanted/had wanted) for years to find out what their spouses are doing online.
8. The software manufacturers (have sold/had sold) many copies of their "detective" to suspicious husbands and wives.
9. One woman bought the software after her husband (has started/had started) spending hours on the computer every evening.
10. If she (has hoped/had hoped) to restore trust to their marriage, she was probably disappointed.

◆ PRACTICE 17.10

Fill in the appropriate tense (past or past perfect) of the verb in parentheses.

Example: After she ___had eaten___ (ate) tomatoes every day for five months, she began to get tired of them.

(1) When she was a young woman, my grandmother ____________ (grow) an impressive vegetable garden every summer. (2) Gardens ____________ (be) not unusual in those days. (3) After the backyard gardeners ____________ (enjoy) their early spring produce, they faced the abundant crops of July and August. (4) At the end of the summer, most people ____________ (can) the extra vegetables they ____________ (raise). (5) My grandmother once claimed that she ____________ (grow) several hundred pounds of tomatoes in a single season. (6) She said that she ____________ (try) to give tomatoes away to relatives, friends, and neighbors, but without success; everyone else also had plenty of tomatoes. (7) I asked her how she ____________ (solve) this problem. (8) "I ____________ (make) enough tomato

sauce and tomato soup to last for several lifetimes," she said. (9) "Then I ________________ (leave) bags and bags of tomatoes on the church steps in the middle of the night." (10) Before she told me this story, I ________________ (admired) my grandmother's quick wits, but since then I have been even more impressed with her ability to solve any problems that come her way.

E Using Past Participles as Adjectives

In addition to functioning as a verb, the past participle can function as an **adjective**, modifing a noun that follows it.

> My aunt sells painted furniture.
>
> I like fried chicken.

The past participle is also used as an adjective after a **linking verb**—*be, become, seem,* and so on.

> Mallory was surprised.
>
> My roommate became depressed.
>
> The applicant seemed qualified for the job.

Writing Tip

A linking verb—such as *seemed* or *looked*—connects a subject to the word that describes it. (See 6E.)

See 20A for more on the use of adjectives as modifiers.

◆ PRACTICE 17.11

The following passage contains errors in past participle forms used as adjectives. Cross out any underlined participle that is incorrect, and write the correct form above it. If the participle form is correct, label it *C*.

Example: A pet should wear identification in case it becomes lost. C

(1) Every year, thousands of pets are abandon in the United States. (2) Sometimes, when a cute puppy or kitten grows up, its owners decide that they are tire of it. (3) In other cases, the unconcern owners, unable to take their pet to a new home, decide that it will be better off in the wild. (4) Then, the poor creature may be thrown out of a car along a highway far from home or leave in a deserted area. (5) These animals are often injure; many do not survive. (6) Animal control groups, usually run by local governments, try to make sure that as many abandoned animals as possible can be save. (7) The animals that are rescue do not

necessarily experience a happy ending, however. (8) Overcrowded animal shelters often have to kill many of these unwanted pets. (9) "No-kill" shelters do exist, but they are often swamp with unwanted animals and in desperate need of funding. (10) Everyone who considers getting a pet must be certain that he or she is committed to caring for the animal.

◆ PRACTICE 17.12

After each of the following verbs, write the correct past participle form. Then, use each of the past participles in one of the phrases listed below the verbs.

Example

break *past participle:* broken

a broken window

1. make *past participle:* ______
2. fry *past participle:* ______
3. register *past participle:* ______
4. defeat *past participle:* ______
5. wear *past participle:* ______
6. hide *past participle:* ______
7. swear *past participle:* ______
8. frost *past participle:* ______
9. cut *past participle:* ______
10. pave *past participle:* ______
11. a ______ road
12. a bouquet of ______ flowers
13. ______ enemies
14. ______ green tomatoes
15. a ______ nurse
16. a bed neatly ______
17. ______ camera
18. a ______ birthday cake
19. the ______ team
20. a ______ patch on the rug

◆ PRACTICE 17.13

In each of the following pairs of sentences, find and underline the past participle that is used as an adjective after a linking verb. Then, combine the two sentences into one longer sentence, with the past participle modifying a noun that follows it.

Example

The lobster was boiled. It was our main course.

The boiled lobster was our main course.

1. The quarterback played for the rest of the quarter. He was injured.

2. The sales clerk was annoyed. She did not want to assist any customers.

3. The figs were dried. Rafika put them in a dish.

4. Anders did not realize he had broken the rules. They were unwritten.

5. His beard was pointed. The baby stared at it for several minutes.

6. My boss was outraged. She wanted to fire us all.

7. His fingers were burned. He put them in his mouth.

8. Mr. Duven keeps his passport in a box. The box is locked.

9. The answers were expected. The students did not give them.

10. The mysterious stranger produced several documents. They were forged.

REVISING AND EDITING

Look back at your response to the Seeing and Writing exercise on page 251. Have you used the present perfect or past perfect tense? If so, underline the helping verbs and past participles. Then, check to make sure that you used these tenses correctly. Cross out any incorrect verb forms, and write your corrections above them.

CHAPTER REVIEW

EDITING PRACTICE

Read the following essay, which contains errors in the use of past participles and the past, present perfect, and past perfect tenses. Decide whether each of the underlined verbs is correct. If it is correct, write *C* above it. If it is not, write in the correct verb form. The first sentence has been corrected for you.

Propaganda or Documentary?

Leni Riefenstahl's name has [C] never ~~became~~ [become] a household word in the United States. However, most people who study filmmaking had heard of Leni Riefenstahl. The documentaries she has made in Germany in the 1930s are still study all over the world. They are consider masterpieces of a certain kind of filmmaking—but what kind? Some people had argued that Riefenstahl created propaganda for the Nazis. Others, including Riefenstahl herself, have said that the films are simply powerful documentaries.

Before becoming a director, Leni Riefenstahl had be a silent film star in Germany in the 1920s. Later, she has began to direct her own films. In the 1930s, when Adolf Hitler come to power, her talent as a director attracted his attention. Hitler hire her, and by the time World War II began, she had made several films for him. In 1934, she shooted her most famous film, *Triumph of the Will.* In Germany today, no one is allow to show this film.

For years, film experts have saw the power of the images in the film. However, these powerful images of marching men in Nazi uniforms has also influence impressionable people. A person who sees the film may conclude that the Nazis are to be admired. Riefenstahl always claimed that making the film was simply a job for her and that she had no special admiration for Hitler and the Nazis. However, many people had accuse her of producing a successful advertisement for joining the Nazi Party.

After World War II, Riefenstahl stopped making films. She is still despise by many people who believe that she had helped the Nazi cause. No one denies that she has been a great director. *Triumph of the Will* and *Olympiad,* her film about the 1936 Berlin Olympics, are consider basic material for film students. However, knowing what she was able to do with a camera, many people were relieve when she retired from the movie business.

◆ COLLABORATIVE ACTIVITIES

1. Form a group of four students. Working on your own, write five verbs on a sheet of paper. Pass the paper to the person next to you, and write the past tense after each verb on the sheet you get. Then, pass the paper again; this time, add the past participle of each verb on the sheet you receive. Pass the paper one final time, and then check one another's work.
2. Working in the same group, choose five of the verbs from your papers in activity 1. Write a sentence for each verb, using the present perfect or past perfect tense, or using the past participle as an adjective.
3. Exchange your sentences from activity 2 with another group. Then, choose two of their sentences and incorporate them into a paragraph that contains at least three other verbs in the present perfect or past perfect tense.

COMPOSING ORIGINAL SENTENCES

4. Working in a group of four students, collaborate to create five sentences that use the present perfect or past perfect tense or that use a past participle as an adjective. Be sure that you use the correct participle for each verb, that the verb tense is appropriate, and that the form of the verb in each sentence is correct. When you have finished, check the sentences again to make sure you have corrected any errors in grammar, punctuation, or spelling.

✓ REVIEW CHECKLIST: Verbs: Past Participles

- The past participle form of a regular verb adds *-d* or *-ed* to the base form of the verb. (See 17A.)
- Irregular verbs usually have irregular past participles. (See 17B.)
- The present perfect tense consists of the present tense of *have* plus the past participle. It shows a continuing action, usually one that began in the past and continues into the present. (See 17C.)
- The past perfect tense consists of the past tense of *have* plus the past participle. It describes a past action that occurred before another past action. (See 17D.)
- The past participle can function as an adjective. (See 17E.)

Nouns

CHAPTER **18**

PREVIEW

In this chapter, you will learn

- to identify nouns (18A)
- to recognize singular and plural nouns (18B)
- to form plural nouns (18C)

SEEING AND WRITING

What objects do you treasure? Why? Look at the picture above, and then write a paragraph in which you answer these questions.

Word Power

memento a reminder of the past; a keepsake (the plural form is *mementos*)

memorabilia objects valued because of their link to historical events or culture

A Identifying Nouns

A **noun** is a word that names a person (*actor, Denzel Washington*), an animal (*elephant, Babar*), a place (*city, Houston*), an object (*game, Monopoly*), or an idea (*theory, Darwinism*).

FOCUS Common and Proper Nouns

Most nouns, called **common nouns**, begin with lowercase (not capital) letters.

prince holiday

Some nouns, called **proper nouns**, name particular people, places, objects, or events. A proper noun always begins with a capital letter.

Prince Charming Memorial Day

◆ PRACTICE 18.1

In each of the following sentences, underline every noun. Label common nouns *C* and proper nouns *P*.

Example: Melvin Stewart, the postman, bit my dog.

1. The incident happened on my birthday, the first Tuesday after Labor Day.
2. The mayor of Springfield, Jana Floyd, loves animals.
3. Ms. Floyd has a statue of a dog in her front yard.
4. The mayor sent letters about the incident to all residents.
5. Mr. Stewart argued that my dog had leaped in the air and snapped at his nose.
6. Postal workers often have stormy relationships with dogs.
7. A bulldog down the street has bitten three postal employees and the man who drives the UPS truck.
8. My poodle hates any person wearing a uniform.
9. The bite did not injure Fluffy; it may teach him a lesson.
10. The front door of my house is now locked when the mail is due.

B Recognizing Singular and Plural Nouns

A **singular noun** names one thing: *book, family.* A **plural noun** names more than one thing: *books, families.*

FOCUS Singular and Plural Nouns

Recognizing whether a noun is singular or plural is particularly important when a noun is the subject of a sentence. This is because subjects and verbs must always be in **agreement**: a singular subject requires a singular verb; a plural subject requires a plural verb.

SINGULAR The book sits on the shelf.

PLURAL The books sit on the shelf.

For more on subject-verb agreement, see Chapter 13.

For more on plural forms of nouns, see 18C.

Because many plural nouns end in *-s*, you can often tell whether a noun is singular or plural by looking at its ending. However, many nouns that end in *-s* are singular (*gas, series, focus*), and some plural nouns do not end in *-s* (*men, women, children*).

Sometimes, a noun is introduced by a **determiner**, a word that specifically identifies the noun or limits its meaning (*this house*, not *that house*). In these cases, the determiner tells you whether the noun is singular (*this house*) or plural (*these houses*).

Writing Tip

Sometimes, a determiner is followed not by a noun but by *of* or *of the:* for example, *each of us, many of the reasons.* Special rules for subject-verb agreement apply in these cases. (See 13E.)

Using Determiners with Nouns

Determiners That Introduce Singular Nouns	Determiners That Introduce Plural Nouns
a	all
an	both
another	few
each	many
every	most
one	several
this	these
that	those
	two, three, etc.

◆ PRACTICE 18.2

In the following passage, fill in the blanks with appropriate singular or plural nouns.

> **Example:** This classroom is too cold.

(1) Every ______ seems to last too long. (2) Most ______ do not expect these ______ to be as long as they are. (3) One ______ can last two or three ______. (4) Most ______ simply do not have enough free time. (5) Several ______ have complained about this ______. (6) I have heard few ______, however. (7) Is there a ______? (8) Each ______ should speak up. (9) One ______ can make a ______. (10) Several ______ can make a ______.

◆ PRACTICE 18.3

In the following paragraph, singular and plural nouns that follow determiners are underlined. Decide whether the correct singular or plural form is used for each underlined noun. If the form is correct, write *C* above the noun. If it is incorrect, cross it out; then write in the correct singular or plural noun form.

> **Example:** One ~~women~~ woman at the United Nations has worked hard for women's rights around the world.

(1) Over twenty years ago, Nafis Sadik was an <u>obstetricians</u> from Pakistan. (2) In 1971, she took a <u>positions</u> with the United Nations Population Fund. (3) At that time, the Population Fund offered few <u>option</u> to women who wanted fewer children. (4) One <u>choices</u> was sterilization, but many <u>woman</u> were unwilling to take such a permanent step. (5) After several <u>year</u> at the Population Fund, Dr. Sadik became the executive director of this <u>program</u>. (6) Population growth is still a <u>problem</u> around the world, but under Dr. Sadik, the U.N. Population Fund found another <u>focus</u>. (7) The Population Fund now supports the right of every <u>women</u> around the world to have access to education and health care. (8) The fund believes that those <u>women</u> who have access to information and

medical care will plan their families wisely. (9) This concept may sound basic, but unfortunately, women in many countrys have very little freedom. (10) Allowing women to make their own choices about family planning still makes many person uncomfortable.

C Forming Plural Nouns

Some nouns form plurals in predictable ways; others do not.

Regular Noun Plurals

Most nouns add *-s* to form plurals. Other nouns, whose singular forms end in *-s, -ss, -sh, -ch, -x,* or *-z,* add *-es* to form plurals. Some nouns that end in *-s* or *-z* double the *s* or *z* before adding *-es*.

Singular	*Plural*
chair	chairs
zoo	zoos
campus	campuses
kiss	kisses
wish	wishes
bunch	bunches
box	boxes
quiz	quizzes

Irregular Noun Plurals

Some nouns form plurals in unusual ways.

- Some nouns have plural forms that are the same as their singular forms.

Singular	*Plural*
one fish	two fish
this species	these species
a series	several series

- Nouns ending in *-f* or *-fe* form plurals by changing the *f* to *v* and adding *-es* or *-s*.

Singular	*Plural*
each half	both halves
one life	nine lives
a thief	many thieves
that loaf	those loaves
the first shelf	several shelves

Exceptions to this rule include the words *roof* (plural *roofs*), *proof* (plural *proofs*), and *belief* (plural *beliefs*).

Writing Tip

When a noun has an irregular plural, the dictionary lists its plural form: *man, men*.

- Most nouns ending in *-y* form plurals by changing the *y* to *ie* and adding *-s*.

Singular	*Plural*
a new baby	more babies
one berry	many berries

Note, however, that when a vowel (the letters *a, e, i, o u,* and *y*) comes before the *y,* the noun has a regular plural form: *turkey* (plural *turkeys*), *day* (plural *days*).

- A **compound noun**—two or more nouns that function as a unit—generally forms the plural just as other nouns do (*baby doll, baby dolls*). However, most hyphenated compound nouns form plurals by adding *-s* to the first word of the compound.

Singular	*Plural*
Ben's brother-in-law	Ben's two favorite brothers-in-law
a husband-to-be	all the husbands-to-be
one runner-up	many runners-up

- Other irregular plurals must be memorized.

Singular	*Plural*
that child	those children
a good man	a few good men
one woman	several women
my left foot	both feet
a wisdom tooth	my two front teeth

◆ PRACTICE 18.4

Next to each of the following singular nouns, write the plural form of the noun. Then, circle the irregular plurals. (If you are not sure of a word's plural form, check the dictionary. Irregular plurals will be listed there.)

Example: hamburger hamburgers goose (geese)

1. lady-in-waiting ____________
2. wolf ____________
3. potato ____________
4. band ____________
5. bench ____________
6. knife ____________
7. calendar ____________
8. boss ____________
9. highway ____________
10. sheep ____________
11. cheese ____________
12. bandit ____________
13. enemy ____________
14. cactus ____________
15. calf ____________
16. mouse ____________
17. tax ____________
18. projector ____________
19. stomach ____________
20. fly ____________

◆ PRACTICE 18.5

Proofread the underlined nouns in the following paragraph, checking for correct singular or plural form. If a correction needs to be made, cross out the noun and write the correct form above it. If the noun is correct, write *C* above it.

Example: The dogs howled as if their ~~lifes~~ lives depended on it.

(1) Hunting foxs is a traditional sport among wealthy people in England (2) In some familys, foxhunting has gone on for generations. (3) Fathers and childrens, sons and daughter-in-laws may all hunt together. (4) The mens and woman, wearing scarlet coates, ride horses and ponys. (5) The riders go out early in the morning, searching for foxes in wooded areaes and green fields where sheeps graze peacefully. (6) Often, a fox is driven from its hiding place by its enemys, the foxhoundes, which bark and howl to alert the peoples on the hunt. (7) The fox is then chased by the dogs, horseman, and horsewoman until it either escapes or is killed. (8) Many activists for animal rights argue that this sport is cruel and should be banned. (9) They believe that the dignified appearance of the riders covers up the fact that they terrorize and kill the creatures and then cut off their tailes with knifes. (10) The activists suggest that men and womens who want to hunt should just dress up and ride around with their dogs instead.

■ REVISING AND EDITING

Look back at your response to the Seeing and Writing exercise on page 271. First, underline every noun. Then, check to be sure you have capitalized every proper noun and formed plurals correctly.

CHAPTER REVIEW

◆ EDITING PRACTICE

Read the following essay, which contains noun errors. Make any editing changes you think are necessary. The first sentence has been edited for you.

Who Needs New?

My Grandmother is a great believer in buying used cars. She is seventy-eight year old and has owned only one new car in her entire life. Many used car she has owned became like old friends to her; she has photoes of some that she shows to me sometimes. She happily discusses the pluss and minus of owning a used car with anyone who asks her.

Grandma pinches pennys, so there is one benefits she always mentions. A used car always costs less than it did when it was new. Every new car, as most peoples know, loses thousands of dollars in value the moment it leaves the lot. My grandmother likes to tell visitors about the time she bought a car from one of her son-in-laws, who had owned it for only six month. "I gave him the market price," grandma says. "He paid a very high price for his six months of ownership!"

Like most woman of her generation, my grandmother is no mechanic. Her biggest worry in buying a used car is whether the car is in good shape or not. She says that all prospective buyer should hire a professional to check every details of a car they want to buy. Cars that break down are not just an inconveniences; they can endanger the lifes of people riding in them. My Aunt's boyfriend, george, is a mechanic, so he has looked at several vehicle for my grandmother.

In many other ways, Grandma feels that used cars and new cars are alike. Used cars can have breakdowns, but new cars can disappoint their owners, too. My grandmother's only new car, which my Grandfather bought for her in the 1960s, was a Lemon. On the other hand, her used Toyota ran for many years and got excellent gas mileage. Many accident can happen whether a car is new or used. Deers can leap out in front of the vehicle, tailgaters can ram into it from behind, and bad weather can make many roads dangerous. Drivers just have to concentrate and refuse to take riskses.

My grandmother has lived a long time, and she offers me this advices: used cars are a wiser economic choice. I don't have the savingses to buy a new car anyway, but she has convinced me to look for a good used car. In our family, used cars have helped to unite the generations.

◆ COLLABORATIVE ACTIVITIES

1. Working in a group, complete the following chart by listing nouns related to each category, writing one noun on each line. If the noun is a proper noun, be sure to capitalize it.

Sports		*Politics*		*Television*		*College*		*Holidays*	
Football	whistel	president	debate	station	switch	campus	library	Christmas	Fourth of July
baseball	glove	senator	Washington DC	channel	programs	students	University Minnesota	Labor Day	Halloween
tennis	racquet	gavener	Bush	remote	viewers	books	professors	St. Patricks	Memorial
hockey	puck	mayor	Regan	screen	Comcast	tution	credits	Martin Luther	Presidents
basketball	net	White House	poll booth	cable	Showtime	grade point	dorms	Valentines Day	Veterans
softball	base	capital	campaign	show	movies	plays	sports	Secretary's Day	Grandparents Day
hunting	gun	ballet	Lincoln	adds	comercials	education	lunches	Easter	Mothers Day

   When you have completed the chart, work together to add the plural form of each singular noun and the singular form of each plural noun to the chart. (Use a different color pen, and write these forms beside the nouns.) If the noun has only one form, circle it.

2. On a sheet of paper, write a sentence using one of the nouns from activity 1. Then, working in the same group, pass the paper to the person next to you; on the sheet you receive, continue the thought, writing a sentence using a different noun. Keep passing the sheets and adding to the story on each page until every page has at least six sentences.
3. From the stories composed in activity 2, choose the one that your group likes best, and work together to complete the story. Then, exchange stories with another group in class. Rewrite the other group's story, substituting a noun from your chart for one of the nouns in each sentence the other group has written. Finally, read the stories to the class, and choose the funniest revision.

COMPOSING ORIGINAL SENTENCES

4. Working in a group, write five sentences. Make sure that you have used at least one proper noun, at least one determiner that introduces a singular noun, at least one determiner that introduces a plural noun, and at least two plural nouns with irregular plurals. Then, check the nouns carefully to be sure that the forms are correct. When you have finished, check the sentences again to make sure you have corrected any errors in grammar, punctuation, or spelling.

✓ REVIEW CHECKLIST: Nouns

- A noun is a word that names a person, animal, place, object, or idea. (See 18A.)
- A singular noun names one thing; a plural noun names more than one thing. (See 18B.)
- Most nouns add *-s* to form plurals. Some nouns have irregular plural forms. (See 18C.)

CHAPTER

19

Pronouns

■ SEEING AND WRITING

If you had a vanity license plate, what would you like it to say? Why? Look at the picture above, and then write a paragraph in which you answer these questions.

PREVIEW

In this chapter, you will learn

- to identify pronouns (19A)
- to understand pronoun-antecedent agreement (19B)
- to solve special problems with pronoun-antecedent agreement (19C)
- to eliminate vague and unnecessary pronouns (19D)
- to understand pronoun case (19E)
- to solve special problems with pronoun case (19F)
- to identify reflexive and intensive pronouns (19G)

A Identifying Pronouns

A **pronoun** takes the place of a noun or another pronoun.

Evan wanted to change his life, so he decided to enlist in the Air Force. (*He* takes the place of *Evan.*)

Without pronouns, you would have to repeat the same nouns over and over again.

Word Power

vanity excessive pride in one's appearance or achievements

vanity plate a license plate that can be customized for an extra charge

Evan wanted to change his life, so Evan decided to enlist in the Air Force.

Pronouns, like nouns, can be singular or plural. Singular pronouns always take the place of singular nouns.

Julia forgot to pick up Max, so she went back to get him. (*She* takes the place of *Julia; him* takes the place of *Max.*)

Plural pronouns always take the place of plural nouns.

Kyle and Mike took their little brother fishing. (*Their* takes the place of *Kyle and Mike.*)

Keep in mind that the pronoun *you* can be either singular or plural.

When the fans met the rock star, they said, "We're crazy about you." The rock star replied, "I couldn't do it without you." (The first *you* is singular; it takes the place of *rock star.* The second *you* is plural; it takes the place of *fans.*)

Writing Tip
Too many pronouns can make a paragraph monotonous, especially when pronouns begin several sentences in a row. Try to vary your sentence openings.

For lists of pronouns, see 19C, 19E, and 19G.

◆ PRACTICE 19.1

In each of the following sentences, underline the pronoun. Then, in the blank after each sentence, write *S* if the pronoun is singular or *P* if the pronoun is plural.

Example: He ate twelve pancakes for breakfast. S

1. She sold flowers on the street corner. _____
2. It was a very dull book. _____
3. We spent seven hours trying to get tickets to the game. _____
4. When the alarm rang, I blinked sleepily. _____
5. The neighborhood is so quiet that it seems deserted. _____
6. Derek, you should try out for the cross-country team. _____
7. The boy was hungry, but he did not ask for any food. _____
8. The room is clean, children, but you forgot to make the beds. _____
9. Strangers turned away when we asked for help. _____
10. If Cathy had married Heathcliff, they might have been happy. _____

B Understanding Pronoun-Antecedent Agreement

As you learned in 19A, a pronoun takes the place of a noun or another pronoun. The word to which the pronoun refers is called its **antecedent.**

In the following sentence, the noun *runner* is the antecedent of the pronoun *he*.

The runner slowed down, but he did not stop.

A pronoun must always agree with its antecedent. If an antecedent is singular, the pronoun must also be singular. In the sentence above, the antecedent *runner* is singular, so the pronoun that refers to it (*he*) is also singular.

If the antecedent is plural, the pronoun must also be plural.

The runners slowed down, but they did not stop.

Here, the antecedent *runners* is plural, so the pronoun that refers to it (*they*) is also plural.

◆ PRACTICE 19.2

In each of the following sentences, a pronoun is underlined. In the blank after each sentence, write the noun that is the antecedent of the underlined pronoun. Then, draw an arrow from the pronoun to its antecedent.

Example: When the kittens were awake, they were eating. kittens

1. The woman spoke out angrily before she left. ______
2. A frog's skin is so thin that it absorbs pesticides. ______
3. The hitchhiker put out a thumb, but his face showed no hope. ______
4. Felicia won her first marathon and took Friday off. ______
5. When the two lawyers fell in love, they decided to stop working together. ______
6. Tino, you cannot graduate without a foreign language credit. ______
7. Esteban saw a film that he hated. ______
8. The boys almost missed their bus to Florida. ______
9. Fries taste good, but they are not very nutritious. ______
10. As Bob crossed the street, a truck narrowly missed him. ______

◆ PRACTICE 19.3

In the following passage, fill in each blank with the appropriate pronoun (*it* or *they*).

Example: When the *Viking 1* spacecraft went to Mars, ___it___ took photographs.

(1) For generations, people on Earth have asked questions about Mars because __________ is the closest planet to us. (2) When the *Viking 1* spacecraft orbited Mars in July 1976, __________ sent photographs back to NASA. (3) Scientists at the space agency looked at the photos, and __________ released the pictures to the public. (4) Some people who saw one of the photographs were surprised when __________ thought it showed a face. (5) The picture showed an area of Mars called Cydonia; __________ is covered with hills and valleys. (6) The face was about a mile long, and __________ appeared to have eyes, a nose, and a mouth. (7) Science fiction fans, who suggested that the face was some kind of monument, wondered if __________ had been built by a former Martian civilization. (8) Although people speculated for years about that face, __________ did not have any further information until 1998. (9) When more detailed photos were taken that year, __________ showed rocky cliffs where the face had been. (10) The Martian face interested a lot of people, but __________ was just an illusion.

◆ PRACTICE 19.4

In the following passage, circle the antecedent of each underlined pronoun. Then, draw an arrow from the pronoun to its antecedent.

Example: Because teachers are poorly paid, they often get little respect.

(1) My parents think that public education in the United States is not good enough, but they cannot agree on a solution. (2) My mother often tells us how she thinks schools should be improved. (3) Public schools are financed by the communities that surround them. (4) If a community is poor, it does not have much money to contribute to the schools. (5) My

mother says that our public school is ineffective because it lacks money. (6) She cares about her children and wants to send us to a private school. (7) Reformers have suggested a voucher system to enable parents to select a school—public or private—of their choice. (8) However, vouchers could take money away from public schools that desperately need it. (9) That is why my father says the voucher system is not for him. (10) We can only hope the public school system will not disappoint us.

C Solving Special Problems with Pronoun-Antecedent Agreement

To make sure pronouns and antecedents agree, you must know whether an antecedent is singular or plural. Certain kinds of antecedents can cause problems for writers because they are not easy to identify as singular or plural. These troublesome groups of antecedents include *compound antecedents, indefinite pronoun antecedents,* and *collective noun antecedents.*

Compound Antecedents

A **compound antecedent** consists of two or more words connected by *and* or *or: England and the United States; Japan or China.* Compound antecedents connected by *and* are always plural. They are always used with plural pronouns.

For more on compound subjects, see 13C.

England and the United States drafted soldiers into their armies.

Compound antecedents connected by *or* may be treated as singular or plural. When both words in a compound antecedent connected by *or* are singular, use a singular pronoun to refer to the compound antecedent.

Did Japan or China send its army to war?

When both words are plural, use a plural pronoun.

Volunteer armies or military drafts both have their supporters.

◆ PRACTICE 19.5

In each of the following sentences, underline the compound antecedent, and circle the connecting word (*and* or *or*). Then, circle the appropriate pronoun in parentheses.

Example: Sadness or even severe depression can take (its/their) toll on residents of northern climates in the winter.

1. Spring and fall are the seasons I like best, but (it/they) can be very unpredictable.

2. In the spring, either crocuses or daffodils are usually the first flowers to show (its/their) faces.
3. Snow and ice can still be present in early spring, but I am always glad to see the last of (it/them).
4. A frost or a light snowfall can damage flower buds, but (it/they) may not hurt any shoots that have come up from the ground.
5. Chilly air and unpredictable weather also appear in the fall, but (its/their) arrival reminds me that winter is coming.
6. Two oak trees and a sugar maple in my yard show off (its/their) fall foliage.
7. When our area has experienced unusually cold weather or a dry spell, (its/their) effect is visible in the colors of the leaves.
8. Winter and summer usually produce more extreme conditions, so I do not like (it/them) as much as the milder seasons.
9. Where I live, the heat and humidity of summer always leave (its/their) victims eager for cool, comfortable fall days.
10. In winter, either the darkness or the bitter cold can make anyone who lives through (it/them) dream of spring.

◆ PRACTICE 19.6

The following passage contains errors in pronoun reference with compound antecedents. Decide whether each underlined pronoun is correct. If it is not, cross out the pronoun, and write the correct pronoun above it. If it is correct, label it *C*.

Example: Perhaps Broadway is running out of ideas and creativity, and without ~~it,~~ *them,* live theater is doomed.

(1) Many filmmakers and theater directors are using the same material for their shows. (2) A successful play or an award-winning musical has always had their uses for Hollywood, and many movies have been based on plays. (3) The play *Who's Afraid of Virginia Woolf* and the musical *The Music Man* were Broadway hits, and later it became successful on film as well. (4) Lately, the hits have moved in the other direction, and now musical films or popular movies have its chance on Broadway.

(5) Zero Mostel and Gene Wilder made their fans laugh in the 1967 film *The Producers*. (6) In 2001, admirers of Nathan Lane and Matthew Broderick could see him sing and dance onstage in *The Producers,* the Broadway musical. (7) Theatergoers might also have seen *The Rocky Horror Show* or *The Lion King* during its Broadway run. (8) Fans who hoped that Tim Curry or James Earl Jones might recreate their film role on Broadway went home disappointed, but the shows were successful anyway. (9) Some critics and theatergoers think a new Broadway play cannot be original enough to entertain them. (10) However, both adaptations of movies (such as *The Full Monty*) and original musicals (such as *Rent*) can be good theater—and can make ticket buyers want to see it.

Indefinite Pronoun Antecedents

Most pronouns refer to a specific person or thing. **Indefinite pronouns**, however, do not refer to any particular person or thing.

For information on subject-verb agreement with indefinite pronouns as subjects, see 13E.

Most indefinite pronouns are singular. When the indefinite pronoun antecedent is singular, use a singular pronoun to refer to it.

> Something was out of its usual place. (*Something* is singular, so it is used with the singular pronoun *its.*)

Singular Indefinite Pronouns

another	everybody	no one
anybody	everyone	nothing
anyone	everything	one
anything	much	somebody
each	neither	someone
either	nobody	something

Writing Tip

Some indefinite pronouns (such as *all, any, more, most, none,* and *some*) can be either singular or plural (*All is lost; All were qualified.*).

FOCUS Singular Indefinite Pronouns with *Of*

The singular indefinite pronouns *each, either, neither,* and *one* are often used in phrases with *of*—*each of, either of, neither of, one of.* In such phrases, these indefinite pronoun antecedents are always singular and take singular pronouns.

> Each of the games has its [not *their*] own rules.

Some indefinite pronouns are plural. When the indefinite pronoun antecedent is plural, use a plural pronoun to refer to it.

The whole group wanted to go swimming, but few had brought their bathing suits. (*Few* is plural, so it is used with the plural pronoun *their.*)

Plural Indefinite Pronouns

both
few
many
others
several

Student Voices

My grammar checker tells me when I've used a word like everyone *with* he. *Then, I use a plural noun like* the people *instead.*

Heather Blaine

FOCUS Using *His* or *Her* with Indefinite Pronouns

Singular indefinite pronouns that refer to people—such as *anybody, anyone, everybody, everyone, somebody,* and *someone*—require a singular pronoun, such as *his.*

However, using the singular pronoun *his* to refer to words such as these suggests that the indefinite pronoun refers to a male. Using *his or her* is an improvement because it suggests that the indefinite pronoun may refer to either a male or a female.

Everyone must revise his or her work.

When used over and over again, however, *he or she, him or her,* and *his or her* can create wordy, repetitive sentences. Often, the best solution is to use a plural noun instead of the indefinite pronoun.

All students must revise their work.

◆ PRACTICE 19.7

In each of the following sentences, circle the indefinite pronoun. Then, circle the pronoun in parentheses that refers to the indefinite pronoun antecedent.

Example: Neither my sister Alyssa nor her best friend can do homework without listening to (her/their) radio.

1. Everyone in the business world has to be able to do several tasks at once at (his or her/their) job.

2. People once said that everything should be done in (its/their) own time, but that idea has been replaced at many offices.
3. Instead, anyone searching the classified ads for (his or her/their) ideal job is likely to see the word *multitasking,* a computer term for doing several things at the same time.
4. Nobody who is unable to divide (his or her/their) attention should apply for a job that requires multitasking.
5. Many of today's adults learned to focus on one job at a time, and few sharpened (his or her/their) ability to multitask.
6. Teenagers, however, seem able to do many things simultaneously, and many can juggle (his or her/their) tasks with apparent ease.
7. Each of my two teenage sisters spends (her/their) evening talking on the telephone, listening to CDs, and reading e-mail at the same time.
8. When our parents objected, both of my sisters insisted that (she/they) could pay attention to all three tasks.
9. Either of them might do (her/their) math assignment in front of the television.
10. Everyone has (his or her/their) opinion about teenagers' multitasking.
11. Although some researchers have studied teenagers' and adults' brains, no one has devoted (his or her/their) research to the effects of multitasking on the brain.
12. Some psychologists are concerned about the way teenagers juggle tasks, and several have published books explaining (his or her/their) worries.
13. Multitasking may affect the ability to concentrate, and anybody who constantly does many simultaneous tasks may not work to (his or her/their) full potential.
14. Still, I expect at least one of my sisters to find (herself/themselves) in demand in the job market someday.
15. Businesses love people who can multitask, so someone will do (his or her/their) company a favor someday by hiring my sisters.

◆ PRACTICE 19.8

In the following passage, fill in each blank with an appropriate pronoun. Then, draw an arrow from the pronoun in the blank to its indefinite pronoun antecedent.

> **Example:** Nobody should forfeit __his or her__ chance to participate in the democratic process.

(1) Everyone who can vote should be sure to cast __________ ballot in an election. (2) My father always said, "Anyone who doesn't vote loses __________ right to complain about the way things are in this country." (3) Unfortunately, few of the people who are eligible to vote make __________ choice known on election day. (4) One of my neighbors devotes __________ time to getting out the vote, and this year I joined him. (5) I telephoned local residents and reminded each of them that __________ should vote on Tuesday. (6) Several who were elderly asked how __________ would get to the polling place. (7) One man, Mr. Jones, told me that either his daughter or his granddaughter would have to come from __________ home thirty miles away to drive him to the polls. (8) I called both and told __________ that I would take Mr. Jones to cast his vote. (9) Many in the United States who are younger take __________ voting responsibilities much less seriously than Mr. Jones. (10) We should all remember that everything we do has __________ consequences; our government works best when we all participate.

◆ PRACTICE 19.9

Edit the following sentences for errors in pronoun-antecedent agreement. In some sentences, substitute *his or her* for *their* when the antecedent is singular and could refer to a person of either gender. In other sentences, replace the antecedent with a plural word or phrase.

> **Example:** Everyone in the restaurant complained to ~~their~~ ^his or her^ waiter.

1. Someone left their key in the lock.
2. Each of the trees grows at their own rate.

3. Everyone on the platform missed their train.
4. Neither of the boys remembers their former home in Oregon.
5. One of the telemarketers hated making their calls at dinnertime.
6. Either Sandra or Emily should sign their name here.
7. Anyone would love to give this encyclopedia to their children.
8. None of these chairs will look as good as they did before the fire.
9. Everyone must e-mail their essays to the professor.
10. Each of us has our own cell phone.
11. Has anybody in this neighborhood lost their dog?
12. Everyone in the office bought their own lottery tickets.
13. Someone hung up without leaving their name or number on the answering machine.
14. Anyone with a drunk-driving conviction ought to have their license revoked.
15. Everyone thought the candidate was charming, but they did not want to vote for him.

Collective Noun Antecedents

Collective nouns are singular words (like *band* and *team*) that name a group of people or things. Because they are singular, collective noun antecedents are used with singular pronouns.

The band was very loud, but it was not very good.

In the sentence above, the collective noun *band* names a group of individual musicians, but it refers to them as a unit. Because *band* is singular, it is used with the singular pronoun *it*.

Frequently Used Collective Nouns

army	committee	government	pack
association	company	group	posse
band	crowd	jury	team
class	family	league	union
club	gang	mob	

Writing Tip

When you refer to a collective noun that is plural—for example, *bands, teams, unions*—you need to use a plural pronoun: *Both teams fired their coaches.*

◆ PRACTICE 19.10

In each of the following sentences, underline the antecedent. If the antecedent is a collective noun, write *coll* above it. Then, circle the correct pronoun in parentheses.

Example: The mob chased (its/their) victim.

1. A wolf pack sometimes tracks (its/their) prey for a long time.
2. Last night, our football team celebrated (its/their) first victory in two years.
3. The officers carried (its/their) guns all the time.
4. The oversight committee holds (its/their) meeting on the first Friday of every month.
5. The gang displayed (its/their) colors proudly.
6. The crowd roared (its/their) encouragement to the runners.
7. The class applauded (its/their) teacher, Mr. Henry, when he was voted Teacher of the Year.
8. The posse made (its/their) way across the plains.
9. The jury gave (its/their) decision to the court clerk.
10. Some people move (its/their) hands rapidly while speaking.

◆ PRACTICE 19.11

Edit the following passage for correct pronoun-antecedent agreement. First, determine the antecedent of each underlined pronoun. (Some antecedents will be compounds, some will be indefinite pronouns, and some will be collective nouns.) Next, cross out any pronoun that does not agree with its antecedent, and write the correct form above it. If the pronoun is correct, write *C*.

Example: Grant Fuhr and Tiger Woods won acclaim for ~~his~~ their athletic abilities.

(1) Golf and hockey are very different sports, but they have one thing in common: its players tend to be white. (2) In golf, this perception is changing; no one has broken the records of their sport more frequently than the golfer Tiger Woods. (3) Because of Woods, everyone has altered their view of what a professional golfer looks like. (4) Hockey, on the

other hand, is still waiting for its version of Tiger Woods; however, black hockey players are becoming more common. (5) Willie O'Ree and Grant Fuhr, for example, have been impressive in his contributions to hockey. (6) The National Hockey League broke their color barrier in 1958 when O'Ree joined the Boston Bruins. (7) O'Ree noticed that American fans and Canadian fans differed in their reactions to him: the Americans were more likely to shout racist remarks. (8) Although O'Ree stopped playing in 1961, the National Hockey League recently hired him to head their Diversity Task Force. (9) The Edmonton Oilers and the Calgary Flames have been fortunate to have Fuhr, who is expected to end up in the Hockey Hall of Fame, as its goalie. (10) Either Fuhr or O'Ree can be a role model for their fans even though they are not as well known as Tiger Woods.

D Eliminating Vague and Unnecessary Pronouns

Vague and unnecessary pronouns clutter up your writing. Eliminating them will make your writing clearer and easier for readers to follow.

Vague Pronouns

A pronoun should always refer to a specific antecedent. When a pronoun has no antecedent, it confuses readers. The pronouns *it* and *they* can be particularly troublesome.

VAGUE PRONOUN It says in today's paper that overcrowded prisons are a serious problem. (Who says overcrowded prisons are a problem?)

VAGUE PRONOUN On the news, they said city workers would strike. (Who said city workers would strike?)

When you use *it* or *they* as the subject of a sentence, check carefully to be sure the pronoun refers to a specific antecedent in the sentence. If it does not, delete it, or replace it with a noun that communicates your meaning to readers.

REVISED An editorial in today's paper says that overcrowded prisons are a serious problem.

REVISED On the news, the reporter said city workers would strike.

Writing Tip

Only an intensive pronoun can come right after its antecedent: *I myself prefer to wait.* (See 19G.)

Unnecessary Pronouns

When a pronoun directly follows its antecedent, it is usually unnecessary.

UNNECESSARY PRONOUN The librarian, he recommended *Beloved.*

In the above sentence, the pronoun *he* serves no purpose. Readers do not need to be directed back to the pronoun's antecedent (the noun *librarian*) because it appears right before the pronoun. The pronoun should therefore be eliminated.

REVISED The librarian recommended *Beloved.*

◆ PRACTICE 19.12

The following sentences contain vague and unnecessary pronouns. Rewrite each sentence correctly on the lines below it.

Example: On the Web site, it claimed that a spaceship was following the comet.

The Web site claimed that a spaceship was following the comet.

1. In Canada, they have many sparsely populated areas.

2. My cat, he likes to play in water.

3. The video game that I bought, it broke almost immediately.

4. In the pamphlet, it explained how AIDS is transmitted.

5. Her granddaughter, she lives in another state.

6. On that game show, they know the answers to very difficult questions.

7. These apples, they were damaged in the hailstorm.

____

____

8. On the sidewalk, they were all watching the television in the store window.

____

____

9. The acrobat, he almost fell off the tightrope.

____

____

10. In her class, they do not explain grammar clearly enough.

____

____

E Understanding Pronoun Case

A **personal pronoun**—a pronoun that refers to a particular person or thing—changes form according to the way it functions in a sentence. Personal pronouns can be *subjective, objective,* or *possessive.*

Personal Pronouns

Subjective Case	Objective Case	Possessive Case
I	me	my, mine
he	him	his
she	her	her, hers
it	it	its
we	us	our, ours
you	you	your, yours
they	them	their, theirs
who	whom	whose
whoever	whomever	

When a pronoun functions as a subject, it is in the **subjective case**.

> She walked along the beach looking for seashells. (The pronoun *She* is the sentence's subject.)

When a pronoun functions as an object, it is in the **objective case**.

> Walking along the beach, Lucia saw them. (The pronoun *them* is the direct object of the verb *saw.*)

FOCUS Objects

A **direct object** is a noun or pronoun that receives the action of the verb.

Lucia saw seashells. (What did Lucia see?)

Lucia saw them. (What did Lucia see?)

An **indirect object** is the noun or pronoun that has received or benefited from the action of the verb.

Lucia brought Greg a seashell. (For whom did Lucia bring a seashell?)

Lucia brought him a seashell. (For whom did Lucia bring a seashell?)

A word or word group introduced by a preposition is called the **object of the preposition**. (See 6C.)

Lucia gave some seashells to Chris and Kelly. (To whom did Lucia give some seashells?)

Lucia gave some seashells to them. (To whom did Lucia give some seashells?)

Lucia brought him a seashell. (The pronoun *him* is the indirect object of the verb *brought.*)

Lucia gave some seashells to them. (The pronoun *them* is the object of the preposition *to.*)

When a pronoun shows ownership, it is in the **possessive case**.

Tuan rode his bike to work. (The bike belongs to Tuan.)

Kate and Alex took their bikes, too. (The bikes belong to Kate and Alex.)

◆ PRACTICE 19.13

Above each of the underlined pronouns, indicate whether it is subjective (S), objective (O), or possessive (P).

Example: She gave me my first kiss. (S, O, P)

1. He played basketball in his first two years of high school.
2. We asked her if she would share her umbrella with us.

3. For a moment, I couldn't remember my name.
4. It gave them great satisfaction to help others.
5. Is this drink mine or yours?
6. You must help me.
7. This is a gift from me to her.
8. The card says, "Happy birthday to you from all of us."
9. Their anniversary is next week, so we are having a party for them at our house.
10. Your car is better than ours or theirs.

PRACTICE 19.14

Above each of the underlined objective case pronouns, indicate whether it is a direct object (DO), an indirect object (IO), or the object of a preposition (OP).

Example: My friends played a good trick on me. (OP)

1. The president gave him a special citation.
2. The package was sent to them by mistake.
3. The transit officer helped us when we got lost.
4. The band dedicated the last song to her.
5. The owner of the wallet rewarded him very generously.
6. All the attention embarrassed us.
7. I mailed you that check weeks ago.
8. The family always looks to her for the final answer.
9. The clerk handed me my change.
10. Stop tickling me.

F Solving Special Problems with Pronoun Case

When you are trying to decide which pronoun case to use, pronouns in *compounds,* pronouns in *comparisons,* and the pronouns *who* and *whom* can sometimes be confusing.

Pronouns in Compounds

Sometimes, a pronoun is linked to a noun or to another pronoun with *and* or *or* to form a **compound**.

The tutor and I met in the writing lab.

He and I worked to revise my paper.

To decide whether to use the subjective or objective case for a pronoun in a compound, follow the same rules you would apply for a pronoun that is not part of a compound.

- If the compound in which the pronoun appears is the subject of the sentence, use the subjective case.

  Kia and I [not *me*] like rap music.

  She and I [not *me*] went to a concert.

- If the compound in which the pronoun appears is the object of the verb or the object of a preposition, use the objective case.

  The personnel office sent my friend and me [not *I*] the application forms. (object of the verb)

  There is a lot of competition between her and me [not *I*] for this job. (object of the preposition)

FOCUS Choosing Pronouns in Compounds

To determine which pronoun case to use in a compound that links a noun and a pronoun, drop the noun and rewrite the sentence with just the pronoun.

Kia and [*I* or *me?*] like rap music.

I like rap music. (not *Me like rap music.*)

Kia and I like rap music.

◆ PRACTICE 19.15

In each blank, write the correct form (subjective or objective) of the pronouns in parentheses.

Example: We want ___her___ (she/her) to admit her mistake.

1. I asked Marisa and __________ (he/him) to the party.
2. My brother and __________ (I/me) are often mistaken for each other.
3. Many people cannot tell __________ (he/him) and __________ (I/me) apart.
4. The boss divided responsibility for the job between __________ (they/them) and __________ (we/us).

5. __________ (She/Her) and her mother have not spoken in years.
6. Nothing could bring my old girlfriend and __________ (I/me) back together again.
7. __________ (They/Them) and __________ (I/me) have nothing in common.
8. The story about the cockroach always amused Liz and __________ (she/her).
9. I think that __________ (they/them) and their grandchildren should see each other more often.
10. This is the last chance for __________ (he/him) and __________ (I/me).

Pronouns in Comparisons

Sometimes, a pronoun appears after the words *than* or *as* in a **comparison**.

Neil is hungrier than I.

Marriage changed Sonia as much as him.

To decide whether to use the subjective or objective case, write in the words needed to complete the comparison. If the pronoun is a subject, use the subjective case.

Neil is hungrier than I [am].

If the pronoun is an object, use the objective case.

Marriage changed Sonia as much as [it changed] him.

FOCUS Choosing Pronouns in Comparisons

Sometimes, the pronoun you choose can change the meaning of your sentence. For example, if you say, "She likes potato chips more than I," you mean that she likes potato chips more than you like potato chips.

She likes potato chips more than I [do].

If, however, you say, "She likes potato chips more than me," you mean that she likes potato chips more than she likes you.

She likes potato chips more than [she likes] me.

◆ PRACTICE 19.16

In each blank, write the correct form (subjective or objective) of the pronouns in parentheses. In brackets, add the word or words needed to complete the comparison.

Example: My sister is very unemotional; the movie *Titanic* affected me much more than *[it affected] her* (she/her).

1. No one could be less qualified than __________ (he/him).
2. Marisol worked harder than __________ (he/him), but he took all the credit.
3. You eat much more than __________ (I/me), so how do you stay so thin?
4. David exercises more regularly than __________ (she/her), and it shows.
5. So many people in my family have died young that a visit to the doctor could not frighten you more than __________ (I/me).
6. I play the piano better than __________ (they/them).
7. The trip to Florida cost you much more than __________ (we/us).
8. Francis has a much larger house than __________ (they/them) even though his family is smaller.
9. Clarence pays you a higher hourly rate than __________ (she/her).
10. In these photos, you look less tired than __________ (we/us).

Who and *Whom*

Who is a pronoun that functions as a subject; *whom* is a pronoun that functions as an object. To determine whether to use *who* or *whom,* you need to know how the pronoun functions within the clause in which it appears.

- When the pronoun is the subject of the clause, use *who.*

  I wonder who teaches that course. (*Who* is the subject of the clause *who teaches that course.*)

- When the pronoun is the object, use *whom*.

  I wonder to whom the course will appeal. (*Whom* is the object of the preposition *to* in the clause *to whom the course will appeal.*)

  Mr. Brennan is the instructor whom we all like. (*Whom* is the direct object of the verb *like* in the clause *whom we all like.*)

Writing Tip

In conversation, people often use *who* for both the subjective case (*I wonder who teaches that course*) and the objective case (*I wonder who this course will appeal to*). In writing, always use *whom* for the objective case: *I wonder to whom this course will appeal.*

◆ PRACTICE 19.17

In each of the following sentences, circle the correct form of *who* or *whom* in parentheses.

Example: Students (who/whom) need a break from studying should try out for the play.

1. Anyone (who/whom) auditioned for the high school musical had to sing and dance.
2. The choreographer with (who/whom) the drama teacher worked had little experience with high school students.
3. Many students (who/whom) enjoyed helping with the production did not want to appear onstage.
4. The girl (who/whom) the music teacher wanted to be the star did not get the part.
5. Ms. Morgan, (who/whom) taught drama, did not want her to star in the musical.
6. Ms. Morgan, (who/whom) complained that the girl had never learned her lines, argued for Janelle, a shy sophomore.
7. Few other teachers knew (who/whom) Janelle was.
8. Fortunately, she turned out to be someone for (who/whom) acting was easy.
9. The boy (who/whom) played her love interest was a football star.
10. He was the actor (who/whom) got the most applause.

G Identifying Reflexive and Intensive Pronouns

Like other pronouns, *reflexive pronouns* and *intensive pronouns* always agree with their antecedents. Although these two kinds of pronouns have different functions, their forms are exactly the same.

Reflexive Pronouns

Reflexive pronouns always end in *-self* (singular) or *-selves* (p
pronouns indicate that people or things did something to them
themselves.

Christina bought herself a new watch.

You need to pace yourself when you exercise.

Eliza and Jill made themselves a plate of nachos.

Intensive Pronouns

Intensive pronouns also end in *-self* or *-selves*. Unlike reflex
however, they always appear directly after their anteceden
pronouns are used for emphasis.

I myself have a friend with an eating disorder.

The actor himself did all the dangerous stunts.

They themselves questioned their motives.

Reflexive and Intensive Pronouns

Singular Forms

Antecedent	*Reflexive or Intensive Pronoun*
I	myself
you	yourself
he	himself
she	herself
it	itself

Plural Forms

Antecedent	*Reflexive or Intensive Pronoun*
we	ourselves
you	yourselves
they	themselves

◆ PRACTICE 19.18

In each of the following sentences, fill in the correct refle
pronoun.

Example: You should take ___yourselves___
to celebrate your anniversary.

1. She ________________ had always walked to
told her children that it would be good for them to d
2. The legislators gave ________________ a raise

3. The cat curled ______________ up on the bedspread and dozed off.
4. Einstein ______________ could not have solved that algebra problem.
5. I caught a frightening glimpse of ______________ in the mirror after my haircut.
6. My sister hates to weigh ______________ at the doctor's office.
7. If you fall, pick ______________ up and start over again.
8. You ______________ told me that this material would not be on the final exam.
9. The toddlers covered ______________ with mud before their mother could stop them.
10. They bought the property for thousands of dollars, but they tore down the house ______________ almost immediately afterward.

REVISING AND EDITING

Look back at your response to the Seeing and Writing exercise on page 281. Underline every pronoun you have used. Then, check your work carefully to be sure that all your pronouns and antecedents agree. (Remember, singular pronouns must refer to singular antecedents, and plural pronouns must refer to plural antecedents.) Then, eliminate any vague or unnecessary pronouns. Finally, check to make sure you have used correct pronoun case.

CHAPTER REVIEW

EDITING PRACTICE

Read the following essay, which contains pronoun errors. Check for errors in pronoun case and pronoun-antecedent agreement as well as for any vague or unnecessary pronouns. Then, make any editing changes you think are necessary. The first sentence has been edited for you.

School Schedules: Time for a New Tradition

~~Every~~ All working ~~parent worries~~ parents worry at least a little about their school-aged children being at home alone every afternoon. On the news every night, they talk about criminals, peer pressure, and drugs that could endanger unsupervised young people. Many parents, they feel guilty about having to be at work while their children are at home after school. Many employers and politicians whom have tried to improve day care have not yet done much to solve the problem of school days that are shorter than work days.

My family illustrates this problem. Me and my younger brother Jaime had strict instructions from our parents about what to do after school. Him and I were supposed to tell callers that our parents were not at home. We had to lock ourself in the apartment after school and not allow anybody to come inside unless we were expecting them. Our parents called us every day at 3:30 even though they worked at a factory where they had trouble getting to a telephone. Jaime always behaved better than me, but both of us were capable of getting into trouble before our parents came home. Any teenager will find themselves tempted by so much free time.

In an article I read, it suggested a solution to this problem: a longer school day and school year. A middle school or high school today still has their school calendar set by the needs of farm families. The school day ends at three o'clock because anyone living on a farm needs the time before dark to do their chores. Summer, it is a time for harvesting, so no school is held during that time. However, they no longer need to schedule school around farming in most parts of the United States today. Very few children whom attend school now live on working farms. Why shouldn't a child be in school during their parents' business day?

This suggestion may horrify every student in the United States, but it could eventually help them. Students in Europe and Japan attend about forty more days of school each year than we American students. A longer

school day could keep young Americans safer, put his or her parents' minds at ease, and perhaps help America become more competitive. Tradition is the only reason for the short school day and short school year in the United States. Perhaps a new tradition is needed.

◆ COLLABORATIVE ACTIVITIES

1. Working in a small group, write a sentence with a compound subject on a sheet of paper, and then pass the sheet to the person on your left. On the sheet you get from the person on your right, write a new sentence that includes a pronoun that refers to the compound subject that student wrote, and then pass your sheet to the person on your left. On the next sheet you get, write a new sentence using *who* or *whom* to refer to the subject on that sheet. Repeat this process until each of you has a paragraph.
2. Choose the paragraph from activity 1 that your group likes best. Then, exchange paragraphs with another group. Check each other's work, making sure that pronoun case and pronoun-antecedent agreement are correct.
3. Turn your group's paragraph from activity 2 into a test for another group in your class. After you receive the corrected version of your paragraph from another group, go through the paragraph and add errors in pronoun-antecedent agreement and pronoun case. Next, exchange paragraphs with a different group. Try to correct every error introduced in the other group's test paragraph.

COMPOSING ORIGINAL SENTENCES

4. Working as a group, write five original sentences. Be sure to use at least one indefinite pronoun, at least one compound subject, and at least one comparison with a pronoun. Then, check pronoun case and pronoun-antecedent agreement carefully. When you have finished, check the sentences again to make sure you have corrected any errors in grammar, punctuation, or spelling.

☑ REVIEW CHECKLIST: Pronouns

- A pronoun is a word that takes the place of a noun or another pronoun. (See 19A.)
- The word to which a pronoun refers is called the pronoun's antecedent. (See 19B.)

(continued on the following page)

(continued from the previous page)

- Compound antecedents connected by *and* are plural and are used with plural pronouns. Compound antecedents connected by *or* may take singular or plural pronouns. (See 19C.)
- Most indefinite pronoun antecedents are singular. Therefore, they are used with singular pronouns. (See 19C.)
- Collective noun antecedents are singular and must be used with singular pronouns. (See 19C.)
- A pronoun should always refer to a specific antecedent. (See 19D.)
- When a pronoun directly follows its antecedent, it is usually unnecessary. (See 19D.)
- Personal pronouns can be in the subjective, objective, or possessive case. (See 19E.)
- Pronouns present special problems when they are used in compounds and comparisons. The pronouns *who* and *whom* also cause problems. (See 19F.)
- Reflexive pronouns and intensive pronouns must agree with their antecedents in person and number. (See 19G.)

CHAPTER

20

Adjectives and Adverbs

PREVIEW

In this chapter, you will learn

- to identify adjectives and adverbs (20A)
- to understand comparatives and superlatives (20B)
- to identify demonstrative adjectives (20C)

SEEING AND WRITING

Look at the picture above, and then write a paragraph in which you describe the costume you would wear to this party. Why would you choose this costume?

Word Power

masquerade (verb) to wear a mask or disguise; (noun) a costume party at which guests wear masks

Student Voices

I used to use the same adjectives—good, nice, unique, bad—*over and over again. Now, I try to think of more specific words.*

Erin Franks

A Identifying Adjectives and Adverbs

Adjectives and adverbs are words that modify—that is, describe or identify—other words. By using these modifying words, you can make your sentences more precise and more interesting.

> **Writing Tip**
>
> Some adjectives, such as *Spanish,* are capitalized because they are formed from proper nouns. (Proper nouns name particular people, animals, places, or things.) For more on proper nouns, see 18A.

Identifying Adjectives

An **adjective** answers the questions *What kind? Which one?* or *How many?* Adjectives modify nouns or pronouns.

> The Spanish city of Madrid has exciting nightlife. (The adjective *Spanish* modifies the noun *city;* the adjective *exciting* modifies the noun *nightlife.*)
>
> It is lively because of its many clubs and tapas bars. (The adjective *lively* modifies the pronoun *it.*)

PRACTICE 20.1

Write an adjective from the list below in each of the blanks in the following paragraph. Cross each adjective off the list as you use it. Be sure to choose an adjective that makes sense in each sentence.

> **Example:** I am *careful* to think before I act.

quick	heavy	unusual	easy	uncomfortable
happy	rude	~~careful~~	brave	noisy

(1) I hardly ever take chances. (2) I am not very ____________, so I try to avoid threatening situations. (3) It is ____________ for me to argue with someone bigger because I am ____________ with any kind of violence. (4) Recently, however, I was annoyed by a ____________ party in the apartment below me. (5) The ____________ sound of the bass guitar came through the floor. (6) Without stopping to think, I made the ____________ decision to go downstairs and complain. (7) The guy who opened the door was six feet five inches tall, covered in leather, chains, and tattoos. (8) This is not going to be ____________, I thought. (9) "Excuse me," I said. (10) "I hate to be ____________, but I would appreciate your turning the music down." (11) The guy in leather looked at me for a minute. (12) Then, he said, "Because you asked so politely, I'll be ____________ to turn the music down."

Identifying Adverbs

An **adverb** answers the questions *How? Why? When? Where?* or *To what extent?* Adverbs modify verbs, adjectives, or other adverbs.

> The huge Doberman barked angrily. (The adverb *angrily* modifies the verb *barked.*)

Still, we felt quite safe. (The adverb *quite* modifies the adjective *safe.*)

Very slowly, we held out a big juicy steak. (The adverb *very* modifies the adverb *slowly.*)

PRACTICE 20.2

Write an adverb from the list below in each of the blanks in the following paragraph. Cross each adverb off the list as you use it. Be sure to choose an adverb that makes sense in each sentence.

Example: I waited ___wearily___ for the train.

quickly	heavily	easily	unusually	uncomfortably
noisily	rudely	bravely	really	~~wearily~~

(1) The subway train screeched ________ into the station. (2) The doors ________ slid open, and departing passengers ________ elbowed their way out. (3) Entering passengers struggled ________ through the narrow doors. (4) It was ________ hot for April, and people were sweating ________ in the steamy underground tunnel. (5) I stood jammed ________ in the middle of the car, praying I'd be able to wriggle out ________ when I reached my stop. (6) What a ________ great way to start the work day!

Telling Adjectives and Adverbs Apart

Many adverbs are formed when the ending *-ly* is added to an adjective.

Adjective	*Adverb*
bad	badly
slow	slowly
nice	nicely
quick	quickly
quiet	quietly
real	really

Writing Tip

Some adjectives—*lovely, friendly,* and *lively,* for example—end in *-ly*. Be careful not to use these words as adverbs.

Because the adjective and adverb forms of these words are so similar, you may sometimes be confused about which form to use in a sentence. Remember, adjectives modify nouns or pronouns; adverbs modify verbs, adjectives, or other adverbs.

ADJECTIVE Kim likes the slow dances. (*Slow* modifies the noun *dances.*)

ADVERB Kim likes to dance slowly. (*Slowly* modifies the verb *dance.*)

Writing Tip

The word *fast* has the same form whether it is used as an adjective or as an adverb. *Tracy has a fast car. It goes as fast as a sportscar.*

ADJECTIVE Mark Twain's real name was Samuel L. Clemens. (*Real* modifies the noun *name.*)

ADVERB It was really generous of him to donate his time. (*Really* modifies the adjective *generous.*)

◆ PRACTICE 20.3

In the following passage, circle the correct form (adjective or adverb) from the choices in parentheses.

> **Example:** Whether they realize it or not, most people take fashion (serious/seriously).

(1) The ways people dress provide (interesting/interestingly) insights into how they view their social roles. (2) Young people who identify themselves (main/mainly) as music fans often dress the part. (3) Those who love punk rock, reggae, and hip-hop wear (different/differently) clothing, shoes, and jewelry. (4) Their fashions are likely to resemble the (particular/particularly) look of the recording stars they admire. (5) Such style serves two purposes: fans of (similar/similarly) music can recognize each other by their outfits, and these young people can also flaunt their status as outsiders. (6) Of course, punk rockers are not the only ones who choose fashions that make others look at them (strange/strangely). (7) Some people (active/actively) try to wear clothes that make them seem dangerous. (8) Those who wear gang colors are an (obvious/obviously) example. (9) Many young people following this fashion hope to move through dangerous neighborhoods (safe/safely). (10) Others (simple/simply) want to belong to a powerful group. (11) Most people with (real/really) power, however, use fashion in other ways. (12) Instead of trying to stand out, they want others to take them (serious/seriously). (13) Therefore, political leaders and business executives tend to dress (conservative/conservatively). (14) Through fashion, (near/nearly) everyone reveals whether or not he or she wants to be a member of mainstream society. (15) For an observer who knows the culture, style can be (extreme/extremely) revealing.

FOCUS *Good* and *Well*

Be careful not to confuse *good* and *well.* Unlike regular adjectives, whose adverb forms add the ending *-ly,* the adjective *good* is irregular. Its adverb form is *well.*

Remember, *good* is an adjective; *well* is an adverb. Use *good* to modify a noun or pronoun; use *well* to modify a verb, an adjective, or another adverb.

ADJECTIVE John Steinbeck was a good writer. (*Good* modifies the noun *writer.*)

ADVERB He wrote particularly well in the novel *The Grapes of Wrath.* (*Well* modifies the verb *wrote.*)

However, always use *well* when you are describing someone's health.

He really didn't feel *well* [not *good*] after the pie-eating contest.

◆ PRACTICE 20.4

In the following passage, circle the correct form (*good* or *well*) in parentheses.

Example: Have Americans treated U.S. veterans (good/well) enough?

(1) Some U.S. veterans of twentieth-century wars were treated (good/well); others, unfortunately, were not. (2) In the 1940s, most American veterans of World War II came home to a (good/well) life. (3) No one doubted that the men and women had done a (good/well) thing by going to war. (4) A grateful nation wanted these former soldiers to be (good/well) provided for. (5) The G.I. Bill made sure that many of them were able to get a (good/well) education. (6) In the prosperous postwar economy, (good/well) jobs were not difficult to find. (7) Unfortunately, times were not nearly as (good/well) for the returning veterans of the Vietnam War. (8) Many citizens of the United States felt that the U.S. involvement in that war was not a (good/well) idea. (9) Some people blamed the soldiers who had gone to Vietnam, even though most of them

had done their jobs as (good/well) as they could. (10) Rather than being (good/well) respected, the returning veterans were sometimes despised. (11) Injured soldiers often ended up in veterans' hospitals that were not (good/well) staffed. (12) These hospitals were rarely a (good/well) place for a wounded soldier to recover. (13) If a patient got (good/well) enough to leave, he or she was unlikely to get the kind of help offered to the veterans of World War II. (14) Many Americans were proud of the U.S. role in World War II, but most, including many Vietnam veterans, did not feel (good/well) about the American participation in the disastrous war in Vietnam. (15) In the future, Americans would do (good/well) to separate their feelings about a war from their feelings about the people who suffer through it.

B Understanding Comparatives and Superlatives

Adjectives and adverbs are sometimes used to compare two or more people or things.The **comparative form** of an adjective or adverb compares two people or things. The **superlative form** of an adjective or adverb compares more than two people or things. Special forms of the adjectives and adverbs are used to indicate these comparisons.

ADJECTIVE These shoes are ugly.

COMPARATIVE The brown shoes are uglier than the black ones.

SUPERLATIVE The purple ones are the ugliest of all.

ADVERB Will you be able to get home soon?

COMPARATIVE I may not be home until midnight, but I will try to get there sooner.

SUPERLATIVE Unfortunately, the soonest I can leave work is 7:30.

FOCUS Adverbs with No Comparative or Superlative Forms

Some adverbs that answer the question *To what degree?*—such as *almost, very, somewhat, quite, extremely, rather,* and *moderately*—do not have comparative or superlative forms.

Forming Comparatives and Superlatives

Adjectives and adverbs form the comparative with *-er* or *more* and the superlative with *-est* or *most.*

ADJECTIVES

To form the comparative of a one-syllable adjective, add *-er.* To form the superlative of a one-syllable adjective, add *-est.*

young   younger   youngest

To form the comparative of an adjective that has two or more syllables, use *more.* To form the superlative of an adjective that has two or more syllables, use *most.*

beautiful   more beautiful   most beautiful

ADVERBS

Most adverbs end in *-ly.* To form the comparative of an adverb that ends in *-ly,* use *more.* To form the superlative of an adverb that ends in *-ly,* use *most.*

slowly   more slowly   most slowly

Some other adverbs form the comparative with *-er* and the superlative with *-est.*

soon   sooner   soonest

Writing Tip

Two-syllable adjectives ending in *-y* do not form the comparative and superlative with *more* and *most*. Instead, they change the *y* to an *i* and then add *-er* or *-est:* for example, *funny, funnier, funniest.*

Solving Special Problems with Comparatives and Superlatives

The following four rules will help you avoid errors with comparatives and superlatives.

1. Never use both *-er* and *more* to form the comparative.

   The comic could have been a lot funnier. (not *more funnier*)

2. Never use both *-est* and *most* to form the superlative.

   Scream was the scariest (not *most scariest*) movie I ever saw.

3. Never use the superlative when you are comparing only two things.

   Beth is the younger (not *youngest*) of the two sisters.

4. Never use the comparative when you are comparing more than two things.

   This is the worst (not *worse*) of my four part-time jobs.

Student Voices

I need to remember that unique *means "the only one." This helps remind me that I can't ever write "more unique" or "most unique."*

Haley Sav

◆ PRACTICE 20.5

In the blank at the right, fill in the comparative form of each adjective or adverb.

Examples

rich ___richer___

embarrassed ___more embarrassed___

1. strong ______
2. playful ______
3. quickly ______
4. traditional ______
5. neat ______
6. neatly ______
7. fair ______
8. mature ______
9. young ______
10. intense ______
11. blue ______
12. new ______
13. easy ______
14. easily ______
15. useful ______
16. poor ______
17. hard ______
18. gently ______
19. deep ______
20. lazy ______

◆ PRACTICE 20.6

In the blank at the right, fill in the superlative form of each adjective or adverb.

Examples

rich ___richest___

embarrassed ___most embarrassed___

1. strong ______
2. playful ______
3. quickly ______
4. traditional ______
5. neat ______
6. neatly ______
7. fair ______
8. mature ______
9. young ______
10. intense ______
11. blue ______
12. new ______
13. easy ______
14. easily ______
15. useful ______
16. poor ______
17. hard ______
18. gently ______
19. deep ______
20. lazy ______

◆ PRACTICE 20.7

Fill in the correct comparative form of the word in parentheses.

Example: Finding time to exercise is no ___more difficult___ (difficult) than finding time to watch television.

1. Working people today often feel ______________ (busy) than ever before.
2. They want to do every task ______________ (efficient).
3. People with desk jobs want to be ______________ (active).
4. Many join gyms to build ______________ (healthy), ______________ (muscular) bodies.
5. Some people hire personal trainers so that they can exercise ______________ (effective).
6. They believe that a workout tailored for their needs will benefit them ______________ (fast) than a generic workout.
7. Looking for a personal trainer online can be ______________ (convenient) than finding one in person.
8. Reputable online sites may ask their trainers to meet ______________ (high) standards than those required by a local gym.
9. Of course, Internet shoppers always need to be ______________ (careful) than other consumers to check claims before making a purchase.
10. Finally, consumers must remember that finding a trainer is much ______________ (easy) accomplished than sticking with an exercise program.

◆ PRACTICE 20.8

Fill in the correct superlative form of the word in parentheses.

Example: Sports fans must be the ___most obsessive___ (obsessive) people in the world.

(1) Extreme sports often seem to be designed to prove which athlete is the ______________ (crazy). (2) The human obsession with extremes is not new, however; records showing who could run the

__________________ (fast) or swim the __________________ (far) go back more than a century. (3) Only the __________________ (tiny) minority of people will ever compete in any sport well enough to approach a world record. (4) Anyone else who wants to be a record-holder must scan the *Guinness Book of World Records* to find the record he or she can __________________ (easy) break. (5) Athletic ability is not the __________________ (necessary) skill for many events in the *Guinness Book of World Records.* (6) One young man simply stayed awake for the __________________ (long) period on record. (7) Another grew to the __________________ (great) height seen in modern times. (8) Of course, his record would be one of the __________________ (difficult) to break. (9) Growing hair and fingernails and peeling an apple will never be Olympic sports, but people have set some of the __________________ (surprising) records in those events. (10) After looking through the *Guinness Book of World Records,* many people conclude that extreme sports are not, after all, the __________________ (bizarre) way a person can spend time.

FOCUS *Good/Well* and *Bad/Badly*

The adjectives *good* and *bad* and their adverb forms, *well* and *badly,* are irregular. They do not form the comparative and superlative in the same way other adjectives and adverbs do. Because their forms are so irregular, you must memorize them.

Adjective	*Comparative Form*	*Superlative Form*
good	better	best
bad	worse	worst

Adverb	*Comparative Form*	*Superlative Form*
well	better	best
badly	worse	worst

◆ PRACTICE 20.9

Fill in the correct comparative or superlative form of *good, well, bad,* or *badly.*

Example: There is nothing <u>worse</u> (bad) than getting one telemarketing call after another.

1. One of the ________ (good) options for people who are tired of getting telemarketing calls is the do-not-call list.
2. The ________ (bad) telemarketing experience of my life was the night I got sixteen calls between 6 and 8 p.m.
3. I had never wanted anything ________ (badly) than I wanted to stop the harassment.
4. I considered changing my telephone number, but a local consumer advocate gave me a ________ (good) idea.
5. That evening, I was the ________ (well) prepared I had ever been for telemarketing calls.
6. The first telemarketer mangled my name even ________ (badly) than usual.
7. When he asked how I was, I told him that I felt ________ (well) than I had in a long time.
8. Mispronouncing my name in several different ways, he garbled it the ________ (badly) just before I interrupted him to ask to be put on the do-not-call list.
9. He reacted ________ (well) than I had expected; he thanked me politely for my time and hung up.
10. The ________ (bad) part of the do-not-call list was waiting thirty days for it to take effect, but since then, my evenings have been peaceful.

C Identifying Demonstrative Adjectives

Demonstrative adjectives do not describe other words. These adjectives—*this, that, these,* and *those*—simply identify particular nouns.

This and *that* identify singular nouns.

<u>This</u> book is much more interesting than <u>that</u> one.

These and *those* identify plural nouns.

<u>These</u> books are novels, but <u>those</u> books are biographies.

◆ PRACTICE 20.10

In the following passage, circle the correct form of the demonstrative adjective in parentheses.

Example: (That/Those) women who read maps well may be unusual.

(1) Many people claim that men's and women's brains work differently and that (this/these) differences can lead to misunderstandings between the sexes. (2) Not everyone believes (this/these) theory. (3) In fact, some people fear that generalizations about men and women make us forget that (this/these) woman or (that/those) man may be much different from the "average" woman or man. (4) A recent study found that men tend to be better at reading maps than women; (this/these) study does not, however, prove that women cannot read maps. (5) A man is more likely to drive aggressively, but (this/these) fact does not mean that every man suffers from road rage. (6) Women are generally more interested in talking about feelings than men are, but some of (that/those) women are more private than others. (7) If a man does not like sports, does (that/those) make him less of a man? (8) (That/Those) people who believe in generalizations must be careful not to conclude too much. (9) They should always be prepared to consider (this/these) or (that/those) person as an exception to the rule. (10) Every person has unique characteristics, and (this/these) are not always consistent with expectations based on gender.

■ REVISING AND EDITING

Look back at your response to the Seeing and Writing exercise on page 307. First, underline every adjective and adverb. Have you used any comparatives or superlatives? Any demonstrative adjectives? If so, check to be sure you have used the correct forms. Then, add or substitute descriptive words you need to make your writing more precise and more interesting.

CHAPTER REVIEW

EDITING PRACTICE

Read the following essay, which contains errors in the use of adjectives and adverbs. Make any changes necessary to correct adjectives that are incorrectly used instead of adverbs, adverbs that are incorrectly used instead of adjectives, errors in the use of comparatives and superlatives, and errors in the use of demonstrative adjectives. You may also add adjectives or adverbs that you feel would make the writer's ideas clearer or more specific. The first sentence has been edited for you.

Satanic Corporations?

These days, most people have heard that those ~~real~~ *really* bizarre stories about kidney thieves and microwaved pets are simply urban legends. This myths are everywhere—in newspapers, on the radio, and on the Internet. Some of the unbelievablest urban legends make people suspicious right away. However, incredible large numbers of people are still willing to believe rumors about a big corporation. The more outrageouser the claims about the corporation, the more likely it is that people will put out the word to boycott the company's products.

The famousest urban legend about a corporation claims that the president of Procter & Gamble appeared on television in the 1980s to say that he was a Satanist. These executive also reportedly said that he gave 10 percent of the company's profits to the Church of Satan. These comments were supposedly made to a talk show host—sometimes reported to be Merv Griffin, but most oftenest said to be Phil Donahue. Of course, no Procter & Gamble executive had appeared on any talk show, and no sane businessperson would say such things on television, but the story spread quick. These rumors damaged the company name really bad.

As a result, Procter & Gamble issued publicly statements denying the comments. The company changed its century-old logo because some people believed that the moon and stars on the company's packages were a symbol of the Church of Satan. None of these tactics worked very good, so finally, Procter & Gamble began to sue people who spread these story without any proof. One Kansas City couple eventual paid Procter & Gamble $75,000 for their part in spreading the rumor. Since then, the company has been doing more better.

More recent, McDonald's and other companies have been targeted with similar stories about Satanism. Who starts these maliciously rumors? Some people suspect business rivals who could make financial gains from this urban legends, but no one really knows. Why do people believe such things? Perhaps they believe subconsciously that big corporations are badly for consumers. Perhaps they do not trust business executives. Whatever the reason, many people do believe the rumors, and Procter & Gamble and other companies have found them more hard to disprove than any competitor's advertisement.

COLLABORATIVE ACTIVITIES

1. Working on your own, write five simple sentences on a sheet of paper. Then, working in a group of three, pass your page to another student in your group. Add one adjective and one adverb to one of the sentences on the paper you receive. Keep passing the pages among the three of you until modifying words have been added to every sentence on each sheet. Then, working together, check to make sure all the adjectives and adverbs are used correctly.
2. Working in the same group, choose the sentence from each page that is most unusual or interesting. Work together to write a one- or two-paragraph story using all three sentences. When you have finished, try to add several more adjectives and adverbs to the story.
3. Exchange stories from activity 2 with another group. Then, rewrite the other group's story by changing every adjective and adverb you can find. Make the story as different from the original as you can. When you have finished, exchange the stories again and make any necessary corrections.

COMPOSING ORIGINAL SENTENCES

4. Working in a group of three, write five original sentences. Make sure each sentence contains at least one adverb and at least one adjective. In addition, include at least one comparative form of an adjective or adverb, at least one superlative form of an adjective or adverb, and at least one demonstrative adjective. Then, check the adjectives and adverbs carefully to be sure you have used them correctly. When you have finished, check the sentences again to make sure you have corrected any errors in grammar, punctuation, or spelling.

☑ REVIEW CHECKLIST: Adjectives and Adverbs

- Adjectives modify nouns or pronouns. (See 20A.)
- Adverbs modify verbs, adjectives, or other adverbs. (See 20A.)
- To compare two people or things, use the comparative form of an adjective or adverb. To compare more than two people or things, use the superlative form of an adjective or adverb. (See 20B.)
- Adjectives and adverbs form the comparative with *-er* or *more* and the superlative with *-est* or *most.* (See 20B.)
- The adjectives *good* and *bad* and their adverb forms, *well* and *badly,* have irregular comparative and superlative forms. (See 20B.)
- Demonstrative adjectives—*this, that, these,* and *those*—identify particular nouns. (See 20C.)

CHAPTER

21 Grammar and Usage Issues for ESL Writers

PREVIEW

In this chapter, you will learn

- to include subjects in sentences (21A)
- to avoid special problems with subjects (21B)
- to identify plural nouns (21C)
- to understand count and noncount nouns (21D)
- to use determiners with count and noncount nouns (21E)
- to understand articles (21F)
- to form negative statements and questions (21G)
- to indicate verb tense (21H)
- to recognize stative verbs (21I)
- to place adjectives in order (21J)
- to choose correct prepositions (21K)
- to use prepositions in familiar expressions (21L)
- to use prepositions in two-word verbs (21M)

SEEING AND WRITING

Do you think U.S. ballots should include languages other than English? If not, why not? If so, what languages should be represented? Why? Look at the picture above, and then write a paragraph that answers these questions.

Word Power

ballot a written or printed paper on which voters indicate their choices in an election

Learning English as a second language involves more than just learning grammar. In fact, if you have been studying English as a second language, you may know as much English grammar as many native speakers do. Still, you will need to learn conventions and rules that are second nature to most (although by no means all) native speakers. This chapter covers the grammar and usage issues that give nonnative speakers the most trouble.

A Including Subjects in Sentences

In almost all cases, English requires that every sentence state its subject. In fact, every dependent clause must also have a subject.

INCORRECT My parents do not make much money although work hard. (Who works hard?)

CORRECT My parents do not make much money although they work hard.

English even requires a false or "dummy" subject to fill the subject position in sentences like this one.

It is hot here.

It is not correct to write just *Hot here* or *Is hot here.*

◆ PRACTICE 21.1

Each of the following sentences is missing the subject of a dependent or an independent clause. On the lines after each sentence, rewrite it, adding an appropriate subject.

Example: The essay was interesting even though had some errors.

The essay was interesting even though it had some errors.

1. Will rain all day tomorrow.

2. She was excited after answered a question in class.

3. Javier studied so that could become an American citizen.

4. Was not my fault.

5. Sofia watched television programs for children when was learning English.

6. Is a very difficult problem.

____

____

7. She waited until was sure they were gone.

____

____

8. He missed the bus because overslept that morning.

____

____

9. After Jean scored the winning goal, went out to celebrate with his friends.

____

____

10. Is quieter than usual in the library today.

____

____

B Avoiding Special Problems with Subjects

> **Writing Tip**
> Special dictionaries help nonnative speakers answer usage questions. Your college librarian or English instructor can help you find a dictionary that meets your needs.

Some languages commonly begin a sentence with a word or phrase that has no grammatical link to the sentence but that states clearly what the sentence is about. If you speak such a language, you might write a sentence like this one.

INCORRECT Career plans I am studying to be a computer scientist.

A sentence like this cannot occur in English. The phrase *career plans* cannot be a subject because the sentence already includes one: the pronoun *I,* which agrees with the verb *am studying.* In addition, *career plans* is not connected to the rest of the sentence in any other way. One way to revise this sentence is to rewrite it so that *career plans* is the subject.

For more on subjects, see 6A.

CORRECT My career plans are to be a computer scientist.

Another way to revise the sentence is to make *career plans* the object of a preposition.

CORRECT In terms of my career plans, I am studying to be a computer scientist.

Standard English also does not permit a two-part subject in which the second part is a pronoun referring to the same person or thing as the first part.

INCORRECT My sister she is a cardiologist.

CORRECT My sister is a cardiologist.

When the real subject follows the verb, and the normal subject position before the verb is empty, it must be filled by a "dummy" subject, such as *there.*

INCORRECT Are tall mountains in my country.

CORRECT There are tall mountains in my country.

◆ PRACTICE 21.2

The following sentences contain problems with subjects. Rewrite each sentence correctly on the lines provided. (Some of the sentences can be corrected in more than one way.)

Example: Are no roads in the middle of the jungle.

There are no roads in the middle of the jungle.

1. The old woman she sells candles in the shop downstairs.

2. Are six kinds of rice in the cupboard.

3. Dmitri he rides his bicycle ten miles every day.

4. The doctor says is hope for my father.

5. My neighbor she watches my daughter in the evenings.

6. My former home I grew up in a village near the Indian Ocean.

7. My job it starts at six o'clock in the morning.

____

____

8. Plans for the future Mr. Esposito hopes to buy his own taxi someday.

____

____

9. The best thing in my life, I feel lucky that my family is together again.

____

____

10. My brother's big problem at school he is afraid of his teacher.

____

____

C Identifying Plural Nouns

In English, most nouns add *-s* to form plurals. Every time you use a noun, ask yourself whether you are talking about one item or more than one, and choose a singular or plural form accordingly. Consider this sentence.

For more on singular and plural nouns, see Chapter 18.

CORRECT The books in both branches of the library are deteriorating.

The three nouns in this sentence are underlined: one is singular (*library*), and the other two are plural (*books, branches*). You might think that the word *both* is enough to indicate that *branch* is plural, and that it is obvious that there would have to be more than one book in any branch of a library. But even if the sentence includes information that tells you that a noun is plural, you must always use a form that shows explicitly that a noun is plural.

◆ PRACTICE 21.3

In each of the following sentences, underline the plural nouns.

Example: Her daughters love to tease their friends.

1. Elena has twin toddlers and two older children.
2. She works two jobs, and her feet hurt every evening.
3. Bella and Mikhail are teenagers with typical teen interests and hobbies.

4. Bella loves animals and keeps a cat, a gerbil, and three white mice.
5. Mikhail is interested in sports and music.
6. The twin girls are three years old.
7. They are identical twins who already love to play tricks on people.
8. They always tell babysitters the wrong names.
9. Elena never dresses them in matching outfits, but sometimes the girls want to wear the same clothes.
10. Elena plans to give them different haircuts.

D Understanding Count and Noncount Nouns

A **count noun** names one particular thing or a group of particular things: *a teacher, a panther, a bed, an ocean, a cloud; two teachers, five panthers, three beds, two oceans, fifteen clouds.* A **noncount noun**, however, names things that cannot be counted: *gold, cream, sand, blood, smoke.*

Count nouns usually have a singular form and a plural form: *cloud, clouds.* Noncount nouns usually have only a singular form: *smoke.* Note how the nouns *cloud* and *smoke* differ in the way they are used in sentences.

CORRECT The sky is full of clouds.

CORRECT The sky is full of smoke.

INCORRECT The sky is full of smokes.

CORRECT I can count ten clouds in the distance.

INCORRECT I can count ten smokes in the distance.

Often, the same idea can be represented with either a count noun or a noncount noun.

Count	*Noncount*
people (plural of *person*)	humanity (not *humanities*)
tables, chairs, beds	furniture (not *furnitures*)
letters	mail (not *mails*)
tools	equipment (not *equipments*)
facts	information (not *informations*)

Some words can be either count or noncount, depending on the meaning intended.

COUNT Students in this course are expected to submit two papers.

NONCOUNT These artificial flowers are made of paper.

Student Voices

The hardest thing about the English language is all the rules.

George Lin

Writing Tip

Sometimes a noncount noun such as *smoke* appears to have a plural form (*smokes*). Although these forms end in *-s,* they are verbs and not plural nouns: *He smokes two cigars a day.*

FOCUS Count and Noncount Nouns

Here are some general guidelines for using count and noncount nouns.

- Use a count noun to refer to a living animal, but use a noncount noun to refer to the food that comes from that animal.

  COUNT There are several live lobsters in the tank.

  NONCOUNT This restaurant specializes in lobster.

- If you use a noncount noun for a substance or class of things that can come in different varieties, you can often make that noun plural if you want to talk about those varieties.

  NONCOUNT Cheese is a rich source of calcium.

  COUNT Many different cheeses come from Italy.

- If you want to shift attention from a concept in general to specific examples of it, you can often use a noncount noun as a count noun.

  NONCOUNT You have a great deal of talent.

  COUNT My talents do not include singing.

◆ PRACTICE 21.4

In each of the following sentences, identify the underlined word as a count or noncount noun. If it is a noncount noun, circle the *N* following the sentence, but do not write in the blank. If it is a count noun, circle the *C*, and then write the plural form of the noun in the blank.

Examples

She was filled with admiration for the turtle. (N) C ________

A seagull watched from a safe distance. N (C) *seagulls*

1. Rosa walked across the sand. N C ________
2. The moon shone brightly. N C ________
3. The moon was reflected in the water. N C ________
4. A sea turtle came out of the waves. N C ________

5. She crawled slowly up the beach and dug a hole for her eggs. N C ________

6. A turtle egg feels like leather. N C ________

7. Rosa felt sympathy for the turtle. N C ________

8. An enemy could be nearby, waiting to attack the turtle or eat her eggs. N C ________

9. The enemy could even be a human being who likes to eat turtle. N C ________

10. Rosa sighed with relief when the turtle finished laying her eggs and swam away. N C ________

E Using Determiners with Count and Noncount Nouns

Determiners are adjectives that *identify* rather than describe the nouns they modify. Determiners may also *quantify* nouns (that is, indicate an amount or a number).

When a determiner is accompanied by one or more other adjectives, the determiner always comes first. For example, in the phrase *my expensive new digital watch, my* is a determiner; you cannot put *expensive, new, digital,* or any other adjective before *my.*

Determiners include the following words.

- Articles: *a, an, the*
- Demonstrative pronouns: *this, these, that, those*
- Possessive pronouns: *my, our, your, his, her, its, their*
- Possessive nouns: *Sheila's, my friend's,* and so on
- *Whose, which, what*
- *All, both, each, every, some, any, either, no, neither, many, most, much, a few, a little, few, little, several, enough*
- All numerals: *one, two,* and so on

A singular count noun must be accompanied by a determiner—for example, *my watch* or *the new digital watch,* not just *watch* or *new digital watch.* Noncount nouns and plural count nouns, on the other hand, sometimes have determiners but sometimes do not. *This honey is sweet* and *Honey is sweet* are both acceptable, as are *These berries are juicy* and *Berries are juicy.* (In each case, the meaning is different.) You cannot say *Berry is juicy,* however; say instead *This berry is juicy, Every berry is juicy,* or *A berry is juicy.*

FOCUS Determiners

Some determiners can be used only with certain types of nouns.

- *This* and *that* can be used only with singular nouns (count or noncount): *this berry, that honey.*
- *These, those, a few, few, many, both,* and *several* can only be used with plural count nouns: *these berries, those apples, a few ideas, few people, many students, both sides, several directions.*
- *Much* and *a little* can be used only with noncount nouns: *much affection, a little honey.*
- *Some* and *enough* can be used only with noncount or plural count nouns: *some honey, some berries, enough trouble, enough problems.*
- *A, an, every,* and *each* can be used only with singular count nouns: *a berry, an elephant, every possibility, each citizen.*

◆ PRACTICE 21.5

In each of the following sentences, circle the more appropriate choice from each pair of words or phrases in parentheses.

Example: On New Year's Eve, the store sold all of (its/these) imported champagne.

1. (Many/Much) people made big plans for December 31, 1999.
2. (Each/All) countries using the Gregorian calendar prepared for the beginning of the year 2000.
3. Even (a few/a little) places using different calendars planned to celebrate.
4. There was (many/much) talk about the "new millennium"; a *millennium* is one thousand years.
5. Although the new millennium would not officially begin until 2001, people showed (few/little) concern about that fact.
6. (Many big, exciting/Big many, exciting) celebrations happened in public places around the world.
7. Before the New Year, some people had expressed (a few/a little) anxiety about how computers would handle the date *2000*.
8. (Most/Much) computers in 1995 read the date as *95* so everyone assumed computers would read *2000* as *00*.

9. Most people found (every/enough) information to solve possible computer problems.

10. When the date became January 1, 2000, (few/little) computer disasters occurred.

F Understanding Articles

The definite article *the* and the indefinite articles *a* and *an* are determiners that tell readers whether the noun that follows is one they can identify (*the book*) or one they cannot yet identify (*a book*).

Definite Articles

When the definite article *the* is used with a noun, the writer is saying to readers, "You can identify which particular thing or things I have in mind. The information you need to make that identification is available to you. Either you have it already, or I am about to supply it to you."

Readers can find the necessary information in the following ways.

- By looking at other information in the sentence.

  Meet me at the corner of Main Street and Lafayette Road.

  In this example, *the* is used with the noun *corner* because other words in the sentence tell readers which particular corner the writer has in mind: the one located at Main and Lafayette.
- By looking at information in other sentences.

  Aisha ordered a slice of pie and a cup of coffee. The pie was delicious. She asked for a second slice.

  Here, *the* is used before the word *pie* in the second sentence to indicate that it is the same pie identified in the first sentence. Notice, however, that the noun *slice* in the third sentence is preceded by an indefinite article (*a*) because it is not the same slice referred to in the first sentence. There is no information that identifies it specifically.
- By drawing on general knowledge.

  The earth revolves around the sun.

  Here, *the* is used with the nouns *earth* and *sun* because readers are expected to know which particular things the writer is referring to.

In the following cases, *the* is always used rather than *a* or *an*.

- Before the word *same: the same day*
- Before the superlative form of an adjective: *the youngest son*
- Before a number indicating order or sequence: *the third time*

For information on the superlative forms of adjectives and adverbs, see 20B.

Indefinite Articles

When an indefinite article is used with a noun, the writer is saying to readers, "I don't expect you to have enough information right now to identify a particular thing that I have in mind. I do expect you to recognize that I'm referring to only one item."

Consider the following sentences.

We need a table for our computer.

I have a folding table; maybe you can use that.

In the first sentence, the writer has a hypothetical table, but no actual one, in mind. Because the table is indefinite to the writer, it is clearly indefinite to the reader, so *a* is used, not *the.* The second sentence refers to an actual table, but because the writer does not expect the reader to be able to identify the table specifically, it is also used with *a* rather than *the.*

> **FOCUS Indefinite Articles**
>
> Unlike the definite article, the indefinite articles *a* and *an* occur only with singular count nouns. *A* is used when the next sound is a consonant, and *an* is used when the next sound is a vowel. In choosing *a* or *an,* pay attention to sounds rather than to spelling: *a house, a year, a union,* but *an hour, an uncle.*

No Article

For more on count and noncount nouns, see 21D.

Only noncount and plural count nouns can stand without articles: *butter, chocolate, cookies, strawberries* (but *a cookie* or *the strawberry*).

Nouns without articles can be used to make generalizations.

Infants need affection as well as food.

Here, the absence of articles before the nouns *infants, affection,* and *food* indicates that the statement is not about particular infants, affection, or food but about infants, affection, and food in general. Remember not to use *the* in such sentences; in English, a sentence like *The infants need affection as well as food* can only refer to particular, identifiable infants, not to infants in general.

Articles with Proper Nouns

For more on proper nouns, see 24A.

Proper nouns split into two classes: names that take *the* and names that take no article.

- Names of people usually take no article unless they are used in the plural to refer to members of a family, in which case they take *the: Napoleon, Mahatma Gandhi,* but *the Kennedys.*

- Names of places that are plural in form usually take *the: the Andes, the United States.*
- The names of most places on land (cities, states, provinces, and countries) take no article: *Salt Lake City, Mississippi, Alberta, Japan.* The names of most bodies of water (rivers, seas, and oceans, although not lakes or bays) take *the: the Mississippi, the Mediterranean, the Pacific,* but *Lake Erie* and *San Francisco Bay.*
- Names of streets take no article: *Main Street.* Names of highways take *the: the Belt Parkway.*

◆ PRACTICE 21.6

In the following passage, decide whether each blank space needs a definite article (*the*), an indefinite article (*a* or *an*), or no article. If a definite or indefinite article is needed, write it in the space provided. If no article is needed, leave the space blank.

Example: Julia's plane arrived at <u>the</u> airport early Tuesday morning.

(1) ____ first time Julia visited New York City, she had ____ memorable experience. (2) Although ____ city has ____ efficient subway system, Julia was afraid to take ____ subway. (3) Fortunately, New York is ____ city that is enjoyable for ____ pedestrians, so Julia walked everywhere. (4) One day, she wandered into ____ unfamiliar neighborhood and got lost. (5) She saw that she was on ____ Broadway, but ____ buildings were small and shabby. (6) In her purse, she carried ____ wallet containing ____ money, ____ passport, and ____ driver's license. (7) She was worried about ____ crime, so she held ____ purse tightly. (8) Suddenly, she saw ____ face of ____ man in ____ dim alleyway. (9) She gasped as he stepped out of ____ shadows and walked toward her. (10) ____ man said, "You look lost." (11) He told her how to get back to ____ hotel where she was staying and even gave her ____ subway map. (12) Now, Julia likes to tell ____ people how friendly and helpful ____ New Yorkers can be.

G Forming Negative Statements and Questions

Negative Statements

To form a negative statement, add the word *not* directly after the first helping verb of the complete verb.

For more on helping verbs, see 6F.

Global warming has been getting worse.

Global warming has not been getting worse.

When there is no helping verb, a form of the verb *do* must be inserted before *not*.

Automobile traffic contributes to pollution.

Automobile traffic does not contribute to pollution.

For information on subject-verb agreement with the verb do, *see 13B.*

Remember that when *do* is used as a helping verb, the form of *do* used must match the tense and number of the original main verb. Note that in the negative statement above, the main verb loses its tense and appears in the base form (*contribute,* not *contributes*).

Questions

To form a question, move the helping verb that follows the subject to the position directly before the subject.

The governor is trying to compromise.

Is the governor trying to compromise?

The governor is working on the budget.

Is the governor working on the budget?

As with negatives, when the verb does not include a helping verb, you must supply a form of *do*. To form a question, put *do* directly before the subject.

The governor works hard.

Does the governor work hard?

A helping verb never comes before the subject if the subject is a question word or contains a question word.

Who is talking to the governor?

Which bills have been vetoed by the governor?

◆ PRACTICE 21.7

Rewrite each of the following sentences in two ways: first, turn the sentence into a question; then, rewrite the original sentence as a negative statement.

Example: Moths are living in my closet.

Question: Are moths living in my closet?

Negative statement: Moths are not living in my closet.

1. The sparrows are searching for winter food.

   Question: ________________________

   Negative statement: ________________________

2. Wild raspberries grow all along these dirt roads.

   Question: ________________________

   Negative statement: ________________________

3. I answered her e-mail immediately.

   Question: ________________________

   Negative statement: ________________________

4. Shiho felt sick after eating the pizza.

   Question: ________________________

   Negative statement: ________________________

5. The porcupine attacked my dog.

   Question: ________________________

   Negative statement: ________________________

6. Final exams will be given during the last week of school.

   Question: ________________________

   Negative statement: ________________________

   ____

7. Gunnar saw the robbery at the convenience store.

   Question: ________________________

   Negative statement: ________________________

   ____

8. The telephone has been ringing all morning.

   Question: ________________________

   Negative statement: ________________________

9. He is working on the problem right now.

   Question: ________________________

   Negative statement: ________________________

10. She dropped the box of dishes on the concrete floor.

Question: ________________________________

Negative statement: ________________________________

____

H Indicating Verb Tense

For more on verb tense, see Chapters 16 and 17.

In English, a verb's form must always indicate when the action referred to by the verb took place (for instance, in the past or in the present). Use the appropriate tense of the verb, even if the time is obvious or if the sentence includes other indications of time (such as *two years ago* or *at present*).

CORRECT Yesterday, I got a letter from my sister Yunpi.

INCORRECT Yesterday, I get a letter from my sister Yunpi.

I Recognizing Stative Verbs

Stative verbs usually tell us that someone or something is in a state that will not change, at least for a while.

Hiro knows American history very well.

The **present progressive** tense consists of the present tense of *be* plus the present participle (*I am going*). The **past progressive** tense consists of the past tense of *be* plus the present participle (*I was going*). Most English verbs show action, and these action verbs can be used in the progressive tenses. Stative verbs, however, are rarely used in the progressive tenses.

INCORRECT Hiro is knowing American history very well.

FOCUS Stative Verbs

Verbs that are stative often refer to mental states like *know, understand, think, believe, want, like, love,* and *hate.* Other stative verbs include *be, have, need, own, belong, weigh, cost,* and *mean.* Certain verbs of sense perception, like *see* and *hear,* are also stative even though they can refer to momentary events rather than unchanging states.

Many verbs have more than one meaning, and some of these verbs are active with one meaning but stative with another. An example is the verb *weigh.*

ACTIVE The butcher is weighing the meat.

STATIVE The meat weighs three pounds.

In the first sentence above, the verb *weigh* means "to put on a scale"; it is active, not stative, as the use of the progressive shows. In the second sentence, however, the same verb means "to have weight," so it is stative, not active. It would be unacceptable to say, "The meat is weighing three pounds."

◆ PRACTICE 21.8

In each of the following sentences, circle the verb. Then, correct any problems with stative verbs by crossing out the incorrect verb tense and writing the correct verb tense above the line. If a sentence is correct, write *C* in the blank after the sentence.

Example: Ahmed ~~is wanting~~ wants to take advanced calculus next semester ____.

1. Ahmed has been studying mathematics for many years. ____
2. He is also knowing a lot about astronomy. ____
3. He is understanding the movements of planets and stars. ____
4. He was being president of the school's Astronomy Club last year. ____
5. Ahmed is working his way through school. ____
6. He is having a job at a gas station. ____
7. He is hating the boring work there, but he must keep his job. ____
8. Ahmed is needing the money for his tuition. ____
9. Little by little, he is earning enough to help his family. ____
10. Ahmed is planning to quit that job in the near future. ____

J Placing Adjectives in Order

Adjectives and other modifiers that come before a noun usually follow a set order.

Required Order

- Determiners always come first in a series of adjectives: *these fragile glasses*. The determiners *all* or *both* always precede any other determiners: *all these glasses*.

For more on determiners, see 21E.

- If one of the modifiers is a noun, it must come directly before the noun it modifies: *these wine glasses.*
- All other adjectives are placed between the determiners and the noun modifiers: *these fragile wine glasses.* If there are two or more of these adjectives, the following order is preferred.

Preferred Order

- Adjectives that show the writer's attitude generally precede adjectives that merely describe: *these lovely fragile wine glasses.*
- Adjectives that indicate size generally come early: *these lovely large fragile wine glasses.*

◆ PRACTICE 21.9

Arrange each group of adjectives in the correct order, and rewrite the complete phrase in the blank.

Example: (rubber, a, red, pretty) ball

a pretty red rubber ball

1. (family, old, a, pleasant) tradition

____

2. (some, disgusting, work) boots

____

3. (four, pampered, Anita's) poodles

____

4. (three, the, circus, funny) clowns

____

5. (my, annoying, both) sisters

____

6. (son's, his, favorite, television) show

____

7. (a, wedding, delightful, outdoor) party

____

8. (cat, fur-covered, ugly, this) toy

____

9. (birthday, a, wonderful, chocolate) cake

____

10. (traveling, all, these, banjo) players

____

K Choosing Correct Prepositions

A **preposition** links a noun (or a word or word group that functions as a noun) to a verb, an adjective, or another noun in the sentence. Thus, prepositions show the precise relationships between words—for example, whether a book is *on, near,* or *under* a table.

> I thought I left the book on the table or somewhere near the table, but I found it under the table.

The prepositions *at, in,* and *on* sometimes cause problems for nonnative speakers of English. For example, to identify the location of a place or an event, you can use *at, in,* or *on.*

The preposition *at* specifies an exact point in space or time.

> Please leave the package with the janitor at 150 South Street. I will pick it up at 7:30 tonight.

Expanses of space or time are treated as containers and therefore require *in.*

> Jean-Pierre went to school in the 1970s.

On must be used in two cases: with names of streets (but not with exact addresses), and with days of the week or month.

> We will move into our new office on 18th Street either on Monday or on March 12.

▼ Student Voices

Knowing which word to use is the hardest thing about English.

Nirav Patel

L Using Prepositions in Familiar Expressions

Many familiar expressions end with prepositions. Learning to write clearly and *idiomatically*—in keeping with the conventions of written English—means learning which preposition is used in each expression. If you find this difficult, you are not alone—even native speakers of English sometimes have trouble choosing the correct preposition.

The sentences that follow illustrate idiomatic use of prepositions in various expressions. Note that sometimes different prepositions are used with the same word. For example, both *on* and *for* can be used with *wait* to form two different expressions with two different meanings (*He waited on their table; She waited for the bus*). Which preposition you choose depends on your meaning. (In the list that follows, pairs of similar expressions that end with different prepositions are bracketed.)

Expression with Preposition	Sample Sentence
acquainted with	It took the family several weeks to become acquainted with their new neighbors.
addicted to	I think Abby is becoming addicted to pretzels.
agree on (a plan or objective)	It is vital that all members of the school board agree on goals for the coming year.
agree to (a proposal)	Striking workers finally agreed to the terms of management's offer.
angry about or at (a situation)	Taxpayers are understandably angry about (or at) the deterioration of city recreation facilities.
angry with (a person)	When the mayor refused to hire more police officers, his constituents became angry with him.
approve of	Amy's adviser approved of her decision to study in Guatemala.
bored with	Just when Michael was getting bored with his life, he met Sharon.
capable of	Dogs may be able to fetch and roll over, but they certainly aren't capable of complex reasoning.
consist of	The deluxe fruit basket consisted of five pathetic pears, two tiny apples, a few limp bunches of grapes, and one lonely kiwi.
contrast with	Coach Headley's relaxed style contrasts sharply with the previous coach's more formal approach.
convenient for	The proposed location of the new day-care center is convenient for many families.
deal with	Many parents and educators believe it is possible to deal with the special needs of autistic children in a regular classroom.
depend on	Children depend on their parents for emotional as well as financial support.
differ from (something else)	The music of Whitney Houston differs from the music of Britney Spears.
differ with (someone else)	I strongly differ with your interpretation of my dream about *The Wizard of Oz*.
emigrate from	My grandfather and his brother emigrated from the part of Russia that is now Ukraine.
grateful for (a favor)	If you can arrange an interview next week, I will be very grateful for your time and trouble.
grateful to (someone)	Jerry Garcia was always grateful to his loyal fans.
immigrate to	Many Cubans want to leave their country and immigrate to the United States.
impatient with	Keshia often gets impatient with her four younger brothers.

interested in	Diana, who was not very interested in the discussion of the Treaty of Versailles, stared out the window.
interfere with	Sometimes it's hard to resist the temptation to interfere with a friend's life.
meet with	I hope I can meet with you soon to discuss my research paper.
object to	The defense attorney objected to the prosecutor's treatment of the witness.
pleased with	Marta was very pleased with Eric's favorable critique of her speech.
protect against	Nobel Prize winner Linus Pauling believed that large doses of vitamin C could protect people against the common cold.
reason with	When a two-year-old is having a tantrum, it's nearly impossible to reason with her.
reply to	If no one replies to our ad within two weeks, we will advertise again.
responsible for	Parents are not responsible for the debts of their adult children.
similar to	The blood sample found at the crime scene was remarkably similar to one found in the suspect's residence.
specialize in	Dr. Casullo is a dentist who specializes in periodontal surgery.
succeed in	Lisa hoped her M.B.A. would help her succeed in a business career.
take advantage of	Some consumer laws are designed to prevent door-to-door salespeople from taking advantage of buyers.
wait for (something to happen)	Snow White sang while she waited for her prince to arrive.
wait on (in a restaurant)	We sat at the table for twenty minutes before someone waited on us.
worry about	Why worry about things you can't change?

◆ PRACTICE 21.10

In the following passage, fill in each blank with the correct preposition.

Example: Naomi's family lives ___in___ a small house ___on___ Parsons Street.

(1) Naomi emigrated __________ Ghana when she was a teenager. (2) Her family settled __________ New Jersey, __________ the East

Coast of the United States. (3) Naomi had studied English __________ Ghana, but she was not prepared for the kind of English spoken __________ the United States. (4) The other students __________ her class sometimes laughed __________ her pronunciation. (5) She studied hard, and her high school teachers were pleased __________ her progress. (6) Naomi was interested __________ attending college and getting a nursing degree. (7) She knew that she was capable __________ doing well __________ college classes if she could continue to improve her English. (8) Before sending an application __________ her local community college, Naomi met __________ an admissions officer to discuss her application. (9) Everyone __________ the admissions office was encouraging, and Naomi decided to take advantage __________ their offers to help her. (10) __________ April 12, Naomi's mother called her __________ her after-school job to tell her that the community college had accepted her. (11) Naomi was grateful __________ everyone __________ the admissions office __________ their help. (12) Her English gets better every day, and Naomi expects to succeed __________ college and __________ her nursing career.

M Using Prepositions in Two-Word Verbs

Two-word verbs consist of a verb and a preposition. If the preposition introduces a prepositional phrase, the preposition comes right after the verb. In the following sentence, *at* introduces the prepositional phrase *at the video monitor;* therefore, *at* must come right after the verb.

CORRECT Please look at the video monitor.

INCORRECT Please look the video monitor at.

In other two-word verbs, however, the second word does not introduce a prepositional phrase; it is part of the verb. In the following pair of sentences, *off,* the second word of the two-word verb, does not introduce a prepositional phrase. Because the object is a noun (*printer*), the second word of such a verb can come either before the object of that verb or after the object.

CORRECT Please turn off the printer.

CORRECT Please turn the printer off.

When their object is a pronoun, however, these two-word verbs must be split, and the pronoun must come between the two parts.

CORRECT Please turn it off.

INCORRECT Please turn off it.

Other examples of two-word verbs in which the second word does not function as a preposition include *take (it) down, put (it) on, let (it) out,* and *make (it) up.*

◆ PRACTICE 21.11

In each of the following sentences, look closely at the two-word verb. In each case, determine whether the preposition introduces a prepositional phrase or is part of the verb. Then, decide whether the preposition is correctly placed in the sentence. If it is, write *C* in the blank after the sentence. If the preposition needs to be moved, edit the sentence.

Example: Each time a child chose a toy, another child tried to take ~~away it.~~ *it away.* ____

1. All parents worry their children about. ____
2. They want the children to succeed in life. ____
3. A child needs rules, and adults should set up them when the child is very young. ____
4. A child needs to learn manners and will not pick them up without help from an adult. ____
5. Most kids love toys, and adults can give children the responsibility of putting away them. ____
6. Parents should not count children on learning to share by themselves. ____
7. Children like to show off their toys, but they may not want other children to touch the toys. ____
8. To a child, even a dull toy becomes interesting if another child picks up it. ____
9. Children resist sharing toys but can learn to give up them to another child for a little while. ____
10. Adults forgive selfishness in a child, but most do not want to deal it with in an adult. ____

REVISING AND EDITING

Look back at your response to the Seeing and Writing exercise on page 322. Review this chapter; then, make any necessary grammar and usage corrections to your writing. When you have finished, add any additional transitional words and phrases you need to make your ideas clear to your readers.

CHAPTER REVIEW

EDITING PRACTICE

Read the following essay, which contains errors in the use of subjects, articles and determiners, stative verbs, and idiomatic expressions. Check each underlined word or phrase. If it is not used correctly, cross it out and write the correct word or phrase above the line. If the underlined word or phrase is correct, write *C* above it. The first error has been corrected for you.

The Electoral College

Presidential elections in the United States follow rules that are sometimes confusing. Many Americans ~~are believing~~ *believe* that the winning candidate is the person who has gotten the most votes. However, a total number of votes for a candidate may not matter. The Electoral College, an organization consisting with electors from every state, actually selects the president. In forty-eight from the fifty states, the candidate who wins in the state gets all of its electoral votes. When the election is being very close, the person who gets the majority of the popular vote may not win the presidency.

The Continental Congress created the Electoral College on 1787, before George Washington was elected president. Since those time, the United States has depended for the Electoral College to name the president. If the no candidate earns a majority of the Electoral College votes, the House of Representatives decides the election. In 1824, John Quincy

Adams was elected by the House of Representatives; he had received only the third of the popular vote.

Were two more elections in the nineteenth century in which the apparent winner lost in the Electoral College. At 1876, the Electoral College chose Rutherford B. Hayes, who had lost for Samuel Tilden in the popular vote. Many people still have questions to the fairness of that election. In 1888, Benjamin Harrison won fewer votes than Grover Cleveland, but Harrison won more electoral votes and became president for one term.

Americans become more interested of the Electoral College when an election is very close, as in 2000 when George W. Bush narrowly defeated Al Gore. Most Americans think that every vote should be equally important in the democracy. Some people feel that the Electoral College system makes some votes more important than others. Members of Congress have not yet had enough complaints about the Electoral College system to give up it. Perhaps some twenty-first-century Congress will finally object on the system enough to change it.

◆ COLLABORATIVE ACTIVITIES

1. Working in a group of three or four students, write down as many determiners as you can think of. Next, make a list of ten adjectives. Then, list ten nouns. Finally, combine the determiners and adjectives (in the correct order) in front of the nouns. Be as creative, original, and funny as you can. Choose your group's best phrase and write it on the board.
2. Working in the same group, write ten sentences using phrases you wrote in activity 1. Make sure that each sentence contains at least one prepositional phrase. Then, exchange sentences with another group. Look over the other group's sentences, and correct any errors you find.
3. Working in the same group, choose one sentence that your group wrote in activity 2. Then, write a short paragraph that begins with this sentence. Use as many specific, interesting nouns and prepositional phrases as you can, and include at least one two-word verb. Finally, have one member of the group read the paragraph aloud to the class.

COMPOSING ORIGINAL SENTENCES

4. Working in the same group, write five additional original sentences. Make sure that you use at least two plural nouns, at least one noncount noun, at least one negative statement or question, at least one stative verb, and at least one idiomatic expression with a preposition. Check

the articles and prepositions carefully. When you have finished, check the sentences again to make sure you have corrected any errors in grammar, punctuation, or spelling.

✓ REVIEW CHECKLIST: Grammar and Usage Issues for ESL Writers

- In almost all cases, English sentences must state their subjects. (See 21A and 21B.)
- In English, most nouns add *-s* to form plurals. Always use a form that indicates that a noun is plural. (See 21C.)
- English nouns may be count nouns or noncount nouns. A count noun names one particular thing or a group of particular things (*a teacher, oceans*). A noncount noun names something that cannot be counted (*gold, sand*). (See 21D.)
- Determiners are adjectives that identify rather than describe the nouns they modify. Determiners may also indicate amount or number. (See 21E.)
- The definite article *the* and the indefinite articles *a* and *an* are determiners that indicate whether the noun that follows is one readers can identify (*the book*) or one they cannot yet identify (*a book*). (See 21F.)
- To form a negative statement, add the word *not* directly after the first helping verb of the complete verb. To form a question, move the helping verb that follows the subject to the position directly before the subject. (See 21G.)
- A verb's form must indicate when the action referred to by the verb took place. (See 21H.)
- Stative verbs indicate that someone or something is in a state that will not change, at least for a while. Stative verbs are rarely used in the progressive tenses. (See 21I.)
- Adjectives and other modifiers that come before a noun usually follow a set order. (See 21J.)
- The prepositions *at, in,* and *on* sometimes cause problems for nonnative speakers of English. (See 21K.)
- Many familiar expressions end with prepositions. (See 21L.)
- When the preposition in a two-word verb introduces a prepositional phrase, the preposition comes right after the verb. In other two-word verbs, the second word can come before or after the object. (See 21M.)

UNIT FIVE

Understanding Punctuation, Mechanics, and Spelling

CHAPTER

22

Using Commas

PREVIEW

In this chapter, you will learn

- to use commas in a series (22A)
- to use commas to set off introductory phrases (22B)
- to use commas to set off parenthetical words and phrases (22C)
- to use commas with appositives (22D)
- to use commas to set off nonrestrictive clauses (22E)
- to use commas in compound and complex sentences (22F)
- to use commas in dates and addresses (22G)

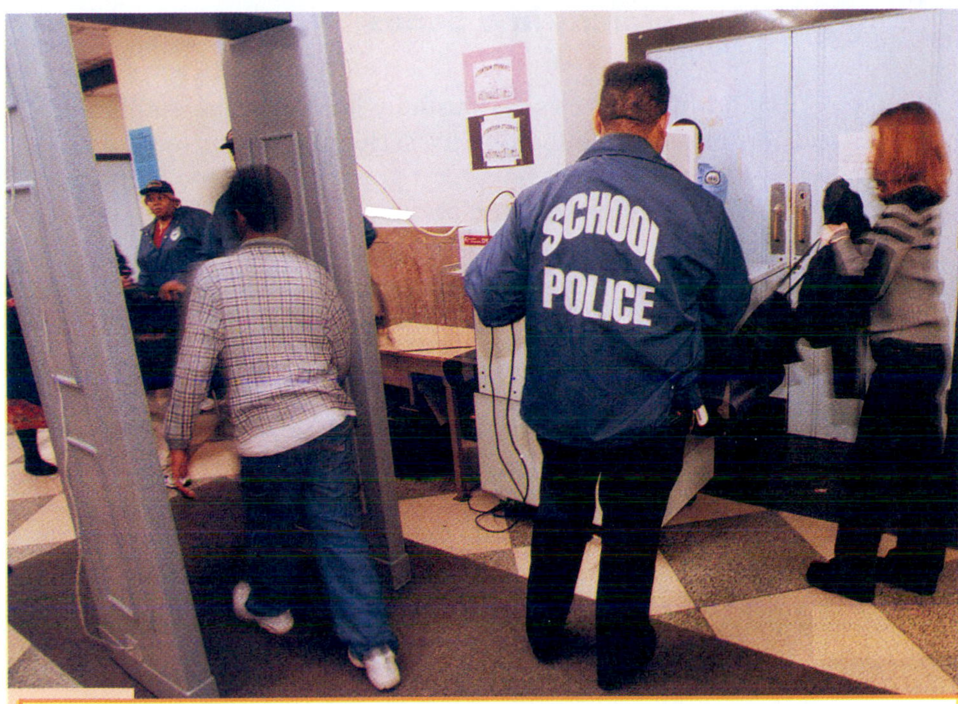

SEEING AND WRITING

What kind of security do you think is needed in America's high schools? Why? Look at the picture above, and then write a paragraph in which you answer these questions.

Word Power

surveillance close observation of a person or a group of people—especially a person or group under suspicion

A **comma** is a punctuation mark that separates words or groups of words within sentences. In this way, commas keep ideas distinct from one another. As you will learn in this chapter, commas also have several other uses.

A Using Commas in a Series

Use commas to separate items in a **series** of three or more words or word groups (phrases or clauses).

● **Writing Tip**

Do not use a comma before the first item in a series or after the last item in a series.

Hamlet, *Macbeth*, and *Othello* are tragedies by William Shakespeare. (series of three nouns linked by *and*)

Hamlet, *Macbeth*, or *Othello* will be assigned this semester. (series of three nouns linked by *or*)

Brian read *Hamlet*, started *Macbeth*, and skimmed Othello. (series of three phrases linked by *and*)

Hamlet is a tragedy, *Much Ado about Nothing* is a comedy, and *Richard III* is a history play. (series of three clauses linked by *and*)

FOCUS Using Commas in a Series

Newspaper and magazine writers usually leave out the comma before the coordinating conjunction in a series of three or more items. However, your writing will be clearer if you use a comma before the coordinating conjunction (*and*, *or*, *but*, and so on).

UNCLEAR The party had 200 guests, great food and rock music blaring from giant speakers. (Did the food as well as the music come from the speakers?)

CLEAR The party had 200 guests, great food, and rock music blaring from giant speakers.

However, do not use *any* commas if all the items in a series are separated by coordinating conjunctions.

The party had 200 guests and great food and rock music blaring from giant speakers.

◆ PRACTICE 22.1

Edit the following sentences for the correct use of commas in a series. If the sentence is correct, write *C* in the blank.

Example: We stowed our luggage, took our seats, and fastened our seat belts. _____

1. The intersection was crowded with buses, cars, and trucks. _____
2. The boys are either in the house, in the yard, or at the park. _____
3. *Star Wars*, *Alien*, and *Blade Runner* are classic science fiction movies. C
4. Jo Ellen took a walk, Roger cleaned the house, and Phil went to the movies. _____
5. A good marriage requires patience, honesty, and hard work. _____

6. Volunteers collected signatures accepted donations and answered phones. ____

7. We did not know whether to laugh, cry, or cheer. ____

8. Owls are outstanding hunters because they are strong, quick and silent. ____

9. The kitchen is to the left the guest room is upstairs and the pool is out back. ____

10. This computer is fast, has plenty of memory, and comes with a large screen. ____

B Using Commas to Set Off Introductory Phrases

Use a comma to set off an **introductory phrase** (a group of words that opens a sentence) from the rest of the sentence.

> For best results, take this medicine with a full glass of water.
>
> In case of fire, keep calm.
>
> After the outdoor concert, we walked home through the park.

Writing Tip

In the case of an introductory prepositional phrase of fewer than three words, you do not need to use a comma: *In 1986 the* Challenger *exploded on takeoff.* However, your sentences will be clearer if you include commas after *all* introductory phrases.

PRACTICE 22.2

Edit the following sentences for the correct use of commas with introductory phrases. If the sentence is correct, write *C* in the blank.

Example: From its first performance,the band was a huge success. ____

1. At the end of the game the bus took the team home. ____

2. Most of the time weather travels from west to east. ____

3. After the holiday season many stores take inventory. ____

4. During chemistry class Thursday, Margaret asked a number of interesting questions. ____

5. Racing against the clock Silvio finished the corporate earnings report. ____

6. Due to a reduction in funding some elementary schools have suspended their music programs. ____

7. Often feared bats are actually helpful creatures. ____

8. According to some experts, eating too much protein can have negative effects. ____

9. Without access to telephones, more than half the world's population depends on face-to-face communication. ____

10. At the current rate of global warming, oceans could rise a foot or more within the next 100 years. ____

C Using Commas to Set Off Parenthetical Words and Phrases

Often, a word or phrase is just an aside or afterthought that the sentence can do without. Because such words and phrases could be enclosed in parentheses, they are known as **parenthetical words and phrases**. Always use commas to set off parenthetical words and phrases.

For lists of some frequently used conjunctive adverbs and transitional expressions, see 7C.

Many parenthetical words and phrases are **conjunctive adverbs** (such as *however* and *therefore*) or **transitional expressions** (such as *in fact* and *for example*).

In fact, Scott Gomez grew up in Alaska.

He is, moreover, a center for the New Jersey Devils.

He plays for the NHL, of course.

Note that parenthetical words and phrases can come at the beginning, in the middle, or at the end of a sentence.

Of course, he plays for the NHL.

He plays, of course, for the NHL.

He plays for the NHL, of course.

Wherever they appear, parenthetical words and phrases must be set off from the rest of the sentence by commas.

FOCUS Using Commas in Direct Address

Always use commas to set off the name of a person (or an animal) whom you are addressing (speaking to directly). Use commas whether the name of the person addressed appears at the beginning, in the middle, or at the end of a sentence.

Spike, roll over and play dead.

Roll over, Spike, and play dead.

Roll over and play dead, Spike.

◆ PRACTICE 22.3

Edit the following sentences for the correct use of commas with parenthetical words and phrases. If the sentence is correct, write *C* in the blank.

Example: The Dallas Cowboys, surely, are one of football's most famous teams. C

1. Bill, how did you do, on the test? _____
2. The plane, therefore, never got off the ground. _____
3. In addition, an exercise class is relatively inexpensive. C
4. We wanted to make a good impression, of course. _____
5. When you give your speech, Jeanne, be sure to speak clearly. _____
6. In fact, even experienced professionals, make mistakes. _____
7. The party, consequently, was a disaster. _____
8. How old are you, anyway? C
9. Don't forget the key to the cabin, Amber. _____
10. However, no one knew, what the outcome would be. _____
11. Furthermore, the team had lost its best defensive player. _____
12. The organization, unfortunately, had suffered a number of scandals. _____
13. What do you suggest we do for Zach, Dr. Chen? _____
14. No one can say, moreover, how the economy will change in the future. C
15. Besides, genetics is the next medical frontier. _____

◆ PRACTICE 22.4

Edit the sentences in the following paragraph for the correct use of commas with parenthetical words and phrases. If the sentence is correct, write *C* in the blank.

Example: Tiger Woods, unlike other golfers, seems to have unlimited talent. _____

(1) For example, Tiger Woods is an exceptional golf player. _____ (2) Moreover, experts say, his skills are nearly perfect. _____ (3) His golf

game, consequently, is difficult to beat. _____ (4) He dominates most of the tournaments he enters, in other words. _____ (5) In fact, Woods is one of the best golf players in history. _C_ (6) After all he has broken many long-standing records. _____ (7) His success, moreover, has come at a young age. _____ (8) Also he finishes ahead of more experienced players. _C_ (9) There may, finally, be no one to challenge him on the golf course. _____ (10) Furthermore, he has increased the popularity of golf among young people. _____

◆ PRACTICE 22.5

Choose five items from the list of words and phrases provided, and then write three sentences for each parenthetical word or phrase—one with the parenthetical expression at the beginning of the sentence, one with the parenthetical expression in the middle, and one with the parenthetical expression at the end.

Examples

In fact, some dinosaurs were highly intelligent creatures.

Some dinosaurs were, in fact, highly intelligent creatures.

Some dinosaurs were highly intelligent creatures, in fact.

after all	in contrast
as a result	in fact
at the same time	in other words
consequently	nevertheless
for example	subsequently
however	therefore
in addition	

1a. ______________________________

____

b. ______________________________

____

c. ______________________________

____

2a. ______________________________

____

b. ______________________________

c. ______________________________

3a. ______________________________

b. ______________________________

c. ______________________________

4a. ______________________________

b. ______________________________

c. ______________________________

5a. ______________________________

b. ______________________________

c. ______________________________

D Using Commas with Appositives

Use commas to set off an **appositive**, a word or word group that identifies or describes a noun or a pronoun.

> Luis Valdez, an award-winning playwright, wrote *Los Vendidos* and *Zoot Suit*. (*An award-winning playwright* is an appositive that describes the noun *Luis Valdez*.)
>
> The Cisco Kid rode in on his horse, a white stallion. (*A white stallion* is an appositive that describes the noun *horse*.)
>
> She, the star of the show, applauded the audience. (*The star of the show* is an appositive that identifies the pronoun *she*.)

FOCUS Using Commas with Appositives

An appositive can appear at the beginning, in the middle, or at the end of a sentence. Wherever it appears, it is always set off from the rest of the sentence by commas.

> A Native American writer, Sherman Alexie wrote the novel *Reservation Blues*.
>
> Alexie's "Defending Walt Whitman," a poem, is about a basketball game.
>
> One of Alexie's books was made into a film, *Smoke Signals*.

◆ PRACTICE 22.6

Edit the following sentences for the correct use of commas to set off appositives. If the sentence is correct, write *C* in the blank.

Example: Hawaii's capital, Honolulu, is on the island of Oahu. _____

1. My mother Sandra Thomas used to work for the city. _____
2. Coca Cola, a popular drink has been around for decades. _____
3. The convention is in Chicago my hometown. _____
4. A rookie he approached the suspect nervously. _____
5. The world's tallest mountain Mount Everest is in Nepal. _____
6. Life on earth could not exist without our nearest star the sun. _____
7. Aloe a common houseplant, has medicinal value. _____
8. An excellent dancer, she won the competition easily. _____
9. Elvis Presley a white singer, was influenced by African-American music. _____
10. Adam Smith was a leading figure in economics the study of wealth and society. _____

◆ PRACTICE 22.7

In each of the following sentences, add an appositive that identifies or describes the noun or pronoun it refers to.

Example: The movie, ___*a western*___, is one of George's favorites.

1. Grace, his aunt, came to visit yesterday.
2. That item, of clothing, is very expensive.
3. My friend John, he passed the test easily.
4. *Alice's Adventures in Wonderland,* the movie, is a classic.
5. Ted enjoyed his meal, it is his favorite dish
6. That building, at the end of the block, used to be a factory.
7. Fresh brewed, coffee is often served in the morning.
8. We like to talk to Suzanne, the parot.
9. Biology, the course, is fascinating.
10. My great-grandmother had carefully folded the garment, and packed it away

E Using Commas to Set Off Nonrestrictive Clauses

Use commas to set off **nonrestrictive clauses**, groups of words that are not essential to a sentence's meaning. Do not use commas to set off **restrictive clauses**.

A **restrictive clause** contains essential information and is therefore *not* set off from the rest of the sentence by commas.

> The artist who was formerly known as Prince is now known as Prince again.

In the above sentence, the clause *who was formerly known as Prince* supplies specific information that is essential to the idea the sentence is communicating. The clause tells readers which particular artist is now known as Prince again. Without the clause *who was formerly known as Prince,* the sentence does not communicate the same idea because it does not specify which particular artist is now once again known as Prince.

> The artist is now known as Prince again.

A **nonrestrictive clause** does not contain essential information; therefore, a nonrestrictive clause *is* set off from the rest of the sentence by commas.

> Violent crime in our cities, which increased steadily for many years, is now decreasing.

Here, the underlined clause provides extra information to help readers understand the sentence, but the sentence communicates the same point without this information.

> Violent crime in our cities is now decreasing.

FOCUS *Who, Which,* and *That*

- *Who* can introduce either a restrictive or a nonrestrictive clause.

RESTRICTIVE Many people who watch *Oprah* buy the books her book club recommends. (no commas)

NONRESTRICTIVE Wally Lamb, who wrote a novel recommended by Oprah's Book Club, saw his book become a bestseller. (clause set off by commas)

- *Which* always introduces a nonrestrictive clause.

NONRESTRICTIVE Natural disasters, which can be terrifying, really appeal to movie audiences. (clause set off by commas)

- *That* always introduces a restrictive clause.

RESTRICTIVE They wanted to see the movie that had the best special effects. (no commas)

◆ PRACTICE 22.8

In each of the following sentences, decide whether the underlined clause is restrictive or nonrestrictive, and then add commas where necessary. If the sentence is correct, write *C* in the blank.

Examples

My boss, who loves fishing, has a picture of his boat in his office. N

The train that derailed yesterday was empty. C

1. Clocks that tick loudly can be irritating. C
2. The reader who graded my essay gave me an A on it. R
3. The camera, which is automatic, often breaks. N
4. Fish that live in polluted water are unsafe to eat. ____
5. The person who painted this picture is famous for her landscapes. R
6. Boxing, which requires quick reflexes, can be exciting to watch. N
7. Rafael, who finishes work at 5:30, met Carla for dinner at 7:00. N

8. The Thai restaurant that opened last month is supposed to be excellent. _____

9. Gray wolves which many ranchers dislike are making a comeback in the West. _____

10. The Broadway star who has also appeared in films has many devoted fans. _____

◆ PRACTICE 22.9

Edit the sentences in the following paragraph so that commas set off all nonrestrictive clauses. (Remember, commas are *not* used to set off restrictive clauses.) If the sentence is correct, write *C* in the blank.

Example: The Weavers Society, which is based in Guyana, runs an Internet business. _____

(1) Many people who live in developing countries have difficulty making a living. _____ (2) Modern technology which includes the Internet is changing that. _____ (3) In fact, businesses that use the Internet can reach customers around the world. _____ (4) For example, a group of women who live in Guyana recently started an Internet business. _____ (5) The women who call themselves the Weavers Society needed customers for their work. _____ (6) Their products which they make themselves are handwoven hammocks. _____ (7) A company that sells satellite telephones donated some phones to the weavers. _____ (8) The same company which also deals in computers helped the women connect to the World Wide Web. _____ (9) The weavers who could find no customers in their own village soon sold many of their hammocks to customers in other regions. _____ (10) These women have changed the economy of a village that had long been in poverty. _____

◆ PRACTICE 22.10

In each of the following sentences, fill in the blank with words that complete the restrictive or nonrestrictive clause.

Example: Movies and video games that *are very violent* have been in the news lately.

1. Action and horror movies, which ________________, often include violent scenes.
2. People who ________________ seem never to get tired of such films.
3. The violence that ________________ is often graphic.
4. Most fans say movie violence, which ________________, is not realistic.
5. They believe movies that ________________ do not pose a danger in real life.
6. However, psychologists who ________________ say viewing on-screen battles can affect people's behavior.
7. They worry that young people who ________________ will use force to settle conflicts in their own lives.
8. Video games that ________________ are the subject of a similar controversy.
9. Many people who ________________ say the games are a safe outlet for strong emotions.
10. The debate over media violence, which ________________, will probably continue for some time.

F Using Commas in Compound and Complex Sentences

In Chapters 7 and 8, you learned how to use commas between the clauses in compound and complex sentences. Here is a brief review.

Compound Sentences

A **compound sentence** is made up of two or more independent clauses (simple sentences) joined by a coordinating conjunction (*and, or, nor, but, for, so, yet*), by a semicolon, or by a conjunctive adverb. When a coordinating conjunction joins the independent clauses, always use a comma before the coordinating conjunction.

Morocco is in North Africa, but Senegal is in West Africa.

Student Voices

I tend to use commas where they aren't necessary.

Becky Bentzel

FOCUS Unnecessary Commas with *And* and *But*

Not every *and* and *but* has a comma before it. Do not use a comma in the following situations.

- Before the coordinating conjunction that separates the two parts of a compound subject

  INCORRECT *The Little Mermaid,* and *Mulan* are two animated films.

  CORRECT *The Little Mermaid* and *Mulan* are two animated films.

- Before the coordinating conjunction that separates the two parts of a compound predicate

  INCORRECT Snoopy ate a dog biscuit, and took a nap.

  CORRECT Snoopy ate a dog biscuit and took a nap.

Complex Sentences

A **complex sentence** is made up of an independent clause and one or more dependent clauses. The clauses are joined by subordinating conjunctions or relative pronouns. Place a comma after the dependent clause when it comes *before* the independent clause.

Although the African-American men called the Buffalo Soldiers fought bravely in World War II, many were never honored for their heroism.

FOCUS Unnecessary Commas in Complex Sentences

Do not use a comma in a complex sentence when the dependent clause comes after the independent clause.

INCORRECT Many people come to the United States, because they are seeking religious or political freedom.

CORRECT Many people come to the United States because they are seeking religious or political freedom.

◆ PRACTICE 22.11

Edit the sentences in the following paragraph for the correct use of commas in compound and complex sentences. If the sentence is correct, write *C* in the blank.

Example: Alaska is a challenging place to live, so its residents must adapt. ____

(1) Alaska is a rugged state and its population is small. ____ (2) Travel there is difficult so people rely on airplanes for transportation. ____ (3) Although many people live in Alaska's cities many others live in small villages. ____ (4) Such villages are scattered across the state and roads do not always reach them. ____ (5) Also, travel by road is not always possible because the state's Arctic weather can be severe. ____ (6) Even though air travel is expensive it is the best option available in some places. ____ (7) Alaska's bush pilots use small planes because these planes can take off and land in tight spots. ____ (8) When a traditional landing strip is not available a pilot may land on snow or open water. ____ (9) Most of Alaska's air passengers are locals, but visiting hunters and sightseers also fly with bush pilots. ____ (10) Until residents find a better means of transportation bush pilots will enjoy a brisk business in Alaska. ____

> **Writing Tip**
> Do not use commas between a month and the number of the day (*December 25*) or year (*December 2001*).

> **Student Voices**
> *I remember where to put the commas in dates and addresses by remembering where commas belong in my own address and my birthday.*
> *Ashley Johns*

> **Writing Tip**
> In addresses, do not use a comma between the building number and the street name.

G Using Commas in Dates and Addresses

Dates

Use commas in dates to separate the day of the week from the month and to separate the day of the month from the year.

The first Christmas Elena's son celebrated was Saturday, December 25, 1999.

When a date that includes commas falls in the middle of a sentence, place a comma after the date.

Saturday, December 25, 1999, was the first Christmas Elena's son celebrated.

Addresses

Use commas in addresses to separate the street address from the city and to separate the city from the state or country.

The British prime minister lives at 10 Downing Street, London, England.

When an address that includes commas falls in the middle of a sentence, place a comma after the address.

> The residence at 10 Downing Street, London, England, has been home to Winston Churchill and Margaret Thatcher.

◆ PRACTICE 22.12

Edit the following sentences for the correct use of commas in dates and addresses. Add any missing commas, and cross out any unnecessary commas. If the sentence is correct, write *C* in the blank.

Examples

Atif was born on August 15, 1965. ____

Islamabad, Pakistan, is near his hometown. ____

1. Atif is from Lahore Pakistan. ____
2. On March 12, 1995 his family moved to the United States. ____
3. Their first home was at 2122 Kent Avenue Brooklyn New York. ____
4. Atif and his wife became citizens of the United States in December, 1999. ____
5. They wanted to move to Boston Massachusetts where Atif's cousins lived. ____
6. On Tuesday June 6 2000 the family moved to the Boston area. ____
7. Their new address was 14 Arden Street Allston Massachusetts. ____
8. His daughters started school there on September 5. ____
9. The school is located at 212 Hope Street, Allston. ____
10. Atif's older daughter will graduate from the sixth grade on Friday June 28 2002. ____

■ REVISING AND EDITING

Look back at your response to the Seeing and Writing exercise on page 349. First, circle every comma in your writing. Then, review this chapter, and decide whether every comma you have used is necessary. If you find any unnecessary commas, cross them out. When you have finished, reread your work again to make sure you have not left out any necessary commas.

Computer Tip

Use the Find or Search command to highlight the commas in your writing. Check to see if you have used the commas correctly.

CHAPTER REVIEW

◆ EDITING PRACTICE

Read the following essay, which contains some errors in the use of commas. Add commas where necessary between items in a series and with introductory phrases, conjunctive adverbs or transitional expressions, appositives, and nonrestrictive clauses. Cross out any unnecessary commas. The first sentence has been edited for you.

The Battles of Elizabeth Cady Stanton

In the 1800s, two human rights campaigns divided public opinion. One was abolition the movement to end slavery. The other was women's suffrage the movement to allow women to vote. Elizabeth Cady Stanton was an important figure in both struggles, and she helped to bring about their ultimate success.

Cady Stanton was a wife, a mother, and a fierce campaigner. As a girl, she showed an interest in the law. Her father was a lawyer and Cady Stanton argued with him about laws that favored men. Her father however felt girls were inferior to boys. Although he respected his daughter's energy, and intelligence he always wished she had been a boy.

Cady Stanton attended a women's seminary in Troy New York. Soon after her graduation she began working to end slavery. Her husband, Henry Stanton opposed slavery. He was in fact a delegate to the World Anti-Slavery Convention in London, England. Cady Stanton admired his speaking talent, liberal values, and good looks. The two were married on May 1 1840.

Her work toward abolition which included lobbying Congress, went on for more than twenty years. Still, she longed to improve the lives of women. Women, who had almost no legal rights, were treated as the property of men. Cady Stanton believed women would never be equal to men, until they had the right to vote.

Suffrage was an uphill fight, but she devoted herself to it for more than fifty years. She wrote to Congress, spoke about women's rights, and published a newspaper called *The Revolution.* Cady Stanton's, work, which she accomplished while caring for seven children, changed women's lives. Her place in history, therefore, should be a prominent one.

◆ COLLABORATIVE ACTIVITIES

1. Working in a group of three or four students, list some of the specific dangers that high school students might be exposed to while in school. Next, list security measures that high schools might take to protect students from these dangers. Once you have completed your lists, work together to write a paragraph that includes at least three dangers to high school students and three possible security measures. Finally, exchange paragraphs with another group. Check one another's paragraphs to be sure commas are used correctly.
2. Bring to class a textbook for one of your courses. Working with a partner, turn to a page in the textbook, and use a pencil to circle every comma on the page. Take turns explaining why each comma is necessary. Next, choose two sentences each. On a separate piece of paper, recopy these sentences without any commas. Then, read them aloud. Do the sentences make sense? Finally, insert commas where they originally appeared, and read the sentences aloud again. Is there a difference?
3. Working with a partner, take turns interviewing each other, and use the information you get as material for a brief biography of your partner. Find out when and where your partner was born, where he or she has lived, the schools he or she has attended, and so on. Then, write a paragraph that includes all the information you have gathered, being sure to include transitions where necessary. When you have finished, exchange papers with another group. Check one another's papers to be sure commas are used correctly.

COMPOSING ORIGINAL SENTENCES

4. Imagine that you are writing a handbook for middle school students on the use of commas. Compose seven sample sentences to show the correct use of commas in each of the following situations:
   - in a series
   - to set off an introductory phrase
   - to set off a parenthetical word or phrase
   - to set off an appositive
   - to set off a nonrestrictive clause
   - in a compound sentence before a coordinating conjunction (*and, but, or,* and so on)
   - in a complex sentence that begins with a dependent clause

   When you have finished, check the sentences again to make sure you have corrected any errors in grammar, punctuation, or spelling.

✓ REVIEW CHECKLIST: Using Commas

- Use commas to separate elements in a series of three or more words or word groups. (See 22A.)
- Use commas to set off introductory phrases. (See 22B.)
- Use commas to set off parenthetical words and phrases. (See 22C.)
- Use commas to set off an appositive from the rest of the sentence. (See 22D.)
- Use commas to set off nonrestrictive clauses. (See 22E.)
- Use commas in compound and complex sentences. (See 22F.)
- Use commas to separate parts of dates and addresses. (See 22G.)

CHAPTER

23

Using Apostrophes

PREVIEW

In this chapter, you will learn

- to use apostrophes to form contractions (23A)
- to use apostrophes to form possessives (23B)
- to revise the incorrect use of apostrophes (23C)

■ SEEING AND WRITING

Do you believe men and women are equally qualified for all jobs, or do you think some jobs should be "men's jobs" or "women's jobs"? Look at the picture above, and then write a paragraph in which you explain your position.

Word Power

tradition behavior or custom handed down from generation to generation

traditional relating to tradition

An **apostrophe** is a punctuation mark that is used in two situations: to form a contraction, and to form the possessive of a noun or an indefinite pronoun.

Writing Tip

Even though contractions are used in speech and informal writing, they are not acceptable in most college or business writing situations.

A Using Apostrophes to Form Contractions

A **contraction** is a word that uses an apostrophe to combine two words. The apostrophe takes the place of the letters that are left out.

I <u>didn't</u> [did not] understand the question.

<u>It's</u> [it is] sometimes hard to see the difference between right and wrong.

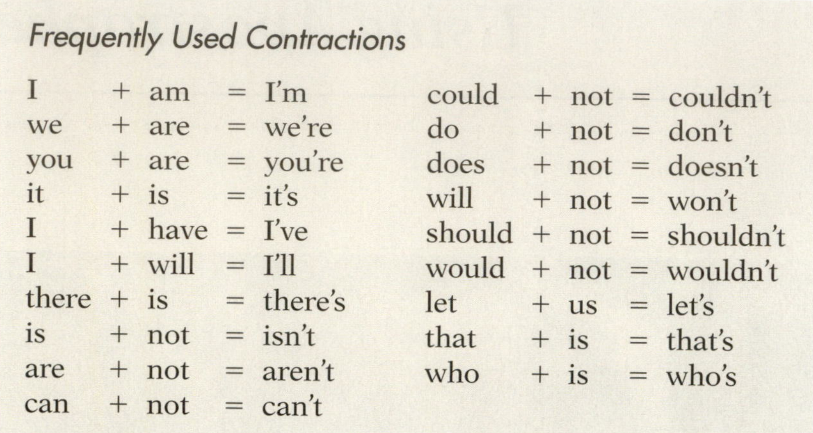

Frequently Used Contractions

I	+ am	= I'm		could	+ not	= couldn't
we	+ are	= we're		do	+ not	= don't
you	+ are	= you're		does	+ not	= doesn't
it	+ is	= it's		will	+ not	= won't
I	+ have	= I've		should	+ not	= shouldn't
I	+ will	= I'll		would	+ not	= wouldn't
there	+ is	= there's		let	+ us	= let's
is	+ not	= isn't		that	+ is	= that's
are	+ not	= aren't		who	+ is	= who's
can	+ not	= can't				

Writing Tip

Note that *won't* is different from the other contractions because its spelling is irregular.

PRACTICE 23.1

Edit the following paragraph so that apostrophes are used correctly in contractions.

Example: Emil ~~cant~~ can't skateboard because he ~~doesnt~~ doesn't practice.

(1) Skateboarding looks easy, but it isnt. (2) Most people cant just pick up a board and go. (3) Theyll need to practice first. (4) Some couldnt manage even if they did practice. (5) Skateboarders dont have that problem. (6) Theyre masters of balance and quick moves. (7) In many cases, theyve spent thousands of hours refining their skills. (8) And theres a lot to learn. (9) Its a sport filled with difficult twists, turns, and jumps. (10) Still, most skateboarders say theyd rather practice than do anything else.

PRACTICE 23.2

In each of the following sentences, add apostrophes to contractions if needed, and edit to make sure all apostrophes are placed correctly. If a sentence is correct, write *C* in the blank.

Example: Television ~~didnt~~ didn't become popular until the 1950s, but ~~its~~ it's very popular now. _____

1. Television is'nt a luxury in many homes; its a necessity. ____
2. Most people cant imagine life without television, and they dont want to try. ____
3. Theyll argue that theres plenty of high-quality programming on television. ____
4. However, television shows are'nt always the best way to get information. ____
5. Theyre designed to appeal to as many people as possible. ____
6. Wouldn't most people prefer to be entertained rather than informed? ____
7. The average American doesnt read nearly as much as he or she watches television. ____
8. It wouldnt hurt us to read more. ____
9. Fifty years ago, people could'nt have imagined how attached wed become to our television sets. ____
10. A generation from now, wholl remember a world where theres no television? ____

B Using Apostrophes to Form Possessives

Possessive forms show ownership. Nouns (names of people, animals, places, objects, or ideas) and indefinite pronouns (words like *everyone* and *anything*) do not have special possessive forms. Instead, they use apostrophes to show ownership.

> **Writing Tip**
>
> Possessive pronouns have special forms, such as *its* and *his*. These forms never include apostrophes. For more on possessives, see 19E.

Singular Nouns and Indefinite Pronouns

To form the possessive of singular nouns (including names), add an apostrophe plus an *s*.

The game's score [the score of the game] was very close.

Coach Nelson's goal [the goal of Coach Nelson] was to win.

Some singular nouns end in *-s*. Even if a singular noun already ends in *-s*, add an apostrophe plus an *s* to form the possessive.

The class's new computers were unpacked on Tuesday.

Carlos's computer crashed on Wednesday.

> **Student Voices**
>
> *I never know what to do about the possessive when I'm dealing with a word that ends in an s.*
>
> *Nicole Walsh*

For more on indefinite pronouns, see 19C.

FOCUS Indefinite Pronouns

Indefinite pronouns—words like *everyone* and *anything*—form possessives in the same way singular nouns do: they add an apostrophe and an *s*.

> Rodney was <u>everyone's choice</u> [the choice of everyone] for quarterback.

Plural Nouns

Most nouns form the plural by adding *s*. To form the possessive of plural nouns (including names) that end in *-s*, add just an apostrophe. Do *not* add an apostrophe plus an *s*.

> The two <u>televisions'</u> features [the features of the two televisions] were very different.
>
> The <u>Thompsons' house</u> [the house of the Thompsons] is on the corner.

For a list of some irregular plural nouns, see 18C.

Some irregular plural nouns do not end in *-s*. If a plural noun does not end in *-s*, add an apostrophe plus an *s* to form the possessive.

> The children's room is upstairs.

◆ PRACTICE 23.3

Rewrite the following groups of words, changing the singular noun or indefinite pronoun that follows *of* to the possessive form.

Example: the plot of the book *the book's plot*

1. the owner of the shop ______________________
2. the pilot of the plane ______________________
3. the cat of the neighbor ______________________
4. the desk of the manager ______________________
5. the computer of Indira ______________________
6. the engine of the truck ______________________
7. the sister of Chris ______________________
8. the guess of anyone ______________________
9. the opinion of the class ______________________
10. the waiting room of the doctor ______________________

◆ PRACTICE 23.4

Rewrite the following groups of words, changing the plural noun or indefinite pronoun that follows *of* to the possessive form.

Example: the rhythm of the dancers *the dancers' rhythm*

1. the bags of the travelers ______
2. the quills of the porcupines ______
3. the faces of the women ______
4. the room of the children ______
5. the car of the ministers ______
6. the bills of the customers ______
7. the apartment of the Huangs ______
8. the voice of the people ______
9. the first meeting of the lawyers ______
10. the telephone number of the Smiths ______

◆ PRACTICE 23.5

In each of the following sentences, fill in the blank with a possessive noun that completes the sentence.

Example: We listened to the *orchestra's* fine performance.

1. The ______ finances are in good order.
2. Tamika bought the ______ clothes on sale.
3. ______ answer made no sense at all.
4. We watched the ______ speech on television last night.
5. The noise made by ______ dog is unbearable.
6. Her ______ letter came in the mail on Friday.
7. ______ last movie was quite successful.
8. Someone found a ______ hat on the sidewalk.
9. ______ interests include water polo and hang gliding.
10. Halfway through the ______ hike, it started to rain.

◆ PRACTICE 23.6

In each of the following sentences, edit the underlined possessive nouns and indefinite pronouns so that apostrophes are used correctly. If a correction needs to be made, cross out the noun or pronoun, and write the correct form above it. If the possessive form is correct, write *C* above it.

Example: A ~~business'~~ business's success depends on the founder's (C) hard work and good luck.

1. In 1888, Lee Kee Lo opened a business in New Yorks Chinatown.
2. He was one of the neighborhoods' best-known grocers.
3. Lee's son, Harold, expanded his fathers' business.
4. He met many customer's financial needs, such as currency exchange.
5. Harold Lees' bank also filled business owners' requests for loans.
6. Then, Harolds' son Arthur changed the business' mission again.
7. He was the familys'—and Chinatowns'—first insurance agent.
8. If someones' property needed to be insured, Arthur Lee's agency took the job.
9. The insurance agencys' office is now run by Arthurs' children.
10. The Lee's business continues to flourish in Lee Kee Lo's original storefront.

C Revising the Incorrect Use of Apostrophes

Writing Tip

Never use an apostrophe with a plural noun unless the noun is possessive.

Watch out for the following problems with apostrophes.

- Be careful not to confuse a plural noun (*girls*) with the singular possessive form of the noun (*girl's*). Do not use apostrophes to form noun plurals.

In the following sentences, the nouns are plural, not possessive. Therefore, no apostrophes are used.

Cats [not *cat's*] can be wonderful pets [not *pet's*].

The Diazes [not *Diaz's*] went to Disney World.

Writing Tip

Remember that *it's* is not a possessive pronoun. It is a contraction that means *it is*.

- Never use apostrophes with **possessive pronouns** that end in *-s*.

Possessive Pronouns	*Incorrect Spelling*
hers	her's
its	it's
ours	our's
yours	your's
theirs	their's

- Do not confuse possessive pronouns with sound-alike contractions. Remember, possessive pronouns never include apostrophes.

Possessive Pronoun	*Contraction*
The dog licked its paw.	It's [it is] not fair.
This apartment is theirs.	There's [there is] the bus.
Whose turn is it?	Who's [who is] there?
Is this your hat?	You're [you are] absolutely right.

Computer Tip

Your computer's spell checker will not tell you when you have used a contraction for a possessive form—*it's* for *its*, for example. If you are not sure you have used the correct form, consult a dictionary.

PRACTICE 23.7

In each of the following sentences, circle the correct form (contraction or possessive pronoun) in parentheses.

Example: This is (you're/your) last chance.

1. The elephant sprayed water from (it's/its) trunk.
2. (There's/Theirs) something wrong with this engine.
3. According to the newspaper, (it's/its) supposed to rain tomorrow.
4. The Nelsons say the yellow rake is (there's/theirs).
5. The building was restored to (it's/its) former beauty.
6. (Who's/Whose) in charge of refreshments?
7. Harriet says (you're/your) an excellent softball player.
8. Does anyone know (who's/whose) sweater this is?
9. I never use that vase because (it's/its) an antique.
10. (You're/Your) suggestion was the best one given at the meeting.

Student Voices

I always get its *and* it's *confused. I try to remember that* its *is a possessive pronoun like* his, *and* his *has no apostrophe.*

Lenny Fox

PRACTICE 23.8

In each of the following sentences, check the underlined words to be sure apostrophes are used correctly. If a correction needs to be made, cross out the word, and write the correct version above it. If the noun or pronoun is correct, write *C* above it.

Example: Tulips grew along the garden's (C) edge, even in ~~it's~~ (its) shadiest spots.

1. Songs about lover's trials and triumphs are always popular.
2. The worlds' population won't stop growing for some time.

3. Its a lovely evening, don't you think?
4. Children are quick to say which toys are there's.
5. The committee reported it's findings in today's newsletter.
6. All the government agency's were closed.
7. Whose coming to your party?
8. If your such an expert, why can't you fix Lois' dishwasher?
9. You'll need five hundred resident's signatures on you're petition.
10. Both of Henrys sister's made the dresses they're wearing.

◆ PRACTICE 23.9

Write an original sentence for each of these possessive pronouns: *its, your, theirs*. Then, write a sentence for each of these contractions: *it's, you're, there's*. Be sure to use apostrophes only in contractions, not in possessive pronouns.

1. its

____

____

2. your

____

____

3. theirs

____

____

4. it's

____

____

5. you're

____

____

6. there's

____

____

◆ PRACTICE 23.10

Write a short paragraph that includes all these words: *it's, its, birds, bird's nest.*

____

____

____

____

____

■ REVISING AND EDITING

Look back at your response to the Seeing and Writing exercise on page 367. First, circle every apostrophe in your writing. Then, review this chapter to make sure that all the apostrophes in your response are used correctly and that you have not forgotten any necessary apostrophes.

CHAPTER REVIEW

◆ EDITING PRACTICE

Read the following essay, which contains some errors in the use of apostrophes. Edit it to eliminate errors by crossing out incorrect words and writing corrections above them. (Note that this is an informal essay, so contractions are acceptable.) The first sentence has been edited for you.

Dolphins: People with Fins?

Tame ~~dolphin's~~ dolphins are a common sight at aquariums and water shows. People are fascinated by the dolphins friendly behavior. Many wild dolphins, too, seem comfortable around people. In some ways, the social patterns of dolphins are'nt so different from those of humans. Maybe dolphins are attracted to humans because their social behavior is similar to our's.

Like people, dolphins socialize in different groups at different times. Their not limited to a small set of companions. Humans shift from one group of friends or family members to another, and so do dolphins. Also like humans, dolphins tend to have several mates during their lives. The dolphins mating pattern isnt just biological. It's social as well. In fact, its sort of like the human practice of dating.

Dolphin family's also show some human traits. For example, young dolphins stay close to their mother's for several years. The mothers sometimes work together in groups to guard their calves safety. One mother might even babysit for another while shes busy elsewhere. And the family bond does'nt end when the offspring grow up. A mature dolphin may return to it's mothers side when the mother is giving birth to a new calf.

Finally, dolphins seem to pick their friends the same way people do. Dolphins tend to spend time with other's who are the same sex and age. In fact, many dolphins have one or two companions, similar to best friends, who's company they prefer. Male dolphins, especially, tend to have a couple of buddies their often found with. With so many things in common, its no wonder dolphins and humans seem to get along well.

◆ COLLABORATIVE ACTIVITIES

1. Working in a group of four and building on each of your responses to the Seeing and Writing exercise at the beginning of the chapter, think about how the definitions of "men's jobs" and "women's jobs" have changed in recent decades. Then, make two lists:

   - jobs that were once held only by men but are now also performed by women (such as firefighter)
   - jobs that were once held only by women but are now also performed by men (such as nurse)

2. Consulting the lists your group developed in activity 1, work in pairs, with one pair of students in each group listing reasons why there should be "men's jobs" and "women's jobs" and one pair listing reasons why both men and women should be able to do any sort of work they choose. Use possessive forms whenever possible—for example, *women's earnings* rather than *the earnings of women.*

3. Bring to class a book, magazine, or newspaper whose style is informal—for example, a popular novel, an entertainment magazine, or the sports section of a newspaper. Working in a group, circle every contraction you can find on one page of each publication. Then, replace each contraction with the words that combine to form it. Are your substitutions an improvement? (You may want to read a few paragraphs aloud before you reach a conclusion.)

COMPOSING ORIGINAL SENTENCES

4. Work together with your group to write a total of seven original sentences. Three sentences should have contractions of a pronoun and a verb using an apostrophe (for example: *it's* = *it is*). Four sentences should use singular and plural nouns in the possessive form. Use at least one noun that ends in *-s* and at least one indefinite pronoun (for example: *everyone*). When you have finished, check the sentences again to make sure you have corrected any errors in grammar, punctuation, or spelling.

✓ REVIEW CHECKLIST: Using Apostrophes

- Use apostrophes to form contractions. (See 23A.)
- Use an apostrophe plus an *s* to form the possessive of singular nouns and indefinite pronouns. Even when a noun ends in *-s*, use an apostrophe plus an *s* to form the possessive. (See 23B.)
- Use an apostrophe alone to form the possessive of most plural nouns, including names. (See 23B.)
- Do not use apostrophes with plural nouns unless they are possessive. Do not use apostrophes with possessive pronouns. (See 23C.)

CHAPTER

24 Understanding Mechanics

PREVIEW

In this chapter, you will learn

- to capitalize proper nouns (24A)
- to punctuate direct quotations (24B)
- to set off titles of books, stories, and other works (24C)

■ SEEING AND WRITING

Look at the picture above. Then, write a paragraph in which you describe your favorite contemporary or classic cartoon. Be sure to name the most important characters and to quote some dialogue that you remember.

Word Power

contemporary current; modern

A Capitalizing Proper Nouns

A **proper noun** names a particular person, animal, place, object, or idea. Proper nouns are always capitalized. The list that follows explains and illustrates the rules for capitalizing proper nouns. It also includes some important exceptions to these rules.

> **Writing Tip**
> The words *black* and *white* are generally not capitalized when they refer to racial groups. However, *African American* and *Caucasian* are always capitalized.

- Always capitalize names of races, ethnic groups, tribes, nationalities, languages, and religions.

  The census data revealed a diverse community of Caucasians, African Americans, and Asian Americans, with a few Latino and Navajo residents. Native languages include English, Korean, and Spanish. Most people identified themselves as Catholic, Protestant, or Muslim.

- Capitalize names of specific people and any titles that go along with those names. In general, do not capitalize titles that are used without a name.

  In 2000, President Vicente Fox was elected to lead Mexico.

  The student body president met with the dean.

- Capitalize names of specific family members and their titles. Do not capitalize words that identify family relationships, including those introduced by possessive pronouns.

  Cousin Matt and Cousin Susie are the children of Mom's brother, Uncle Bill.

  My cousins Matt and Susie are the children of my mother's brother Bill, who is my uncle.

- Capitalize names of specific countries, cities, towns, bodies of water (lakes, rivers, oceans), streets, and so on. Do not capitalize words that identify unnamed places.

  The Liffey runs through Dublin.

  The river runs through the city.

- Capitalize names of specific geographical regions. Do not capitalize such words when they refer to a direction.

  Louis L'Amour's novels are set in the American West.

  We got lost after we turned west off the freeway.

- Capitalize names of specific buildings and monuments. Do not capitalize general references to buildings and monuments.

  He drove past the Space Needle and toward Pike's Market.

  He drove past the monument and toward the market.

- Capitalize names of specific groups, clubs, teams, and associations. Do not capitalize general references to groups of individuals.

  Members of the Teamsters' Union worked at the Democratic Party convention, the Backstreet Boys concert, and the Sixers-Pacers game.

  Members of the union worked at the party's convention, the rock group's concert, and the basketball team's game.

For information on capitalizing titles of books, essays, and so on, see 24C.

- Capitalize names of specific historical periods, events, and documents. Do not capitalize general references to periods, events, or documents.

The Emancipation Proclamation was signed during the Civil War, not during Reconstruction.

The document was signed during the war, not during the post-war period.

- Capitalize names of businesses, government agencies, schools, and other institutions. Do not capitalize nonspecific references to such institutions.

  Our local Burger King and McDonald's want to hire students from Lincoln High School and Brooklyn College.

  Our local fast-food restaurants want to hire high school and college students.

Student Voices

I have to fight the urge to capitalize a word just because I think it's important.

Lenny Fox

Writing Tip

Trade names that have been part of the language for many years—*nylon,* for example—are no longer capitalized.

- Capitalize brand names. Do not capitalize general references to kinds of products.

  Jan put on her Rollerblades and skated off to Xerox her paper.

  Jan put on her in-line skates and skated off to photocopy her paper.

- Capitalize titles of specific academic courses. Do not capitalize names of general academic subject areas, except for proper nouns—for example, the name of a language or a country.

  Calvin registered for English 101 and Psychology 302.

  Calvin registered for English and psychology.

- Capitalize days of the week, months of the year, and holidays. Do not capitalize the names of the seasons (*summer, fall, winter, spring*).

  Christmas, Chanukah, and Kwanzaa all fall in December.

  Christmas, Chanukah, and Kwanzaa all fall in the winter.

◆ PRACTICE 24.1

Edit the following sentences, capitalizing letters and changing capitals to lowercase letters where necessary.

Example: Archaeologists study the Ojibwa at M mackinac State Historic Park in M michigan, a s State where many members of the group live.

1. The Ojibwa are the largest native american group in north america.
2. Today, they live near the Great lakes in the united states and canada.
3. The ojibwa made maple syrup that was something like the syrup sold in shoprite or safeway.
4. The Ojibwa migrated to the midwest from their original homes near the atlantic ocean.

5. A century before the revolutionary war, Europeans traveled West and met the native peoples who lived there.
6. Many modern Ojibwa live in michigan in the cities of Detroit and duluth and on rural Reservations.
7. The american indian movement is an Organization that calls attention to unfair treaties, such as the treaty of 1854.
8. Activist Winona LaDuke, who served as the Principal of an Ojibwa school, is also active in national politics.
9. In November 2000, LaDuke ran for Vice President on the green party ticket.
10. My cousin, aunt Sara's son, learned about the Ojibwa in American history 240.

◆ PRACTICE 24.2

Write a sentence that includes each of the following pairs of words. Capitalize where necessary. Each sentence should be at least six or seven words long.

Example: valentine's day/holiday

Stella's least favorite holiday is Valentine's Day.

1. aunt mary/aunt

____

2. johnson's department store/store

____

3. dr. casey/doctor

____

4. reverend jackson/minister

____

5. american history 210/history

____

6. donald duck/duck

____

B Punctuating Direct Quotations

A **direct quotation** reproduces the *exact* words of a speaker or writer. Direct quotations are always placed within quotation marks.

> Brian said, "I've decided to go to business school."
>
> Tolstoy wrote, "Happy families are all alike; every unhappy family is unhappy in its own way."

When a quotation is a complete sentence, as it is in the two examples above, it begins with a capital letter and ends with appropriate end punctuation (a period, a question mark, or an exclamation point). When a quotation falls at the end of a sentence, as it does in the examples above, the period is placed *inside* the quotation marks. If the quotation is a question or an exclamation, the question mark or exclamation point is also placed *inside* the quotation marks.

> Regis asked, "Is that your final answer?"
>
> When the vampire attacked, Ted cried, "Help me!"

FOCUS Identifying Tags

A direct quotation is usually accompanied by an **identifying tag**, a phrase—such as *Mike said* or *asked Jeanine*—that identifies the person whose words are being quoted. Identifying tags can appear in a variety of places in a sentence.

Identifying Tag at the Beginning

When the identifying tag comes before the quotation, it is followed by a comma.

> Jamie announced, "I really need to cut up all my credit cards."

Identifying Tag at the End

When the identifying tag comes at the end of a sentence, it is followed by a period. A comma (or, sometimes, a question mark or exclamation point) inside the closing quotation marks separates the quotation from the identifying tag.

> "I really need to cut up all my credit cards," announced Jamie.
>
> "Do I really need to cut up all my credit cards?" asked Jamie.

Identifying Tag in the Middle

When the identifying tag comes in the middle of a quoted sentence, it is followed by a comma. The first part of the quotation is

(continued on the following page)

(continued from the previous page)

also followed by a comma, which is placed *inside* the quotation marks. Because the part of the quotation that follows the tag is not a new sentence, it does not begin with a capital letter.

> "I'll cut up all my credit cards," Jamie promised, "and then I'll start over."

Identifying Tag between Two Sentences

When the identifying tag comes between two quoted sentences, it is followed by a period, and the second quoted sentence begins with a capital letter.

> "Doing without credit cards will be good for me," Jamie decided. "Paying cash for everything will help me stick to my budget."

FOCUS Indirect Quotations

Be careful not to confuse direct and indirect quotations. A direct quotation reproduces someone's *exact* words, but an **indirect quotation** simply summarizes what was said or written.

Indirect quotations are not placed within quotation marks.

DIRECT QUOTATION Martin Luther King Jr. said, "I have a dream."

INDIRECT QUOTATION Martin Luther King Jr. said that he had a dream.

Writing Tip

Note that an indirect quotation is introduced by the word *that*.

◆ PRACTICE 24.3

Rewrite each of the following sentences twice. In the first version, place the identifying tag at the end of the sentence. In the second version, place the identifying tag in the middle of the sentence. Be sure to check punctuation and capitalization carefully.

Example: Joe said, "The grapes don't taste as good as they look."

"The grapes don't taste as good as they look," Joe said.

"The grapes," Joe said, "don't taste as good as they look."

1. Sue said, "These clothes are too small for me."

______

______

2. Pasqual claimed, "I won the team's soccer match all by myself."

____

____

3. The instructor said, "The exam should not be too difficult."

____

____

4. Councilman Gonzalez announced, "I will do my best to defeat the new tax law."

____

____

____

____

5. The poet Emily Dickinson wrote, "Tell all the truth but tell it slant."

____

____

◆ PRACTICE 24.4

In the following sentences containing direct quotations, first underline the identifying tag. Then, punctuate the quotation correctly, adding capital letters where necessary.

Example: "Injustice anywhere," said Dr. Martin Luther King Jr., "is a threat to justice everywhere."

1. Dorothy Parker said the cure for boredom is curiosity.
2. The guide announced whatever you do, don't leave the group.
3. Why does it always rain on my birthday Patrice asked.
4. Move along, everyone the officer shouted.
5. If you lose this tape Rebecca insisted I'll never lend you anything again.
6. The game isn't over till it's over said baseball legend Yogi Berra.
7. When I walked in, the instructor was saying please be sure to arrive on time.
8. If we get separated Paul asked where should I meet you?

9. High school Kurt Vonnegut observed is closer to the core of the American experience than anything I can think of.

10. I not only use all the brains that I have said Woodrow Wilson but all that I can borrow.

◆ PRACTICE 24.5

The following quotations are followed in parentheses by the names of the people who wrote or said them. On the blank lines, write a sentence that includes the quotation and places the identifying tag in the position that the directions specify. Be sure to punctuate and capitalize correctly.

Example: Let's ask for directions before we get lost. (said by Michelle)

Identifying tag in the middle: "Let's ask for directions," Michelle said, "before we get lost."

1. Fiction is the truth inside the lie. (said by Stephen King)

   Identifying tag at the beginning: ______________________

   ____

2. What's up? (asked by Hector)

   Identifying tag at the end: ______________________

   ____

3. Express yourself. (said by Madonna)

   Identifying tag at the end: ______________________

   ____

4. Brevity is the soul of wit. (written by William Shakespeare)

   Identifying tag at the beginning: ______________________

   ____

5. I am the greatest! (proclaimed by heavyweight champion Muhammad Ali)

   Identifying tag at the end: ______________________

   ____

6. Why is this bag of rice in the refrigerator? (asked by Juan's sister)

   Identifying tag at the beginning: ______________________

   ____

7. No one can make you feel inferior without your consent. (written by Eleanor Roosevelt)

   Identifying tag at the end: ______________________________

   ____

8. Taku is not home. He went to the movies. (said by Hannah)

   Identifying tag in the middle: ______________________________

   ____

9. The best way to have a good idea is to have lots of ideas. (said by scientist Linus Pauling)

   Identifying tag in the middle: ______________________________

   ____

10. Get plenty of rest. You should feel better in a week or so. (said by Dr. Jagu)

    Identifying tag in the middle: ______________________________

    ____

C Setting Off Titles of Books, Stories, and Other Works

Some titles are *italicized* (or underlined to indicate italics). Others are enclosed in quotation marks. In general, underline titles of books and other long works, and enclose titles of shorter works (stories, essays, poems, and so on) in quotation marks.

The following chart shows which titles should be italicized and which should be enclosed in quotation marks.

Italicized Titles

Books: *The Joy Luck Club*
Newspapers: the *Los Angeles Times*
Magazines: *Newsweek, Latina*
Record albums: *Marc Anthony*
Long poems: *Paradise Lost*
Plays: *Our Town, Fences*
Films: *Jurassic Park*
Television and radio series: *Eyes on the Prize*

Titles in Quotation Marks

Book chapters: "Writing a Paragraph"
Short stories: "The Lottery"
Essays and articles: "Shooting an Elephant"
Songs: "I Need to Know"
Short poems: "The Road Not Taken"
Songs: "The Star-Spangled Banner"
Individual episodes of television or radio series: "The Montgomery Bus Boycott" (episode of *Eyes on the Prize*)

Writing Tip

When you type one of your own papers, do not underline your title or enclose it in quotation marks. Only titles of *published works* are set off in this way.

FOCUS Capitalizing in Titles

Capitalize the first letters of all important words in titles. Do not capitalize an **article** (*a, an,* or *the*), a **preposition** (*to, of, around,* and so on), or a **coordinating conjunction**—unless it is the first or last word of the title (*On the Road, No Way Out*).

◆ PRACTICE 24.6

In each of the following sentences, underline or insert quotation marks around titles. (Remember that titles of books and other long works are underlined, and titles of stories, essays, and other shorter works are enclosed in quotation marks.)

Example: Late Blooming Flowers, a book of stories by Anton Chekhov, includes "The Little Trick" and "A Visit to Friends."

1. The show A Prairie Home Companion has been on the radio for many years.
2. Soul Coughing's first album, Ruby Vroom, contained their hit song Supra Genius.
3. Did you see the article Earthquake Predictions Made in the Los Angeles Times?
4. Essays of E. B. White, a collection published in 1977, includes Death of a Pig and Once More to the Lake.
5. The song I Could Have Danced All Night was written for the musical My Fair Lady.
6. Sylvia Plath's poem The Moon and the Yew Tree was published in Ariel, her best-known book.
7. The textbook Foundations First includes the chapter Understanding Mechanics.
8. When the movie The Perfect Storm first appeared in theaters, Newsweek featured a review of the film.
9. After studying Shakespeare's play Hamlet, we will read John Milton's book-length poem Paradise Lost.

10. The Orphan Trains is a program in the television series The American Experience.

◆ PRACTICE 24.7

Edit the following sentences, capitalizing letters where necessary in titles.

Example: The movie *charley* was based on the short story "flowers for algernon."

1. Lucy's favorite novel is *for whom the bell tolls.*
2. Jack London's short story "to build a fire" is a classic.
3. Recent television cartoons created for adults include *the simpsons* and *king of the hill.*
4. The soundtrack for the movie *the matrix* features songs such as "ultrasonic sound" and "wake up."
5. The articles "stream of consciousness" and "school's out" in *wired* magazine focus on new technology.

■ REVISING AND EDITING

Look back at your response to the Seeing and Writing exercise on page 378. Check your work carefully. Have you capitalized all proper nouns? Have you used quotation marks correctly to set off direct quotations? Have you punctuated direct quotations correctly? Have you underlined the title of the cartoon you chose to write about and used capital letters throughout? Edit where necessary.

CHAPTER REVIEW

◆ EDITING PRACTICE

Read the following passage, which contains errors in capitalization and in the use of direct quotations and titles. Then, edit the passage to correct the errors. The first sentence has been edited for you.

Until recently, minority actors had trouble finding work in hollywood, where most films starred actors who had european backgrounds. This was true even when the characters they played were Asian, native american, or Hispanic. One example is the movie "West Side Story." Natalie Wood, who was Anglo, played the character Maria, who was Puerto Rican. Wood assumed a Puerto Rican accent when she sang songs such as *I Feel Pretty* and *Tonight*.

Anna May Wong was an exception to the rule. For years, she was the most famous Chinese actress in hollywood. She grew up in Los Angeles, california, and began appearing in movies when she was twelve years old. In the 1920s, Wong played her first major role in *The Thief of Bagdad*. Her real name was Liu Tsong. An Executive at a movie studio changed her name to make it sound more American.

As late as the 1980s, movie executives were cautious about casting actors from other cultures. Andy Garcia, who was born in Cuba, had trouble getting roles until he starred in the film *the Mean Season*. He went on to star in movies such as *The Untouchables* and "The Godfather, Part III." Garcia decided to become an actor when he was a student in College. He said, "That was when my true calling came out." Even though he has lived in the United States since he was a young child, Garcia feels a connection to his Cuban heritage. "Over the years, he said, I've realized how much my feelings about Cuba define my sense of self."

◆ COLLABORATIVE ACTIVITIES

1. Working in a small group, make a list of at least fifteen famous people, places, and historical or news events you have heard of or read about recently. Be sure to capitalize all proper nouns. Next, choose three of the items on your list, and work together to write a sentence about each person, place, or event, explaining why it is important. Then, exchange papers with another group. Check one another's papers to be sure capital letters are used correctly.
2. Imagine that you and the other members of your group are in charge of creating the American Entertainment Hall of Fame. Make lists of your favorite songs, movies, and television shows. When you have finished,

choose one item from each person's list. Then, write a sentence explaining why that song, movie, or television show belongs in the American Entertainment Hall of Fame. When you have finished, exchange papers with another group. Check one another's papers to be sure capitals, quotation marks, and underlining are used correctly.

3. Working in a group of four, choose two people in the group to take different positions on a topic such as the drinking age, gun control, or required college courses. Next, have these two people present their views and discuss alternatives. While the discussion is going on, each of the two remaining group members should record a few key statements by each participant. After the discussion has ended, work together to write a paragraph that includes the viewpoints of both participants. Place all direct quotations within quotation marks, and include identifying tags that clearly indicate which person is speaking. When you have finished, exchange paragraphs with another group. Finally, check one another's papers to be sure capitals and quotation marks are used correctly, and make sure all quotations are punctuated correctly.

COMPOSING ORIGINAL SENTENCES

4. Working in a group of four, write a five- or six-sentence paragraph about your city or neighborhood, capitalizing proper nouns to identify important places, public officials, schools, and natural features. Include at least one direct quotation and one title of a local newspaper and an article in that paper. (The quotation and the article title can be made up.) Then, exchange paragraphs with another group. Check one another's work to be sure capitals and quotation marks are used correctly, and make sure all quotations are punctuated correctly. When you have finished, check your group's paragraph again to make sure you have corrected any errors in grammar, punctuation, or spelling.

✓ REVIEW CHECKLIST: Understanding Mechanics

- Capitalize proper nouns. (See 24A.)
- Always place direct quotations within quotation marks. (See 24B.)
- In titles, capitalize all important words, as well as the first and the last words. Use quotation marks or underline to set off titles. (See 24C.)

CHAPTER

25

Understanding Spelling

PREVIEW

In this chapter, you will learn

- to become a better speller (25A)
- to know when to use *ie* and *ei* (25B)
- to understand prefixes (25C)
- to understand suffixes (25D)

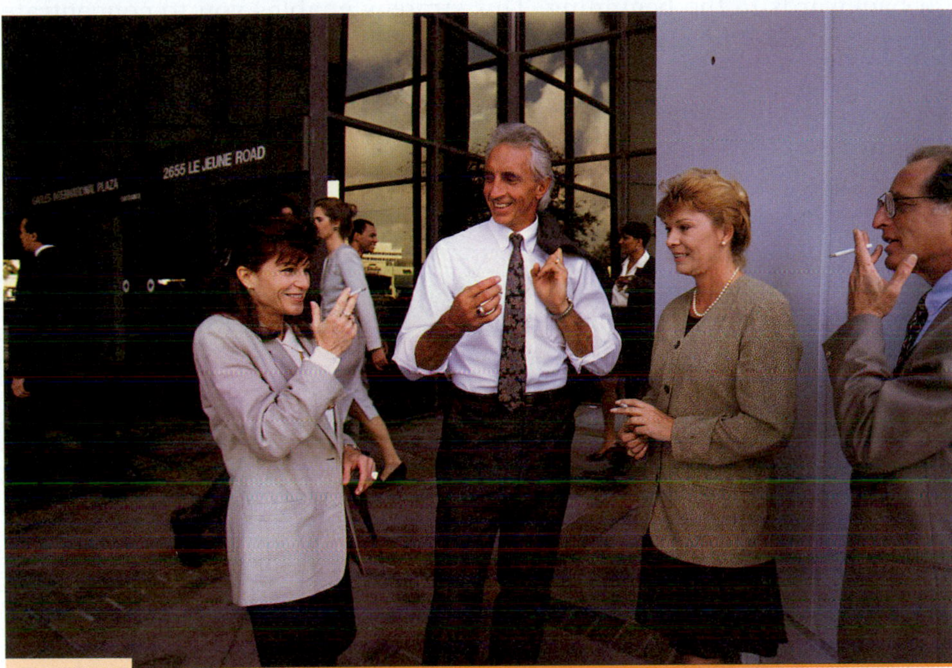

SEEING AND WRITING

Do you think local, state, and federal governments are right to pass laws that prohibit smoking in public places? Look at the picture above, and then write a paragraph in which you answer this question.

Word Power

prohibit to forbid

ostracize to exclude from a group

carcinogen something that causes cancer

obligation a course of action demanded of a person by law or conscience

A Becoming a Better Speller

Teachers and employers will expect you to be able to recognize and correct misspelled words. The following suggestions can help you become a better speller.

Student Voices

I love my spell checker.

Frank Palmer

- *Use a spell checker.* Always use a spell checker if you are writing on a computer. It will identify and correct most typos and misspelled words.

However, keep in mind that spell checkers have limitations. For one thing, they will not identify some misspelled words—for example, some foreign words and proper nouns. In addition, they do not identify typos that create words (*form* instead of *from*) or words that you have used incorrectly (*there* for *their*).

- *Use a dictionary.* As you proofread, circle words whose spellings you are not sure of. Look these words up in a dictionary to make sure they are spelled correctly.
- *Proofread carefully.* Proofread first for your biggest problem and then go back and check for all other errors. If spelling is your biggest problem, proofread first for misspellings. (You might try checking your spelling by starting with the last sentence of your paper and reading backwards to the beginning. This strategy enables you to concentrate on one word at a time without being distracted by the logic and sequence of your ideas.)
- *Keep a personal spelling list.* Write down all the words you misspell. If you keep a writing journal, set aside a few pages in the back for a spelling list. Keep a record of the words your spell checker highlights, and write down any misspelled words that your instructor identifies. (These will usually be circled or marked *sp.*)
- *Look for patterns in your misspellings.* Do you have trouble forming plurals? Do you misspell words with *ei* combinations? Once you have identified these problems, you can focus on eliminating them.
- *Learn the basic spelling rules.* Memorize the spelling rules outlined in this chapter. Each rule you learn can help you spell many words correctly.
- *Review commonly confused words.* Study the commonly confused words in Chapter 26. If any of these words give you trouble, add them to your personal spelling list.
- *Make flash cards.* Copy down words that constantly give you trouble on 3 × 5 cards. Review these words when you have time.
- *Use memory cues.* Think of a memory cue that will help you remember how to spell each particularly troublesome word. For example, remembering that *definite* contains the word *finite* will help you remember that *definite* is spelled with an *i,* not an *a.*
- *Learn the most frequently misspelled words.* Study the words on the following list. If a word gives you trouble, add it to your personal spelling list.

Writing Tip

The best place to check spelling is a good college dictionary, which will also tell you how to pronounce a word and which syllables to stress. For more on using a dictionary, see Appendix A of this book, "Building Word Power."

Frequently Misspelled Words

across	benefit	definitely	everything
address	calendar	dependent	exercise
all right	cannot	describe	experience
a lot	careful	develop	finally
argument	careless	disappoint	forty
beautiful	cemetery	early	fulfill
becoming	certain	embarrass	generally
beginning	crowded	entrance	government
believe	definite	environment	grammar

(continued on the following page)

(continued from the previous page)

harass	occasion	probably	tomato
height	occur	professor	tomatoes
holiday	occurred	receive	truly
integration	occurrences	recognize	until
intelligence	occurring	reference	usually
interest	occurs	restaurant	Wednesday
interfere	personnel	roommate	weird
judgment	possible	secretary	window
loneliness	potato	sentence	withhold
medicine	potatoes	separate	woman
minute	prejudice	speech	women
necessary	prescription	studying	writing
noticeable	privilege	surprise	written

FOCUS Vowels and Consonants

Knowing which letters are vowels and which are consonants will help you understand the spelling rules presented in this chapter.

VOWELS *a, e, i, o, u*

CONSONANTS *b, c, d, f, g, h, j, k, l, m, n, p, q, r, s, t, v, w, x, z*

The letter *y* may be considered either a vowel or a consonant, depending on how it is pronounced. In *young, y* acts as a consonant because it has the sound of *y;* in *truly,* it acts as a vowel because it has the sound of *ee.*

B Deciding between *ie* and *ei*

Memorize this rule: *i* before *e,* except after *c,* or when *ei* sounds like *ay* as in *neighbor* and *weigh.*

i before e	*except after c*	*or when ei is pronounced ay*
achieve	ceiling	eight
believe	conceive	freight
friend	deceive	neighbor
		weigh

FOCUS Exceptions to the "*i* before *e*" Rule

There are some exceptions to the "*i* before *e*" rule. The exceptions follow no pattern, so you must memorize them.

ancient	either	leisure	seize
caffeine	foreign	neither	species
conscience	height	science	weird

◆ PRACTICE 25.1

In each of the following sentences, proofread the underlined words for correct spelling. If a correction needs to be made, cross out the incorrect words and write the correct spelling above it. If the word is spelled correctly, write *C* above it.

Example: The winner of the college science (C) competition will ~~recieve~~ receive a full scholarship.

1. If you believe in yourself, you will find it easier to acheive your goals.
2. Sometimes an emergency can turn nieghbors into friends.
3. Niether one of these dresses fits, and the colors aren't flattering either.
4. The frieght charge depends on the wieght of the package.
5. In the future, people will have more leisure than we can conceive of.
6. The children could not control thier grief over the death of the dog.
7. The prosperous soceity of ancient Rome depended on the labor of slaves.
8. The hieght of the cieling was impressive.
9. A criminal may confess to releive a guilty conscience.
10. That unusual species of butterfly must have migrated here from a foriegn country.

C Understanding Prefixes

A **prefix** is a group of letters added to the beginning of a word that changes the word's meaning. Adding a prefix to a word never changes the spelling of the original word.

dis + service = disservice
un + able = unable
co + operate = cooperate

pre + heat = preheat
un + natural = unnatural
over + rate = overrate

◆ PRACTICE 25.2

Write in the blank the new word that results when the given prefix is added to each of the following words.

Example: pre + view = *preview*

1. un + easy = ____________
2. dis + satisfied = ____________
3. over + cook = ____________
4. co + exist = ____________
5. un + wind = ____________
6. dis + respect = ____________
7. under + pay = ____________
8. non + sense = ____________
9. pre + war = ____________
10. tele + communications = ____________

D Understanding Suffixes

A **suffix** is a group of letters added to the end of a word that changes the word's meaning or its part of speech. Adding a suffix to a word can cause changes in the spelling of the original word.

Words Ending in Silent *-e*

A **silent *e*** is an *e* that is not pronounced. If a word ends with a silent *-e*, drop the *e* if the suffix begins with a vowel.

DROP THE *E*

hope + ing = hoping
continue + ous = continuous

dance + er = dancer
insure + able = insurable

EXCEPTIONS

change + able = changeable
notice + able = noticeable

courage + ous = courageous
replace + able = replaceable

Keep the *e* if the suffix begins with a consonant.

KEEP THE *E*

hope + ful = hopeful
excite + ment = excitement
bore + dom = boredom
same + ness = sameness

EXCEPTIONS

argue + ment = argument
judge + ment = judgment
true + ly = truly
nine + th = ninth

◆ PRACTICE 25.3

Write in the blank the new word that results when the given suffix is added to each of the following words.

Examples

decide + ing = *deciding*

lone + ly = *lonely*

1. adore + able = __________
2. definite + ly = __________
3. judge + ment = __________
4. care + ful = __________
5. whistle + ed = __________
6. invite + ation = __________
7. true + ly = __________
8. dine + ing = __________
9. insure + ance = __________
10. dedicate + ion = __________
11. sense + less = __________
12. disgrace + ful = __________
13. notice + able = __________
14. become + ing = __________
15. amuse + ment = __________
16. write + er = __________
17. imagine + ation = __________
18. place + ment = __________
19. microscope + ic = __________
20. simple + ly = __________

Words Ending in *-y*

When you add a suffix to a word that ends in *-y,* change the *y* to an *i* if the letter before the *y* is a consonant.

CHANGE *Y* TO *I*

beauty + ful = beautiful
try + ed = tried
busy + ly = busily
friendly + er = friendlier

EXCEPTIONS

Keep the *y* if the suffix starts with an *i.*

cry + ing = crying
baby + ish = babyish

Keep the *y* when you add a suffix to some one-syllable words.

shy + er = shyer   dry + ness = dryness

Keep the *y* if the letter before the *y* is a vowel.

KEEP THE *Y*

annoy + ance = annoyance   enjoy + ment = enjoyment
play + ful = playful   display + ed = displayed

EXCEPTIONS

day + ly = daily   say + ed = said
gay + ly = gaily   pay + ed = paid

◆ PRACTICE 25.4

Write in the blank the new word that results when the given suffix is added to each of the following words.

Examples

cry + ed = *cried*

fry + ing = *frying*

employ + ment = *employment*

1. try + ing = ________
2. pay + ed = ________
3. noisy + ly = ________
4. buy + er = ________
5. destroy + ed = ________
6. annoy + ance = ________
7. dry + ness = ________
8. play + ful = ________
9. tiny + er = ________
10. happy + ness = ________
11. busy + ly = ________
12. marry + es = ________
13. reply + ed = ________
14. fifty + eth = ________
15. thirty + ish = ________
16. lonely + ness = ________
17. joy + ful = ________
18. spy + ed = ________
19. day + ly = ________
20. lively + hood = ________

Doubling the Final Consonant

When you add a suffix that begins with a vowel—for example, *-ed, -er,* or *-ing*—double the final consonant in the original word if (1) the last three letters of the word have a consonant-vowel-consonant pattern (cvc), and (2) the word has one syllable, or the last syllable is stressed.

▼ **Student Voices**

All I have to remember is CVC.

Geraldine Smith

FINAL CONSONANT DOUBLED

cut	+	ing	=	cutting (cvc—one syllable)
bat	+	er	=	batter (cvc—one syllable)
pet	+	ed	=	petted (cvc—one syllable)
commit	+	ed	=	committed (cvc—stress is on last syllable)
occur	+	ing	=	occurring (cvc—stress is on last syllable)

FINAL CONSONANT NOT DOUBLED

answer	+	ed	=	answered (cvc—stress is not on last syllable)
happen	+	ing	=	happening (cvc—stress is not on last syllable)
act	+	ing	=	acting (no cvc)

◆ PRACTICE 25.5

Write in the blank the new word that results when the given suffix is added to each of the following words.

Examples

hit + ing = *hitting*

slow + er = *slower*

1. shop + er = ______
2. squeak + ing = ______
3. prefer + ed = ______
4. thin + est = ______
5. climb + ed = ______
6. wrap + ing = ______
7. fair + est = ______
8. regret + ed = ______
9. begin + ing = ______
10. star + ed = ______
11. write + en = ______
12. swim + er = ______
13. appeal + ing = ______
14. excel + ed = ______
15. exist + ing = ______
16. occur + ed = ______
17. run + er = ______
18. commit + ed = ______
19. trap + er = ______
20. occur + ence = ______

■ REVISING AND EDITING

Type your response to the Seeing and Writing exercise on page 391 if you have not already done so. Then, run a spell check. Did the computer pick up all the errors? Which did it identify? Which did it miss? Correct all the spelling errors in your Seeing and Writing exercise.

CHAPTER REVIEW

◆ EDITING PRACTICE

Read the following essay, which contains spelling errors. As you read, identify the words you think are misspelled; then, check the list on pages 392–93. If you do not find them there, check a dictionary. Finally, cross out each incorrectly spelled word, and write the correct spelling above the line. The first sentence has been corrected for you.

Body Language

When I was invited to a job ~~interveiw~~ interview last month, I decided to prepare by learning from the ~~expereinces~~ experiences of others. I asked my freinds what to wear, what to say, and how to show that I was qualifyed. An aquaintance who works in a personell department gave me an article titled "Body Language Tips: Get Your Dream Job!" Naturaly, I read the article and got a few more helpful hints. Because I got the job, I asume my strategies worked, so let me pass them along.

Body language, or body and facial movments, can certanly reveal alot about a person. In fact, some sceintists claim that body language comunicates more than speech does. Gestures, smiles, posture, eye contact, and even the position of one's head, arms, and legs all can revele whether a person is honest or lying, interested or bored, defensive or coperative.

The article explained how to use body language to do well in an interview. The advice was to maintain eye contact, but not to stare at the interviewer. The point is to look intrested without harrassing the interviewer. The experts also said to use hand gestures to show enthusiasm. Again, the trick is not to overdo this, because it can make you seem agressive or just plain wierd. A suprising warning was not to cross your legs or arms, which can make you look stubborn. Finaly, at the end of the interview, give the interviewer a firm handshake to show that you are honest and trustworthy.

These tips on body language came in handy at my job interview. And, as they say, sucess speaks for itself.

◆ COLLABORATIVE ACTIVITIES

1. Working with a partner, test each other on the list of frequently misspelled words on pages 392–93. Then, make a list of the words you misspelled, and study these words, using flash cards and memory cues if necessary. Retake the test until you have learned all the misspelled words.
2. Create a personal spelling list, checking a dictionary for the correct spelling of each word. Then, try to identify patterns in your misspelling habits, and memorize the rules and exceptions that apply to your misspellings. Working with a partner, test each other on these words.
3. Work in a small group to create a spelling test for another group. The test can be a list of words, or it can be a paragraph in which you have intentionally misspelled some words. Correct the other group's test.

COMPOSING ORIGINAL SENTENCES

4. Choose ten of the most troublesome words from your personal spelling list. Then, write a sentence using each word. When you have finished, exchange sentences with another student, and correct any errors in grammar, punctuation, or spelling.

✓ REVIEW CHECKLIST: Understanding Spelling

- Follow the steps to becoming a better speller. (See 25A.)
- *I* comes before *e*, except after *c* or in any *ay* sound, as in *neighbor* and *weigh*. (See 25B.)
- Adding a prefix to a word never affects the word's spelling. (See 25C.)
- Adding a suffix to a word may change the word's spelling. (See 25D.)
- When a word ends with a silent *-e*, drop the *e* if the suffix begins with a vowel. Keep the *e* if the suffix begins with a consonant. (See 25D.)
- When you add a suffix to a word that ends with a *-y*, change the *y* to an *i* if the letter before the *y* is a consonant. Keep the *y* if the letter before the *y* is a vowel. (See 25D.)
- When you add a suffix that begins with a vowel, double the final consonant in the original word if (1) the last three letters of the word have a consonant-vowel-consonant pattern (cvc), and (2) the word has one syllable, or the last syllable is stressed. (See 25D.)

CHAPTER

26

Learning Commonly Confused Words

PREVIEW

- In this chapter, you will learn to identify word pairs that are often confused.

SEEING AND WRITING

What does America mean to you? Look at the picture above, which depicts a naturalization ceremony, and then write a paragraph in which you answer this question.

Word Power

multicultural of or relating to many cultures

mobility the movement of people from one social group, class, or level to another

naturalization the process of gaining citizenship

Some English words cause spelling problems because they look or sound like other words. The following word pairs are often confused. Learning them can help you become a better speller.

Computer Tip

Delete commonly confused words from your computer's spell checker so they will always be flagged as possible errors.

Accept/Except *Accept* means "to receive something." *Except* means "with the exception of" or "to leave out or exclude."

> "I accept your challenge," said Alexander Hamilton to Aaron Burr.
>
> Everyone except Darryl visited the museum.

Affect/Effect *Affect* is a verb meaning "to influence." *Effect* is a noun meaning "result" and sometimes a verb meaning "to bring about."

> Jodi's job could affect her grades.

Overexposure to sun can have a long-term effect on skin.

Commissioner Williams tried to effect changes in police procedure.

All ready/Already *All ready* means "completely prepared." *Already* means "previously, before."

Serge was all ready to take the history test.

Gina had already been to Italy.

Brake/Break *Brake* means "a device to slow or stop a vehicle." *Break* means "to smash" or "to detach."

Peter got into an accident because his foot slipped off the brake.

Babe Ruth bragged that no one would ever break his home-run record.

Buy/By *Buy* means "to purchase." *By* is a preposition meaning "close to" or "next to" or "by means of."

Tina wanted to buy a laptop computer.

He drove by but didn't stop.

He stayed by her side all the way to the hospital.

Malcolm X wanted "freedom by any means necessary."

◆ PRACTICE 26.1

Proofread the underlined words in the following sentences for correct spelling. If a correction needs to be made, cross out the incorrect word, and write the correct spelling above it. If the word is spelled correctly, write *C* above it.

Example: The ~~breaks~~ *brakes* on this car work well, except *C* on icy roads.

1. The sign in the shop read, "If you break any glass item, you have to buy it."
2. Brad was already for the beach except for having forgotten his sunglasses.
3. Some medications effect a person's ability to drive by causing drowsiness.
4. If we hope to affect change in our government, we have to except our obligation to vote.
5. The talented college basketball player had already accepted an offer from a professional team by the end of his junior year.
6. Gervase plans to buy a car with anti-lock breaks.

7. Buy the way, I've all ready taken that course.

8. Mild stress, such as the excitement before a test, can effect a person in a positive way, whereas long-term stress usually has a negative affect.

9. The excited contestant was all ready to accept the prize money she had won.

10. Participating in sports can affect young people strongly and affect a change for the better in their attitudes and ability to get along with others.

Conscience/Conscious *Conscience* refers to the part of the mind that urges a person to choose right over wrong. *Conscious* means "aware" or "deliberate."

> After he cheated at cards, his conscience started to bother him.
>
> As she walked through the woods, she became conscious of the hum of insects.
>
> Elliott made a conscious decision to stop smoking.

Everyday/Every day *Everyday* is a single word that means "ordinary" or "common." *Every day* is two words that mean "occurring daily."

> *I Love Lucy* was a successful comedy show because it appealed to everyday people.
>
> Every day, Lucy and Ethel would find a new way to get into trouble.

Fine/Find *Fine* means "superior quality" or "a sum of money paid as a penalty." *Find* means "to locate."

> He sang a fine solo at church last Sunday.
>
> Demi had to pay a fine for speeding.
>
> Some people still use a willow rod to find water.

Student Voices

My parents come from Vietnam and don't speak English well, so I pay a lot of attention to language.

Din Ngoc Dang

Hear/Here *Hear* means "to perceive sound by ear." *Here* means "at or in this place."

> I moved to the front so I could hear the speaker.
>
> My great-grandfather came here in 1883.

Its/It's *Its* is the possessive form of *it*. *It's* is the contraction of *it is* or *it has*.

> The airline canceled its flights because of the snow.
>
> It's twelve o'clock, and we're late.
>
> Ever since it's been in the accident, the car has rattled.

◆ PRACTICE 26.2

Proofread the underlined words in the following sentences for correct spelling. If a correction needs to be made, cross out the incorrect word, and write the correct spelling above it. If the word is spelled correctly, write *C* above it.

Example: Every day, we ~~fine~~ find new challenges to face.

1. Sarita became conscience of someone staring at her and turned to discover that it was Tony.
2. "Its been a long time since I've seen you here," Tony remarked to Sarita.
3. Sarita smiled as she said, "Its a great place to here jazz."
4. Paul hated paying the fine for parking in a disabled spot, but his conscious bothered him more than losing the money.
5. Everyday, the dog eats it's dinner at precisely 12:00 noon.
6. As soon as a child becomes conscious of right and wrong, his or her conscience begins to develop.
7. This week, everyday has been fine weather.
8. You will fine an outstanding collection of American art right hear in the college museum.
9. The airline made a conscience effort to enforce it's "no smoking" policy.
10. The wind had stopped its roaring, but in my mind, I could still hear it.

Know/Knew/New/No *Know* means "to have an understanding of" or "to have fixed in the mind." *Knew* is the past tense form of the verb *know. New* means "recent or never used." *No* expresses a negative response.

I know there will be a lunar eclipse tonight.

He knew how to install a new light switch.

Yes, we have no bananas.

Lie/Lay *Lie* means "to rest or recline." The past tense of *lie* is *lay. Lay* means "to put or place something down." The past tense of *lay* is *laid.*

Every Sunday I lie in bed until noon.

They lay on the grass until it began to rain, and then they went home.

Tammy told Carl to lay his cards on the table.

Brooke and Cassia finally laid down their hockey sticks.

Loose/Lose *Loose* means "not fastened" or "not attached securely." *Lose* means "to mislay" or "to misplace."

In the 1940s, many women wore loose-fitting pants.

Sometimes I lose my keys.

Mine/Mind *Mine* is a possessive pronoun that indicates ownership. *Mind* can be a noun meaning "human consciousness" or "intelligence" or a verb meaning "to obey" or "to attend to."

> That red mountain bike is mine.
>
> A mind is a terrible thing to waste.
>
> "Mind your manners when you visit your grandmother," Dad said.

Passed/Past *Passed* is the past tense of the verb *pass*. It means "moved by" or "succeeded in." *Past* is a noun meaning "earlier than the present time."

> The car that passed me must have been doing more than eighty miles an hour.
>
> David finally passed his driving test.
>
> The novel was set in the past.

Peace/Piece *Peace* means "the absence of war" or "calm." *Piece* means "a part of something."

> The prime minister thought he had achieved peace with honor.
>
> My peace of mind was destroyed when the flying saucer landed.
>
> "Have a piece of cake," said Marie.

◆ PRACTICE 26.3

Proofread the underlined words in the following sentences for correct spelling. If a correction needs to be made, cross out the incorrect word, and write the correct spelling above it. If the word is spelled correctly, write *C* above it.

Example: Heads of state ~~no~~ know that peace C is hard to achieve.

1. Everyone was amazed when the troops lay down their weapons and went home in peace.
2. The child new he should not eat another peace of candy, but he did it anyway.
3. In the passed, it was more important to mine one's manners than it is today.
4. Jamal past his chemistry final with a high grade, as we knew he would.
5. I loose my way every time I drive to the mall.
6. The car passed us as if there were know speed limit.
7. Janet decided to lay on a lounge chair and enjoy the peace of the garden.

8. The violinist was able to finish playing the piece even though one string had come loose from his bow.
9. The new dog had to be trained not to lay on the couch.
10. The children were warned to mine the babysitter, or they would loose their television-watching privileges.

Plain/Plane *Plain* means "simple, not elaborate." *Plane* is the shortened form of *airplane.*

Sometimes the Amish are referred to as the plain people.

Chuck Yeager was the first person to fly a plane faster than sound.

Principal/Principle *Principal* means "first" or "highest" or "the head of a school." *Principle* means "a law or basic assumption."

She had the principal role in the movie.

I'll never forget the day the principal called me into his office.

It was against his principles to tell a lie.

Quiet/Quit/Quite *Quiet* means "free of noise" or "still." *Quit* means "to leave a job" or "to give up." *Quite* means "actually" or "very."

Jane looked forward to the quiet evenings at the lake.

Sammy quit his job and followed the girls into the parking lot.

"You haven't quite got the hang of it yet," she said.

After practicing all summer, Tamika got quite good at softball.

Raise/Rise *Raise* means "to elevate" or "to increase in size, quantity, or worth." The past tense of *raise* is *raised. Rise* means "to stand up" or "to move from a lower position to a higher position." The past tense of *rise* is *rose.*

Carlos raises his hand when the teacher asks for volunteers.

They raised the money for the down payment.

The fans rise every time their team scores a touchdown.

Sarah rose before dawn so she could see the sunrise.

Right/Write *Right* means "correct" or "the opposite of left." *Write* means "to form letters with a writing instrument."

If you turn right at the corner, you will be going in the right direction.

All students are required to write three short papers.

Sit/Set *Sit* means "to assume a sitting position." The past tense of *sit* is *sat. Set* means "to put down or place" or "to adjust something to a desired position." The past tense of *set* is *set.*

I usually sit in the front row at the movies.

They sat at the clinic waiting for their names to be called.

Every semester I set goals for myself.

Elizabeth set the mail on the kitchen table and left for work.

Suppose/Supposed *Suppose* means "to consider" or "to assume." *Supposed* is both the past tense and the past participle of *suppose*. *Supposed* also means "expected" or "required." (Note that when *supposed* has this meaning, it is followed by *to*.)

Suppose researchers found a cure for AIDS tomorrow.

We supposed the movie would be over by ten o'clock.

You were supposed to finish a draft of the report by today.

◆ PRACTICE 26.4

Proofread the underlined words in the following sentences for correct spelling. If a correction needs to be made, cross out the incorrect word, and write the correct spelling above it. If the word is spelled correctly, write *C* above it.

Example: Everyone in the creative writing class was ~~suppose~~ supposed to write (C) a short autobiography.

1. According to Miss Manners, you are supposed to raise from your seat when an older person enters the room.
2. The school board hasn't quite selected a new principle for the high school yet.
3. The dress Lindsay is making started out rather plane but is now quite fancy.
4. We watched as the plane raised slowly and disappeared in the clouds.
5. All she wanted was a quite place to set and think for a while.
6. I suppose I should sit this glass on a coaster so as not to damage the wood table.
7. Set the dial to the right level for the kind of fabric you are ironing.
8. Although Yuki was quiet by nature, she spoke out strongly in defense of her principals.
9. Do you suppose that Raoul will be chosen for the principle role in the play?
10. If the candidate cannot rise enough money, she will have to quite the race for mayor.

Their/There/They're *Their* is the possessive form of *they*. *There* means "at or in that place." *There* is also used in the phrases *there is* and *there are*. *They're* is a contraction meaning "they are."

Jane Addams wanted poor people to improve their living conditions.

I put the book over there.

There are three reasons why I will not eat meat.

They're the best volunteer firefighters I've ever seen.

Then/Than *Then* means "at that time" or "next in time." *Than* is used to introduce the second element in a comparison.

He was young and naive then.

I went to the job interview and then stopped off for a double chocolate shake.

My dog is smarter than your dog.

Writing Tip
Do not use the informal spelling *thru* for *through*.

Threw/Through *Threw* is the past tense of *throw*. *Through* means "in one side and out the opposite side" or "finished."

Satchel Paige threw a baseball faster than ninety-five miles an hour.

It takes almost thirty minutes to go through the tunnel.

"I'm through," said Clark Kent, storming out of Perry White's office.

To/Too/Two *To* means "in the direction of." *Too* means "also" or "more than enough." *Two* denotes the numeral 2.

During spring break, I am going to Disney World.

My roommates are coming too.

The microwave popcorn is too hot to eat.

"If we get rid of the tin man and the lion, the two of us can go to Oz," said the scarecrow to Dorothy.

Use/Used *Use* means "to put into service" or "to consume." *Used* is both the past tense and the past participle of *use*. *Used* also means "accustomed." (Note that when *used* has this meaning, it is followed by *to*.)

I use a soft cloth to clean my glasses.

"Hey! Who used all the hot water?" he yelled from the shower.

Mary had used all the firewood during the storm.

After living in Alaska for a year, they got used to the short winter days.

◆ PRACTICE 26.5

Proofread the underlined words in the following sentences for correct spelling. If a correction needs to be made, cross out the incorrect word, and write the correct spelling above it. If the word is spelled correctly, write *C* above it.

Example: ~~Their~~ There are at least two C good reasons not to rent that apartment.

1. It was hard to get use to the cold when they first came to New York from there home in Puerto Rico.
2. The shortstop threw the ball to second base, but it flew on through the air and landed in the bleachers.
3. I'm threw with the two of them and all they're nonsense!
4. Her blind date was more fun then she expected although it was too early to tell if she really liked him.
5. "They're used to staying up until nine," Mrs. Tsang told the babysitter.
6. Four-year-old Zachary got spaghetti sauce all over his face and than use his T-shirt to clean it off.
7. If they had known then what problems there car would have, they never would have bought it.
8. As a new teacher, Spencer use to feel tired at the end of the day.
9. Is there any reason to risk driving after drinking to much at a party?
10. I don't like the food at that restaurant, and it's two expensive too.

Weather/Whether *Weather* refers to the state of the atmosphere with respect to temperature, humidity, precipitation, and so on. *Whether* means "if it is so that; if the cause is that."

The *Farmer's Almanac* says that the weather this winter will be severe.

Whether or not this prediction will be correct is anyone's guess.

Where/Were/We're *Where* means "at or in what place." *Were* is the past tense of *are*. *We're* is a contraction meaning "we are."

Where are you going, and where have you been?

Charlie Chaplin and Mary Pickford were popular stars of silent movies.

We're doing our back-to-school shopping early this year.

Whose/Who's *Whose* is the possessive form of *who*. *Who's* is a contraction meaning "who is" or "who has."

My roommate asked, "Whose book is this?"

"Who's there?" squealed the second little pig as he leaned against the door.

Who's been in my room?

Your/You're *Your* is the possessive form of *you*. *You're* is a contraction meaning "you are."

> "You should have worn your running shoes," said the hare as he passed the tortoise.
>
> "You're too kind," said the tortoise sarcastically.

◆ PRACTICE 26.6

Proofread the underlined words in the following sentences for correct spelling. If a correction needs to be made, cross out the incorrect word, and write the correct spelling above it. If the word is spelled correctly, write *C* above it.

Example: We're (C) not sure ~~weather~~ whether or not this is the right road to take.

1. "Whose going to the party," Tracey asked, "and whose car are we taking?"
2. Orlando, were we went on vacation, has good weather, fine beaches, and many tourist attractions.
3. "Your late for you're appointment," the receptionist said.
4. Someone who's experienced at buying cameras can tell you whether or not to buy that one.
5. Where you surprised at the sudden change in the weather?
6. Do you know whose left this laptop computer were anyone might take it?
7. By the time your finished with school and work, your energy is all gone.
8. Whether you like it or not, no one is going to make you're decisions for you.
9. Who's car is parked in the spot were my car usually is?
10. Were you excited when you're letter to the editor was printed in the newspaper?

■ REVISING AND EDITING

Look back at your response to the Seeing and Writing exercise on page 401. Make sure you have not misused any of the words listed in this chapter. If you are writing on a computer, use the Search or Find function to locate any words you think you may have misused.

CHAPTER REVIEW

◆ EDITING PRACTICE

Read the following student essay, which contains spelling errors. Identify the words you think are misspelled; then, look them up in a dictionary. Finally, cross out each incorrectly spelled word, and write the correct spelling above the line. The first sentence has been edited for you.

The Minimum Wage

As a student who has worked at her share of minimum wage jobs, I strongly believe in the ~~principal~~ principle of a "living wage." How, in good conscious, can employers not pay workers enough to support themselves? To this question, many employers reply that rising the minimum wage would have a negative affect on they're businesses. If the minimum wage were set too high, they might have to close up shop. Some small business owners feel that the minimum wage is all ready to high and that they cannot make a fair profit because of labor costs.

Most labor leaders and working peeple, including myself, do not except this argument. We believe that a minimum wage is suppose to reflect the basic needs of an individual for food, clothing, shelter, and transportation to and from work. The present minimum wage, in my opinion, doesn't provide for these basic necessities. However, I realize that what a fair amount would be depends on whose making the estimate. If your an employer, your estimate might differ greatly from mine. Their is also the question of whether the minimum hourly wage should be enough to support just an individual or a family.

In the United States, about forty states have minimum wage laws or boards that set minimum wages. The first state to pass such a law was Massachusetts in 1912. The federal government first past a minimum wage law in 1938. About eighty percent of all private industries are all ready covered by the federal law. But self-employed workers and employees of small businesses are often not protected by this law.

This is a complex problem that will not be easily layed to rest. As lawmakers struggle to fine a solution, they should investigate just how someone making minimum wage and working a full forty-hour week can survive on that amount of money.

◆ COLLABORATIVE ACTIVITIES

1. After completing the practice exercises in the chapter, make a list of the words that you found confusing, and study their meanings and the sample sentences. Then, have a partner quiz you on these words.
2. Working in a small group, choose one section of this chapter and write a test on the material it discusses. (Use the practices in this chapter as a model for your test.) Each of your sentences should contain one of the commonly confused words. When you have finished, exchange tests with another group, and take their test. Finally, correct the other group's work on your test.
3. Divide into two teams, and stage a spelling bee. Each team should prepare a list of twenty words and quiz the other, with students on the two teams alternating to try to spell each word. The team that spells the most words correctly is the winner.

COMPOSING ORIGINAL SENTENCES

4. Working with a partner, choose the five commonly confused word pairs that give you the most trouble. Write sample sentences for the two words in each pair to illustrate the correct use of the commonly confused words.

Examples

1. Don't drop that vase or it will break.
2. I hit the brake suddenly to avoid hitting the deer.

When you have finished, check the sentences to make sure you have corrected any errors in grammar, punctuation, or spelling.

✓ REVIEW CHECKLIST: Learning Commonly Confused Words

- Memorize the most commonly confused words.

UNIT SIX

Learning College Reading Skills

CHAPTER

27

Becoming an Active Reader

PREVIEW

In this chapter, you will learn

- how to approach a reading assignment (27A)
- how to highlight a reading assignment (27B)
- how to annotate a reading assignment (27C)
- how to outline a reading assignment (27D)

■ SEEING AND WRITING

When you read your textbooks, you will understand them better if you mark the pages as this student has done.

Word Power

annotating making explanatory notes

Reading is essential to all your college courses. To get the most out of your college reading, you should read *actively*. Being an **active reader** means approaching a reading assignment with a clear understanding of your purpose, highlighting the selection, annotating it, and perhaps outlining it—all *before* you begin to discuss or write about what you have read.

A Approaching a Reading Assignment

Even before you start reading, you should ask yourself some questions about your purpose—why you are reading. The answers to these questions will help you understand what kind of information you hope to get out of your reading and how you will use this information.

Questions about Purpose

- Will you be expected to discuss the reading selection in class?
- Will you be expected to discuss the reading selection in a one-on-one conference with your instructor?
- Will you have to write about the reading selection? If so, will you be expected to write an informal response (for example, in a journal entry) or a more formal one (for example, in an essay)?
- Will you be tested on what you read?

Keeping these questions in mind, **preview** the assigned reading by quickly skimming the entire selection. As you skim, your goal is to get a sense of the selection's most important information: the writer's main point and key supporting ideas. You do this by looking for various **visual signals**:

Visual Signals for Previewing a Reading

- Look at the essay's title.
- Look at the essay's opening and closing paragraphs.
- Look at each paragraph's topic sentence.
- Look at headings.
- Look at *italicized* and **boldfaced** words.
- Look at numbered lists.
- Look at bulleted lists (like this one).
- Look at illustrations (graphs, charts, tables, photographs, and so on).
- Look at any information that is boxed.
- Look at any information that is in color.

When you have finished previewing, you should have a general sense of what the writer wants to communicate.

◆ PRACTICE 27.1

Following is a brief newspaper article by Nathan Black, a Colorado high school student. Preview the article in preparation for class discussion as well as for the other activities that will be assigned throughout this chapter.

As you read, try to identify the writer's main point and key supporting ideas, and write that information on the blank lines following the article.

AFTER A SHOOTING

Nathan Black

High school students in Littleton now have a new excuse to get out 1
of class for a few extra minutes: the lockdown drill. My school had its

first last year. While most students sat quietly in locked classrooms, a few teachers responded to simulated crises, like a student injury. It's one of many new features of life in Littleton since the Columbine High shootings of 1999. Most people have tried to move on, but some aspects of our lives have changed forever.

That reality will soon face the people of Santee, California, where two students were killed on Monday. And the shooting yesterday of a girl by a schoolmate in Pennsylvania, and the arrest this week of two boys in Twentynine Palms, California, after police found a "hit list" of their classmates, suggest that Columbine's experience will become still more common. 2

Apart from lockdown drills, there have been few changes in security procedures. The greatest change has been the increase of paranoia. For example, a few weeks after the shooting I was working on a graph assignment with a friend. We arranged the points on the graph to spell out a humorous but inappropriate message. 3

A month earlier, my friend would have said, "The teacher's going to be mad." This time he said, "If we turn this in, we'll be expelled." 4

There's the difference. The worst case I've heard of took place in Canada. A boy had written and performed, for class, a dark, vengeful monologue. After his performance, rumors swirled about hit lists, and the boy was arrested. The police said he had made death threats. No hard evidence appears to have been found in the boy's home—just the monologue. His story has now entered the larger tale of Littleton and its aftermath. 5

Only time can ease this paranoia. I wish time would hurry up about it. 6

Yet good changes have also occurred. The killings at Columbine and elsewhere have been a pitiless wake-up call to adults. Last April, 1,500 of my peers gathered at a local college to discuss education. Adults want our perspective. They may want it now because of fear, but they want it. 7

Such conversations have to continue. Violence is still happening, 8
and as long as my school needs a lockdown drill, we need to keep asking: Why do kids kill each other and how can we stop them? There's no answer yet. But the fact that we're looking makes me feel a little less helpless.

Author's main point

____

____

Key supporting ideas

1. ______________________________
2. ______________________________
3. ______________________________
4. ______________________________

B Highlighting a Reading Assignment

After you have previewed a reading selection, read it again, this time more carefully. Now, your goals are to identify connections between one idea and another and to follow the writer's line of thought.

As you read, make sure you have a pen (or a highlighter pen) in hand so you can *highlight*. When you **highlight**, you use underlining and symbols to identify key words and ideas. This active reading strategy will help you understand what you are reading.

The number and kinds of highlighting symbols you use when you read are up to you. All that matters is that your symbols be clear, meaningful, and easy to remember.

Highlighting Symbols

- Underline or highlight key ideas—for example, topic sentences.
- Box or circle words or phrases you want to remember.
- Place a check mark (✔) or star (✱) next to an important idea.
- Place a double check mark (✔✔) or double star (✱✱) next to an especially significant idea.
- Draw lines or arrows to connect related ideas.
- Put a question mark (?) beside a word or idea that you do not understand.
- Number the writer's key supporting points or examples.

Highlight freely, but try not to highlight too much. Remember, you will eventually be rereading every highlighted word, phrase, and sentence—and your study time is limited. Highlight only the most important, most useful information.

FOCUS Knowing What to Highlight

You want to highlight what's important—but how do you *know* what's important? As a general rule, you should look for the same visual signals you looked for when you did your previewing. Many of the ideas you will need to highlight will probably be found in material that is visually set off from the rest of the text—topic sentences, opening and closing paragraphs, lists, and the like. Also, look for **verbal signals**—words and phrases like *however, therefore, another reason, the most important point,* and so on—which often introduce key points. Together, these visual and verbal signals will give you clues to the writer's meaning and emphasis.

Student Voices

Before I highlight a chapter in a textbook, I look for a review box at the end of the chapter. This gives me an idea of what's important.

Amanda Thomas

Here is how a student highlighted an excerpt from a newspaper column, "Some Truths behind Those Statistics" by Joyce Purnick.

The theories are many, but the experts all agree that the end of the crack epidemic came from the streets up.* 1

Crack was a central cause of crime in the 1980's. It destroyed families, provoked drive-by shootings, generated crack houses. In 1989, things started to turn around. 2

?

"Most important, the reason crack is in remission is that for reasons still unclear, youngsters, especially those born after 1970, essentially avoided its use even though they are not very articulate about why," said Bruce D. Johnson, a director at the National Development and Research Institutes, a nonprofit organization. 3

Federally financed drug tests of people arrested in Manhattan showed that among those 18 to 20 years old, 70 percent had crack or cocaine in their urine in 1988. In 1991 that figure had tumbled to 31 percent and in 1996 to 22 percent, where experts believe it to be now. People born before 1970 still tested positive in high percentages. 4

"The major story was a major split in the use of crack," said Mr. 5
Johnson. Why the generational division?

One theory is rejection, the "older-brother syndrome." Young people 6
saw families destroyed, older brothers imprisoned, paralyzed by bullets, living on the streets. "They said 'I don't want to be like that,'" according to Mr. Travis. "It was a self-protective, healthy instinct."

In addition, dealers discouraged crack use because their sellers 7
were consuming the profits. Community and church groups organized to fight the drug. And the country changed; it got wealthier, more conservative, less tolerant.

In New York, the authorities mobilized. As Richard S. Curtis, pro- 8
fessor at John Jay College of Criminal Justice, observed, "The city reasserted itself." Police strategies broke up drug networks, forced dealers to go inside instead of hawking on the streets; more guns were confiscated.

There is no doubt that many factors led to the changes, including 9
effective law enforcement. But criminologists question how successful those would have been without community rejection of the crack culture.

The student who highlighted this passage was preparing to write an essay about the relationship between drug use and crime in his neighborhood. He began by underlining and starring Purnick's main idea: "the end of the crack epidemic came from the streets up." He went on to underline sentences that briefly compared the status of crack use in the 1970s, 1980s, and 1990s. Next, he starred Purnick's key question ("Why the generational division?") and numbered and underlined the five theories she presents to answer this question. Finally, he put a double line and a star in the margin to highlight the conclusion, which restates Purnick's main idea.

FOCUS Building Word Power

Note that the student who highlighted the Purnick passage also circled four words whose meanings he did not know—*remission, syndrome, mobilized,* and *reasserted.* He placed a question mark beside each of these words to remind himself to look them up.

◆ PRACTICE 27.2

Review the highlighted passage by Joyce Purnick (pp. 419–20). How would your own highlighting of this passage be similar to or different from the sample student highlighting?

◆ PRACTICE 27.3

Reread "After a Shooting" (pp. 416–18). As you read, highlight the passage by underlining and starring main ideas, boxing and circling key words, and checkmarking important points. Also, circle each unfamiliar word, and put a question mark in the margin beside it.

C Annotating a Reading Assignment

As you highlight, you should also *annotate* what you are reading. **Annotating** a passage means making notes—of questions, reactions, reminders, and ideas for discussion or writing—in the margins or between the lines. Keeping an informal record of ideas as they occur to you will help prepare you to discuss the reading with your classmates—and, eventually, to write about it.

Asking yourself the following questions as you read will help you write useful annotations.

Questions for Annotating

- What is the writer saying?
- What is the writer's purpose—his or her reason for writing?
- What kind of audience is the writer addressing?
- Is the writer responding to another writer's ideas?
- What is the writer's main point?
- How does the writer support his or her points? With facts? Opinions? Both facts and opinions? What kinds of supporting details and examples does the writer use?
- Does the writer include enough supporting details and examples?
- Do you understand the writer's vocabulary?
- Do you understand the writer's ideas?
- Do you agree with the points the writer is making?
- Do you see any connections between this reading selection and something else you have read?

The following passage reproduces the student's highlighting from pages 419–20 and also illustrates his annotations.

Who are these experts?

1 The theories are many, but the experts all agree that the end of the crack epidemic came from the streets up.*

80s vs. 90s

2 Crack was a central cause of crime in the 1980's. It destroyed families, provoked drive-by shootings, generated crack houses. In 1989, things started to turn around.

lessening of intensity or degree

3 "Most important, the reason crack is in remission is that for reasons still unclear, youngsters, especially those born after 1970, essentially avoided its use even though they are not very articulate about why," said Bruce D. Johnson, a director at the National Development and Research Institutes, a nonprofit organization.

Overall crack use declined in 90s as younger people stopped using it.

4 Federally financed drug tests of people arrested in Manhattan showed that among those 18 to 20 years old, 70 percent had crack or cocaine in their urine in 1988. In 1991 that figure had tumbled to 31 percent and in 1996 to 22 percent, where experts believe it to be now. People born before 1970 still tested positive in high percentages.

5 "The major story was a major split in the use of crack," said Mr. Johnson. Why the generational division? *

group of symptoms of a disease or disorder

Which of these was most important?

6 (1) One theory is rejection, the "older-brother syndrome." Young people saw families destroyed, older brothers imprisoned, paralyzed by bullets, living on the streets. "They said 'I don't want to be like that,'" according to Mr. Travis. "It was a self-protective, healthy instinct."

7 (2) In addition, dealers discouraged crack use because their sellers (3) were consuming the profits. Community and church groups organized (4) to fight the drug. And the country changed; it got wealthier, more conservative, less tolerant.

prepared for action

Did crack use decline in other cities too?

took forceful action

8 (5) In New York, the authorities mobilized. As Richard S. Curtis, professor at John Jay College of Criminal Justice, observed, "The city reasserted itself." Police strategies broke up drug networks, forced dealers to go inside instead of hawking on the streets; more guns were confiscated.

What happened after 1996?

9 * There is no doubt that many factors led to the changes, including effective law enforcement. But criminologists question how successful those would have been without community rejection of the crack culture.

In his annotations, this student wrote down brief definitions of the four words—*remission, syndrome, mobilized,* and *reasserted*—he had identified in his highlighting. In the margins, he also summarized some statistics and recorded questions he intended to explore further.

▼ Student Voices

To remember how to spell new words, I keep a personal spelling list.

Joellen Baird

◆ PRACTICE 27.4

Reread "After a Shooting" (pp. 416–18). As you reread, refer to the Questions for Annotating (p. 421), and use them to help you annotate the passage by writing your own thoughts and questions in the margins. Note where you agree or disagree with the writer, and briefly explain why. Quickly summarize any points you think are particularly important. Take time to look up any unfamiliar words you have circled, and write brief definitions for them.

◆ PRACTICE 27.5

Trade workbooks with another student, and read over his or her highlighting and annotating of "After a Shooting." How are your written responses similar to the other student's? How are they different? Do your classmate's responses help you see anything new about the article?

D Outlining a Reading Assignment

Another technique you can use to help you understand a passage better is **outlining**. Unlike a **formal outline**, which must follow fairly strict conventions, an **informal outline** is easy to make, and it can be a valuable reading tool: it shows you which ideas are more important than others, and it shows you how ideas are related.

To make an informal outline of a reading assignment, follow these guidelines.

Computer Tip

Use your computer's tab keys to set up your outline.

FOCUS Making an Informal Outline

1. Write or type the passage's main idea across the top of a sheet of paper.
2. At the left margin, write down the most important idea of the first paragraph or section of the passage.
3. Indent the next line a few spaces, and list the examples or details that support this idea.
4. As ideas become more specific, indent further. (Ideas that have the same degree of importance are indented the same distance from the left margin.)
5. Repeat this process with each paragraph or section of the passage.

The student who highlighted and annotated the passage from Joyce Purnick's "Some Truths behind Those Statistics" made the following informal outline of the ideas in the passage.

```
Main idea: "The end of the crack epidemic came from the
streets up."
     1980s
     Crack = main cause of crime
          --ruined families
          --drive-by shootings
          --crack houses
     1990s
     Crack use declined
          --those born after 1970 avoided crack
          --among 18- to 20-year-olds arrested, % with
            crack in blood went down
               • in 1988, 70%
               • in 1991, only 31%
               • in 1996, only 22%
     "Why the generational division?"
               • "older-brother syndrome"
               • dealers discouraged crack use
               • community and church groups organized
                 against crack use
               • United States got richer and more con-
                 servative
               • N.Y.C. authorities (police, etc.) took
                 action
Conclusion: "Community rejection of the crack culture" =
most important factor in decline
```

◆ PRACTICE 27.6

Working on your own or in a small group, make an informal outline of "After a Shooting" (pp. 416–18). Refer to your highlighting and annotations as you construct the outline. When you have finished, check to make sure your outline indicates the writer's emphasis and the relationships among his ideas.

☑ REVIEW CHECKLIST: Becoming an Active Reader

- ☐ Understand your purpose before you begin to read. (See 27A.)
- ☐ Highlight your reading assignment. (See 27B.)
- ☐ Annotate your reading assignment. (See 27C.)
- ☐ Outline your reading assignment. (See 27D.)

CHAPTER 28

Readings for Writers

The following twenty essays by student and professional writers are designed to give you interesting material to read, react to, think critically about, discuss, and write about. Each essay is accompanied by a short introduction that tells you something about the reading and its author. Definitions of some of the words used in the essay appear in **Word Power** boxes in the margins.

Following each essay are four **Thinking about the Reading** discussion questions, some of which can be done collaboratively. (These are marked in the text with a star.) With your instructor's permission, you can discuss your responses to these questions with other students, and then share them with the class. Three **Writing Practice** activities also follow each essay.

As you read each of these essays, highlight and annotate them to help you understand what you are reading. (Highlighting and annotating are discussed in Chapter 27.) Then, reread them more carefully in preparation for class discussion and for writing.

TRIGGER-HAPPY BIRTHDAY

Kiku Adatto

Kiku Adatto is writing a book about how childhood is changing in modern America. In this essay, she describes her own experience with paintball birthday parties for children and questions whether they are appropriate for twelve-year-olds like her son.

Some months ago, my 12-year-old son received a brightly colored invitation to a friend's birthday party, which was being held someplace called Boston Paintball. A few days later, I received a more somber missive: "This is a Release of Liability—read before signing." 1

Word Power

missive a letter or message

liability a financial and legal responsibility; a debt that must be paid

A couple of clauses stood out. No. 1: "The risk of injury from the activity and weaponry involved in paintball is significant, including the potential for permanent disability and death." No. 4: "I, for myself and on behalf of my heirs, assigns, personal representatives and next of kin, *hereby release . . . the American Paintball League (A.P.L.), Boston Paintball . . . with respect to any and all injury, disability, death. . . .*" 2

Welcome to today's birthday party. And by the way, if your kid is killed at the party, it's not our fault. Call me an old-fashioned mother, but I just couldn't sign. Apparently all the other parents did, however; my son's friends told him that everyone had a great time. 3

I decided to visit Boston Paintball to check it out. Located in an old converted warehouse, the place was teeming with white suburban boys. Over at one end, I found another birthday party, for a kid named Max and 10 or so friends. 4

With their parents' help, the kids were putting on safety gear—chest protectors, neck guards and "Star Wars"–style masks. "It's fun," said Max's mom encouragingly, "like a video game." Then a referee held up a paintball gun (which looked like a real semiautomatic) and shot off a few rounds. The boys quickly lined up to get their weapons. 5

Next came the safety orientation. "First rule: don't lift off the masks on the field. We shoot balls at 100 miles an hour. Lift a mask, you'll lose an eye. Second rule: on the field, no shooting point-blank. No taking hostages. No using dead guys as shields. No hitting with fists or with gun butts." Max's dad snapped a few photos and handed out the ammunition. 6

Word Power

orientation a meeting in which participants are introduced to a new situation, such as a new school, job, or other activity

sporadic infrequent; happening from time to time

adrenaline a hormone in the body that produces a "rush" of energy and excitement in the face of danger

The referee gave the signal, and the game began. 7

But nothing happened. The boys huddled behind the bunkers. Eventually some of them poked their heads out; sporadic shots were fired. A few brave souls ventured into the open. 8

I was watching with the other parents from behind a window in the viewing area. Suddenly a paintball bullet hit the window with a dull thud. I started back. My adrenaline was pumping, but my mind said, "Trust the plexiglass." More bullets splattered the window. It sounded like real gunfire. "Hey, it looks like one of the kids is shooting at us," joked one of the mothers. We all laughed. And moved back from the window. 9

There was a release of tension after the first game. Max appeared in the lobby flushed and jubilant. "It was awesome," he said. "I hit someone." Max's parents laid out pizza. Spirits were high. "I killed a person," a boy said as he downed a Coke. 10

While they ate, I visited the gift shop. Along the back wall were racks of paintball guns—all looking like assault weapons—from the Sniper II at $249.99 to the Express Pro Autococker at $749.99. Even without these sou- 11 venirs, paintball is pricey: $29 for kids ($39 for adults), with numerous extra fees. A birthday party for 10 boys with pizza can run $450.

Back at Max's party, one boy was pressing a cold Coke can against a welt. I asked Max's mom about the cost. "Max has contributed a hundred bucks of his birthday money to help pay for the party," she said fondly. Suddenly she spotted a welt on another boy's chin. "Oh, my God. How did that happen?" She turned back to me. "He's a little warrior," she said. 12

When paintball was invented 19 years ago in New Hampshire, it was played by adults who focused less on simulated violence than on self-reliant survival. Today, it is reportedly a billion-dollar business in North America alone, with outdoor theme parks featuring mock Vietcong villages and bases named the Rambo Hotel. It's a business that proudly markets itself as an all-purpose sport: the Boston Paintball Web site said it was great for "stress relief, confidence, company outings, morale boosting" and, of course, "birthdays." 13

Some of the mothers in attendance that day said that paintball is no different from the war games their brothers played a generation ago. I disagree. True, when I was a kid, my friends and I spun violent fantasies, some (like cowboys and Indians) as troubling as the new high-tech games. But there were differences. We didn't pay for admission. The guns weren't lethal. We used our imaginations. And our parents didn't open the paper several times a year to read about kids firing guns in school. 14

Word Power
lethal capable of killing

As I was pulling out of the paintball parking lot, the attendant, a guy in his 40's, asked if I had played. I said no. "I don't think it's good, kids and paintball," he said. "They don't realize that they can hurt somebody with those guns." 15

Well I'm with the parking-lot attendant. And as for the contract, I still couldn't sign. 16

Thinking about the Reading

1. In the Release of Liability, what does Boston Paintball say it will *not* be responsible for?
2. Why does Boston Paintball want parents to sign this Release of Liability? Why does Adatto refuse to sign?
3. Compare Adatto's reaction to the paintball game she watches with the reaction of Max's parents. How are their reactions different?

*4. According to Adatto, how is paintball different from the war games children have played in the past? Do you agree with her?

Writing Practice

1. Imagine that you are the parent of a 12-year-old boy who has just been invited to a paintball party. Would you sign the Release of Liability and allow him to participate? Explain your decision.
2. The author seems to make a connection between the violent game of paintball, which is played with weapons that look like real semiautomatics, and the problem of "kids firing guns in school" (paragraph 14). Do you agree or disagree that paintball might encourage violent behavior in real life? Give reasons for your answer.
3. Why do you think paintball is so popular among both children and adults? Do you agree that violent games fulfill a useful function in society, such as preventing real-life violence or relieving stress and building confidence, as the Boston Paintball people claim? Explain your position.

FRIENDS

Justin Brines

Have you ever experienced an unlikely friendship that brought unexpected rewards? Student writer Justin Brines describes his friendship with an unforgettable character, Lula May Johnston, who shared with him her unique approach to life.

"Magic dust and persimmon tips—those are the things that keep you fit." 1
That was her favorite saying, and she would mumble it every time she passed by me in the retail store where I worked. Mrs. Lula May Johnston was the only homeless person I've ever known on a personal level.

Perhaps the most memorable quality that May (that was what she pre- 2
ferred to be called) possessed was her smell. It was not a loud smell, and it was not an offensive smell either. It was more of a sweet, almost honey-like aroma that followed her everywhere she went. This was surprising to me because my narrow mind assumed that all homeless people smelled bad. Another trademark was her long brown hair; however, usually it was not visible because it was covered with a burgundy hat in both winter and summer. May said that her brain needed padding. You see, she was a little eccentric, and I think that was what made me like her so much.

Word Power

eccentric having odd or whimsical ways; behaving in ways that are not usual or customary

commotion a noisy disturbance

Whenever May came into the store, she was always pushing an old steel 3
shopping cart that was covered in rust. Inside the cart were three items. In the child's seat was May's dog, Charlie. According to her, Charlie was a "hundred-percent full-blooded basset hound." The store manager never minded her bringing Charlie into the store because Charlie never barked or caused any kind of commotion. Charlie was only a stuffed animal, but you would never have known it from the way May treated him. She talked to him, petted him, and even fed him "magic dust and persimmon tips."

This brings me to the next item in May's cart: a little blue bag with two 4
glass bottles in it. To me, the bottles looked empty. To May, however, they contained her lifeblood. She told me that without her magic dust and persimmon tips she could not live. Every so often, she would turn each bottle up and take a big gulp of the imaginary concoction, acting as though it tasted terrible. (I never tried them.) I once asked her where she got these two substances that were so important in her life. "It's all in your heart, son," she answered. I never asked again.

Word Power

concoction a mixture of several ingredients

The third, and probably most important, item in May's cart was her 5
Bible. It was old and worn, and the cover was almost torn off the front. She once told me that all a person needed to survive was God Almighty, a friend, and a heart. May possessed all three of these things; in fact, they were on public display in her cart.

May came into the store once a week, always on Tuesday, and walked 6
around. However, she never bought anything. I think the purpose of her ritual walk was to remind me to eat my lunch on the loading dock that day. There, every Tuesday, the store I worked for would trash its damaged items in a large Dumpster. May knew this, and I could always find her rummaging through the refuse.

This was when May talked to me most; I suppose it was because she 7
was in her setting, on her terms. She told me that she was from Kannapolis and had lived there all her life. She had never been married and did not have any children. She had worked for the mill in town but was laid off around 1962 and had not worked since. "I'm not crazy," May insisted.

"People think I am, but I'm perfectly normal." She had strong feelings about welfare and about taking money from other people. "I could work if I wanted to," she told me, "but I just don't feel like it. But I'm not going to take money from hard-working people, and I don't expect them to support me." May also believed that people should live in the simplest way possible, and I guess that's what she did.

On my last day in the store, I stopped by the Christian Supply on my way to work and bought May a new Bible. On the front, I had the words "Mrs. Lula May Johnston" embossed. When I got to the store, she was waiting for me out front. 8

Word Power

embossed decorated with raised, printed letters or designs

"You're running late, son," she said. 9

"I know," I replied. "I had to stop and get you a present." 10

"For me?" May asked as I handed her the package. She opened her gift and looked at the Bible. "Nobody's ever given me anything before," she said. Then she looked at Charlie (sitting, as he always was, in the child's seat of May's shopping cart) and added, "Our friend's leaving us, boy. Our friend's leaving us." 11

"It's my last day," I explained. "Well, I guess I'll see you around." 12

"Yep," May said. She leaned over and gave me a hug. I didn't realize a little woman could squeeze so hard. Finally, she let go and said, "You know, I was almost ready to get rid of Charlie." 13

"Why?" I asked. 14

"Well, you were my friend, and I didn't need Charlie anymore. I guess it's a good thing I kept him." May turned around and began walking away. "Magic dust and persimmon tips, those are the things that keep you fit," she whispered to herself. I watched May until she was out of sight, and that was the last time I saw her. 15

Thinking about the Reading

1. Justin Brines states that the most memorable thing about May was her smell. How did she smell? Why do you think Justin chose to focus on that detail? What does May's smell suggest about her personality?
2. What do the three items in May's shopping cart reveal about her personality and beliefs?
3. In what ways does May differ from your idea of a typical homeless person? In what ways does she fit this stereotype?

*4. Justin seems to think of May as a wise person even though others might consider her crazy. What examples does he give of her wisdom? Do you consider May a wise woman? Why or why not?

Writing Practice

1. May claimed she could not live without "magic dust and persimmon tips," which she found in her heart. What are two things that you cannot live without? Why?
2. Write a description of someone you consider to be eccentric. It might be someone you know or a character in a movie or story. Include specific details that show what the person looks like and what he or she says and does.
3. What effect do you think Justin's friendship with May had on him? What effect do you think their friendship had on May? (Some of these effects are stated in the essay, but others are left for you to figure out.)

> **Word Power**
> **weathering** passing through safely; surviving

WEATHERING PREJUDICE

Richard G. Carter

Richard G. Carter, an African-American journalist and a columnist for the New York *Daily News,* has been married for many years to an award-winning white journalist. In this essay, he documents how he and his wife have "weathered" the disapproval their interracial marriage provokes in both whites and blacks.

The fortyish white woman, fur collar up around her neck against the chill winds of a still-dark morning in January, stepped into the airport bus and made her way to an empty double seat on the left side of the aisle. The driver, a burly white man of about 55, approached and asked her destination. 1

"Two for La Guardia," she replied. 2

"Two?" he said. 3

"Yes. I'm waiting for my husband. He should be here shortly." 4

The driver smiled, accepted her money and gave her a receipt. 5

About five minutes later, a tall black man trotted up to the bus, climbed aboard and glanced at the huddled passengers. 6

"Are you looking for your wife?" the driver asked. 7

"Yes, I am," I answered. 8

"She's halfway back on the left," said the driver, smiling. 9

> **Word Power**
> **mundane** ordinary; commonplace
> **civil** polite; courteous

This mundane incident points up a recent subtle change in America. A dozen years ago, chances are that a white bus driver wouldn't have realized that my wife was the white woman. Or, if he had come to that conclusion, probably wouldn't have behaved in a civil manner. 10

I know. I lived it. In 1978, in Cleveland, I "married white" despite some friends' telling me that a black man who does so better have a high boiling point, which they knew I didn't. They reminded me that such a man can't expect to live happily ever after. 11

In those days, it seemed a lot of people had nothing better to do than come to attention when Janice and I appeared. It happened when the lights went up in a movie house on Friday night, in a supermarket line on Saturday morning, a realtor's office in the afternoon or a football crowd on Sunday. White folks craned their necks to see us and bent sideways to hear us. From black men, there were knowing winks at me; from black women, icy stares at Janice. 12

Of course, as a black man in America, I had always known about racism. But my marriage to Janice made me more acutely aware of it—to the point that we decided against having children because we didn't want them subjected to the taunts offspring of interracial parents often endure. 13

> **Word Power**
> **confront** to face a challenger or a challenge

The hurt and humiliation we felt on any number of occasions was always followed by anger, which caused us to confront the offender by openly questioning the motive and meaning of his or her comment. This often resulted in an argument—odd, because we simply wanted to go about our business. But we were determined not to accept abuse. 14

There was the treatment we received in several cities while eating out. Typically, we'd be seated next to a serving area or the kitchen or in an unromantic corner—the better not to be seen by other diners. We'd usually counter by waiting for our order to be taken and then asking for another table. Or by leaving a minuscule tip. Or walking out before ordering. 15

As time went on, we found that our antagonists could be black as well as white. 16

For example, there was a nearly violent encounter with a black man in a Japanese restaurant that features communal dining. This fellow took umbrage at our declining to sit with him, his wife, their young children and another woman. He shouted a few nasty names our way to let us know how he felt about *our kind* of twosome. 17

It wasn't race, but the children that had kept us from the table. We'd each put in a particularly harrowing work day and did not at that particular time want to deal with young kids. 18

And yet, while "marrying white" has resulted in discomfort at work (some coworkers and bosses have openly disapproved) and has carried a social penalty, it has also proved a personal blessing to both of us. 19

For example, through Janice I am better able to understand some of the trepidation of whites in reacting to affirmative action programs they feel go too far in favor of blacks. She described the gut-wrenching insecurity of a blue-collar neighbor who feared for his job. And through her eyes I can empathize with whites who, when encountering young black males in some situations, may fear that a mugging or worse is in the offing. 20

And I also have learned why Janice, a tall, beautiful woman, makes sure to look her best when we are out together. She is consciously combating the unfortunate stereotype that says a black man will go out with a white woman—no matter how unattractive she is—simply because she is white. And my wife is no stereotype. 21

For her part, Janice has learned to understand my exasperation when, during my lunch hour, I was unable to find a downtown barber who knew how to cut my hair. And she came to know the importance of the role of predominantly black colleges—one of which I attended for a year—in providing quality education, forging self-pride and engendering the ideals of black self-help. 22

Through my career ups and downs, my wife has seen that for a black man the job options are limited and chances to succeed are hard to come by. 23

And I take pride in nurturing in my wife an appreciation of original black rhythm and blues music—which she'd never heard. Owing to my record collection dating back to the late 1940's and my writing on the subject, she now knows that before Elvis, the Beatles, Rolling Stones, and the Motown Sound, there were Big Joe Turner, Ivory Joe Hunter, the Orioles, Clovers and Spaniels. 24

Professionally, I've always been proud of my wife, an award-winning journalist who now works in corporate public relations, and I've never been shy about letting others know it. One evening in Cleveland, at my company's holiday party in a big hotel, I expressed this pride to a white colleague from out of town. He was so impressed that I was married to a well-known reporter that he dragged people over to meet her. It never occurred to him that many of the white executives and their wives were not eager to exchange pleasantries with us. And their disdain showed. 25

And I can't count the number of times Janice and I were drawn into staring contests with blue-collar ethnic types, button-down WASP's and the omnipresent gray-haired grandmothers. But it went with the territory we'd staked out. 26

Along about 1984, after six years of fighting the stares, subtle slights and flagrant insults, Janice and I stopped being so confrontational and 27

Word Power

antagonist an opponent; a person with whom one is in conflict

umbrage offense; resentment **to take umbrage** to take offense

Word Power

trepidation fear, dread

began rolling with the punches. In addition, leaving the Middle West for Manhattan, we left behind a place that tolerated us grudgingly for a city where our abilities and perseverance mean more to other people than our interracial marriage. A city where the driver of an airport bus acted with sensitivity.

Yet two highly publicized events of the last several years involving suspected interracial relationships—the 1989 murder of 16-year-old Yusuf Hawkins in Bensonhurst and the vicious beating in early June of 17-year-old Jermaine Ewell on Long Island—have lately caused me to look over my shoulder occasionally when out with my wife. It's the same way I felt in 1980 when I learned of the near-fatal shooting in Indiana of the National Urban League's Vernon Jordan after he left the company of a white woman. I pray we aren't returning to such mindless violence. 28

Which is why, when we heard the words "Jungle Fever"—title of the controversial Spike Lee film—yelled at us from a passing truck on a recent Saturday night in midtown Manhattan, we cringed. The jungle is for animals. Our humanity is what counts. And pride. The marriage we have embraced permits us to endure bigotry, insults and insensitivity, and to press on. 29

Thinking about the Reading

1. What does the incident with the airport bus driver show about Americans' changing attitudes toward interracial marriage?
2. The author cites many examples of incidents that caused him and his wife to feel "hurt and humiliation" (paragraph 14). How has the couple's reaction to these incidents changed over the years? Why has their reaction changed?
*3. Carter states that "our antagonists could be black as well as white" (paragraph 16). Give at least two examples from his essay in which African Americans showed their disapproval of the interracial relationship. In each case, tell why you think they disapproved.
4. How has the relationship between Richard and Janice been a "blessing" (paragraph 19) to both of them? Give examples.

Writing Practice

1. Have you ever been treated with prejudice or been discriminated against? If so, describe one or more such incidents, and tell how you reacted.
2. In this essay, Carter describes how he and his wife confronted incidents of prejudice and discrimination. What other tactics might they have used besides confrontation? Choose two of the incidents that Carter describes, and propose other ways of dealing with them besides angry confrontation.
3. In spite of the difficulties, Carter believes that his interracial marriage has been "a personal blessing to both of us" (paragraph 19). Write about how a relationship with a person of a different race, ethnic group, religion, or economic or social class has been a personal blessing to you. (You might also choose to apply this question to your relationship with a person who has different abilities or who holds political opinions different from yours.)

CAN YOU IMAGINE?

Jared Esposito

Student writer Jared Esposito compares and contrasts life before and after cellular phones and computers became an important part of our existence. He examines the positive and negative effects of these two inventions and comes to a conclusion that you may or may not agree with.

A few days ago, my grandmother talked to me about how much things have changed since she was a girl. "Can you imagine," she asked, "what life without television was like?" Of course I could not; I have grown up with television. Like people in my grandmother's generation, those in my generation have seen many changes during our lifetimes. And our children will find it difficult to imagine what life was like before cell phones and computers. 1

Ten years ago, the only people who had cell phones were people like doctors whose jobs required them to be on call twenty-four hours a day. Average people could not afford the high cost of cell phones, and they were impressed when they saw someone use these devices. If parents went out to a movie or a restaurant, they would have to call home several times during the evening to find out how their children were. If there was an emergency, the babysitter would have to call the theater or the restaurant and hope that the parents could be located. If a car broke down on the way home, the driver would have to hope that a police cruiser would come by or that another motorist would stop. If that did not happen, someone would have to hike to the nearest phone booth. 2

Now, everyone seems to have a cell phone. These items are so inexpensive that many phone companies simply give them away if a customer signs up for service. Now, people can be reached anywhere. If there is an emergency at home, a babysitter can get hold of the parents wherever they are. If someone has car trouble, all he or she has to do is get out a trusty cell phone and call the auto club or a gas station. Of course, the availability of cell phones has some drawbacks. The ringing of cell phones constantly interrupts movies, and restaurants are filled with people talking loudly on their cell phones. In fact, some restaurants have even put up signs asking patrons to turn their phones off when they enter. The biggest drawback of having a cell phone is that a person never can be completely out of reach. No matter where a person is—at the beach, at a ball game, or even at church—someone can call. 3

Much the same situation exists with computers. Only a few years ago, most people did not own computers. When someone wanted to write a letter, he or she had to type it or write it by hand, mail it, and then wait several days for it to arrive. If the writer wanted to take some words out or add a sentence, he or she would have to copy or type the letter over. The same was true for schoolwork. As every student knows, essays and reports have to go through several drafts. Before word processing, each draft had to be typed or hand written. Then, students would have to correct small mistakes in spelling or grammar with correction tape or Wite-Out. If students needed to look up a fact or find information for their papers, they would have to go to the library to use the card catalog or to look through periodical indexes. 4

Now, almost everyone has access to a computer. People who do not own computers can go to the public library or to a community center and use one. Some rest stops on the turnpike even have computers that patrons can use without cost. E-mail makes it possible for people to type and send letters in a matter of minutes. After a letter is finished, the spell checker and a grammar checker can identify mistakes, and the writer can correct them with a few keystrokes. Computers have also made schoolwork easier. Now, students can write drafts of an essay or a report quickly and easily. Word-processing programs enable them to add and delete material and to move whole blocks of text. No longer do students have to type and retype material before they submit it. If students have to find information for their papers, they can get on the Internet and access an online encyclopedia, a library's online card catalog, or a magazine article. 5

Cell phones and computers have changed our world forever—for better and for worse. They make it possible for us to communicate almost instantly over great distances. And, by enabling us to write more efficiently, they make us more productive workers. Still, even with their obvious advantages, there are certain drawbacks. For example, cell phones have almost destroyed our privacy, and e-mail has almost eliminated thoughtful writing and editing. These drawbacks have led me to conclude that although life might have been more difficult before cell phones and computers, in some ways it might also have been better. 6

Thinking about the Reading

*1. What are the advantages of cell phones? What are their disadvantages? Discuss the advantages and disadvantages mentioned in the essay as well as some from your own experiences and observations.

*2. How have computers made writing and researching for school easier? How have they made communication easier?

3. In the final paragraph, Jared states his opinion about whether these inventions have, on the whole, made our lives better or worse. What is his conclusion? Tell why you agree or disagree with it.

4. How does Jared organize his essay? How do the two paragraphs on cell phones differ? How do the two paragraphs on computers differ? Why do you think he organized his ideas the way he did?

Writing Practice

1. Write about how your life was different before and after one of the following: beginning college, the birth of a sibling or child, a move, a new responsibility, or a new hobby.
2. Write about two careers you are considering. What are their advantages and disadvantages?
3. What are the advantages and disadvantages of both marriage and the single life? Consider your own experiences and the experiences of friends and family members.

WHAT I DID FOR LOVE

Macarena del Rocío Hernández

Do you believe in fortune tellers, love potions, or psychic advisers? Journalist Macarena Hernández did not think she did until love made her change her mind. Hernández is a staff writer for the *San Antonio Express-News*.

I know what I will be serving at my wedding. My mother's neighbor Doña Ester García will make carne guisada, beef stew, for the main course. My uncle has volunteered one of his steers. I am wondering whether it should be a huge affair, a la Mexicana,[1] with a guest list including the mailman and distant relatives of my second cousin's inlaws. Or a simple, more Americanized ceremony, with only those by my side who have been part of my most recent life. I have some time to work out the details since I still don't have the groom. 1

I'm a 25-year-old Mexican American whose relationships wilt faster than orchids in the Texas sun. And that, according to my aunts and cousins, makes me an old maid. 2

Never mind that I've spent the last seven years living and working in major cities throughout the United States where women tend to get married in their late 20s and early 30s. Whenever I come back home to La Joya, Texas, my family is quick to remind me that time is running out. My love life, or lack of it, is especially troubling to my aunts, most of whom have children who are at least seven years younger than I and already married. 3

I know about the chisme[2] that the aunts swap as they huddle over the kitchen table making tamales. 4

"She studies way too much. All that work can't be good for her head," says one as she spreads masa on a cornhusk and tops it with a spoonful of beef. 5

"Maybe she doesn't like men. You know, in San Francisco where she used to live, there are a lot of gay people," another tía[3] adds. 6

I suspect they also talk about me while they watch their favorite Spanish-language soap operas, overwrought stories that always involve a poor girl crying crocodile tears as she calls out, "Carlos José! No me dejes. Yo te amo." (Carlos José! Don't leave me. I love you.) 7

It was probably during one of those pain-filled telenovelas[4] that one of my tias had an epiphany. Something, she realized, must have happened to me during my childhood, some awful trauma that has made it impossible for me to keep a man. 8

Word Power

epiphany a sudden flash of insight

trauma an injury or wound, either physical or emotional

I'll admit I can scare men off. But I think it has more to do with growing up with four older brothers who rarely spoke to me unless they wanted a shirt ironed or dinner cooked. At an early age, I began to equate marriage with slavery. I couldn't see myself spending the rest of my life washing someone else's underwear. 9

My relatives view my attitude on the subject as a disease that seems to be getting worse. 10

It's no secret that my mother has been praying for years for a "good man who can take care of you." And if all that prayer hasn't helped, my Tía Nelly concluded, I must be cursed. 11

1. In the Mexican style.
2. Gossip.
3. Aunt.
4. Television soap operas.

Word Power

anemic weak; lacking vitality

Word Power

vixen slang for a tempting, sexy woman; can also mean a bad-tempered woman. The original meaning is "female fox."

She knew the perfect person to help me: a curandera, a healer who can cure a person of lovelessness just as easily as colic. 12

"I don't believe in it," my cousin said to me, "but maybe you should go." 13

I thought about it for a week. If I went, I'd be admitting that I have a problem. If I didn't, I might miss out on a cure. 14

I picked a Friday afternoon. I decked myself out in a short black dress and red lipstick so the curandera couldn't blame my anemic love life on the way I dressed. Tía Nelly and I drove 35 minutes to Rio Grande City and the curandera's storefront office. 15

I hid my truck in an alley so nobody I knew would see it. The store looked like a herb shop one might find on South Street in Philadelphia, except this one inhabited an old grocery. Inside were long aisles of neatly displayed candles, religious statuettes, soaps and good luck charms. One wall offered packages of herbs and spices. 16

In Latino neighborhoods curanderas are considered not only healers, but also spiritual advisers. They are like doctors, psychiatrists and priests rolled into one. 17

I am told my father's grandfather, Emeterio Chasco, was a curandero. He didn't charge his clients money; in exchange for banishing a fright, bad luck or a rash, he'd receive chickens, boxes of fruit and personal favors. 18

The only curandero I'd ever met was El Papi, one of my mother's younger cousins. A dark-skinned man who never married and lived with his parents in Mexico, El Papi had big crooked teeth that you saw even when he wasn't smiling. My mother doubted his spiritual powers, but people from nearby towns and ranches consulted with him in his bedroom, which was also the family living room. Nonetheless, I expected my curandera to be an older woman, with hands as worn and soft as my grandmother's. Her touch, I imagined, would be magical enough to cure anything. 19

But this curandera greeted me wearing a tight purple shirt and black pants that hugged a killer figure—curves that the bottle-blond healer told me were the product of hours at the gym. She was a middle-age vixen, not a grandmotherly adviser. A thoroughly modern healer who drives a white convertible and recently divorced her husband of more than 20 years. 20

She performed her consults in the area once designated "for employees only." For $20 she gave me a card reading that she said would give us both a better handle on mi problema.[5] She asked me to shuffle the tarot cards and then split the deck into three stacks. She instructed me to use my left hand to place the different piles back into one. I kept my left hand on the pile. She covered it with her left hand and prayed. Then she began to deal the cards. Her long, pearl-colored acrylic nails made clicking noises every time she placed one down, face up. She spread the cards out on her desk. "Your problem," she said, "is a sentimental one." 21

No one could hear our conversation, so I decided to be honest. "My aunt said maybe you could help me because I can't seem to find the right guy or even keep the bad ones I date." 22

"This is not logical. You are very pretty," she said, looking me straight in the eye. "Men are desgraciados [ingrates]. You can give everything except your heart, because they will hurt you." 23

After a few more minutes of reading my life in the cards, she looked at me as if to say: "This is more serious than I thought." 24

"There was a woman about five years ago, and her name starts with the letter M," she said. "There was money paid to keep men away from you, 25

5. My problem.

and it was probably done in Mexico because they will do anything over there."

But that was all she could tell me. I would, she said, have to come back the next morning so she could start doing some work on me. She asked for $48 to buy 40 candles that she'd burn while she prayed that night in hopes that everything we needed to know about the mysterious M would reveal itself. I would also need to pay $20 for a barrida, a cleansing ritual. 26

The next day the curandera was 10 minutes late—she had just finished a two-hour workout. She said she had news for me. Her overnight mediation had revealed two more letters of the mystery woman's name: A and R. 27

"Do you know anyone whose name starts with M-A-R?" she asked. Half of the Latinas I know have names that start with M-A-R: Maria, Martina, Marisa, Marisela, Marielena, Marina, Marta, Margarita. 28

Well, she said, the woman in question now dyes her hair guerro, blond. That only disqualified half. 29

"Last night," she said, "I saw a small black-and-white photo, probably from a yearbook." 30

Then the curandera explained what was wrong. The evil MAR woman, she said, had loved someone I was dating and had paid a dark man from Mexico to curse me, to keep men from sticking around. 31

The curse, she said, could be removed for $275, and even if I opted to go somewhere else, she advised me to get help as soon as possible. I couldn't remember dating anyone within the last five years who was so special that another woman would pay to have him. But I told her she could give me a barrida. 32

That, she promised, would definitely make me feel better, but I still needed to have the curse removed. 33

For the barrida, she had me stand just outside her office, facing south, in the middle of a circle that looked as if it had been burned into the floor. She instructed me to stretch my arms over my head as if I were singing or praising the Lord at church. 34

She doused her hands with lavender-scented alcohol and touched my neck, arms, hands and legs. She then began making the sign of the cross with a brown-shelled egg that she said had been laid by a black hen. The egg was cold. I couldn't help but wonder whether it had lost its magic while sitting in the refrigerator. 35

The curandera prayed, fast and in Spanish, imploring the bad spirits to leave. She then lighted a candle and walked around me, asking some invisible power to illuminate me. She put the candle down and crumbled some dried leaves around the circle and poured alcohol on them. She grabbed the candle and set the circle on fire. 36

Her praying was so fervent and so rapid that I could understand only a few phrases: "Give her a pure love," "send her a good man." Essentially, the same thing my mom had been asking for. 37

It was getting hot. The flames were inching closer to my toes and there was smoke. Just when I thought I might melt I heard her say: "Jump over the flame." I did. 38

For the next three days, she said, before I ate anything else I was to drink half a cup of water mixed with sugar followed by a single banana cut into slices and covered with honey. She sold me two $10 candles that I was supposed to light and pray to. 39

Then she calmly reminded me that I still had to come back to get the curse removed. 40

> **Word Power**
>
> **contradiction** a statement, situation, or personality in which two opposites are true

41 But I'd had enough. I had no intention of drinking sugar water, eating honey-coated slices of banana or lighting candles. Maybe I was afraid to rely on some vague magic I didn't understand.

42 Or maybe I believed in it too much, and couldn't bear the thought that it might not work.

43 When you live squeezed between two cultures, two languages, you are often a walking contradiction. Sometimes there is little you can do to keep both worlds at peace.

44 For days after the barrida I thought about everything the curandera told me. I held on to the things I wanted to believe—that I was too pretty not to attract men, that I would eventually end up with a successful, good man. And weighed those I didn't—that unless I reversed the curse there was no hope.

45 I wondered why a modern woman like me should listen to a curandera, even a with-it one clad in spandex. And then I remembered the words of another curandero: El Papi.

46 I was in the fourth grade and we were visiting his family in Nuevo Leon.

47 He and I were standing in the middle of the woods and I was watching him break an egg over a pile of sticks he was about to set on fire.

48 "Can you make someone fall in love with someone else?" I asked.

49 He looked up.

50 "Yes. I can," he said. "But that wouldn't be true love. You can't force love. You just have to wait for it to happen."

Thinking about the Reading

1. How does Hernández's attitude toward being single at age 25 differ from her family's attitude toward her marital status? In what way does she seem to agree with them?
2. Why do you think the author describes her experience with the curandera in great detail? What do these details reveal about the curandera and her methods?
*3. Hernández describes herself as a "walking contradiction" (paragraph 43). What does she mean by this? Cite some examples from the article that reveal contradictions in her personality.
4. In what ways does Hernández poke fun at herself, her family, and the curandera?

Writing Practice

1. Hernández is embarrassed by her trip to the curandera. To make herself feel better about the experience, she describes it with humor. Write about an embarrassing situation you experienced. Use humor to describe the situation and your feelings at the time.
2. Are you a "walking contradiction" like Hernández? Most of us are, even if we do not live in two cultures. Do you sometimes think one way and then act a different way? Describe the ways in which you are a contradiction—for example, in your personality traits or beliefs.
3. Hernández presents several details that show the importance of love and marriage in her culture, such as the custom of huge weddings and the popularity of Spanish-language soap operas. Write about how love and marriage are viewed in your culture. What customs and celebrations show their importance?

HOW BOYS BECOME MEN

Jon Katz

Journalist and mystery novelist Jon Katz examines the experiences that shape the typical male character in American culture. Katz uses examples from his own boyhood to explain why men seem to have trouble expressing feelings and accepting help. This essay originally appeared in *Glamour,* a magazine for young women.

Two nine-year-old boys, neighbors and friends, were walking home from school. The one in the bright blue windbreaker was laughing and swinging a heavy-looking book bag toward the head of his friend, who kept ducking and stepping back. "What's the matter?" asked the kid with the bag, whooshing it over his head. "You chicken?" 1

His friend stopped, stood still and braced himself. The bag slammed into the side of his face, the thump audible all the way across the street where I stood watching. The impact knocked him to the ground, where he lay mildly stunned for a second. Then he struggled up, rubbing the side of his head. "See?" he said proudly. "I'm no chicken." 2

Word Power
audible able to be heard

No. A chicken would probably have had the sense to get out of the way. This boy was already well on the road to becoming a *man,* having learned one of the central ethics of his gender: Experience pain rather than show fear. 3

Word Power
ethics a code of right and wrong behavior

Women tend to see men as a giant problem in need of solution. They tell us that we're remote and uncommunicative, that we need to demonstrate less machismo and more commitment, more humanity. But if you don't understand something about boys, you can't understand why men are the way we are, why we find it so difficult to make friends or to acknowledge our fears and problems. 4

Boys live in a world with its own Code of Conduct, a set of ruthless, unspoken, and unyielding rules: 5

Word Power
unyielding not giving in; not giving way to persuasion

> Don't be a goody-goody.
>
> Never rat. If your parents ask about bruises, shrug.
>
> Never admit fear. Ride the roller coaster, join a fistfight, do what you have to do. Asking for help is for sissies.
>
> Empathy is for nerds. You can help your best buddy, under certain circumstances. Everyone else is on his own.
>
> Never discuss anything of substance with anybody. Grunt, shrug, dump on teachers, laugh at wimps, talk about comic books. Anything else is risky.

Word Power
empathy sensitivity to the thoughts and emotions of other people

Boys are rewarded for throwing hard. Most other activities—reading, befriending girls, or just thinking—are considered weird. And if there's one thing boys don't want to be, it's weird. 6

More than anything else, boys are supposed to learn how to handle themselves. I remember the bitter fifth-grade conflict I touched off by elbowing aside a bigger boy named Barry and seizing the cafeteria's last carton of chocolate milk. Teased for getting aced out by a wimp, he had to reclaim his place in the pack. Our fistfight, at recess, ended with my knees buckling and my lip bleeding while my friends, sympathetic but out of range, watched resignedly. 7

When I got home, my mother took one look at my swollen face and screamed. I wouldn't tell her anything, but when my father got home I cracked and confessed, pleading with them to do nothing. Instead, they called Barry's parents, who restricted his television for a week. 8

The following morning, Barry and six of his pals stepped out from behind a stand of trees. "It's the rat," said Barry. 9

I bled a little more. *Rat* was scrawled in crayon across my desk. 10

They were waiting for me after school for a number of afternoons to follow. I tried varying my routes and avoiding bushes and hedges. It usually didn't work. 11

I was as ashamed for telling as I was frightened. "You did ask for it," said my best friend. Frontier Justice has nothing on Boy Justice. 12

In panic, I appealed to a cousin who was several years older. He followed me home from school, and when Barry's gang surrounded me, he came barreling toward us. "Stay away from my cousin," he shouted, "or I'll kill you." 13

After they were gone, however, my cousin could barely stop laughing. "You were afraid of *them?*" he howled. "They barely came up to my waist." 14

Men remember receiving little mercy as boys; maybe that's why it's sometimes difficult for them to show any. 15

"I know lots of men who had happy childhoods, but none who have happy memories of the way other boys treated them," says a friend. "It's a macho marathon from third grade up, when you start butting each other in the stomach." 16

"The thing is," adds another friend, "you learn early on to hide what you feel. It's never safe to say 'I'm scared.' My girlfriend asks me why I don't talk more about what I'm feeling. I've gotten better at it, but it will *never* come naturally." 17

You don't need to be a shrink to see how the lessons boys learn affect their behavior as men. Men are being asked, more and more, to show sensitivity, but they dread the very word. They struggle to build their increasingly uncertain work lives but will deny they're in trouble. They want love, affection, and support but don't know how to ask for them. They hide their weaknesses and fears from all, even those they care for. They've learned to be wary of intervening when they see others in trouble. They often still balk at being stigmatized as weird. 18

Word Power

balk to resist abruptly and strongly

stigmatized described or identified as having a shameful or unacceptable trait or background

Some men get shocked into sensitivity—when they lose their jobs, their wives, or their lovers. Others learn it through a strong marriage, or through their own children. 19

It may be a long while, however, before male culture evolves to the point that boys can learn more from one another than how to hit curve balls. Last month, walking my dog past the playground near my house, I saw three boys encircling a fourth, laughing and pushing him. He was skinny and rumpled, and he looked frightened. One boy knelt behind him while another pushed him from the front, a trick familiar to any former boy. He fell backward. 20

When the others ran off, he brushed the dirt off his elbows and walked toward the swings. His eyes were moist and he was struggling for control. 21

"Hi," I said through the chain-link fence. "How ya doing?" 22

"Fine," he said quickly, kicking his legs out and beginning his swing. 23

Thinking about the Reading

*1. Are there any rules in the "Code of Conduct" (paragraph 5) that you think are *not* part of American boys' culture? Which rules would you eliminate or change because they do not reflect real life? Which rules, if any, do you think are missing?

2. Do you agree or disagree with the claim that men find it difficult to make friends and to admit their "fears and problems" (paragraph 4)? What negative effects might these attitudes have on men's lives?

*3. Do you agree or disagree with the claim that men are "remote and uncommunicative" and "need to demonstrate . . . more commitment, more humanity" (paragraph 4)? Give examples to support your position.

4. Think about a man you have known or read about who does not fit the stereotype presented in this essay. Why do you think he is different?

Writing Practice

1. If you are male, write a response to Katz's version of the Code of Conduct. Has the Code affected your life? If so, how? If you are female, list three rules that govern the lives of female teens. Explain how these rules have affected your life.
2. If you are male, choose one of the rules in Katz's Code of Conduct and tell how this rule caused you to act in a specific situation. Be sure to include the results of that action. If you are female, choose one of the rules in Katz's Code of Conduct and tell how this rule has affected your relationships with men in general or with one specific male.
3. Write about some rules that you think should be part of an ideal Universal Code of Conduct for all people. What do you think the results would be if everyone actually followed these rules?

HOW TO WRITE A PERSONAL LETTER

Garrison Keillor

Humorist Garrison Keillor is the creator of the National Public Radio variety show *A Prairie Home Companion.* This essay was written as an advertisement for the International Paper Company in 1987. Keillor mixes humor with practical advice on how to express oneself in letters to friends and family members.

We shy persons need to write a letter now and then, or else we'll dry up and blow away. It's true. And I speak as one who loves to reach for the phone, dial the number, and talk. I say, "Big Bopper here—what's shakin', babes?" The telephone is to shyness what Hawaii is to February, it's a way out of the woods, *and yet:* a letter is better. 1

Such a Sweet Gift

Such a sweet gift—a piece of handmade writing, in an envelope that is not a bill, sitting in our friend's path when she trudges home from a long day spent among wahoos and savages, a day our words will help repair. They don't need to be immortal, just sincere. She can read them twice and again tomorrow: *You're someone I care about, Corinne, and think of often and every time I do you make me smile.* 2

We need to write, otherwise nobody will know who we are. They will have only a vague impression of us as A Nice Person, because frankly, we don't shine at conversation, we lack the confidence to thrust our faces forward and say, "Hi, I'm Heather Hooten, let me tell you about my week." Mostly we say "Uh-huh" and "Oh really." People smile and look over our shoulder, looking for someone else to talk to. 3

So a shy person sits down and writes a letter. To be known by another person—to meet and talk freely on the page—to be close despite distance. To escape from anonymity and be our own sweet selves and express the music of our souls. 4

Word Power

anonymity the state of being unknown; not named or identified

Same thing that moves a giant rock star to sing his heart out in front of 123,000 people moves us to take ballpoint in hand and write a few lines to our dear Aunt Eleanor. *We want to be known.* We want her to know that we have fallen in love, that we quit our job, that we're moving to New York, and we want to say a few things that might not get said in casual conversation: *Thank you for what you've meant to me, I am very happy right now.* 5

Skip the Guilt

The first step in writing letters is to get over the guilt of *not* writing. You don't "owe" anybody a letter. Letters are a gift. The burning shame you feel when you see unanswered mail makes it harder to pick up a pen and makes for a cheerless letter when you finally do. *I feel bad about not writing, but I've been so busy,* etc. Skip this. Few letters are obligatory, and they are *Thanks for the wonderful gift* and *I am terribly sorry to hear about George's death* and *Yes, you're welcome to stay with us next month,* and not many more than that. Write those promptly if you want to keep your friends. Don't worry about the others, except love letters, of course. When 6

Word Power

obligatory required; necessary

your true love writes *Dear Light of My Life, Joy of My Heart, O Lovely Pulsating Core of My Sensate Life,* some response is called for.

Some of the best letters are tossed off in a burst of inspiration, so keep your writing stuff in one place where you can sit down for a few minutes and *Dear Roy, I am in the middle of an essay for International Paper but thought I'd drop you a line. Hi to your sweetie too* dash off a note to a pal. Envelopes, stamps, address book, everything in a drawer so you can write fast when the pen is hot. 7

A blank white 8" x 11" sheet can look as big as Montana if the pen's not so hot—try a smaller page and write boldly. Or use a note card with a piece of fine art on the front; if your letter ain't good, at least they get the Matisse. Get a pen that makes a sensuous line, get a comfortable typewriter, a friendly word processor—whichever feels easy to the hand. 8

Word Power
sensuous appealing to the senses (in this case, sight and touch)

Sit for a few minutes with the blank sheet in front of you, and meditate on the person you will write to, let your friend come to mind until you can almost see her or him in the room with you. Remember the last time you saw each other and how your friend looked and what you said and what perhaps was unsaid between you, and when your friend becomes real to you, start to write. 9

Tell Us What You're Doing

Write the Salutation—*Dear* You—and take a deep breath and plunge in. A simple declarative sentence will do, followed by another and another and another. Tell us what you're doing and tell it like you were talking to us. Don't think about grammar, don't think about lit'ry style, don't try to write dramatically, just give us your news. Where did you go, who did you see, what did they say, what do you think? 10

If you don't know where to begin, start with the present moment: *I'm sitting at the kitchen table on a rainy Saturday morning. Everyone is gone and the house is quiet.* Let your simple description of the present moment lead to something else, let the letter drift gently along. 11

Take It Easy

The toughest letter to crank out is one that is meant to impress, as we all know from writing job applications; if it's hard work to slip off a letter to a friend, maybe you're trying too hard to be terrific. A letter is only a report to someone who already likes you for reasons other than your brilliance. Take it easy. 12

Don't worry about form. It's not a term paper. When you come to the end of one episode, just start a new paragraph. You can go from a few lines about the sad state of rock 'n roll to the fight with your mother to your fond memories of Mexico to your cat's urinary tract infection to a few thoughts on personal indebtedness to the kitchen sink and what's in it. The more you write, the easier it gets, and when you have a True True Friend to write to, a *compadre,* a soul sibling, then it's like driving a car down a country road, you just get behind the keyboard and press on the gas. 13

Word Power
sibling a brother or sister

Don't tear up the page and start over when you write a bad line—try to write your way out of it. Make mistakes and plunge on. Let the letter cook along and let yourself be bold. Outrage, confusion, love—whatever is in your mind, let it find a way to the page. Writing is a means of discovery, always, and when you come to the end and write *Yours ever* or *Hugs and Kisses,* you'll know something you didn't when you wrote *Dear Pal.* 14

Word Power

relic a valued object from the past

An Object of Art

Probably your friend will put your letter away, and it'll be read again a few 15
years from now—and it will improve with age. And forty years from now, your friend's grandkids will dig it out of the attic and read it, a sweet and precious relic of the ancient Eighties that gives them a sudden clear glimpse of you and her and the world we old-timers knew. You will then have created an object of art. Your simple lines about where you went, who you saw, what they said, will speak to those children and they will feel in their hearts the humanity of our times.

You can't pick up a phone and call the future and tell them about our 16
times. You have to pick up a piece of paper.

Thinking about the Reading

1. Why, according to Keillor, is writing letters especially important for shy people? How is a letter, like a telephone, "a way out of the woods" (paragraph 1)?
2. Do you agree with Keillor that letters express "the music of our souls" (paragraph 4)? Why or why not?

*3. This selection was written in 1987, before the widespread use of e-mail. How do you think e-mail will affect the future of letter writing?

4. What does Keillor mean when he writes, "when your friend becomes real to you, start to write" (paragraph 9)?

Writing Practice

1. Write a letter to a good friend or a family member updating them about your recent life. Let them know how school and work are going, and share your feelings about your activities, teachers, and friends. Use Keillor's advice to help you get started.
2. List the steps in a favorite recipe or the steps in some other process, such as cleaning or repairing something. Then, use your list to explain in writing how to do this activity. Include advice and comments to give your writing interest and personality.
3. Think of something you enjoy doing—anything from playing pickup basketball to designing Web sites. Write an e-mail message to a friend about this activity. Try to convince your friend that your hobby is an activity he or she, too, might enjoy.

TAKE ME OUT OF THEIR BALL GAME

Maria Guhde Keri

A "sports mom" herself, Maria Guhde Keri believes that parents today are too involved in the sports activities of their children. She questions whether this involvement is good for parents or children, or for the family as a whole. As you read her essay, notice how she uses humor to make her point.

My son's baseball team had just lost their last game of the season—they were out of the tournament. We losing parents tried our best to look glum, while the winning parents attempted to hide their jealousy. By the time we arrived at our cars, the lucky losers were excitedly discussing vacations we could take, projects we could begin, and friends we could finally see. Baseball season was over! We were free! 1

"At least until soccer season," one mom reminded us. "We're playing football this year," another added, rolling her eyes, and I couldn't block an image of parents and children all suited up in matching football uniforms, complete with pads. As a veteran sports mom, I knew exactly why she had used the plural *we*. 2

When one child in the family plays a sport, it is indeed a family affair. I think maybe the team photos should include us parents, derrieres parked in lawn chairs, arms laden with water bottles, diaper bags, and Barbie carry-alls. 3

> **Word Power**
> **derrière** a French word for backside, rear end, buttocks

We want to be there for our kids, to take an interest in what's important to them. This is what good parents do, right? Maybe. When I was young, kids rode their bikes or were dropped off for their games and practices. Only later would Mom or Dad ask how it went. My father was a coach, but I don't remember being dragged along to my brother's games. In fact, the kids on my dad's teams would converge on our house to be driven to the games in our 12-seater station wagon. No parents required. 4

> **Word Power**
> **dilute** to water down; make weaker or thinner

Sometimes I think that being so involved in our kids' sports, we dilute their experience. After all, it's not *their* win, it's *our* win. Do all the valuable lessons—losing, striking out, missing the winning shot—have the same impact when Mom and Dad are there to immediately say it's OK? 5

Of course we need to make sure Michael is listening to the coach and the coach is listening to Michael, and to ensure that Lauren is getting off the bench but not being pushed too hard. And psycho sports parents are obviously a problem: the dad who screams at his son for every fumble, the mom who reacts to the 14-year-old umpire's bad call as if it were a threat to world peace. We know they are wacko. 6

But then there are the rest of us, the good parents. Are we cramping our kids' style? Maybe they just want to get together and play a game. 7

> **Word Power**
> **animated** lively; full of energy and spirit

Did you ever walk into a room where kids are playing, say, a board game? They're animated, excited, totally focused on what they're doing. When you appear, they stiffen, grow quiet, and appear confused. An adult is watching, and suddenly the game and rules are changed—maybe even ruined. Now imagine 40 of us adults descending on a ball game. Do we really believe we can make it more fun for our children? 8

I'm essentially a non-athlete; my only "sport" was cheerleading. I don't remember my mother ever coming to my games, much less shouting from the stands "Good, honey, but smile more!" or "Doing great, but you were 9 late on that last turn." I think I would have told her to either shut up or stay home.

10 And don't the siblings deserve a well-balanced, un-rushed dinner once in a while? To play in their own neighborhood, their own yard? What are they learning when life revolves around Lauren's soccer games, and family harmony ranks a distant second?

11 Maybe we parents should be doing more constructive things: cutting the lawn, painting the dining room, volunteering, writing a book—in short, getting a life instead of just driving our children to theirs. Our time is important, too; we need to show our children that moms and dads can and need to do more than watch. Certainly, our involvement depends on our children's ages and personalities. My 5-year-old T-ball player will surely not be so enthusiastic about my seeing his every hit when he is 15. My 8-year-old daughter, on the other hand, already seems relieved when we miss one of her soccer games. Somewhere there is a perfect balance between not caring at all and caring too much. As parents, we know that at some point we need to make it *their* game, *their* recital, *their* grades. If we share every element of their lives, we're cheating them out of part of it.

12 We need to shut up. And sometimes—not always—we need to stay home. As hard as it is to risk missing her first home run, or not being there to comfort him after the missed foul shot, at some point we need to take ourselves out of their ball game. Because this is what good parents do.

Thinking about the Reading

1. Keri opens her essay with a short discussion of how she felt when her son's baseball season finally ended. What do you think the author's purpose was in beginning her essay with this story?
2. Why does Keri believe that "good parents" (paragraph 4) should become involved in their children's sports activities? What negative effects of such involvement does she mention?
*3. How convincing are Keri's arguments that children might prefer their parents to be less involved in their sports lives? Do her examples support your own experiences and observations?
4. Keri is serious about her topic but uses humor in many of her examples and comments. What effect does the use of humor in this essay have on you, the reader?

Writing Practice

1. Do you agree or disagree with Keri's claim that parents are "cheating" (paragraph 11) their children by involving themselves in every aspect of the children's lives? State your point of view, and support it with examples.
2. Write about an aspect of modern life that annoys you. Introduce your topic with a brief story (true or made-up) that illustrates your point. Your writing can be humorous or serious.
3. Write about a time in your childhood when you learned a valuable lesson on your own.

WHEN LIFE IMITATES VIDEO

John Leo

Columnist, author, and social observer John Leo has written widely on popular culture, politics, and relationships between men and women. In this essay, Leo argues that violent video games have a negative influence on unstable young people, causing some to become cold-blooded mass murderers. How convincingly does he argue his case?

1 Was it real life or an acted-out video game?

2 Marching through a large building using various bombs and guns to pick off victims is a conventional video-game scenario. In the Colorado massacre, Dylan Klebold and Eric Harris used pistol-grip shotguns, as in some video-arcade games. The pools of blood, screams of agony, and pleas for mercy must have been familiar—they are featured in some of the newer and more realistic kill-for-kicks games. "With each kill," the *Los Angeles Times* reported, "the teens cackled and shouted as though playing one of the morbid video games they loved." And they ended their spree by shooting themselves in the head, the final act in the game Postal, and, in fact, the only way to end it.

Word Power

scenario a plot outline; a sequence of events, often imaginary

3 Did the sensibilities created by the modern video kill games play a role in the Littleton massacre? Apparently so. Note the cool and casual cruelty, the outlandish arsenal of weapons, the cheering and laughing while hunting down victims one by one. All of this seems to reflect the style and feel of the video killing games they played so often.

Word Power

sensibilities feelings; attitudes

4 No, there isn't any direct connection between most murderous games and most murders. And yes, the primary responsibility for protecting children from dangerous games lies with their parents, many of whom like to blame the entertainment industry for their own failings.

5 But there is a cultural problem here: We are now a society in which the chief form of play for millions of youngsters is making large numbers of people die. Hurting and maiming others is the central fun activity in video games played so addictively by the young. A widely cited survey of 900 fourth-through-eighth-grade students found that almost half of the children said their favorite electronic games involve violence. Can it be that all this constant training in make-believe killing has no social effects?

Word Power

maiming depriving someone of an arm or leg

6 The conventional argument is that this is a harmless activity among children who know the difference between fantasy and reality. But the games are often played by unstable youngsters unsure about the difference. Many of these have been maltreated or rejected and left alone most of the time (a precondition for playing the games obsessively). Adolescent feelings of resentment, powerlessness, and revenge pour into the killing games. In these children, the games can become a dress rehearsal for the real thing.

Word Power

obsessively in an excessive and unreasonable way

7 Psychologist David Grossman of Arkansas State University, a retired Army officer, thinks "point and shoot" video games have the same effect as military strategies used to break down a soldier's aversion to killing. During World War II, only 15 to 20 percent of all American soldiers fired their weapons in battle. Shooting games in which the target is a man-shaped outline, the Army found, made recruits more willing to "make killing a reflex action."

Word Power

aversion an avoidance of something as a result of extreme dislike

Video games are much more powerful versions of the military's primitive discovery about overcoming the reluctance to shoot. Grossman says Michael Carneal, the schoolboy shooter in Paducah, Ky., showed the effects of video-game lessons in killing. Carneal coolly shot nine times, hitting eight people, five of them in the head or neck. Head shots pay a bonus in many video games. Now the Marine Corps is adapting a version of Doom, the hyperviolent game played by one of the Littleton killers, for its own training purposes. 8

More realistic touches in video games help blur the boundary between fantasy and reality—guns carefully modeled on real ones, accurate-looking wounds, screams, and other sound effects, even the recoil of a heavy rifle. Some newer games seem intent on erasing children's empathy and concern for others. Once the intended victims of video slaughter were mostly gangsters or aliens. Now some games invite players to blow away ordinary people who have done nothing wrong—pedestrians, marching bands, an elderly woman with a walker. In these games, the shooter is not a hero, just a violent sociopath. One ad for a Sony game says: "Get in touch with your gun-toting, testosterone-pumping, cold-blooded murdering side." 9

Word Power

sociopath a person who exhibits antisocial behavior of a criminal nature; a mentally ill or unstable person who feels no social or moral obligations to others

These killings are supposed to be taken as harmless over-the-top jokes. But the bottom line is that the young are being invited to enjoy the killing of vulnerable people picked at random. This looks like the final lesson in a course to eliminate any lingering resistance to killing. 10

SWAT teams and cops now turn up as the intended victims of some video-game killings. This has the effect of exploiting resentments toward law enforcement and making real-life shooting of cops more likely. This sensibility turns up in the hit movie *Matrix:* world-saving Keanu Reeves, in a mandatory Goth-style, long black coat packed with countless heavy-duty guns, is forced to blow away huge numbers of uniformed law-enforcement people. 11

"We have to start worrying about what we are putting into the minds of our young," says Grossman. "Pilots train on flight simulators, drivers on driving simulators, and now we have our children on murder simulators." If we want to avoid more Littleton-style massacres, we will begin taking the social effects of the killing games more seriously. 12

Thinking about the Reading

*1. Leo introduces his topic by describing the similarities between the plot and actions of some violent video games and the massacre in Littleton, Colorado, in 1999. Do you think this comparison is an effective and convincing way for the author to present his main idea? In your own words, state this main idea.

2. How does Leo support his claim that violent video games can break down people's aversion to killing and even make them more efficient killers?

*3. Leo states that video games are getting worse in terms of promoting random violence because the newer ones target law-enforcement officers and innocent people rather than "gangsters or aliens" (paragraph 9). How does Leo support this statement? Explain why you agree or disagree with this view of the newest video games.

4. Do the arguments and support in this essay convince you that we should "begin taking the social effects of the killing games more seriously" (paragraph 12)? Discuss why you are or are not convinced.

Writing Practice

1. Do you think violent video games are a bad influence on young people in our society? Explain your views, presenting support from your own reading, observations, and experience.
2. Using facts and examples from your own experience, try to support the position that violent video games have a useful function in the lives of young people.
3. Write a letter to the editor of your local newspaper suggesting ways to prevent violent behavior in young people.

BLACK AND LATINA—FACE IT!

Odalys Martínez

People of mixed heritage often suffer from lack of acceptance by one or more of the ethnic groups in their background. Odalys Martínez, a dark-skinned young woman of Cuban and African-American ancestry, wrote this essay to make Hispanics (and all other Americans) aware of the discrimination she has experienced as a "black Latina." Her essay appeared in *Latina,* a magazine for young Hispanic women.

"Say something in Spanish," I'm often asked. It's always a dare or a test. 1
That's because I don't seem to fit some people's idea of what a Hispanic should look like—or what a black person should sound like, for that matter. I happen to be a brown-skinned black (my maternal grandfather was black American) Hispanic (my Cuban father was considered mestizo). I guess that for some people, blacks have no business speaking Spanish, or Hispanics looking black.

Word Power

mestizo a person of mixed European and American Indian ancestry

For most of my life I have had to endure comments such as "You don't 2
look Spanish. . . ." On the other hand, I really can't blame people for their ignorance when the only Cubans they may be familiar with are Ricky Ricardo[1] and Gloria Estefan. I also can't blame them if all they see on television are blacks, whites, Asians, and a few light-skinned Hispanics—no in-betweens, no mixtures. I watch the Latino networks such as Telemundo and Univision and note that a minute number of the Latinos represented are dark-skinned (let's say approximately 10 percent on a good day). I remember, as a child, watching the maids on the telenovelas[2] portrayed by white Latinas in blackface. Mind you, this was in the 1960s and 1970s. I can honestly tell you that there was no one on television with whom I could identify—with the exception of Celia Cruz.[3]

Word Power

minute tiny

When I was growing up in Harlem, there was no such thing as color 3
inside my home. After all, when it comes to my family, skin shades range from light pecan to caramel to bronze to dark brown. I have some *parientes*[4] who look Caucasian, and some with Asian features. But once I went out into the real world, it was as if I had to choose sides in order to make it easier for others.

Word Power

Caucasian (noun) a person of European, North African, or southwest Asian ancestry; (adjective) relating or belonging to Caucasians

I remember having to complete those stupid forms—you know, the 4
ones on which you had to check off whether you were white, black, Asian, or Indian, as well as the ever popular "other." This used to give me major headaches when I was a kid. I'd agonize over which one best applied to me. My teachers would argue with me and tell me to check off "black," while friends and family would tell me I wasn't black and to check off "other," which would ultimately be the one I chose—with guilt. Nowadays I have more of a choice: white (non-Hispanic), black (non-Hispanic), or Hispanic. An improvement, but it still feels wrong, since Hispanic is not a race.

As a teenager in the late 1970s, I felt it best just to pretend that I wasn't 5
Hispanic at all. That way I didn't have to prove I was part of their club. I

1. A character in the 1950s television comedy *I Love Lucy* (played by the Cuban-American musician and actor Desi Arnaz).
2. Television soap operas.
3. A popular Latina singer.
4. Relatives.

associated only with black people and spoke no Spanish outside the home. There was no salsa, no Latin hustle, no *frijoles.*[5] Nada. I was all soul and sisterhood.

I dated the darkest guys I could find. The only thing is that when they found out about my Hispanic side, suddenly I turned into a trophy girlfriend. Their standard introduction was, "This is Odalys. She's Cuban." Then, nudging me, they'd add, "Go ahead, say something in Spanish." And I would say something in Spanish—to myself. 6

I bristled whenever I was automatically excluded based on my looks. I'd go to parties or clubs where Latin music was played, and no one would ask me to dance, but they'd ask my light-skinned girlfriend. I had to endure ordering *café con leche*[6] and being served American coffee at Latino *cafeterías.*[7] Time after time, someone would ask everyone in the room, except me, for directions in Spanish. My all-time favorite is when I'm asked where did I "get" my last name. "Uh... my father?" I answer. 7

I still resent that I'm not considered by some to be Latina enough merely because of the color of my skin. I still get tired of proving that I am and that there is no such thing as a "typical" Latina. but after years of berating myself for letting other people's opinions govern me, I decided that enough is enough. 8

Word Power
berating scolding

I'm both black and Hispanic. It's up to others to deal with it. I no longer feel that I have to go to one side or the other. I am what I am—whether or not it matches the picture in the beholder's mind. I've lost that "How can I join the club?" feeling, for I finally realized that I am, and always have been, a member in good standing. 9

Thinking about the Reading

1. Why does Martínez feel that it is "a dare or a test" when people ask her to "say something in Spanish" (paragraph 1)? Why have African-American boyfriends asked her to speak Spanish to their friends? Why is she a "trophy girlfriend" (paragraph 6) to them?
2. What do the members of Martínez's family look like? Why would it be difficult to characterize them as members of one "race" only? Do they all belong to the same race, or is each one different, even though they all come from the same group of ancestors?
3. How has being a "black Latina" affected Martínez's life? Why do you think she pretended that she was not Hispanic when she was a teenager?

*4. What conclusion does Martínez reach in the final paragraph of her essay? How do you think this attitude will affect her life in the future?

Writing Practice

1. Many people, including some scientists, are seriously questioning the whole concept of "race." They believe that there is too much variety and too little consistency among human groups to divide people neatly into races. They argue that the constant mixing of groups makes it

5. Beans.
6. Coffee with milk.
7. Coffeehouses.

almost impossible to assign many individuals to a single race. In fact, the U.S. Census Bureau now permits Americans to check more than one category of race. Do you see yourself as belonging to one particular ethnic or racial group or to more than one? Why?

2. Describe a favorite food from your own or another ethnic group. Begin by defining the food item or dish. Then, describe it in greater detail, presenting examples of the occasions on which it is eaten. Conclude with a story about your own experience with this food.
3. In her essay, Martínez shows readers how she is misjudged and discriminated against because of her physical appearance. Write about a time when your own physical appearance or dress caused people to misjudge you or discriminate against you. Or, write about a time you formed an opinion about someone else (based solely on their appearance) that turned out to be untrue.

BEFORE AIR CONDITIONING

Arthur Miller

Pulitzer Prize–winner Arthur Miller is considered one of America's greatest playwrights. His dramas *Death of a Salesman, All My Sons,* and *The Crucible* are classics of the modern theater. Here, Miller recalls his youth in New York City during the days before air conditioning became common.

Exactly what year it was I can no longer recall—probably 1927 or '28— 1
there was an extraordinarily hot September, which hung on even after school had started and we were back from our Rockaway Beach bungalow. Every window in New York was open, and on the streets venders manning little carts chopped ice and sprinkled colored sugar over mounds of it for a couple of pennies. We kids would jump onto the back steps of the slow-moving, horse-drawn ice wagons and steal a chip or two; the ice smelled vaguely of manure but cooled palm and tongue.

People on West 110th Street, where I lived, were a little too bourgeois 2
to sit out on their fire escapes, but around the corner on 111th and farther uptown mattresses were put out as night fell, and whole families lay on those iron balconies in their underwear.

Word Power

bourgeois middle-class and proper in attitudes

Even through the nights, the pall of heat never broke. With a couple of 3
other kids, I would go across 110th to the park and walk among the hundreds of people, singles and families, who slept on the grass, next to their big alarm clocks, which set up a mild cacophony of the seconds passing, one clock's ticks syncopating with another's. Babies cried in the darkness, men's deep voices murmured, and a woman let out an occasional high laugh beside the lake. I can recall only white people spread out on the grass; Harlem began above 116th Street then.

Later on, in the Depression thirties, the summers seemed even hotter. 4
Out West, it was the time of the red sun and the dust storms, when whole desiccated farms blew away and sent the Okies,[1] whom Steinbeck immortalized, out on their desperate treks toward the Pacific. My father had a small coat factory on Thirty-ninth Street then, with about a dozen men working sewing machines. Just to watch them handling thick woolen winter coats in that heat was, for me, a torture. The cutters were on piecework, paid by the number of seams they finished, so their lunch break was short—fifteen or twenty minutes. They brought their own food: bunches of radishes, a tomato perhaps, cucumbers, and a jar of thick sour cream, which went into a bowl they kept under the machines. A small loaf of pumpernickel also materialized, which they tore apart and used as a spoon to scoop up the cream and vegetables.

Word Power

desiccated dried-up

immortalized made famous forever

treks difficult journeys

The men sweated a lot in those lofts, and I remember one worker who 5
had a peculiar way of dripping. He was a tiny fellow, who disdained scissors, and, at the end of a seam, always bit off the thread instead of cutting it, so that inch-long strands stuck to his lower lip, and by the end of the day he had a multicolored beard. His sweat poured onto those thread ends and dripped down onto the cloth, which he was constantly blotting with a rag.

1. Oklahoma farmers forced to abandon their farms during the dust storms of the 1930s; subject of the 1939 Pulitzer Prize–winning novel *The Grapes of Wrath* by John Steinbeck.

Word Power
physique the structure or form of a person's body

Given the heat, people smelled, of course, but some smelled a lot worse than others. One cutter in my father's shop was a horse in this respect, and my father, who normally had no sense of smell—no one understood why—claimed that he could smell this man and would address him only from a distance. In order to make as much money as possible, this fellow would start work at half past five in the morning and continue until midnight. He owned Bronx apartment houses and land in Florida and Jersey, and seemed half mad with greed. He had a powerful physique, a very straight spine, a tangle of hair, and a black shadow on his cheeks. He snorted like a horse as he pushed through the cutting machine, following his patterns through some eighteen layers of winter-coat material. One late afternoon, he blinked his eyes hard against the burning sweat as he held down the material with his left hand and pressed the vertical, razor-sharp reciprocating blade with his right. The blade sliced through his index finger at the second joint. Angrily refusing to go to the hospital, he ran tap water over the stump, wrapped his hand in a towel, and went right on cutting, snorting, and stinking. When the blood began to show through the towel's bunched layers, my father pulled the plug on the machine and ordered him to the hospital. But he was back at work the next morning, and worked right through the day and into the evening, as usual, piling up his apartment houses. 6

There were still elevated trains then, along Second, Third, Sixth, and Ninth Avenues, and many of the cars were wooden, with windows that opened. Broadway had open trolleys with no side walls, in which you at least caught the breeze, hot though it was, so that desperate people, unable to endure their apartments, would simply pay a nickel and ride around aimlessly for a couple of hours to cool off. As for Coney Island on weekends, block after block of beach was so jammed with people that it was barely possible to find a space to sit or to put down your book or your hot dog. 7

My first direct contact with an air conditioner came only in the sixties, when I was living in the Chelsea Hotel. The so-called management sent up a machine on casters, which rather aimlessly cooled and sometimes heated the air, relying, as it did, on pitchers of water that one had to pour into it. On the initial filling, it would spray water all over the room, so one had to face it toward the bathroom rather than the bed. 8

A South African gentleman once told me that New York in August was hotter than any place he knew in Africa, yet people here dressed for a northern city. He had wanted to wear shorts but feared that he would be arrested for indecent exposure. 9

High heat created irrational solutions: linen suits that collapsed into deep wrinkles when one bent an arm or a knee, and men's straw hats as stiff as matzohs,[2] which, like some kind of hard yellow flower, bloomed annually all over the city on a certain sacred date—June 1 or so. Those hats dug deep pink creases around men's foreheads, and the wrinkled suits, which were supposedly cooler, had to be pulled down and up and sideways to make room for the body within. 10

The city in summer floated in a daze that moved otherwise sensible people to repeat endlessly the brainless greeting "Hot enough for ya? Ha-ha!" It was like the final joke before the meltdown of the world in a pool of sweat. 11

2. Large, flat, crisp bread eaten during the Jewish holiday of Passover.

Thinking about the Reading

1. The opening paragraphs describe how poor people coped with extreme heat in the 1920s. Was Miller's family poor? Which details in the essay answer this question?
*2. Why do you suppose New York businessmen in the 1920s wore suits instead of cooler, more comfortable clothes? How has men's summer business wear changed since the days Miller writes about?
3. Why do you think Miller chose to focus on the man in his father's factory who smelled like a horse? How does Miller seem to feel about this man? Which details reveal his attitude?
4. Why do you think Miller decided to write about life before air conditioning? Does he accomplish his purpose?

Writing Practice

1. Write a description of a time when you or someone you know had to live without a modern convenience, such as a refrigerator, a telephone, or electricity. How did you (or the other person) cope? As an alternative, imagine a day in your life without one of these conveniences, and write about how your life would be affected.
2. Write a description of your workplace, focusing on the physical appearance, actions, and attitudes of one employee in particular.
3. Write a description of a time when you were physically uncomfortable—hot, cold, exhausted, or in pain or discomfort. What did you do to make yourself feel better?

WHY WE NEED ANIMAL EXPERIMENTATION

Thuy Nguyen

Student writer Thuy Nguyen argues that animal experimentation is necessary to improve medical technology and thus to save human lives. Thuy supports her position with three main points. As you read this essay, note the specific examples she supplies to support these points.

With our advanced medical technology today, medicine has helped save many lives. The advances in medical technology that have saved these lives, for the most part, have been developed from animal experimentation. However, some people have claimed that animal experimentation is cruel and should not be continued. In my opinion, because medical research is so dependent on it, animal experimentation should be continued. It provides preventive measures to protect humans against getting diseases, helps discover cures and treatments for diseases, and helps surgeons to perfect the surgical techniques that are needed to save human lives. 1

First of all, animal experimentation provides preventive measures to protect humans from getting diseases. With the help of medical research on animals, scientists have found useful applications of vaccines to prevent many diseases. For example, the vaccines for polio, typhoid, diphtheria, tetanus, tuberculosis, measles, mumps, and rubella were all developed through animal experimentation. In addition, the principle of sterilization came out of Pasteur's[1] discovery, through animal experimentation, that microbes cause diseases. As a result, nowadays, medical professionals know that it is extremely important to sterilize medical tools such as gloves and syringes in order to keep them bacteria-free and to prevent patients from getting infections. Also, from experiments on rats, the connection between smoking and lung cancer was conclusively proved. This led many people to quit smoking and avoid getting cancer. 2

Word Power

sterilization the process of making something free of germs

microbes germs

Besides leading to preventive measures, animal experimentation also leads to the discovery of cures and treatments for many diseases. For instance, it has helped with the treatment of diabetic patients who are in need of insulin. Through experiments on cows and pigs, researchers have found the usefulness of cows' and pigs' insulin for treating diabetes. In addition, many drugs discovered through animal tests have been proven to cure ill patients. For example, a number of antibiotics, such as penicillin and sulfonamides, which were found from animal experimentation, help cure many infections. Also, many antihypertension medicines, which were developed in experiments on cats, help control blood pressure in hypertensive patients. Similarly, anticancer drugs were developed from tests on rats and dogs. 3

Word Power

hypertensive having high blood pressure

Besides providing preventive measures to protect humans from getting diseases and helping discover cures and treatments for many diseases, animal experimentation also helps surgeons to perfect the surgical techniques needed to save human lives. Surgeons have always been searching for better techniques to make surgery safer and more effective for their patients. One good way to perfect these techniques is to practice them on 4

1. Louis Pasteur (1822–1895) was a French chemist.

animals. From experiments on cats, researchers have found suturing techniques for transplants. Similarly, techniques for open heart surgery were perfected through many years of animal experimentation. Animal research programs have also helped surgeons to refine their techniques for kidney dialysis needed by patients with kidney failure.

5 Animal experimentation should be continued because it provides preventive measures to protect humans against diseases, helps to discover cures and treatments for diseases, and helps surgeons to perfect their surgical techniques. Therefore, animal experimentation is vital for the medical research that saves human lives.

Word Power

suturing surgical stitching in which fiber is used to close up wounds or to connect two parts of the body

Thinking about the Reading

1. What are the three arguments Thuy Nguyen uses to support her position that animal experimentation is essential to medical research?
2. What does the first paragraph of this essay accomplish? Where does Thuy first state each of her reasons for continuing animal experimentation? Where does she support each of these points? What does the last paragraph achieve?

*3. Are the examples Thuy presents convincing? Does she present enough support? Do any of the following elements appear in this essay?

- An explanation of what animal experimentation entails
- Expert opinions on the subject of animal experimentation
- A response to possible arguments against Thuy's point of view

If not, how would the addition of these elements improve the essay?

*4. Do you agree with Thuy's position on animal experimentation? What objections do you have? Support your position with facts and examples from your reading and experience.

Writing Practice

1. Revise Thuy's essay to give it more personal appeal for the reader. For example, make some of the examples come alive with narratives about people who have been helped by medical research.
2. Write an editorial that takes a position against the use of animal experimentation. Consider some of the following points made by opponents of animal experimentation:

   - The same medical results could be obtained by means other than animal experimentation.
   - Some animal experimentation is not necessary to medical research and could be eliminated.
   - Animal experimentation is not humane.

3. Choose an issue that is important to you, and write an essay supporting your position on that issue. Use facts and examples from your reading and experience to support your point of view.

THE LITTLE PRETZEL LADY

Sara Price

For some children, adult responsibility comes early in life. Student writer Sara Price recounts her experience as a ten-year-old working a Saturday job with her brother. For three years, to help their financially strapped family, Sara and her brother sold pretzels in a local shopping center.

When I was ten years old, selling pretzels at the corner of a shopping center was not my favorite weekend activity. Unfortunately, however, I had no alternative. My father had recently been injured on the job, and we had been experiencing severe financial difficulties. His disability payments and my mother's salary were not enough to support four children and my grandparents. When my parents could not pay our monthly mortgage, the bank threatened to take our house. 1

Knowing we had to find jobs to help, my older brother and I asked the local soft pretzel dealer to give us work on Saturdays. At first he refused, saying we were too young. But we simply would not take "no" for an answer because our parents desperately needed financial help. When we persisted, the pretzel dealer agreed to let us start the next week. In return for his kindness, my brother and I agreed to work faithfully for the next three years. 2

Word Power

persist to continue to do something in spite of setbacks

On the first Saturday morning, my brother and I reported promptly to our positions in front of the Cool-Rite appliance shop at the Academy Plaza shopping center. When Tom, our dealer, arrived with three hundred pretzels, he set up the stand and gave us instructions to sell each pretzel for a quarter, and five for a dollar. Then, Tom wished us luck and said he would be back later to pick up the table and the money. The arrangement with him was that we would get one-third of the total sales. 3

On that first Saturday, after selling our three hundred pretzels, my brother and I earned ten dollars each. (We also received a two-dollar tip from a friendly man who bought fifteen pretzels.) Our first day was considered a good one because we sold out by 4 p.m. However, the days that followed were not always as smooth as the first. When the weather was bad, meaning rain or snow, sales decreased; there were times when we had to stay as late as 7 p.m. until the last pretzel was sold. 4

To my regular customers, I was the little pretzel lady. But to my classmates, I was the target of humiliation. My worst nightmare came true when they found out that I ran a pretzel stand. Many of the boys made fun of me by calling out nasty names and harassing me for free pretzels. It was extremely embarrassing to see them walk by and stare while I stood like a helpless beggar on the street. I came to dread weekends and hate the sight of pretzels. But I was determined not to give up because I had a family that needed support and a three-year promise to fulfill. With that in mind, I continued to work. 5

Although winter was the best season for sales, I especially disliked standing in the teeth-chattering cold. I still remember that stinging feeling when the harsh wind blew against my cheeks. In order to survive the hours of shivering, I usually wore two or three pairs of socks and extra-thick clothing. Many times, I felt like a lonesome, leafless tree rooted to one spot and unable to escape from the bitter cold of winter. 6

7 The worst incident of my pretzel career occurred when I was selling alone because my brother was sick. A pair of teenage boys came up to the stand, called me offensive names, and squirted mustard all over the pretzels. My instant reaction was total shock, and before I could do anything else, they quickly ran away. A few minutes later, I discarded the pretzels, desperately fighting back the tears. I felt helpless and angry because I could not understand their actions.

8 The three years seemed like forever, but finally they were over. Even though selling pretzels on the street was the worst job I ever had, I was grateful for it. The money I earned each Saturday accumulated over the three years and helped my family. Selling pretzels also taught me many important values, such as responsibility, teamwork, independence, and appreciation for hard-earned money. Today, as I pass the pretzel vendors on my way to school, I think of a time not too long ago when I was the little pretzel lady.

Word Power

offensive hurtful; disagreeable; unpleasant

accumulate to gather or pile up little by little

Thinking about the Reading

1. What emotions did you experience as you read "The Little Pretzel Lady"? Which incidents or statements caused these emotions?
2. It is a well-known fact that children are often cruel to one another. What do you think caused the cruelty that Sara Price experienced?
3. Sara says that she sometimes felt like "a lonesome, leafless tree rooted to one spot and unable to escape from the bitter cold of winter" (paragraph 6). Explain how this image suits Sara's situation.

*4. Do you think that Sara's experience as a "pretzel lady" was more hurtful than beneficial to her? State reasons to support your answer.

Writing Practice

1. Write about a time in your childhood when you felt "different" and vulnerable to teasing or cruelty by other children.
2. Write about the "little pretzel lady" and her experiences from the point of view of a clerk in the Cool-Rite appliance shop who watches the two children sell pretzels every Saturday.
3. Write about an experience you had at work that made you like or dislike your job. Be sure to include details about the workplace, your job responsibilities, the other people involved in the situation, and any conversations that occurred.

SAY SOMETHING

Lucie Prinz

Lucie Prinz urges adults to lose their fear of teenagers and dare to "say something" when they encounter unacceptable behavior. Is she making a courageous moral statement, or is she encouraging meddling, or even harassment? You be the judge.

I was sitting on the subway a few weeks ago when I looked up and saw a baby, just a little less than a year old, swinging from the overhead bar. She was flanked by two young teenage girls who thought this was a great way to entertain their little sister. As the train began to move, I could visualize the baby flying across the car. Without really thinking, I said to the girls, "Hey, that's not a good idea. That baby is going to get hurt. You better sit down with her on the seat." The kids gave me one of those "Who do you think you are?" looks they reserve for meddling adults, but they took the baby off the bar and sat down. 1

I was suddenly struck by the silence in the subway car. The normal hum of conversation had vanished. My fellow passengers, who had witnessed my encounter with the kids, were now engrossed in their newspapers and books or staring at something fascinating on the subway-tunnel wall. The car was not very crowded, and everyone had seen that endangered baby just as clearly as I had, but they had chosen not to get involved. Although most of them now avoided eye contact with me, a few treated me to the kind of disdain reserved for troublemakers. Could it be that my fellow passengers didn't care about that baby? Or were they just afraid to interfere? 2

We've all heard the old African saying "It takes a whole village to raise a child." Americans have adopted it, and I understand why. It expresses some things that we can all easily accept: family values, shared responsibility, community spirit. But do we really believe in it as a guiding principle for our lives? When we repeat it, are we pledging ourselves to carry out its imperative? I don't think so. 3

Word Power
imperative a command that must be obeyed

Americans are known for generosity. We're ready to rescue the suffering children of the world. We send food to Ethiopia after our television screens show us little kids with huge eyes and distended bellies. We help the victims of floods, and we fund agencies to take care of refugees and abandoned children. We are the nation that invented the poster child and the telethon. These nameless suffering children touch our hearts—but they do not touch our lives. 4

Word Power
plight an unfortunate or difficult situation

The same adults who are profoundly moved by the plight of children they will never know seem to be willing to ignore the children they encounter every day, even if it is obvious that these children are in trouble or that they need a little adult guidance. I've watched adults actually move away from children they see approaching. I'm not talking about hostile, swaggering gangs of teenage boys—although even some of them are just exhibiting the high that comes with that first surge of testosterone. I'm talking about the ordinary, harmless children we all come in contact with every day on the streets of our cities, towns, and, yes, villages. 5

I'm keeping score, counting the number of times I find myself the only person in a crowd who dares to interact with a child she doesn't know. 6

A few days after the swinging-baby incident I was waiting on a crowded subway platform when someone pushed me from behind. I 7 turned to see three teenage girls, giggling, ebullient, and so eager to get on the train just pulling into the station that they were shoving. Again I reacted without thinking. "Stop pushing—we'll all get on," I said. After a few murmured remarks along the lines of "Get lost, lady," they stopped. So did the conversation around me. Eyes swiveled away. I felt a collective intake of breath. Disapproval hung in the air, but mainly I sensed fear.

Word Power
ebullient lively and enthusiastic

8 Seconds later the train doors opened, and we all stepped in. The woman who dropped into the seat next to me said, "Wow, that was a brave thing to do." When I suggested that it was no such thing, she said, "Well, you can't be too careful these days." That's just it, I thought. You *can* be too careful.

9 In both these encounters I treated harmless children as if they were indeed harmless. They may have been foolish, thoughtless, rambunctious, rude, or annoying. But the only one in any danger was that baby swinging on the bar.

Word Power
rambunctious unruly; full of uncontrolled energy

10 I live in a big city. I know that there are violent armed children, hopeless and desperate kids out there. There is no way that I can attack the serious urban problems we all hear about on the evening news. But I am convinced that I can contribute to the larger solutions by refusing to recoil from kids just because they are acting like kids. A lost child who encounters fear instead of concern is twice lost. By responding to these children we may begin to build a village where they will flourish and adults can live without fear.

Word Power
recoil to shrink away from something in fear or disapproval

Thinking about the Reading

*1. When Prinz confronted the girls who were endangering the baby, the other adults in the subway car reacted with fear or disapproval. Do you think these reactions are typical? Give examples from your own observations and experience to support your answer.

*2. What does Prinz mean when she writes, "The same adults who are profoundly moved by the plight of children they will never know seem to be willing to ignore the children they encounter every day" (paragraph 5)? Why might it be easier to help a child or teenager we will never meet personally?

3. What does the woman in the subway car mean when she says to Prinz, "You can't be too careful these days" (paragraph 8)? Do you agree with her or with Prinz, who believes that "you *can* be too careful"? Give reasons for your answer.

*4. Why does Prinz think that all adults should "say something" if they see children or teenagers behaving in an unacceptable way? Do you think this would make life better for the youngsters as well as for the adults?

Writing Practice

1. Write about a time when your childish actions were misinterpreted by an adult. Could a more understanding adult have made the situation better? Give examples to support your answer.
2. According to Prinz, most Americans agree with the idea that "It takes a whole village to raise a child" (paragraph 3). Write about how your town or neighborhood might help children and teenagers develop into responsible adults. Give at least two examples of how this might be accomplished.
3. Write about a time when you chose not to get involved in a situation you were witnessing. Explain your reasons for not getting involved, and tell how you would act in that situation today.

THE DOG ATE MY DISK, AND OTHER TALES OF WOE

Carolyn Foster Segal

Word Power
woe sadness

Carolyn Foster Segal, assistant professor of English at Cedar Crest College in Pennsylvania, has heard practically every student excuse for handing in late papers. In this humorous essay, she divides student excuses into categories. This article appeared in a journal for college teachers called *The Chronicle of Higher Education.*

Word Power
feline (noun) a member of the cat family; (adjective) catlike

Taped to the door of my office is a cartoon that features a cat explaining to his feline teacher, "The dog ate my homework." It is intended as a gently humorous reminder to my students that I will not accept excuses for late work, and it, like the lengthy warning on my syllabus, has had absolutely no effect. With a show of energy and creativity that would be admirable if applied to the (missing) assignments in question, my students persist, week after week, semester after semester, year after year, in offering excuses about why their work is not ready. Those reasons fall into several broad categories: the family, the best friend, the evils of dorm life, the evils of technology, and the totally bizarre. 1

Word Power
veracity truthfulness

The Family. The death of the grandfather/grandmother is, of course, the grandmother of all excuses. What heartless teacher would dare to question a student's grief or veracity? What heartless student would lie, wishing death on a revered family member, just to avoid a deadline? Creative students may win extra extensions (and days off) with a little careful planning and fuller plot development, as in the sequence of "My grandfather/grandmother is sick"; "Now my grandfather/grandmother is in the hospital"; and finally, "We could all see it coming—my grandfather/grandmother is dead." 2

Word Power
conjure up to bring to mind

Another favorite excuse is "the family emergency," which (always) goes like this: "There was an emergency at home, and I had to help my family." It's a lovely sentiment, one that conjures up images of Louisa May Alcott's little women rushing off with baskets of food and copies of *Pilgrim's Progress,* but I do not understand why anyone would turn to my most irresponsible students in times of trouble. 3

The Best Friend. This heartwarming concern for others extends beyond the family to friends, as in, "My best friend was up all night and I had to (a) stay up with her in the dorm, (b) drive her to the hospital, or (c) drive to her college because (1) her boyfriend broke up with her, (2) she was throwing up blood [no one catches a cold anymore; everyone throws up blood], or (3) her grandfather/grandmother died." 4

Word Power
adjunct an instructor at an institution of higher education who is not a permanent staff member; any temporary employee

At one private university where I worked as an adjunct, I heard an interesting spin that incorporated the motifs of both best friend and dead relative: "My best friend's mother killed herself." One has to admire the cleverness here: A mysterious woman in the prime of her life has allegedly committed suicide, and no professor can prove otherwise! And I admit I was moved, until finally I had to point out to my students that it was amazing how the simple act of my assigning a topic for a paper seemed to drive large numbers of otherwise happy and healthy middle-aged women to their deaths. I was careful to make that point during an off week, during which no deaths were reported. 5

The Evils of Dorm Life. These stories are usually fairly predictable; almost always feature the evil roommate or hallmate, with my student in 6 the role of the innocent victim; and can be summed up as follows: My roommate, who is a horrible person, likes to party, and I, who am a good person, cannot concentrate on my work when he or she is partying. Variations include stories about the two people next door who were running around and crying loudly last night because (a) one of them had boyfriend/girlfriend problems; (b) one of them was throwing up blood; or (c) someone, somewhere, died. A friend of mine in graduate school had a student who claimed that his roommate attacked him with a hammer. That, in fact, was a true story; it came out in court when the bad roommate was tried for killing his grandfather.

The Evils of Technology. The computer age has revolutionized the student story, inspiring almost as many new excuses as it has Internet businesses. Here are just a few electronically enhanced explanations: 7

- The computer wouldn't let me save my work.
- The printer wouldn't print.
- The printer wouldn't print this disk.
- The printer wouldn't give me time to proofread.
- The printer made a black line run through all my words, and I know you can't read this, but do you still want it, or wait, here, take my disk. File name? I don't know what you mean.
- I swear I attached it.
- It's my roommate's computer, and she usually helps me, but she had to go to the hospital because she was throwing up blood.
- I did write to the newsgroup, but all my messages came back to me.
- I just found out that all my other newsgroup messages came up under a diferent name. I just want you to know that its really me who wrote all those messages, you can tel which ones our mine because I didnt use the spelcheck! But it was yours truely :) Anyway, just in case you missed those messages or dont belief its my writting. I'll repeat what I sad: I thought the last movie we watched in clas was borring.

The Totally Bizarre. I call the first story "The Pennsylvania Chain Saw Episode." A commuter student called to explain why she had missed my morning class. She had gotten up early so that she would be wide awake for class. Having a bit of extra time, she walked outside to see her neighbor, who was cutting some wood. She called out to him, and he waved back to her with the saw. Wouldn't you know it, the safety catch wasn't on or was broken, and the blade flew right out of the saw and across his lawn and over her fence and across her yard and severed a tendon in her right hand. So she was calling me from the hospital, where she was waiting for surgery. Luckily, she reassured me, she had remembered to bring her paper and a stamped envelope (in a plastic bag, to avoid bloodstains) along with her in the ambulance, and a nurse was mailing everything to me even as we spoke. 8

That wasn't her first absence. In fact, this student had missed most of the class meetings, and I had already recommended that she withdraw from the course. Now I suggested again that it might be best if she dropped the class. I didn't harp on the absences (what if even some of this story were true?). I did mention that she would need time to recuperate and that making up so much missed work might be difficult. "Oh, no," she said, "I can't drop this course. I had been planning to go on to medical school and become a surgeon, but since I won't be able to operate because 9

Word Power

harp on to repeat over and over again

of my accident, I'll have to major in English, and this course is more important than ever to me." She did come to the next class, wearing—as evidence of her recent trauma—a bedraggled Ace bandage on her left hand.

You may be thinking that nothing could top that excuse, but in fact I 10
have one more story, provided by the same student, who sent me a letter to explain why her final assignment would be late. While recuperating from her surgery, she had begun corresponding on the Internet with a man who lived in Germany. After a one-week, whirlwind Web romance, they had agreed to meet in Rome, to rendezvous (her phrase) at the papal Easter Mass. Regrettably, the time of her flight made it impossible for her to attend class, but she trusted that I—just this once—would accept late work if the pope wrote a note.

Word Power

rendezvous (verb) to meet at a prearranged place and time; (noun) a meeting of this kind

Thinking about the Reading

1. What categories does Segal identify? Can you think of others she does not mention?
*2. Sarcasm involves remarks that mean the opposite of what they say and are usually meant to mock or poke fun at someone or something. In what ways does Segal use sarcasm? Give some examples.
*3. Do you think this essay is funny? Do you find it offensive in any way? Explain.
4. Would you have been interested in reading a serious essay on Segal's topic? Why or why not?

Writing Practice

1. Write about the strangest excuse you have ever been given by someone for not doing something he or she was supposed to do. Tell about the circumstances of this excuse in a humorous manner.
2. Discuss one of the following topics (or a similar topic of your own choice):

   - Ways to turn down a date
   - Types of behavior by a baby, child, or pet
   - Types of students at your school

3. Write a letter to Carolyn Foster Segal explaining why your English term paper will be late. Admit that you have read her essay about various categories of student excuses, but insist that *your* excuse is true.

THE COLORS

Gary Soto

The work of Mexican-American poet and short story writer Gary Soto is popular with children and adults alike. He often writes about his memories of growing up in Fresno, California, in the 1950s and 1960s. In *A Summer Life,* a book of short essays from which "The Colors" is taken, Soto describes the sights, sounds, smells, and textures of his childhood world.

Grandfather's favorite color was the green of dollar bills. On summer evenings he watered his lawn, the jet of water cooling his thumb from eight hours of stapling wooden crates at Sun Maid Raisin. He knew that his house, pink as it was, was worth money. He knew that if he kept the rose bushes throwing out buds of sweet flowers, the value of the house would increase. The fruit trees would grow and thicken with branches to feed his family and neighbor. 1

Grandmother was also fond of green but preferred the silver shine of coins that made her eyebrows jump up and down. She showed me a nickel slug from the county fair stamped: MILK IS GOOD. She could not read or write in Spanish or English and thought the coin was worth more than a brown child realized. I wanted to say that it was nothing. It could sparkle in the sun or make a nice necklace, but it was no rare coin. I drank my purple Kool-Aid, crunched spines of air trapped in the ice cubes, and made my eyebrows jump up and down like hers. 2

Word Power

slug a coin-shaped metal disk that has no monetary value

Yellow was her favorite color. Yellow roses floated in a bowl on the windowsill. The yellow sunshine clock hummed on the wall, and her yellow refrigerator, the first on the block, blended well with the floor, a speckled affair with some yellow but mostly black. From a top shelf of the hallway closet, she took down a shoe box of papers, including a single stock certificate from a sewing machine company. I looked closely at the yellowed paper and noted "one share" and the date "1939." It was now 1961, and even though I was young, nine at the time, I guessed that the stock was worth the memory of hope but little else. 3

Word Power

speckled spotted with dots of color

"When you marry, honey, I will give this to you," she said, shaking the paper at me. "You'll be a rich man." 4

My eyebrows jumped up and down, and I went outside to the backyard to play with my favorite color, mud. At my grandparents' house there were no toys, no pets, no TV in English, so when I stayed there I had to come up with things to do. I tried rolling summer-warmed oranges around the yard in a sort of bowling game in which I tried to knock over sparrows that had come in search of worms. But after twenty minutes of this I was bored. I did chin-ups on the clothesline pole, but that was sweaty work that bored me even more. 5

So I fashioned mud into two forts and a great wall on which I stuck flags of straw-like weeds. When the mud dried hard as a turtle, I pounded the hell out of the forts and wall, imagining that a Chinese war had come. I made bomb sounds and moaned for the dying. My thumb pressed a red ant, and I said, "Too bad." 6

Mud was a good color, and the purple of plums made my mouth water. Peaches did the same, and the arbor of greenish grapes that I spied in the neighbor's yard. Their German Shepherd, ears erect, spied me too, so I 7 couldn't climb the fence and help myself. But looking was almost like eating, and noon was near.

The brown of *frijoles*[1] was our favorite color as steam wavered in our faces. Grandfather, who came home for lunch, left his shoes near the door, smothered his beans with a river of chile and scooped them with big rips of tortilla.[2] I ate with a fork and a tortilla, savoring little mouthfuls of beans with a trickle of chile. The clear color of water washed it all down, and the striped candy cane left over from Christmas sweetened the day. Grandfather, patting his stomach, smiled at me and turned on the radio to the Spanish station. For dessert, there was dark coffee and a powdered donut on a white plate. Grandmother sipped coffee and tore jelly-red sweetness from a footprint-sized Danish.[3] 8

While Grandfather played a game of solitaire, I fooled with the toothpicks in the wooden, pig-shaped holder, the only thing that resembled a toy in the house or yard. I swept the crumbs from the table and pinched the donut crumbs from Grandfather's plate. Grandmother did the dishes, ever mindful of the sweep of the sunshine clock. "Viejo,"[4] she said, "it's time." 9

I walked Grandfather to the front yard, where he stopped and said to me, "A pink house is worth lot of money, m'ijo."[5] We both stood admiring the house, trimmed with flowers and a wrought-iron gate, a plastic flamingo standing one-legged in front of a geranium. This was home, the color of his life. We started up the block, me taking two steps for every one of his, and he said no one's lawn was as green as his. When we looked back, when Grandfather said I should go because it was time to work, Grandmother was at the front window beating the dusty windowsills with a dish towel, waving goodbye until later. 10

Thinking about the Reading

1. Circle all the color words in this essay. What do these words add to the memories of Soto's childhood?

*2. What do these characters' favorite colors suggest about them?

- Grandfather—green
- Grandmother—silver and yellow
- boy—mud brown

3. Why do you think Soto chose to describe the colors of the food at lunch rather than the smells or tastes?
4. In describing his grandfather's house, Soto says, "This was home, the color of his life" (paragraph 10). What do the colors in this essay suggest about the grandfather's life?

1. Beans.
2. A round, thin, flat cake of cornmeal or wheat, usually filled with meat, cheese, or other foods.
3. A large pastry containing a fruit or cheese filling.
4. Old man.
5. Shortened form of *mi hijo,* meaning "my boy" or "my son."

Writing Practice

1. Write a description of a meal, emphasizing the colors as well as the tastes and textures of each dish.
2. Write a description of a place, focusing on the colors. You might want to emphasize either the variety of colors in that place or the sameness of the colors.
3. Describe a memory you have of a grandparent or older person who was important to you when you were a child. Place the person in a setting that shows what the person's life was like, such as his or her home, work, or place of worship.

TAKE-OUT RESTAURANT

Kimsohn Tang

In this essay, student writer Kimsohn Tang examines the life of her Uncle Meng, the owner of a Chinese take-out restaurant. As Kim describes the stresses and risks that go with this demanding job, she asks whether the high income is worth the problems that Uncle Meng endures.

Word Power
profanity curses; vulgar, abusive language

1 My Uncle Meng owns the New Phoenix Take-Out Restaurant at the corner of Main Street and Landfair Avenue in North Philadelphia, a dangerous place. Words of profanity and various kinds of graffiti are written on the wall outside his restaurant. On his windows are black bars just like those on the windows of prisons. Inside his take-out, bulletproof glass separates the customers' area from the workers' area. Every day, Uncle Meng works in his restaurant with his wife and a cook. He must prepare the food, carry it to the cooking area, take orders, run back and forth to get things, cook the food, and satisfy his customers. Although he earns a decent salary, his job not only takes him away from his family but is also stressful, hard, and dangerous.

Word Power
wholesaler a person who sells large amounts of merchandise to stores or individuals, who then resell it

marinating letting meat, fish, or vegetables soak in a sauce to make them more flavorful or tender

2 Uncle Meng works long hours, from 11 a.m. to midnight. He is constantly working. Even before he opens the restaurant, he has to prepare the food by getting the raw food from the wholesaler, marinating and putting bread crumbs on fifty pounds of chicken, coloring rice, making soup, and carrying heavy pots and pans of food to the cooking area. After he opens the take-out, the customers come in, and now Uncle Meng has to take orders; cook the food; put the food in containers, place sodas, drinks and food in bags; and hand the customers the bags through the little hole in the bulletproof glass. Throughout the day and into the night, Uncle Meng continues to work. Even at midnight, after the take-out is closed, his work is not finished because he has to clean up the place.

3 Because of his long working hours, Uncle Meng has little time to spend with his family, especially his two children, a sixteen-year-old daughter and a thirteen-year-old son. Most of his time is spent in his restaurant. The only time he is free is on Sunday, when the restaurant is closed; this is the only time he and his family actually spend together. On regular school days, if he has time, Uncle Meng brings his children to and from school; otherwise, his sister or one of his other relatives takes them. When his children get home, they stay in their apartment above the take-out and only come down once in a while. Because Uncle Meng is so busy, he does not even have time to help his children with their homework.

Word Power
pertaining to relating to or having to do with

4 Having little time to spend with his family is not the worst thing about his job; the stress from customers is even worse. Customers will yell out, "Man, where's my food? Why is it taking so long? I can't wait all day, you know!" Uncle Meng must have a lot of patience with the customers and not yell back at them. If the customers complain about getting different food from what they have ordered, Uncle Meng has to calm them down and make another dish for them. In addition, the customers are always asking for various things, such as more forks, spoons, or napkins, which is hard for Uncle Meng to handle. When a customer has a question pertaining to a dish on the menu, Uncle Meng also has to explain what ingredients are in the dish. He has to satisfy the customers and give them what they want, or else they will give him more trouble.

5 Uncle Meng's working conditions are the worst aspect of his job. Because the cooking area is always hot, Uncle Meng is never comfortable. The working area is also a dangerous place to be in; if he is not cautious while frying, he can get burns from the splattering oil. Lifting heavy pans while stir-frying, which requires a great amount of strength, causes Uncle Meng a lot of pain in his arms and wrists. In addition, because he has to stand on his feet all day and run all over the take-out to get food, he often gets pains in his legs. By the time the take-out is closed, Uncle Meng is always exhausted.

6 Uncle Meng works long hard hours at difficult, physical labor. Although the take-out brings in a lot of money, it is a stressful and risky environment. Money is worthless compared to family and health. Even though money can buy many things, it cannot buy strong family relationships or good health. Working in a take-out, therefore, is not a desirable job.

Thinking about the Reading

1. How do job stresses harm Uncle Meng's health? Give examples.
2. In what ways is Uncle Meng's job dangerous? Describe how both the working conditions at the restaurant and the neighborhood in which it is located are dangerous.
3. How does Uncle Meng's job affect his family life? Give examples.

*4. Why do you think Kim chose to write about her Uncle Meng? What does she think of her uncle's way of life?

Writing Practice

1. Imagine that you are Meng's teenage son or daughter. Write a letter to your father telling him how you feel about the sacrifices he is making by working at the restaurant.
2. Have you ever worked at a job that was stressful or dangerous? Give examples of the stresses and dangers and the effect they had on you. If you have never held a job that fits this description, write about a stressful or dangerous situation that you have experienced—or about a friend's or relative's job.
3. Kim states, "Money is worthless compared to family and health" (paragraph 6). Explain why you agree or disagree with this statement. Give examples from your own experience and observation of the world to support your position.

Word Power

linguist a scholar who studies the history and forms of languages and other aspects of human communication

novice a beginner

paradox a statement that seems contradictory or opposed to common sense but may still be true

GENDER GAP IN CYBERSPACE

Deborah Tannen

Deborah Tannen is a linguist and social scientist who has written several popular books that analyze the various ways in which men and women talk to each other. In this essay, she examines the different ways in which women and men use computers.

I was a computer pioneer, but I'm still something of a novice. That paradox is telling. 1

I was the second person on my block to get a computer. The first was my colleague Ralph. It was 1980. Ralph got a Radio Shack TRS-80; I got a used Apple II+. He helped me get started and went on to become a maven,[1] reading computer magazines, hungering for the new technology he read about, and buying and mastering it as quickly as he could afford. I hung on to old equipment far too long because I dislike giving up what I'm used to, fear making the wrong decision about what to buy, and resent the time it takes to install and learn a new system. 2

My first Apple came with videogames; I gave them away. Playing games on the computer didn't interest me. If I had free time I'd spend it talking on the telephone to friends. 3

Ralph got hooked. His wife was often annoyed by the hours he spent at his computer and the money he spent upgrading it. My marriage had no such strains—until I discovered e-mail. Then I got hooked. E-mail draws me the same way the phone does: it's a souped-up[2] conversation. 4

E-mail deepened my friendship with Ralph. Though his office was next to mine, we rarely had extended conversations because he is shy. Face to face he mumbled so, I could barely tell he was speaking. But when we both got on e-mail, I started receiving long, self-revealing messages; we poured our hearts out to each other. A friend discovered that e-mail opened up that kind of communication with her father. He would never talk much on the phone (as her mother would), but they have become close since they both got online. 5

Word Power

obliqueness indirectness; lack of straightforwardness

Why, I wondered, would some men find it easier to open up on e-mail? It's a combination of the technology (which they enjoy) and the obliqueness of the written word, just as many men will reveal feelings in dribs and drabs while riding in the car or doing something, which they'd never talk about sitting face to face. It's too intense, too bearing-down on them, and once you start you have to keep going. With a computer in between, it's safer. 6

Word Power

balk to resist abruptly and strongly

It was on e-mail, in fact, that I described to Ralph how boys in groups often struggle to get the upper hand whereas girls tend to maintain an appearance of cooperation. And he pointed out that this explained why boys are more likely to be captivated by computers than girls are. Boys are typically motivated by a social structure that says if you don't dominate you will be dominated. Computers, by their nature, balk; you type a perfectly appropriate command and it refuses to do what it should. Many boys and men are incited by this defiance: "I'm going to whip this into line and teach it who's boss! I'll get it to do what I say!" (and if they work hard 7

1. An expert; someone who is very knowledgeable about a particular subject.
2. A slang expression meaning "speeded up" or "made more powerful."

enough, they always can). Girls and women are more likely to respond, "This thing won't cooperate. Get it away from me!"

Although no one wants to think of herself as "typical"—how much nicer to be *sui generis*[3]—my relationship to my computer is—gulp—fairly typical for a woman. Most women (with plenty of exceptions) aren't excited by tinkering with the technology, grappling with the challenge of eliminating bugs or getting the biggest and best computer. These dynamics appeal to many men's interest in making sure they're on the top side of the inevitable who's-up-who's-down struggle that life is for them. E-mail appeals to my view of life as a contest for connections to others. When I see that I have fifteen messages, I feel loved. 8

I once posted a technical question on a computer network for linguists and was flooded with long dispositions, some pages long. I was staggered by the generosity and the expertise, but wondered where these guys found the time—and why all the answers I got were from men. 9

Like coed classrooms and meetings, discussions on e-mail networks tend to be dominated by male voices, unless they're specifically women-only, like single-sex schools. Online, women don't have to worry about getting the floor (you just send a message when you feel like it), but, according to linguists Susan Herring and Laurel Sutton, who have studied this, they have the usual problems of having their messages ignored or attacked. The anonymity of public networks frees a small number of men to send long, vituperative, sarcastic messages that many other men either can tolerate or actually enjoy, but that turn most women off. 10

Word Power

vituperative verbally abusive; viciously critical

The anonymity of networks leads to another sad part of the e-mail story: there are men who deluge women with questions about their appearance and invitations to sex. On college campuses, as soon as women students log on, they are bombarded by references to sex, like going to work and finding pornographic posters adorning the walls. 11

Most women want one thing from a computer—to work. This is significant counterevidence to the claim that men want to focus on information while women are interested in rapport. That claim I found was often true in casual conversation, in which there is no particular information to be conveyed. But with computers, it is often women who are more focused on information, because they don't respond to the challenge of getting the equipment to submit. 12

Once I had learned the basics, my interest in computers waned. I use it to write books (though I never mastered having it do bibliographies or tables of contents) and write checks (but not balance my check book). Much as I'd like to use it to do more, I begrudge the time it would take to learn. 13

Ralph's computer expertise costs him a lot of time. Chivalry requires that he rescue novices in need, and he is called upon by damsel novices far more often than knaves. More men would rather study the instruction booklet than ask directions, as it were, from another person. "When I do help men," Ralph wrote (on e-mail, of course), "they want to be more involved. I once installed a hard drive for a guy, and he wanted to be there with me, wielding the screwdriver and giving his own advice where he could." Women, he finds, usually are not interested in what he's doing; they just want him to get the computer to the point where they can do what they want. 14

3. A Latin phrase meaning "of its own kind" or "unique."

Which pretty much explains how I managed to be a pioneer without 15
becoming an expert.

Thinking about the Reading

1. How is Tannen's attitude toward her computer different from that of her fellow worker, Ralph?
*2. In what ways do you think Tannen's and Ralph's contrasting relationships with their computers are typical of most women and men?
3. According to Tannen, why does shy Ralph pour out his heart (paragraph 5) when he writes e-mail? Read Jon Katz's essay "How Boys Become Men" (p. 439). How does Katz's essay help explain why Ralph is able to communicate via e-mail but not face to face?
*4. Review Tannen's discussion of how women and men act when the messages they post online are attacked. What basic differences in attitudes and behavior do these reactions reveal? Do you think women are more vulnerable online than men? Explain.

Writing Practice

1. Evaluate yourself as a computer user. Are you more like the typical male or female user? If you differ from the stereotype Tannen considers typical of your gender, explain what may account for this difference.
2. Do your observations suggest that young or adolescent girls and boys differ in their attitudes toward computers? Explain the reasons for any differences you observe.
3. Choose an area in which you believe men's and women's attitudes, behavior, or goals differ. You can write about dating, marriage, careers, or any other area in which you see major differences. Explore these differences in either a serious or a humorous way.

ONE LIAR'S BEGINNINGS

Brady Udall

Almost all of us have told a lie at one time or another. Fear, self-protection, convenience, and personal gain can all be seen as justification for a lie. But how many of us remember our first lie? Here, Brady Udall, an award-winning writer of essays and fiction, recalls how a lifetime of lying began.

Before all else, let me make my confession: I am a liar. For me, admitting to being a liar is just about the most difficult confession I could make; as a rule, liars don't like to admit to anything. But I'm trying to figure out how I came to be this way—what influences, what decisions at what forked roads have led me to be the devious soul I am today. And as any clergyman worth a nickel can tell you, before you can discover the truth about yourself, first you must confess. 1

> **Word Power**
> **devious** lying; sneaky; cunning

I can't say I remember the first lie I ever told. It's been so long, and there have been so many lies in between. But I can only believe that my first steps, first day of school, first kiss—all those many firsts we love to get so nostalgic about—none of them was in any way as momentous as that first lie I ever told. 2

It's a dusty summer day. I am three years old, and in the Udall household there is going to be hell to pay; some fool has gone and eaten all the cinnamon red-hots my mother was going to use to decorate cupcakes for a funeral luncheon. 3

Down in the basement, I am bumping the back of my head against the cushion of the couch. This peculiar habit, *head-bouncing* we called it in our house, was something I liked to do whenever I was nervous or bored. I was most satisfied with the world when I could sit on that couch and bounce my head against the back cushion—you know, really get up a good rhythm, maybe a little Woody Woodpecker on the TV—and not have anyone bother me about it. Along with worrying that their son might be retarded on some level, my parents also became concerned about the living room couch—all this manic head-bouncing of mine was wearing a considerable divot in the middle cushion (my preferred section) right down to the foam. So my father, after trying all he could think of to get me to desist, finally threw up his hands and went to the town dump and came back with a prehistoric shaggy brown couch that smelled like coconut suntan oil. He put it down in the basement, out of sight of friends and neighbors, and I was allowed to head-bounce away to my heart's content. 4

> **Word Power**
> **manic** excessively enthusiastic
>
> **desist** to stop an action

So there I am down on the couch, really going at it, while my mother stomps around up above. She is looking for the red-hots thief, and she is furious. My mother is beautiful, ever-smiling and refined, but when she is angry she could strike fear into the heart of a werewolf. 5

As for me, I am thoroughly terrified, though not too terrified to enjoy the last of the red-hots. I put them in my mouth and keep them there until they turn into a warm, red syrup that I roll around on my tongue. 6

My mother is yelling out all the kids' names: *Travis! Symonie! Brady! Cord!* But none of us is dumb enough to answer. Finally, she stomps down the steps and sees me there on my couch, bobbing back and forth like the peg on a metronome, trying not to look her way, hoping that if I can keep my eyes off her long enough she just might disappear. 7

"Brady, did you eat those red-hots?" she asks, her mouth set hard. I begin to bounce harder. 8

"Hmmm?" I say. 9

"Did you eat them?" 10

I imagine for a second what my punishment will be—maybe spending the rest of the afternoon cooped up in my room, maybe being forced to watch while the rest of the family hogs down the leftover cupcakes after dinner—or maybe she will have mercy on me and opt for a simple swat on the butt with a spatula. 11

"Did you eat them?" 12

I don't really think about it, don't even know where it comes from—I look my mother straight in the eye, say it loud and clear as you please: "No." 13

She doesn't press me, just takes my answer for what it is. Why would she suspect anything from me, a baby who's never lied before, innocent as can be, a sweet little angel who doesn't know any better than to spend all his free time banging his head against the back cushion of a couch from the dump. 14

"All right," she says, smiling just a little now. She can't help herself—I am that innocent and cute. "Why don't you come upstairs and have a cupcake?" 15

Right then I stop bouncing altogether. It feels as if there is light blooming in my head, filling me up, giving me a sensation I've never had before, a feeling of potency and possibility and dominion. With a word as simple as "no" I can make things different altogether; no, it wasn't me who ate those red-hots; no, it's not me who deserves a swat on the butt or no cartoons for the rest of the afternoon. What I deserve is a cupcake. 16

It's a wonderful epiphany: with a lie I can change reality; with a lie I can change the world. 17

Word Power

potency power

dominion rule; authority

epiphany a sudden flash of insight

Thinking about the Reading

1. What caused three-year-old Brady Udall to lie to his mother?
2. What does Udall mean when he writes that his first lie gave him "a feeling of potency and possibility and dominion" (paragraph 16)?
3. How does Udall support his statement that his mother "is beautiful, ever-smiling and refined, but when she is angry she could strike fear into the heart of a werewolf" (paragraph 5)?

*4. What does Udall mean when he writes, "with a lie I can change reality; with a lie I can change the world" (paragraph 17)?

Writing Practice

1. In general, what do you think causes people to tell lies—whether "little white lies" or more serious ones? Write about several kinds of situations and feelings that might tempt a person to lie.
2. What positive and negative effects have lies (yours or other people's) had on your life? Discuss one or two examples in detail.
3. Can you think of any situations in which it is right to lie? Describe such a situation, and explain why you think it justifies a lie.

THE TRANSACTION

William Zinsser

William Zinsser has written many articles and books on improving writing and study skills. He has also had a long career as a professional newspaper and magazine writer, drama and film critic, and author of nonfiction books on subjects ranging from jazz to baseball. This excerpt is from his book *On Writing Well: An Informal Guide to Writing Nonfiction.*

A school in Connecticut once held "a day devoted to the arts," and I was asked if I would come and talk about writing as a vocation. When I arrived I found that a second speaker had been invited—Dr. Brock (as I'll call him), a surgeon who had recently begun to write and had sold some stories to magazines. He was going to talk about writing as an avocation. That made us a panel, and we sat down to face a crowd of students, teachers and parents, all eager to learn the secrets of our glamorous work. 1

Dr. Brock was dressed in a bright red jacket, looking vaguely bohemian, as authors are supposed to look, and the first question went to him. What was it like to be a writer? 2

He said it was tremendous fun. Coming home from an arduous day at the hospital, he would go straight to his yellow pad and write his tensions away. The words just flowed. It was easy. I then said that writing wasn't easy and it wasn't fun. It was hard and lonely, and the words seldom just flowed. 3

Next Dr. Brock was asked if it was important to rewrite. Absolutely not, he said. "Let it all hang out," he told us, and whatever form the sentences take will reflect the writer at his most natural. I then said that rewriting is the essence of writing. I pointed out that professional writers rewrite their sentences over and over and then rewrite what they have rewritten. 4

"What do you do on days when it isn't going well?" Dr. Brock was asked. He said he just stopped writing and put the work aside for a day when it would go better. I then said that the professional writer must establish a daily schedule and stick to it. I said that writing is a craft, not an art, and that the man who runs away from his craft because he lacks inspiration is fooling himself. He is also going broke. 5

"What if you're feeling depressed or unhappy?" a student asked. "Won't that affect your writing?" 6

Probably it will, Dr. Brock replied. Go fishing. Take a walk. Probably it won't, I said. If your job is to write every day, you learn to do it like any other job. 7

A student asked if we found it useful to circulate in the literary world. Dr. Brock said he was greatly enjoying his new life as a man of letters, and he told several stories of being taken to lunch by his publisher and his agent at Manhattan restaurants where writers and editors gather. I said that professional writers are solitary drudges who seldom see other writers. 8

"Do you put symbolism in your writing?" a student asked me. 9

"Not if I can help it," I replied. I have an unbroken record of missing the deeper meaning in any story, play or movie, and as for dance and mime, I have never had any idea of what is being conveyed. 10

"I *love* symbols!" Dr. Brock exclaimed, and he described with gusto the joys of weaving them through his work. 11

Word Power

transaction an exchange or transfer of goods, services, or money; an exchange of thoughts and feelings

Word Power

vocation an occupation; regular employment

avocation a hobby or interest pursued for enjoyment rather than for monetary gain

arduous difficult and tiring; strenuous

Word Power

symbolism the use of a symbol (something that stands for something else) in a work of art or literature

gusto enthusiasm; lively enjoyment

So the morning went, and it was a revelation to all of us. At the end Dr. Brock told me he was enormously interested in my answers—it had never occurred to him that writing could be hard. I told him I was just as interested in *his* answers—it had never occurred to me that writing could be easy. Maybe I should take up surgery on the side. 12

As for the students, anyone might think we left them bewildered. But in fact we probably gave them a broader glimpse of the writing process than if only one of us had talked. For there isn't any "right" way to do such personal work. There are all kinds of writers and all kinds of methods, and any method that helps you to say what you want to say is the right method for you. Some people write by day, others by night. Some people need silence, others turn on the radio. Some write by hand, some by word processor, some by talking into a tape recorder. Some people write their first draft in one long burst and then revise; others can't write the second paragraph until they have fiddled endlessly with the first. 13

But all of them are vulnerable and all of them are tense. They are driven by a compulsion to put some part of themselves on paper, and yet they don't just write what comes naturally. They sit down to commit an act of literature, and the self who emerges on paper is far stiffer than the person who sat down to write. The problem is to find the real man or woman behind all the tension. 14

Ultimately the product that any writer has to sell is not the subject being written about, but who he or she is. I often find myself reading with interest about a topic I never thought would interest me—some scientific quest, perhaps. What holds me is the enthusiasm of the writer for his field. How was he drawn into it? What emotional baggage did he bring along? How did it change his life? It's not necessary to want to spend a year alone at Walden Pond[1] to become deeply involved with a writer who did. 15

This is the personal transaction that's at the heart of good nonfiction writing. Out of it come two of the most important qualities that this book will go in search of: humanity and warmth. Good writing has an aliveness that keeps the reader reading from one paragraph to the next, and it's not a question of gimmicks to "personalize" the author. It's a question of using the English language in a way that will achieve the greatest strength and the least clutter. 16

Can such principles be taught? Maybe not. But most of them can be learned. 17

Thinking about the Reading

1. Why do you think Zinsser chose to use an interview format to compare and contrast his own writing methods and experiences with those of Dr. Brock?
2. What is Zinsser's purpose in comparing his views on the writing process with those of Dr. Brock? In what ways does he suggest that his work and methods are superior to those of the doctor? Contrast this attitude with his statement in paragraph 13 that "any method that helps you to say what you want to say is the right method for you."

1. The place where Henry David Thoreau (1817–1862), an American writer, naturalist, and political activist, lived for two years in a cabin he built himself. He wrote about the experience in his most famous book, *Walden*.

3. Zinsser claims that "rewriting is the essence of writing" (paragraph 4). Use your own experience to support or challenge this statement.
4. Zinsser states, "Ultimately the product that any writer has to sell is not the subject being written about, but who he or she is" (paragraph 15). The writer's ability to draw the reader into his subject is the "personal transaction" or exchange between two people that, according to Zinsser, makes writing come alive. Discuss any of the essays in Chapter 28 that you have read. Which of the essay topics did not really interest you until you were drawn in by the writer's personal view of the topic?

Writing Practice

1. Imagine that you have been asked some of the same questions as Zinsser and Dr. Brock—but about your own experience as a college student. Write your responses. Be sure to include answers to the following questions: What is it like to be a student? What do you do when classes or schoolwork is not going well? Does being depressed or unhappy affect your performance in the classroom? How?
2. In paragraph 13, Zinsser writes, "There are all kinds of writers and all kinds of methods." Describe the kind of writer you are. Do you find writing easy, as Dr. Brock does, or difficult, as Zinsser does? What methods do you use to come up with ideas or to get through a particularly difficult assignment? Do you use any of the methods that Zinsser describes in paragraph 13?
3. Zinsser claims that the most successful pieces of writing are produced when the writer really cares about his or her subject. Write about a topic that interests you—for example, a book, a sport, a famous person, a political opinion, or a religious belief. Why does this topic interest you? How has it affected your life?

APPENDIX **A**

Building Word Power

Building a vocabulary is an important part of your education. Knowing what words mean and how to use them can help you become a better reader and a better writer. As you have worked your way through *Foundations First,* you have encountered one or more Word Power boxes in each chapter; at this point, you may know the meanings of many of these words, and you have probably used some of them in writing or speaking. By continuing to use these and other new words, you can further expand your vocabulary.

One of the best ways to improve your vocabulary is to get into the habit of using a dictionary to help you understand what new words mean and how to use them in your writing. A **dictionary** is an alphabetical list of the words in a language. However, a good dictionary is more than just a collection of words. In addition to showing how to spell and pronounce a word and what its most common meanings are, a dictionary can give you a great deal of other information.

A typical dictionary entry begins with the **entry word**, the word being defined. This word is set in boldface type and divided into syllables by centered dots.

sneak•er

Following the entry word are a pronunciation guide and an abbreviation that identifies the word's **part of speech**—whether it is a noun (*n.*), a verb (*v.*), an adjective (*adj.*), or another kind of word. Next, the entry lists the word's meaning or meanings. (If a word has several meanings, the most common meaning usually comes first.)

sneak•er (snē′ker) *n.* A sports shoe usually made of canvas and having soft rubber soles. Also called *tennis shoe.*

Often, a dictionary entry gives additional information. For example, it may note the word's origin in another language, show alternate spellings of the word, or supply plural forms of nouns or various tenses of verbs (if they are irregular). Some words are followed by **usage labels**, which tell readers that these words are used in particular academic disciplines, occupations, or areas of daily life. For example, in one dictionary the definition of *miniature golf* has the usage label *Games.* Usage labels can also tell you if a word is no longer in use (*archaic*) or if it is *obscene, informal,* or *slang.* (Such words are not appropriate for your college or on-the-job writing.)

Some dictionaries also include extensive notes in some entries. For example, a dictionary entry may list, explain, and illustrate a word's **synonyms**—other words that have similar meanings.

teach (tēch) *v.* **taught** (tôt), **teach•ing**, **teach•es**.—*tr.* **1.** To impart knowledge or skill to: *teaches children.* **2.** To provide knowledge of; instruct in: *teaches French.* **3.** To condition to a certain action or frame of mind: *teaching youngsters to be self-reliant.* **4.** To cause to learn by example or experience: *an accident that taught me a valuable lesson.* **5.** To advocate or preach: *teaches racial and religious tolerance.* **6.** To carry on instruction on a regular basis in: *taught high school for many years.*—*intr.* To give instruction, especially as an occupation. [Middle English *techen,* from Old English *tǣcan.* See **deik-** in Appendix.]

SYNONYMS: *teach, instruct, educate, train, school, discipline, drill.* These verbs mean to impart knowledge or skill. *Teach* is the most widely applicable: *teaching a child the alphabet; teaches political science. "We shouldn't teach great books; we should teach a love of reading"* (B. F. Skinner). *Instruct* usually suggests methodical teaching: *A graduate student instructed the freshmen in the rudiments of music theory. Educate* often implies formal instruction but especially stresses the development of innate capacities that leads to wide cultivation: *"All educated Americans, first or last, go to Europe"* (Ralph Waldo Emerson). *Train* suggests concentration on particular skills intended to fit a person for a desired role: *The young woman attends vocational school, where she is being trained as a computer technician. School* often implies an arduous learning process: *The violinist had been schooled to practice slowly to assure accurate intonation. Discipline* usually refers to the teaching of control, especially self-control: *The writer has disciplined himself to work between breakfast and lunch every day. Drill* implies rigorous instruction or training, often by repetition of a routine: *The French instructor drilled the students in irregular verbs.*

An entry may also provide **regional notes** to explain how a word is used in different areas of the United States.

♦**fry•ing pan** (frī′ĭng) *n.* A shallow, long-handled pan used for frying food. Also called ♦*fry pan,* ♦*skillet,* ♦*spider.*

♦***REGIONAL NOTE:*** The terms *frying pan* and *skillet* are now virtually interchangeable, but there was a time when they were so regional as to be distinct dialect markers. *Frying pan* and the shortened version *fry pan* were once New England terms; *frying pan* is now in general use. *Skillet* seems to have been confined to the Midland section of the country, including the Upper South. Its use is still concentrated there, but it is no longer used in that area alone, probably because of the national marketing of skillet dinner mixes. The term *spider,* orginally denoting a type of frying pan that had long legs to hold it up over the coals, spread from New England westward to the Upper Northern states and down the coast to the South Atlantic states. It is still well known in both these regions, although it is now considered old-fashioned.

A dictionary entry can also explain **word history**.

tax•i (tăk′sē) *n., pl.* **tax•is** or **tax•ies**. A taxicab.—**taxi** *v.* **tax•ied** (tăk′sēd), **tax•i•ing** or **tax•y•ing**, **tax•ies** or **tax•is** (tăk′sēz).—*intr.* **1.** To be transported by taxi. **2.** To move slowly on the ground or on the surface of the water before takeoff or after landing: *an airplane taxiing down the runway.*—*tr.* **1.** To transport (someone or something) by or as if by taxi: *taxied the children to dance class; taxi documents to a law office.* **2.** To cause (an aircraft) to taxi. [Short for TAXIMETER, or TAXICAB.]

WORD HISTORY: "Taxi" is much easier to yell into the traffic than *taximeter cabriolet,* the form from which *taxi* has ultimately been shortened. *Taximeter* comes from the French word *taximètre,* ultimately derived from Medieval Latin *taxāre,* "to tax," and the French combining form *–metre. Taximètre* orginally meant, as did its English companion, "a device for measuring distance traveled," but this device was soon adapted to measure waiting time and compute and indicate the fare as well. *Taximeter,* first recorded in English in 1898 (an earlier form *taxameter,* borrowed through French from German, was recorded in 1894), joined forces with *cab,* a shortening (1827) of *cabriolet,* "a two-wheeled, one-horse carriage." This word, first found in English in 1766, came from French *cabriolet,* of the same meaning, which in turn was derived from *cabriole,* "caper," because the vehicle moves along with a springing motion. *Cab,* the shortened form, was applied to other vehicles as well, including eventually public conveyances. Fitted with a taximeter, such a vehicle, first horse-drawn and then motorized, was known as a *taxameter cab* (1899), a *taximeter cab* (1907), and a *taxicab* (1907), among other names, including *taxi* (1907), a shortening of either *taximeter* or *taxicab*. Interestingly enough, the fullest form possible, *taximeter cabriolet*, is not recorded until 1959.

Finally, some dictionaries provide detailed **usage notes** that discuss changing or disputed uses of words or grammatical constructions.

sneak (snēk) *v.* **sneaked** also **snuck** (snŭk), **sneak•ing, sneaks.**—*intr.* **1.** To go or move in a quiet, stealthy way. **2.** To behave in a cowardly or servile manner.—*tr.* To move, give, take, or put in a quiet, stealthy manner: *sneak candy into one's mouth; sneaked a look at the grade sheet.*—**sneak** *n.* **1.** A person regarded as stealthy, cowardly, or underhanded. **2.** An instance of sneaking; a quiet, stealthy movement. **3.** *Informal.* A sneaker.—**sneak** *adj.* **1.** Carried out in a clandestine manner: *sneak preparations for war.* **2.** Perpetrated without warning: *a sneak attack by terrorists.* [Probably akin to Middle English *sniken*, to creep, from Old English *snīcan*.]

USAGE NOTE: *Snuck* is an Americanism first introduced in the 19th century as a nonstandard regional variant of *sneaked.* But widespread use of *snuck* has become more common with every generation. It is now used by educated speakers in all regions, and there is some evidence to suggest that it is more frequent among younger speakers than *sneaked* is. Formal written English is naturally and properly more conservative than other varieties, of course, and here *snuck* still meets with much resistance. Many writers and editors have a lingering unease about the form, particularly if they recall its nonstandard origins. In fact, our consolidated citations, exhibiting almost 10,000 instances of *sneaked* and *snuck*, indicate that *sneaked* is preferred by a factor of 7 to 2. And 67 percent of the Usage Panel disapproves of *snuck*. Nevertheless, in recent years *snuck* has been quietly establishing itself in formal writing. An electronic search of a wide range of reputable publications turns up hundreds of citations for *snuck*, not just in sports writing but in news columns and commentary: *"He ran up huge hotel bills and then snuck out without paying"* (George Stade). *"In the dressing room beforehand, while the NBC technician was making me up, Jesse Jackson snuck up behind me and began playfully powdering my face"* (Bruce Babbitt). *"Raisa Gorbachev snuck away yesterday afternoon for a 65-minute helter-skelter tour of San Francisco"* (San Francisco Chronicle). *"The Reagan administration snuck in some illegal military assistance before that"* (New Republic). Our citation files also contain a number of occurrences of *snuck* in serious fiction: *"He had snuck away from camp with a cabinmate"* (Anne Tyler). *"I ducked down behind the paperbacks and snuck out"* (Garrison Keillor).

The pages that follow list (in alphabetical order) and define all the words that appear in Word Power boxes in *Foundations First*. You can use this list as a mini-dictionary to help you incorporate these words into your written and spoken vocabulary.

Following the list are several pages on which you can create a personal vocabulary list, your own list of new words (and their definitions) that you encounter in your reading. Space has been provided for you to write an original sentence for each word so you can remember how it is used.

Finally, exercises at the end of this appendix will give you additional practice in using the Word Power feature in *Foundations First.*

1 Word Power

This alphabetical list includes all the words, along with their definitions, that appear in the Word Power boxes throughout *Foundations First.*

accumulate to gather or pile up little by little

adjunct an instructor at an institution of higher education who is not a permanent staff member; any temporary employee

adrenaline a hormone in the body that produces a "rush" of energy and excitement in the face of danger

alienated emotionally withdrawn or unresponsive

altercation a quarrel

anemic weak; lacking vitality

animated lively; full of energy and spirit

annotating making explanatory notes

anonymity the state of being unknown; not named or identified

antagonist an opponent; a person with whom one is in conflict

anticipate to look forward to

apathetic feeling or showing a lack of interest

apathy lack of interest

arduous difficult and tiring; strenuous

audible able to be heard

aversion an avoidance of something as a result of extreme dislike

avocation a hobby or interest pursued for enjoyment rather than for monetary gain

balk to resist abruptly and strongly

ballot a written or printed paper on which voters indicate their choices in an election

berating scolding

bourgeois middle-class and proper in attitudes

brawl a noisy quarrel or fight

carcinogen something that causes cancer

Caucasian (noun) person of European, North African, or southwest Asian ancestry; (adjective) relating or belonging to Caucasians

civil polite; courteous

classic something typical or traditional; something that has lasting importance or worth

commission to place an order for something

commotion a noisy disturbance

concoction a mixture of several ingredients

confront to face a challenger or a challenge

conjure up to bring to mind

contemporary current; modern

contradiction a statement, situation, or personality in which two opposites are true

controversial marked by controversy

controversy a dispute between sides holding different views

dependent relying on another for support

derrière a French word for backside, rear end, buttocks

desiccated dried-up

desist to stop an action

devious lying; sneaky; cunning

dilemma a situation in which one must choose between two courses of action

dilute to water down; make weaker or thinner

dominion rule; authority

ebullient lively and enthusiastic

eccentric having odd or whimsical ways; behaving in ways that are not usual or customary

embossed decorated with raised, printed letters or designs

empathy sensitivity to the thoughts and emotions of other people

envision to imagine

epiphany a sudden flash of insight

estranged separated from someone else by feelings of hostility or indifference

ethics a code of right and wrong behavior

feline (noun) a member of the cat family; (adjective) catlike

gender a person's sex

generation a group of individuals born and living at about the same time

genome a complete set of chromosomes and its associated genes; DNA

gusto enthusiasm; lively enjoyment

harp on to repeat over and over again

heritage something passed down from previous generations

hypertensive having high blood pressure

immortalized made famous forever

imperative a command that must be obeyed

improvise to make do with the tools or resources at hand

independent free from the influence or control of others

institution a well-known person, place, or thing; something that has become associated with a particular place

lethal capable of killing

liability a financial and legal responsibility; a debt that must be paid

linguist a scholar who studies the history and forms of languages and other aspects of human communication

maiming depriving someone of an arm or leg

manic excessively enthusiastic

marinating letting meat, fish, or vegetables soak in a sauce to make them more flavorful or tender

maroon to put ashore on a deserted island

masquerade (verb) to wear a mask or disguise; (noun) a costume party at which guests wear masks

mature full-grown

mellow to gain the wisdom and tolerance that are characteristic of maturity

memento a reminder of the past; a keepsake (the plural form is *mementos*)

memorabilia objects valued because of their link to historical events or culture

mestizo a person of mixed European and American Indian ancestry

metamorphosis a change or transformation

microbes germs

migrate to move from one area or region to another

minute tiny

missive a letter or message

mobility the movement of people from one social group, class, or level to another

monument a structure built as a memorial

multicultural of or relating to many cultures

mundane ordinary; commonplace

naturalization the process of gaining citizenship

newsworthy interesting enough to be worth reporting in the news

novice a beginner

obligation a course of action demanded of a person by law or conscience

obligatory required; necessary

obliqueness indirectness; lack of straightforwardness

obsessively in an excessive and unreasonable way

offensive hurtful; disagreeable; unpleasant

orient to adjust

orientation adjustment to a new environment; a meeting in which participants are introduced to a new situation, such as a new school, job, or other activity

ostracize to exclude from a group

paradox a statement that seems contradictory or opposed to common sense but may still be true

parity equality in power or value

persist to continue to do something in spite of setbacks

pertaining to relating to or having to do with

physique the structure or form of a person's body

plight an unfortunate or difficult situation

potency power

priorities things that deserve extra attention

priority important or urgent goal

profanity curses; vulgar, abusive language

prohibit to forbid

rambunctious unruly; full of uncontrolled energy

recoil to shrink away from something in fear or disapproval

relic a valued object from the past

renaissance rebirth or revival

rendezvous (verb) to meet at a prearranged place and time; (noun) a meeting of this kind

rigor hardship or difficulty

role model a person who serves as a model of behavior for someone else to imitate

scenario plot outline; a sequence of events, often imaginary

self-esteem pride in oneself; self-respect

sensibilities feelings; attitudes

sensuous appealing to the senses

sibling a brother or sister

skepticism a doubtful or questioning attitude

slug a coin-shaped metal disk that has no monetary value

sociopath a person who exhibits antisocial behavior of a criminal nature; a mentally ill or unstable person who feels no social or moral obligations to others

speckled spotted with dots of color

spectacle a public show or exhibition; an unusual sight

sporadic infrequent; happening from time to time

stark bare; harsh; grim

sterilization the process of making something free of germs

stigmatized described or identified as having a shameful or unacceptable trait or background

subsidize to give financial support to a project

surveillance close observation of a person or a group of people—especially a person or group under suspicion

suturing surgical stitching in which fiber is used to close up wounds or to connect two parts of the body

syllabus an outline or summary of a course's main points (the plural form is *syllabi*)

symbol something that represents something else

symbolism the use of a symbol (something that stands for something else) in a work of art or literature

tradition behavior or custom handed down from generation to generation

traditional relating to tradition

transaction an exchange or transfer of goods, services, or money; an exchange of thoughts and feelings

trauma an injury or wound, either physical or emotional

treks difficult journeys

trepidation fear; dread

umbrage offense; resentment **to take umbrage** to take offense

unique one of a kind

unyielding not giving in; not giving way to persuasion

vanity excessive pride in one's appearance or achievements

vanity plate a license plate that can be customized for an extra charge

venue the scene or location at which something takes place

veracity truthfulness

vituperative verbally abusive; viciously critical

vixen slang for a tempting, sexy woman; can also mean a bad-tempered woman. The original meaning is "female fox."

vocation an occupation; regular employment

weathering passing through safely; surviving

wholesaler a person who sells large amounts of merchandise to stores or individuals, who then resell it

woe sadness

2 Your Personal Vocabulary List

On the pages that follow, keep a list of new words you come across in your reading. Write down a brief definition of each word, and then use it in a sentence.

Example

Word: *memento* Definition: *a reminder of the past*

____

Sentence: *I kept a seashell as a memento of our vacation at the beach.*

______________________________.

Word: ______________ Definition: ______________

____

Sentence: ______________________________

______________________________.

Word: ________________ Definition: ____________________________

____

Sentence: ____

____.

Word: ________________ Definition: ____________________________

____

Sentence: ____

____.

Word: ________________ Definition: ____________________________

____

Sentence: ____

____.

Word: ________________ Definition: ____________________________

____

Sentence: ____

____.

Word: ________________ Definition: ____________________________

____

Sentence: ____

____.

Word: ________________ Definition: ____________________________

____

Sentence: ____

____.

Word: ________________ Definition: ____________________________

____

Sentence: ____

____.

Word: ________________ Definition: ____________________________

____

Sentence: ____

____.

Word: ________________ Definition: ____________________________

____

Sentence: ____

____.

Word: ________________ Definition: ____________________________

____

Sentence: ____

____.

Word: ________________ Definition: ____________________________

____

Sentence: ____

____.

Word: ________________ Definition: ____________________________

____

Sentence: ____

____.

Word: ________________ Definition: ____________________________

____

Sentence: ____

____.

Word: ________________ Definition: ____________________________

____

Sentence: ____

____.

Word: ________________ Definition: ______________________________

____

Sentence: ____

____.

Word: ________________ Definition: ______________________________

____

Sentence: ____

____.

Word: ________________ Definition: ______________________________

____

Sentence: ____

____.

Word: ________________ Definition: ______________________________

____

Sentence: ____

____.

◆ PRACTICE 1

In the space next to each definition, write the word (from the list provided below) that best matches that definition. Check the Word Power list on pages 481–86 if necessary.

annotating	immortalized	scenario
antagonist	liability	sterilization
balk	manic	transaction
berating	obliqueness	vituperative
bourgeois	paradox	vixen
carcinogen	plight	

1. ________________ an unfortunate or difficult situation
2. ________________ middle-class and proper in attitudes
3. ________________ excessively enthusiastic
4. ________________ verbally abusive; viciously critical

5. ______________ slang for a tempting, sexy woman; can also mean bad-tempered woman. The original meaning is "female fox."
6. ______________ written or printed paper on which voters indicate their choices in an election
7. ______________ something that causes cancer
8. ______________ making explanatory notes
9. ______________ to resist abruptly and strongly
10. ______________ scolding
11. ______________ indirectness; lack of straightforwardness
12. ______________ an opponent; a person with whom one is in conflict
13. ______________ made famous forever
14. ______________ a statement that seems contradictory or opposed to common sense but may still be true
15. ______________ a financial and legal responsibility; a debt that must be paid
16. ______________ the process of making something free of germs
17. ______________ an exchange or transfer of goods, services, or money; an exchange of thoughts and feelings
18. ______________ plot outline; a sequence of events, often imaginary

◆ PRACTICE 2

Fill in the blank in each of the following sentences with one of the words listed below. Check the definitions in the Word Power list on pages 481–86 if necessary.

brawl	marinating	surveillance
conjure up	naturalization	symbol
dilute	obligatory	tradition
eccentric	orient	umbrage
embossed	rambunctious	venue
heritage	stigmatized	weathering
lethal	subsidize	

1. We had to ______________ the cleanser with water before scrubbing the bathtub.

2. Our _______________ instructor came to class barefoot, wearing a bright Hawaiian shirt.
3. In the fifth grade, I was _______________ by the other students for being the only one who wore glasses.
4. The Puerto Rican Day parade participants displayed pride in their _______________.
5. Everyone at the _______________ ceremony carried American flags.
6. The band played at the Ritz, the fanciest _______________ in town.
7. The bird in that poem is actually a(n) _______________ for freedom.
8. The strikers took _______________ at the mayor's comments.
9. Even the most common medications can be _______________ if you take too much of them.
10. Those songs _______________ memories of high school dances.
11. The hockey game soon became a noisy _______________ when the players started fighting.
12. The _______________ children ran around the room, throwing toys.
13. Once Ben had a chance to _______________ himself to his new office, he settled right in.
14. _______________ a tornado requires more than just an umbrella and some boots.
15. The school agreed to _______________ our play and even provided refreshments during the intermission.
16. Having a Memorial Day barbecue is a _______________ in our family; we do it every year.
17. The bank robber had no idea he was under _______________ by hidden cameras.
18. Eric is _______________ the meat in teriyaki sauce to make it taste better.
19. Maria sent out _______________ invitations for her wedding.
20. Passing this course is _______________ for all English majors, so you should not miss too many lectures.

◆ PRACTICE 3

Use your dictionary to find synonyms for each of the following words.

1. altercation ______________________________
____
2. arduous ______________________________
____
3. civil ______________________________
____
4. devious ______________________________
____
5. epiphany ______________________________
____
6. mature ______________________________
____
7. minute ______________________________
____
8. mundane ______________________________
____
9. novice ______________________________
____
10. offensive ______________________________
____
11. parity ______________________________
____
12. persist ______________________________
____
13. prohibit ______________________________
____
14. rigor ______________________________
____

Writing Tip

Be sure to look for the adjective, not the noun.

15. spectacle ______________________________

____

16. sporadic ______________________________

____

17. stark ______________________________

____

18. vocation ______________________________

____

19. woe ______________________________

____

◆ COLLABORATIVE ACTIVITIES

1. Choose four words from the Word Power list on pages 481–86, and work with another student to write a paragraph that uses all of the words you chose. When you have finished your work, check the definitions to make sure you have used each word correctly.

COMPOSING ORIGINAL SENTENCES

2. Write five original sentences using two of the following words in each sentence. Check the Word Power list on pages 481–86 if necessary.

alienated	migrate
anemic	physique
anticipate	recoil
apathy	self-esteem
ebullient	speckled
estranged	traditional
gusto	trek
improvise	veracity
memento	

APPENDIX **B**

Picture Gallery

The images in this picture gallery give you an opportunity to practice looking at, thinking about, and responding to a wide range of visual images created in a variety of time periods and cultures. Each image is followed by two **Thinking about the Image** questions and one **Writing Practice** activity. The questions are designed to help you move from noticing small details in the pictures to speculating about what those details "say" to you. Through these thinking and writing exercises, you will learn how to describe the mood of a picture and to tell the story of a painting in your own words. You will also learn to speculate about what a person's expression, posture, or clothing tells you about what that person is thinking or feeling. Finally, you will learn to consider how an artist's choice of color and style shapes the story being told or the scene being depicted.

As you look at each of these images, pay attention to details that stand out for you. These can be things that catch your eye in a positive way, or things that confuse you, or even upset you. After you have let your eye take in the whole picture, try to imagine why the artist might have included those particular details.

Marc Chagall. Russian-born French painter.
The Marriage (1932).

Thinking about the Image

1. What is unusual about the scene and the characters in this picture?
2. List all the objects you see in this picture. Which are unexpected or surprising? Why do you think the artist included them?

Writing Practice

Write about a wedding you attended. What was memorable about it? If you painted a picture of this wedding, who would be in it? What details would you include?

Oil on canvas; The Museum of Fine Arts, Boston, The Hayden Collection. Charles Henry Hayden Fund, 35.66.

Edward Hopper. American. *Room in Brooklyn* (1932).

Thinking about the Image

1. Why do you think the woman is sitting alone in the room? What do you think happened before she came to the window?
2. What do you think the woman sees out the window? What is she thinking about? What is she feeling? How do you know?

Writing Practice

Imagine you are the woman in the painting. Think about the last conversation you had with someone important in your life before you came into the room and sat by the window. Write a brief letter to that person about the conversation you had.

Fernando Botero. Colombian. *The Musicians* (1979).

Thinking about the Image

1. What do you notice about each of the musicians' faces? About how they are dressed? Why do you think the artist painted them in this way?
2. What do the following details tell you about the painting: the lights? The bird? The jukebox?

Writing Practice

Who are these musicians? What kind of music do you think they are performing? Where do you think they are playing? Who might their audience be? Write a review of their performance for your local or community newspaper.

Winslow Homer. American. *The Gulf Stream* (1899).

Thinking about the Image

1. How do you think the man in the boat got where he is? What might have happened?
2. How would you describe the mood of this picture? What colors and details in the picture help establish this mood?

Writing Practice

What do you think will happen to the man in the boat? Write a story that tells the events of the next few hours.

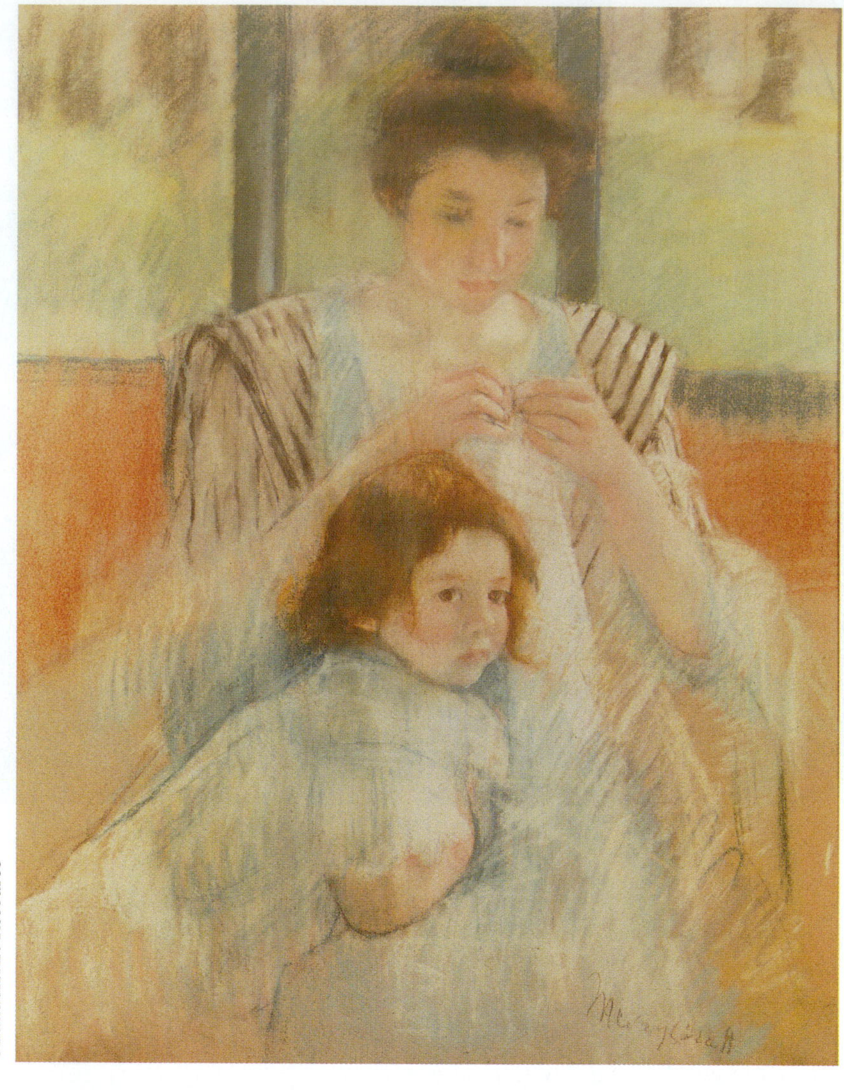

Giraudon/Art Resource

Mary Cassatt. American. *Mother and Child* (1900).

Thinking about the Image

1. How would you describe the look on the girl's face? What do you think she is feeling?
2. What do you think the mother is thinking? Is her mind on her child? On her sewing? On something else?

Writing Practice

Write about an early memory you have of an interaction with a family member. What were the two of you doing at the time? Where were you? Why is this memory important to you? Include as many visual details as you can.

Mural on building at Ninth St. and Indiana Ave., Philadelphia. Photo by Akira Suwa

Jon Lewis. American. *Together We Stand, Divided We Fall* (c. 1983).

Thinking about the Image

1. What story does this picture tell? How do you think the people are related?
2. Consider the use of color and images in the picture. How does the artist use color and images to tell his story?

Writing Practice

Find a detail in the picture that stands out for you. Then, write about what you think that detail is "saying." How does it help you understand the meaning of the picture?

The Newark Museum/Art Resource

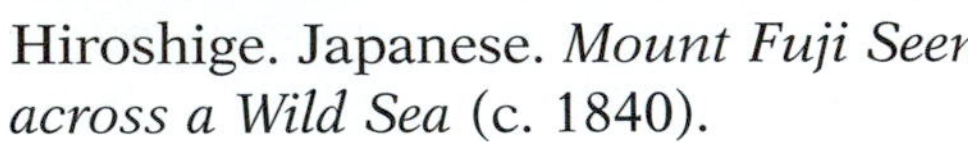

Hiroshige. Japanese. *Mount Fuji Seen across a Wild Sea* (c. 1840).

The Brooklyn Museum of Art, Bequest of Judith and Milton Lowenthal

Georgia O'Keeffe. American.
Ram's Head, White Hollyhock–Hills (1935).

Thinking about the Images

1. Compare the colors and shapes in the two landscapes. What mood is created in each one?
2. How do the ram's head and the flower influence the way you see O'Keeffe's landscape? Why do you think she included them?

Writing Practice

Think of a place you have visited that would have made an interesting photograph, and create a vivid image of the landscape in words for your readers. Describe the place so that your readers can visualize it. Be sure to emphasize the details and colors that best convey the mood of the place.

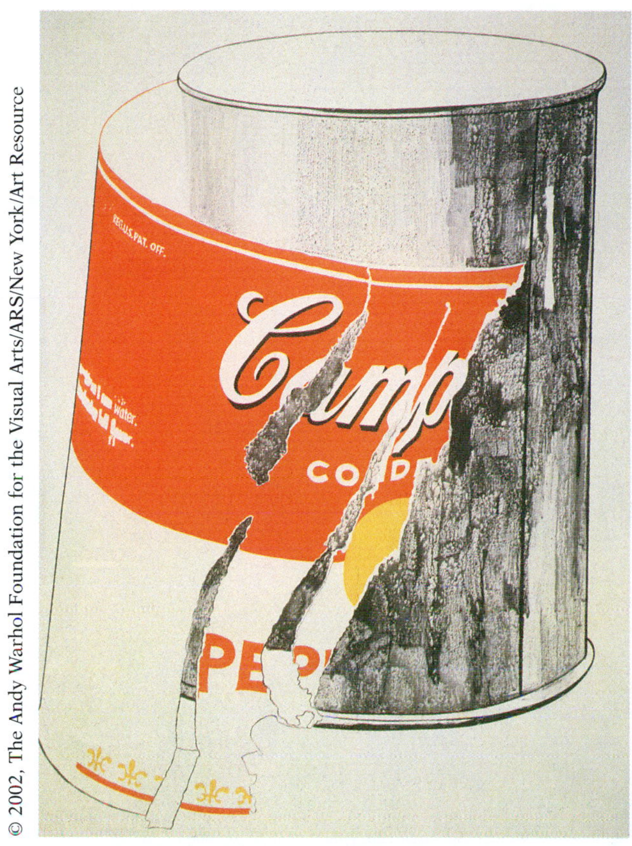

Andy Warhol. American. *Big Torn Campbell Soup Can (Pepper Pot)* (1962).

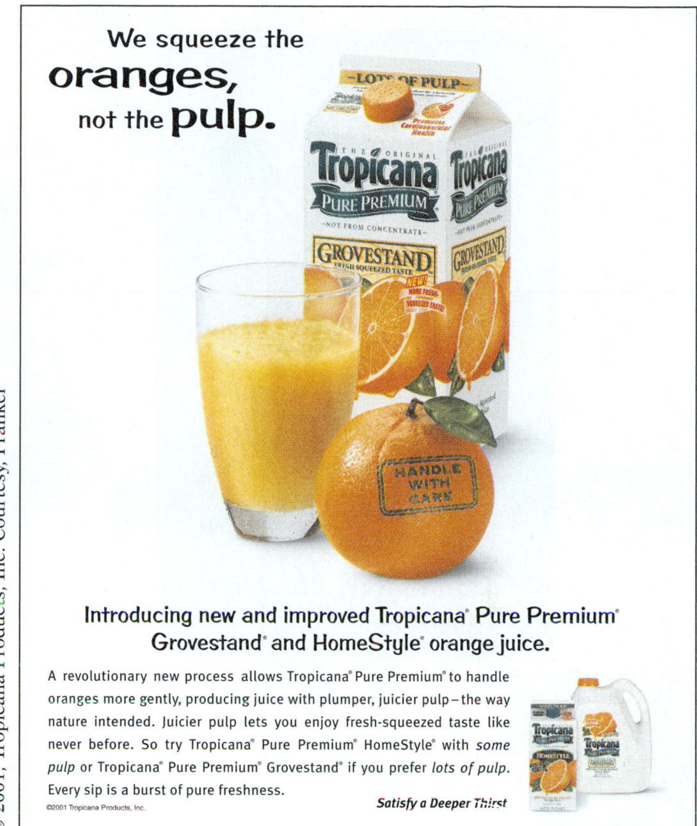

Tropicana advertisement (2001).

Thinking about the Images

1. Read the text in the Tropicana ad. How does it influence the way you look at the picture?
2. Compare the condition of the objects—the soup can and the orange juice carton—in the two pictures. How do you account for the differences? What do you think each artist was trying to achieve?

Writing Practice

The orange juice carton illustrates an ad for Tropicana orange juice. The soup can is considered a work of art. How do you explain why one image is art and the other is not?

The Phillips Collection, Washington, DC

Jacob Lawrence. American. *The Migration of the Negro Panel no. 3* (c. 1940–1941).

Birmingham Museum/Bridgeman Art Library

Ford Madox Brown. British. *The Last of England* (1852–1855).

Thinking about the Images

1. Compare the way people are portrayed in each painting. Why do you think Brown focused on faces while Lawrence painted only silhouettes (dark outlines against a white background)?
2. What do the faces of the people in *The Last of England* suggest about how they feel about their experience? What do the postures of the people in *The Migration of the Negro* suggest about their feelings?

Writing Practice

Imagine that you are a person in one of the paintings, traveling with the people in the picture. Write a journal entry describing what one of your days was like. Give as much detail as possible so your readers can experience what you experienced.

Answers to Odd-Numbered Exercises

Chapter 6

◆ PRACTICE 6.1, page 100

Answers: **1.** One **3.** a man **5.** They **7.** Many viewers **9.** The original show

◆ PRACTICE 6.4, page 102

Answers: **1.** P **3.** S **5.** S **7.** P **9.** S

◆ PRACTICE 6.5, page 103

Answers: **1.** The memorial; singular **3.** More than two and a half million people; plural **5.** Some visitors; plural 7. One man; singular **9.** Spouses, children, parents, and friends; plural

◆ PRACTICE 6.6, page 104

Answers: **1.** Prepositional phrase: for almost seventy-five years; subject: companies **3.** Prepositional phrase: to the person on one end; subject: phone **5.** Prepositional phrase: for the Picturephone; subject: customers **7.** Prepositional phrases: of visual images, after the invention of high-speed DSL lines; subject: transmission **9.** Prepositional phrase: on the other side of the line; subject: people

◆ PRACTICE 6.7, page 105

Answers: **1.** traveled **3.** advertised **5.** packed, joined **7.** wrote **9.** understand

◆ PRACTICE 6.9, page 106

Answers: **1.** leave; action verb **3.** quit; action verb **5.** feels; linking verb **7.** were; linking verb **9.** appreciate; action verb

◆ PRACTICE 6.10, page 107

Answers: **1.** Subject: The night; linking verb: grew; descriptive word: cold **3.** Subject: George W. Bush; linking verb: became; descriptive phrase: the forty-third president of the United States **5.** Subject: Many people; linking verb: were; descriptive phrase: outraged at the mayor's announcement **7.** Subject: The fans; linking verb: appear; descriptive phrase: exhausted by their team's defeat **9.** Subject: Charlie; linking verb: got; descriptive word: sick

◆ PRACTICE 6.11, page 108

Answers: **1.** Helping verb: may; verb: risk **3.** Helping verbs: has been; verb: thinking **5.** Helping verbs: could have; verb: risk **7.** Helping verb: have; verb: wondered **9.** Helping verb: has; verb: loved

◆ PRACTICE 6.12, page 109

Answers: **1.** Verb: wanted **3.** Helping verb: were; verb: suspected **5.** Verb: dyed **7.** Helping verbs: would have; verb: hidden **9.** Helping verbs: can be; verb: seen

Chapter 7

◆ PRACTICE 7.1, page 113

Answers: **1.** [Speech is silver], *but* [silence is golden]. **3.** [The house was dark], *so* [he didn't ring the doorbell]. **5.** [They will not surrender], *and* [they will not agree to a cease-fire]. **7.** [She had lived in California for years], *yet* [she remembered her childhood in Kansas very clearly]. **9.** [Melody dropped French], *and* [then she added Italian].

◆ PRACTICE 7.2, page 115

Answers: **1.** but/yet **3.** and **5.** so **7.** and **9.** and

◆ PRACTICE 7.8, page 123

Answers: **1.** Today, adults need computer skills to get a good job; consequently, education experts want young people to learn how to use computers. **3.** Even some elementary schools have computer labs; in fact, some kindergarten children are learning to use computers. **5.** Some scientists think children need to play; in addition, they need to develop social skills. **7.** Many adults now spend their free time online; as a result, they do not get enough exercise. **9.** Young Americans need to understand technology; still, they need to understand other human beings as well.

◆ PRACTICE 7.9, page 124

Possible edits: **1.** Every year, unusual weather makes news somewhere in the United States; for example, there may be droughts on the East Coast or floods in the Midwest. **3.** Winters are generally cold in this country; therefore, people plan for snow and ice. **5.** Weather is always changing; as a result, big changes in weather patterns are hard to see. **7.** Fortunately, most parts of the country have at least a century of weather records; consequently, analysts can tell that the weather has gotten warmer in the last hundred years. **9.** Some scientists say that the warming is insignificant; however, others see a potential for disaster.

Chapter 8

◆ PRACTICE 8.1, page 132

Possible edits: **1.** Although **3.** Even if **5.** When **7.** unless **9.** Now that

◆ PRACTICE 8.3, page 134

Answers: **1.** More than six million Firestone tires were recalled in 2000 because the treads peeled off the surface of the tires. **3.** Correct **5.** Correct **7.** Some customers were buying the recalled tires so that they could turn them in to Firestone and get brand-new replacements. **9.** If the tires catch fire, they burn uncontrollably and pollute the air.

◆ PRACTICE 8.4, page 135

Possible edits: **1.** Although many Westerners rarely think about problems in Africa, the lack of money for medical supplies should concern everyone. **3.** When an outbreak of Ebola virus appeared in northern Uganda in 2000, doctors and nurses caring for Ebola patients lacked disinfectants and latex gloves. **5.** Because the Ebola virus makes a patient bleed profusely, medical workers without gloves face grave danger. **7.** The virus is named for the Ebola river in Zaire where it first appeared in human beings. **9.** Even though a doctor and several nurses died of the Ebola virus, more than half of the patients survived.

◆ PRACTICE 8.6, page 137

Answers: **1.** Dependent clause: *that* there is no such thing as bad publicity; modifies: idea **3.** Dependent clause: *whom* talk-show hosts humiliate; modifies: people **5.** Dependent clause: *that* they need to live a normal life; modifies: privacy **7.** Dependent clause: *who* wanted to be alone; modifies: Sean Penn **9.** Dependent clause: *which* many people think will make them happy; modifies: Money and fame

◆ PRACTICE 8.7, page 138

Answers: **1.** Nonrestrictive. Working women, who have more career opportunities today than ever before, are successful in many fields. **3.** Nonrestrictive. After getting a position of power, which almost always involves supervising other employees, women may face additional problems. **5.** Restrictive. Workers admitted unhappiness with their female bosses on surveys that questioned both male and female employees. **7.** Restrictive; punctuation correct **9.** Restrictive. People who admire a tough attitude in a man may not like the same attitude in a woman.

◆ PRACTICE 8.8, page 139

Possible edits: **1.** In the nineteenth century, American whalers, who had very dangerous jobs, sailed around the world to hunt whales. **3.** Today, U.S. laws protect several species of whale that are considered to be in danger of extinction. **5.** Whale hunting is the focus of a disagreement between the United States and Japan, which have different ideas about whaling. **7.** Some of the whales killed in the Japanese hunt, which include minke whales, Bryde's whales, and sperm whales, are considered by the U.S. government to be endangered. **9.** The U.S. government argues that the Japanese whale hunt is not for research, but for businesses that want whale meat to sell to restaurants.

Chapter 9

◆ PRACTICE 9.2, page 146

Possible edits: **1.** With their cuddly teddy-bear looks, giant pandas are a favorite animal for people of all ages. **3.** Saving the panda has been a priority for wildlife conservation experts for decades, but it is not an easy task. **5.** Wilderness areas are increasingly rare in China, the giant panda's home. **7.** Some endangered wild animals have been saved by breeding programs in zoos, but panda-breeding programs have struggled. **9.** The cub, known as Hua Mei, is the first giant panda to be born outside of China. **11.** Now, wildlife conservationists hope that Hua Mei's success story will help them increase the numbers of giant pandas.

◆ PRACTICE 9.3, page 147

Possible answers: **1.** School Day Parade; Uncle Sam; stiltwalker wearing red-and-white-striped pants that were ten feet long **3.** plump tuba player for Marion High School's marching band; red wool jacket **5.** the Millard sisters, four dark-haired look-alikes in identical satin cowgirl costumes—one red, one blue, one yellow, and one green; brown and white horses

◆ **PRACTICE 9.6, page 150**

Possible edits: **1.** Protesters disrupted the World Trade Organization's meeting in Seattle in 1999. **3.** Some violent incidents happened in Seattle. **5.** Some of the protesters were mainly interested in protecting the environment. **7.** The Seattle protest was not an isolated event. **9.** Many young people are getting involved in these because they believe a global economy should help the poor as much as the wealthy.

◆ **PRACTICE 9.7, page 151**

Answers and possible edits: **1.** A few years ago, antibacterial cleaning products were introduced to the American market. **3.** The ads try to make people afraid of the germs in their homes. **5.** When the ads appeared, frightened people immediately began buying antibacterial soap, to kill off the invisible germs. **7.** But new research suggests that antibacterial products may kill good germs. **9.** Scientists have warned that children who grow up in germ-free homes may get sick from normally harmless bacteria.

◆ **PRACTICE 9.8, page 152**

Answers and possible edits: **1.** Clichés: take to; like a duck to water. Americans love health fads. **3.** Cliché: as strong as an ox. Weight training, which can make a person very strong, is now as common among students and homemakers as it is among athletes. **5.** Cliché: have worn out their welcome. Meanwhile, smokers are no longer welcome in many office buildings. **7.** Cliché: go off the deep end. Dr. Ruth Clifford Engs, a professor of applied health science, believes that once about every eighty years, Americans develop a strong desire to be physically and morally healthy. **9.** Cliché: like the plague. They exercise, eat foods they think are healthy, and completely avoid alcohol and cigarettes.

Chapter 10

◆ **PRACTICE 10.1, page 157**

Answers: **1.** sudden; unexpected; destructive **3.** lie down; take a nap **5.** expanded the parking lot; added a deli counter **7.** a bath; a bottle; a lullaby **9.** A beautiful voice; acting ability

◆ **PRACTICE 10.2, page 158**

Answers: **1.** Hundreds of people wanted to be on a game show that required them to live on an island, catch their own food, and have no contact with the outside world. **3.** Parallel **5.** The contestants held their breath underwater, rowed a canoe, and ate rats and caterpillars. **7.** Each week, the television audience saw one person win a contest, and another person get voted off the island. **9.** Parallel

◆ **PRACTICE 10.3, page 160**

Answers: **1.** I wanted to find my old friend's address and telephone number. **3.** Her telephone numbers had been written and then crossed out in my address book. **5.** Searching the Internet for her address was easier than getting the information any other way. **7.** She had used the Internet to find information on the disease and to learn if she was at risk. **9.** Other sites were developed by crackpots or put together by people who knew little about the disease.

◆ **PRACTICE 10.5, page 161**

Suggested answers: **1.** Young people in the 1930s, 1940s, and 1950s read about the adventures of Nancy Drew and the Hardy Boys. **3.** The Hardy Boys' father was a former policeman, a good father, and a famous detective. **5.** Frank and Joe Hardy found smugglers, thieves, and counterfeiters all over their town, but it also seemed like a nice place to live. **7.** Nancy Drew was blond, attractive, and wealthy. **9.** Nancy was both a sleuth and a loyal friend to Bess and George.

Chapter 11

◆ **PRACTICE 11.1, page 170**

Answers: **1.** Correct **3.** Run-on **5.** Comma splice **7.** Correct **9.** Run-on

◆ **PRACTICE 11.2, page 173**

Possible edits: **1.** Flatbread is bread that is flat; usually, it does not contain yeast. **3.** The tortilla is a Mexican flatbread; tortillas are made of corn or wheat. **5.** Italians eat focaccia, but when they put cheese on a focaccia, it becomes a pizza. **7.** Indian cooking has several kinds of flatbreads, and all of them are delicious. **9.** Fifty years ago, most people ate only the flatbreads from their native land; today, flatbreads are becoming internationally popular.

◆ **PRACTICE 11.3, page 173**

Possible edits: **1.** Some Americans have serious drug problems that can be difficult to treat. **3.** Richard Nixon, who was president of the United States at the time, realized that drug-addicted soldiers were a problem. **5.** Even though drugs such as marijuana and cocaine were illegal during the 1960s and 1970s, drug use was ignored or tolerated by many Americans. **7.** After laws against illegal drugs became stricter, possession of small amounts of many drugs was enough to send a young person to jail. **9.** The "Just Say No" drug policy, which was widespread in the 1980s, tried to convince young people to avoid drugs.

◆ **PRACTICE 11.4, page 174**

Possible edits: **1.** Older generations may not approve of rap; however, it appears to be here to stay. **3.** However, this music still has its critics. Many feel that rap lyrics are too violent. **5.** Another issue is the crude language that many rap artists use. **7.** Rappers use crude language to discuss unpleasant topics; students can talk about this strategy. **9.** Rap cannot reach every student, but some people do not relate to Shakespeare, either.

Chapter 12

◆ PRACTICE 12.2, page 180

Answers: **1.** Fragment **3.** Correct **5.** Fragment **7.** Correct **9.** Fragment
Rewrite: According to some people who frequently use lip balm, this product is addictive. The purpose of lip balm is to keep the lips from getting chapped. Can people become dependent on lip balm? Some users say yes. However, the makers of lip balm deny the possibility of addiction.

◆ PRACTICE 12.3, page 181

Answers: **1.** Correct **3.** Fragment **5.** Fragment **7.** Fragment **9.** Fragment
Rewrite: Hikers often wear bells to make noise on the trail, especially in areas populated by bears. Bears can hear very well but cannot see long distances. Sometimes, bears can be frightened by humans and attack them. However, a bear may hear a person coming and then is very likely to avoid the person. This is why experienced hikers never go hiking without bells.

◆ PRACTICE 12.5, page 184

Answers: **1.** Fragment **3.** Correct **5.** Correct **7.** Correct **9.** Correct **11.** Correct
Rewrite: In August 2000, the Kahiki closed its doors forever. This Columbus landmark was famous for its tropical drinks, grass huts, giant tiki gods, and indoor rainstorms. The restaurant was built in a more innocent time, the 1950s. The outside of the building was impressive, with its wooden idols and canoe-shaped roof. The Kahiki had recently been added to the National Register of Historic Places. Now, the building will be replaced by something more modern, a drugstore.

◆ PRACTICE 12.6, page 185

Answers: **1.** Fragment **3.** Fragment **5.** Fragment **7.** Fragment **9.** Fragment
Rewrite: In 1999, the Kansas State Board of Education voted to change the standards for science education in the state's public schools. The board members voted to stop teaching students about evolution. This decision horrified science teachers across the country and had economic consequences. Some technology companies decided not to move to Kansas, a place where future workers might not have a good science background.

◆ PRACTICE 12.7, page 187

Answers and possible edits: **1.** My sister has forgotten the house where we used to live. **3.** The baby has been crying ever since you left. **5.** Vivian and her daughters have gone to the supermarket to pick up some groceries for dinner. **7.** Until yesterday, the choir had never sung a hymn that featured two soloists. **9.** More and more airplanes are flying over this neighborhood every day.

◆ PRACTICE 12.8, page 189

Answers: **1.** This young man has a very promising future. **3.** A box turtle was trying to find water. **5.** Most people think of themselves as good drivers. **7.** Frequent-flier miles can sometimes be traded for products as well as for airline tickets. **9.** She searched the crowd frantically.

Chapter 13

◆ PRACTICE 13.1, page 197

Answers: **1.** sit **3.** needs **5.** requires **7.** enjoy **9.** works **11.** stop **13.** think **15.** see

◆ PRACTICE 13.2, page 198

Answers: **1.** blows **3.** reach **5.** come **7.** cause **9.** want

◆ PRACTICE 13.3, page 199

Answers: **1.** is **3.** am **5.** are **7.** is **9.** are

◆ PRACTICE 13.4, page 200

Answers: **1.** have **3.** has **5.** have **7.** has **9.** have

◆ PRACTICE 13.5, page 200

Answers: **1.** does **3.** do **5.** does **7.** do **9.** do

◆ PRACTICE 13.6, page 201

Answers: **1.** is **3.** has **5.** has **7.** are **9.** does **11.** have **13.** are **15.** is **17.** are

◆ PRACTICE 13.7, page 202

Answers: **1.** are **3.** work **5.** share **7.** make **9.** save

◆ PRACTICE 13.8, page 203

Answers: **1.** is **3.** have **5.** contains **7.** is **9.** costs

◆ PRACTICE 13.9, page 204

Answers: **1.** Prepositional phrase: of one of China's cities; subject: resident; verb: goes **3.** Prepositional phrase: with a huge, heavy frame; subject: bicycle; verb: has **5.** Prepositional phrase: of China; subject: economy; verb: is **7.** Prepositional phrase: with a long commute; subject: worker; verb: does **9.** Prepositional phrase: under age thirty; subject: people; verb: do

◆ PRACTICE 13.10, page 204

Answers: **1.** Prepositional phrase: of these plants; subject: roots; verb: go **3.** Prepositional phrase: on the night shift; subject: Firefighters; verb: take **5.** Prepositional phrase: with a hundred guests; subject: wedding; verb: costs **7.** Prepositional phrase: about chimpanzees; subject: book; verb: was **9.** Prepositional phrase: to this week's performance; subject: Tickets; verb: are

◆ PRACTICE 13.11, page 206

Answers: **1.** wants **3.** looks **5.** remembers **7.** knows **9.** seems

◆ PRACTICE 13.12, page 207

Answers: **1.** is **3.** are **5.** are **7.** are **9.** is

◆ PRACTICE 13.13, page 207

Answers: **1.** Subject: program; verb: is **3.** Subject: dormitory; verb: is **5.** Subject: tests; verb: are **7.** Subject: people; verb: are **9.** Subject: student; verb: does

◆ PRACTICE 13.14, page 209

Answers: **1.** Subject: mother; verb: watches **3.** Subject: newscasters; verb: smile **5.** Subject: citizens; verb: need **7.** Subject: juice; verb: leaves **9.** Subject: panels; verb: charge

◆ PRACTICE 13.15, page 210

Answers: **1.** Subject: researchers; verb: study **3.** Subject: cartoon; verb: shows **5.** Subject: shootings; verb: were **7.** Subject: theaters; verb: show **9.** Subject: teenagers; verb: are

Chapter 14

◆ PRACTICE 14.1, page 215

Answers: **1.** Verbs: ordered, takes; correction: *takes* becomes *took* **3.** Correct **5.** Correct **7.** Verbs: offered, tells; correction: *tells* becomes *told* **9.** Correct

◆ PRACTICE 14.2, page 216

Answers: **1.** Correct **3.** Lincoln needed 300,000 more men. **5.** For example, a rich man could pay a "commutation fee" that allowed him to pay someone else to fight so that he could stay at home. **7.** On June 12, 1863, the first draftees were named, and soon mobs began to form. **9.** Correct

◆ PRACTICE 14.3, page 217

Answers: **1.** The students learned that they needed to use proper lab technique. **3.** I worked on an assembly line where I could not spend more than thirty seconds on each task. **5.** His boss told him that he had to be on time for work every day. **7.** Correct **9.** His brother said that he could find almost anything on the Internet.

◆ PRACTICE 14.4, page 218

Answers: **1.** My brother found out that he had to get tickets for the high school graduation so that his family could attend. **3.** If more than two family members wanted to come to the graduation, they had to sit in the gym, where they could hear the speeches but not see anything. **5.** One of his friends, who had graduated the year before, said that he should check the bulletin boards. **7.** My brother did not understand how he could walk up to another student and say, "Is it true that only one person wants to come to your graduation?" **9.** He could not believe that he had to deal with ticket scalpers for a high school graduation.

◆ PRACTICE 14.5, page 219

Answers: **1.** The lawyers discussed a settlement, but the defendant refused it. **3.** Roberto signed up for calculus, so he bought a new calculator. **5.** As the waves battered the beach, a gasping young man clutched a surfboard. **7.** When Brandon met Jane, he asked her for a date. **9.** Kathy mowed her grandfather's lawn, and she also did his yardwork.

◆ PRACTICE 14.6, page 220

Answers: **1.** I kept this book beside my bed, and I read it every night before I went to sleep. **3.** I loved Poe's "Annabel Lee," and I also enjoyed his poem "The Bells." **5.** Maybe that book explains why I like reading poetry and why I like writing my own poems.

Chapter 15

◆ PRACTICE 15.1, page 225

Answers: **1.** Present participle modifier: fearing for his life; modifies: soldier **3.** Present participle modifier: smiling professionally; modifies: winner **5.** Present participle modifier: Standing in the barbershop doorway; modifies: men **7.** Present participle modifier: ringing loudly at 2 a.m.; modifies: telephone **9.** Present participle modifier: blowing his whistle loudly in my ear; modifies: foreman

◆ PRACTICE 15.2, page 226

Answers: **1.** Present participle modifier: Appearing at picnics and other outdoor gatherings; modifies: yellow jackets **3.** Present participle modifier: causing allergic reactions in many people; modifies: stings **5.** Present participle modifier: Looking for food; modifies: females **7.** Present participle modifier: overflowing with trash; modifies: garbage can **9.** Present participle modifier: Pollinating flowers and eating other harmful insects; modifies: yellow jackets

◆ PRACTICE 15.4, page 228

Answers: **1.** Present participle modifier: Plastered with bumper stickers; modifies: car **3.** Present participle modifier: covered with mosquito bites; modifies: legs **5.** Present participle modifier: buried under two feet of snow; modifies: roof **7.** Present participle modifier: Shattered in its fall from the mantle; modifies: vase **9.** Present participle modifier: rejected by six publishers; modifies: book

◆ **PRACTICE 15.5, page 228**

Answers: **1.** Present participle modifier: committed in Fall River, Massachusetts; modifies: crime **3.** Present participle modifier: Horrified at the news of this murder; modifies: people **5.** Present participle modifier: changed repeatedly; modifies: story **7.** Present participle modifier: discussed in every home in town; modifies: motive **9.** Present participle modifier: faced with a circumstantial case; modifies: jury

◆ **PRACTICE 15.7, page 230**

Possible answers: **1.** Hanging by one hand from the edge of the roof, he could not reach the fire escape. **3.** Frightened by the alligator, I almost turned over my canoe. **5.** Sitting on the dock in the bay, he caught many fish. **7.** Given a second chance, she ran out of luck. **9.** Feeling sick to her stomach, she was too far away to reach the bathroom in time.

◆ **PRACTICE 15.9, page 233**

Possible answers: **1.** The angry bull with a ring in its nose threw every rodeo rider. **3.** The bathroom door was quickly closed by Henry, blushing furiously. OR: Blushing furiously, Henry quickly closed the bathroom door. **5.** A car kept in a garage is not likely to be damaged by rust. **7.** A bartender with long hair served strong drinks. **9.** A white limousine waited as the director, blowing kisses, emerged from the restaurant.

Chapter 16

◆ **PRACTICE 16.1, page 240**

Answers: **1.** Verb: sings; tense: present **3.** Verb: protested; tense: past **5.** Verb: cried; tense: past **7.** Verb: gurgled; tense: past **9.** Verb: pool; tense: present

◆ **PRACTICE 16.2, page 241**

Answers: **1.** walked **3.** smelled **5.** loved **7.** followed **9.** chased

◆ **PRACTICE 16.3, page 241**

Answers: **1.** slept **3.** gave **5.** rose **7.** tore **9.** hurt

◆ **PRACTICE 16.4, page 243**

Answers: **1.** bought **3.** took **5.** told **7.** made **9.** left

◆ **PRACTICE 16.5, page 244**

Answers: **1.** were **3.** were **5.** was **7.** were **9.** was

◆ **PRACTICE 16.6, page 244**

Answers: **1.** was **3.** was **5.** were **7.** Correct; were **9.** Correct; correct

◆ **PRACTICE 16.7, page 246**

Answers: **1.** would **3.** would **5.** could **7.** can **9.** could

◆ **PRACTICE 16.8, page 247**

Answers: **1.** can **3.** would **5.** can; could **7.** would **9.** will; would

Chapter 17

◆ **PRACTICE 17.1, page 252**

Answers: **1.** Present: agrees; past: agreed; past participle: agreed **3.** Present: drops; past: dropped; past participle: dropped **5.** Present: work; past: worked; past participle: worked **7.** Present: gargles; past: gargled; past participle: gargled **9.** Present: confuses; past: confused; past participle: confused

◆ **PRACTICE 17.2, page 253**

Answers: **1.** feared **3.** watched **5.** attacked **7.** gained **9.** prevented

◆ **PRACTICE 17.3, page 257**

Answers: **1.** Present: goes; past: went; past participle: gone **3.** Present: drink; past: drank; past participle: drunk **5.** Present: feels; past: felt; past participle: felt **7.** Present: keeps; past: kept; past participle: kept **9.** Present: understands; past: understood; past participle: understood

◆ **PRACTICE 17.4, page 258**

Answers: **1.** made **3.** kept **5.** found **7.** been **9.** heard

◆ **PRACTICE 17.5, page 259**

Answers: **1.** Correct **3.** spent **5.** begun **7.** written **9.** gone **11.** given

◆ **PRACTICE 17.6, page 260**

Answers: **1.** has put **3.** have gotten **5.** have become **7.** had drawn **9.** saw, had become

◆ **PRACTICE 17.7, page 261**

Answers: **1.** have enjoyed **3.** played **5.** saw; have never seen **7.** have ever had; has ever thrown **9.** moved **11.** played

◆ **PRACTICE 17.8, page 262**

Answers: **1.** was; went **3.** left **5.** has become **7.** has been **9.** loved; have become

◆ **PRACTICE 17.9, page 263**

Answers: **1.** have invested **3.** have allowed **5.** has made **7.** have wanted **9.** had started

◆ **PRACTICE 17.10, page 264**

Answers: **1.** grew **3.** had enjoyed **5.** had grown **7.** had solved **9.** left

◆ **PRACTICE 17.11, page 265**

Answers: **1.** abandoned **3.** unconcerned **5.** injured **7.** rescued **9.** swamped

◆ **PRACTICE 17.12, page 266**

Answers: **1.** made **3.** registered **5.** worn **7.** sworn **9.** cut **11.** paved **13.** sworn **15.** registered **17.** hidden **19.** defeated

◆ **PRACTICE 17.13, page 267**

Answers: **1.** Past participle: injured. The injured quarterback played for the rest of the quarter. **3.** Past participle: dried. Rafika put the dried figs in a dish. **5.** Past participle: pointed. The baby stared at his pointed beard for several minutes. **7.** Past participle: burned. He put his burned fingers in his mouth. **9.** Past participle: expected. The students did not give the expected answers.

Chapter 18

◆ **PRACTICE 18.1, page 272**

Answers: **1.** incident (common); birthday (common); Tuesday (proper); Labor Day (proper) **3.** Ms. Floyd (proper); statue (common); dog (common); yard (common) **5.** Mr. Stewart (proper); dog (common); air (common); nose (common) **7.** bulldog (common); street (common); employees (common); man (common); truck (common) **9.** bite (common); Fluffy (proper); lesson (common)

◆ **PRACTICE 18.2, page 274**

Possible answers: **1.** class **3.** class; hours **5.** people; problem **7.** solution **9.** voice; sound

◆ **PRACTICE 18.3, page 274**

Answers: **1.** obstetrician **3.** options **5.** years; correct **7.** woman **9.** concept; countries

◆ **PRACTICE 18.4, page 276**

Answers: **1.** ladies-in-waiting (irregular) **3.** potatoes **5.** benches **7.** calendars **9.** highways **11.** cheeses **13.** enemies (irregular) **15.** calves (irregular) **17.** taxes **19.** stomachs

◆ **PRACTICE 18.5, page 277**

Answers: **1.** Hunting foxes is a traditional sport among wealthy people in England. **3.** Fathers and children, sons and daughters-in-law may all hunt together. **5.** The riders go out in early morning, searching for foxes in wooded areas and green fields where sheep graze peacefully. **7.** The fox is then chased by the dogs, horsemen, and horsewomen until it either escapes or is killed. **9.** They believe that the dignified appearance of the riders covers up the fact that they terrorize and kill the creatures and then cut off their tails with knives.

Chapter 19

◆ **PRACTICE 19.1, page 282**

Answers: **1.** She (singular) **3.** We (plural) **5.** it (singular) **7.** he (singular) **9.** we (plural)

◆ **PRACTICE 19.2, page 283**

Answers: **1.** Antecedent: woman; pronoun: she **3.** Antecedent: hitchhiker; pronoun: his **5.** Antecedent: lawyers; pronoun: they **7.** Antecedent: Esteban; pronoun: he **9.** Antecedent: Fries; pronoun: they

◆ **PRACTICE 19.3, page 284**

Answers: **1.** it **3.** they **5.** it **7.** it **9.** they

◆ **PRACTICE 19.4, page 284**

Answers: **1.** Antecedent: parents; pronoun: they **3.** Antecedent: schools; pronoun: them **5.** Antecedent: school; pronoun: it **7.** Antecedent: parents; pronoun: their **9.** Antecedent: father; pronoun: him

◆ **PRACTICE 19.5, page 285**

Answers: **1.** Compound antecedent: Spring and fall; connecting word: and; pronoun: they **3.** Compound antecedent: Snow and ice; connecting word: and; pronoun: them **5.** Compound antecedent: Chilly air and unpredictable weather; connecting word: and; pronoun: their **7.** Compound antecedent: unusually cold weather or a dry spell; connecting word: or; pronoun: its **9.** Compound antecedent: heat and humidity; connecting word: and; pronoun: their

◆ **PRACTICE 19.6, page 286**

Answers: **1.** Correct **3.** they **5.** Correct **7.** Correct **9.** Correct

◆ **PRACTICE 19.7, page 288**

Answers: **1.** Indefinite pronoun antecedent: Everyone; pronoun: his or her **3.** Indefinite pronoun antecedent: anyone; pronoun: his or her **5.** Indefinite pronoun antecedent: few; pronoun: their **7.** Indefinite pronoun antecedent: Each; pronoun: her **9.** Indefinite pronoun antecedent: Either; pronoun: her **11.** Indefinite pronoun antecedent: no one; pronoun: his or her **13.** Indefinite pronoun antecedent: anybody; pronoun: his or her **15.** Indefinite pronoun antecedent: someone; pronoun: his or her

◆ **PRACTICE 19.8, page 290**

Answers: **1.** Pronoun: his or her; antecedent: Everyone **3.** Pronoun: their; antecedent: few **5.** Pronoun: he or she; antecedent: each **7.** Pronoun: her; antecedent: either **9.** Pronoun: their; antecedent: Many

◆ **PRACTICE 19.9, page 290**

Possible edits: **1.** Someone left his or her key in the lock. **3.** All of the people on the platform missed their train. **5.** One of the telemarketers hated making his or her calls at dinnertime. **7.** Anyone would love to give this encyclopedia to his or her children. **9.** All of the students must e-mail their essays to the professor. **11.** Ha anybody in this neighborhood lost his or her d **13.** Someone hung up without leaving his or her nam the answering machine. **15.** The voters thought the candidate was charming, but they did not want to vote for him.

◆ PRACTICE 19.10, page 292

Answers: **1.** Antecedent: pack (collective); pronoun: its **3.** Antecedent: officers; pronoun: their **5.** Antecedent: gang (collective); pronoun: its **7.** Antecedent: class (collective); pronoun: its **9.** Antecedent: jury; pronoun: its

◆ PRACTICE 19.11, page 292

Answers: **1.** Correct; their **3.** his or her **5.** their **7.** Correct **9.** their

◆ PRACTICE 19.12, page 294

Answers: **1.** Canada has many sparsely populated areas. **3.** The video game that I bought broke almost immediately. **5.** Her granddaughter lives in another state. **7.** These apples were damaged in the hailstorm. **9.** The acrobat almost fell off the tightrope.

◆ PRACTICE 19.13, page 296

Answers: **1.** He: subjective; his: possessive **3.** I: subjective; my: possessive **5.** mine: possessive; yours: possessive **7.** me: objective; her: objective **9.** Their: possessive; we: subjective; them: objective; our: possessive

◆ PRACTICE 19.14, page 297

Answers: **1.** him: indirect object **3.** us: direct object **5.** him: direct object **7.** you: indirect object **9.** me: indirect object

◆ PRACTICE 19.15, page 298

Answers: **1.** him **3.** him; me **5.** She **7.** They; I **9.** they

◆ PRACTICE 19.16, page 300

Answers: **1.** he [is] **3.** I [eat] **5.** [it frightens] me **7.** [it costs] us **9.** [he pays] her

◆ PRACTICE 19.17, page 301

Answers: **1.** who **3.** who **5.** who **7.** who **9.** who

◆ PRACTICE 19.18, page 302

Answers: **1.** herself **3.** itself **5.** myself **7.** yourself [or yourselves] **9.** themselves

Chapter 20

◆ PRACTICE 20.1, page 308

Answers: **1.** I hardly ever take chances. **3.** It is unusual for me to argue with someone bigger because I am uncomfortable with any kind of violence. **5.** The heavy sound of the bass guitar came through the floor. **7.** The guy who opened the door was six feet five inches tall, covered in leather, chains, and tattoos. **9.** "Excuse me," I said. **11.** The guy in the leather looked at me for a minute.

◆ PRACTICE 20.2, page 309

Answers: **1.** The subway train screeched noisily into the station. **3.** Entering passengers struggled bravely through the narrow doors. **5.** I stood jammed uncomfortably in the middle of the car, praying I'd be able to wriggle out quickly when I reached my stop.

◆ PRACTICE 20.3, page 310

Answers: **1.** interesting **3.** different **5.** similar **7.** actively **9.** safely **11.** real **13.** conservatively **15.** extremely

◆ PRACTICE 20.4, page 311

Answers: **1.** well **3.** good **5.** good **7.** good **9.** well **11.** well **13.** well **15.** well

◆ PRACTICE 20.5, page 314

Answers: **1.** stronger **3.** more quickly **5.** neater **7.** fairer **9.** younger **11.** bluer **13.** easier **15.** more useful **17.** harder **19.** deeper

◆ PRACTICE 20.6, page 314

Answers: **1.** strongest **3.** most quickly **5.** neatest **7.** fairest **9.** youngest **11.** bluest **13.** easiest **15.** most useful **17.** hardest **19.** deepest

◆ PRACTICE 20.7, page 315

Answers: **1.** busier **3.** more active **5.** more effectively **7.** more convenient **9.** more careful

◆ PRACTICE 20.8, page 315

Answers: **1.** craziest **3.** tiniest **5.** most necessary **7.** greatest **9.** most surprising

◆ PRACTICE 20.9, page 316

Answers: **1.** best **3.** worse **5.** best **7.** better **9.** better

◆ PRACTICE 20.10, page 318

Answers: **1.** these **3.** this; that **5.** this **7.** that **9.** this; that

Chapter 21

◆ PRACTICE 21.1, page 323

Answers: **1.** It will rain all day tomorrow. **3.** Javier studied so that he could become an American citizen. **5.** Sofia watched television programs for children when she was learning English. **7.** She waited until she was sure they were gone. **9.** After Jean scored the winning goal, he went out to celebrate with his friends.

◆ **PRACTICE 21.2, page 325**

Possible answers: **1.** The old woman sells candles in the shop downstairs. **3.** Dmitri rides his bicycle ten miles every day. **5.** My neighbor watches my daughter in the evenings. **7.** My job starts at six o'clock in the morning. **9.** The best thing in my life is that my family is together again.

◆ **PRACTICE 21.3, page 326**

Answers: **1.** toddlers; children **3.** teenagers; interests; hobbies **5.** sports **7.** twins; tricks; people **9.** outfits; girls; clothes

◆ **PRACTICE 21.4, page 328**

Answers: **1.** Noncount **3.** Noncount **5.** Count; beaches **7.** Noncount **9.** Noncount

◆ **PRACTICE 21.5, page 330**

Answers: **1.** Many **3.** a few **5.** little **7.** a little **9.** enough

◆ **PRACTICE 21.6, page 333**

Answers: **1.** The; a **3.** a; blank **5.** blank; the **7.** blank; the **9.** the **11.** the; a

◆ **PRACTICE 21.7, page 334**

Answers: **1.** Question: Are the sparrows searching for winter food? Negative statement: The sparrows are not searching for winter food. **3.** Question: Did I answer her e-mail immediately? Negative statement: I did not answer her e-mail immediately. **5.** Question: Did the porcupine attack my dog? Negative statement: The porcupine did not attack my dog. **7.** Question: Did Gunnar see the robbery at the convenience store? Negative statement: Gunnar did not see the robbery at the convenience store. **9.** Question: Is he working on the problem right now? Negative statement: He is not working on the problem right now.

◆ **PRACTICE 21.8, page 337**

Answers: **1.** Verb: has been studying. Correct **3.** Verb: is understanding. He understands the movement of planets and stars. **5.** Verb: is working. Correct **7.** Verb: is hating. He hates the boring work there, but he must keep his job. **9.** Verb: is earning. Correct

◆ **PRACTICE 21.9, page 338**

Answers: **1.** a pleasant old family tradition **3.** Anita's four pampered poodles **5.** both my annoying sisters **7.** a delightful outdoor wedding party **9.** a wonderful chocolate birthday cake

◆ **PRACTICE 21.10, page 341**

Answers: **1.** from **3.** in; for; in **5.** with **7.** of; in **9.** in; of **11.** to; in; for

◆ **PRACTICE 21.11, page 343**

Answers: **1.** All parents worry about their children. **3.** A child needs rules, and adults should set them up when the child is very young. **5.** Most kids love toys, and adults can give children the responsibility of putting them away. **7.** Correct **9.** Children resist sharing toys but can learn to give them up to another child for a little while.

Chapter 22

◆ **PRACTICE 22.1, page 350**

Answers: **1.** The intersection was crowded with buses, cars, and trucks. **3.** Correct **5.** A good marriage requires patience, honesty, and hard work. **7.** Correct **9.** The kitchen is to the left, the guest room is upstairs, and the pool is out back.

◆ **PRACTICE 22.2, page 351**

Answers: **1.** At the end of the game, the bus took the team home. **3.** After the holiday season, many stores take inventory. **5.** Racing against the clock, Silvio finished the corporate earnings report. **7.** Often feared, bats are actually helpful creatures. **9.** Without access to telephones, more than half the world's population depends on face-to-face communication.

◆ **PRACTICE 22.3, page 353**

Answers: **1.** Bill, how did you do on the test? **3.** Correct **5.** When you give your speech, Jeanne, be sure to speak clearly. **7.** The party, consequently, was a disaster. **9.** Don't forget the key to the cabin, Amber. **11.** Furthermore, the team had lost its best defensive player. **13.** What do you suggest we do for Zach, Dr. Chen? **15.** Besides, genetics is the next medical frontier.

◆ **PRACTICE 22.4, page 353**

Answers: **1.** For example, Tiger Woods is an exceptional golf player. **3.** His golf game, consequently, is difficult to beat. **5.** Correct **7.** His success, moreover, has come at a young age. **9.** There may, finally, be no one to challenge him on the golf course.

◆ **PRACTICE 22.6, page 356**

Answers: **1.** My mother, Sandra Thomas, used to work for the city. **3.** The convention is in Chicago, my hometown. **5.** The world's tallest mountain, Mount Everest, is in Nepal. **7.** Aloe, a common houseplant, has medicinal value. **9.** Elvis Presley, a white singer, was influenced by African-American music.

◆ **PRACTICE 22.8, page 358**

Answers: **1.** Correct **3.** The camera, which is automatic, often breaks. **5.** Correct **7.** Rafael, who finishes work at 5:30, met Carla for dinner at 7:00. **9.** Gray wolves, which many ranchers dislike, are making a comeback in the West.

◆ **PRACTICE 22.9, page 359**

Answers: **1.** Correct **3.** Correct **5.** The women, who call themselves the Weavers Society, needed customers for their work. **7.** A company that sells satellite telephones donated some phones to the weavers. **9.** The weavers, who could find no customers in their own village, soon sold many of their hammocks to customers in other regions.

◆ **PRACTICE 22.11, page 361**

Answers: **1.** Alaska is a rugged state, and its population is small. **3.** Although many people live in Alaska's cities, many others live in small villages. **5.** Correct **7.** Correct **9.** Correct

◆ **PRACTICE 22.12, page 363**

Answers: **1.** Atif is from Lahore, Pakistan. **3.** Their first home was at 2122 Kent Avenue, Brooklyn, New York. **5.** They wanted to move to Boston, Massachusetts, where Atif's cousins lived. **7.** Their new address was 14 Arden Street, Allston, Massachusetts. **9.** Correct

Chapter 23

◆ **PRACTICE 23.1, page 368**

Answers: **1.** Skateboarding looks easy, but it isn't. **3.** They'll need to practice first. **5.** Skateboarders don't have that problem. **7.** In many cases, they've spent thousands of hours refining their skills. **9.** It's a sport filled with difficult twists, turns, and jumps.

◆ **PRACTICE 23.2, page 368**

Answers: **1.** Television isn't a luxury in many homes, it's a necessity. **3.** They'll argue that there's plenty of high-quality programming on television. **5.** They're designed to appeal to as many people as possible. **7.** The average American doesn't read nearly as much as he or she watches television. **9.** Fifty years ago, people couldn't have imagined how attached we'd become to our television sets.

◆ **PRACTICE 23.3, page 370**

Answers: **1.** the shop's owner **3.** the neighbor's cat **5.** Indira's computer **7.** Chris's sister **9.** the class's opinion

◆ **PRACTICE 23.4, page 371**

Answers: **1.** the travelers' bags **3.** the women's faces **5.** the minister's car **7.** the Huangs' apartment **9.** the lawyers' first meeting

◆ **PRACTICE 23.6, page 371**

Answers: **1.** New York's **3.** Correct; father's **5.** Harold Lee's; correct **7.** family's; Chinatown's **9.** agency's; Arthur's

◆ **PRACTICE 23.7, page 373**

Answers: **1.** its **3.** it's **5.** its **7.** you're **9.** it's

◆ **PRACTICE 23.8, page 373**

Answers: **1.** lovers' **3.** It's; correct **5.** its; correct **7.** Who's **9.** Correct; residents'; your

Chapter 24

◆ **PRACTICE 24.1, page 380**

Answers: **1.** The Ojibwa are the largest Native American group in North America. **3.** The Ojibwa made maple syrup that was something like the syrup sold in Shoprite or Safeway. **5.** A century before the Revolutionary War, Europeans traveled west and met the native peoples who lived there. **7.** The American Indian Movement is an organization that calls attention to unfair treaties, such as the Treaty of 1854. **9.** In November 2000, LaDuke ran for vice president on the Green Party ticket.

◆ **PRACTICE 24.3, page 383**

Answers: **1.** "These clothes are too small for me," Sue said. "These clothes," Sue said, "are too small for me." **3.** "The exam should not be too difficult," the instructor said. "The exam," the instructor said, "should not be too difficult." **5.** "Tell all the truth but tell it slant," the poet Emily Dickinson wrote. "Tell all the truth," the poet Emily Dickinson wrote, "but tell it slant."

◆ **PRACTICE 24.4, page 384**

Answers: **1.** Identifying tag: Dorothy Parker said. Dorothy Parker said, "The cure for boredom is curiosity." **3.** Identifying tag: Patrice asked. "Why does it always rain on my birthday?" Patrice asked. **5.** Identifying tag: Rebecca insisted. "If you lose this tape," Rebecca insisted, "I'll never lend you anything again." **7.** Identifying tag: the instructor was saying. When I walked in, the instructor was saying, "Please be sure to arrive on time." **9.** Identifying tag: Kurt Vonnegut observed. "High school," Kurt Vonnegut observed, "is closer to the core of the American experience than anything I can think of."

◆ **PRACTICE 24.6, page 387**

Answers: **1.** The show *A Prairie Home Companion* has been on the radio for many years. **3.** Did you see the article "Earthquake Predictions Made" in the *Los Angeles Times*? **5.** The song "I Could Have Danced All Night" was written for the musical *My Fair Lady*. **7.** The textbook *Foundations First* includes the chapter "Understanding Mechanics." **9.** After studying Shakespeare's play *Hamlet*, we will read John Milton's book-length poem *Paradise Lost*.

◆ **PRACTICE 24.7, page 388**

Answers: **1.** Lucy's favorite novel is *For Whom the Bell Tolls*. **3.** Recent television cartoons created for adults include *The Simpsons* and *King of the Hill*. **5.** The articles "Stream of Consciousness" and "School's Out" in *Wired* magazine focus on new technology.

Chapter 25

◆ PRACTICE 25.1, page 394

Answers: **1.** Correct; achieve **3.** Neither; correct **5.** Correct; correct **7.** society; correct **9.** relieve; correct

◆ PRACTICE 25.2, page 395

Answers: **1.** uneasy **3.** overcook **5.** unwind **7.** underpay **9.** prewar

◆ PRACTICE 25.3, page 396

Answers: **1.** adorable **3.** judgment **5.** whistled **7.** truly **9.** insurance **11.** senseless **13.** noticeable **15.** amusement **17.** imagination **19.** microscope

◆ PRACTICE 25.4, page 397

Answers: **1.** trying **3.** noisily **5.** destroyed **7.** dryness **9.** tinier **11.** busily **13.** replied **15.** thirtyish **17.** joyful **19.** daily

◆ PRACTICE 25.5, page 398

Answers: **1.** shopper **3.** preferred **5.** climbed **7.** fairest **9.** beginning **11.** written **13.** appealing **15.** existing **17.** runner **19.** trapper

Chapter 26

◆ PRACTICE 26.1, page 402

Answers: **1.** Correct; correct **3.** affect; correct **5.** Correct; correct; correct **7.** By; already **9.** Correct; correct

◆ PRACTICE 26.2, page 403

Answers: **1.** conscious **3.** It's; hear **5.** Every day; its **7.** every day; correct **9.** conscious; its

◆ PRACTICE 26.3, page 405

Answers: **1.** laid; correct **3.** past; mind **5.** lose **7.** lie; correct **9.** Correct; lie

◆ PRACTICE 26.4, page 407

Answers: **1.** Correct; rise **3.** plain; correct **5.** quiet; sit **7.** Correct; correct **9.** Correct; principal

◆ PRACTICE 26.5, page 408

Answers: **1.** used; their **3.** through; correct; their **5.** Correct; correct **7.** Correct; their **9.** Correct; too

◆ PRACTICE 26.6, page 410

Answers: **1.** Who's; correct **3.** You're; your **5.** Were; correct **7.** you're; correct **9.** Whose; where

Appendix A

◆ PRACTICE 1, page 489

Answers: **1.** plight **3.** manic **5.** vixen **7.** carcinogen **9.** balk **11.** obliqueness **13.** immortalized **15.** liability **17.** transaction

◆ PRACTICE 2, page 490

Answers: **1.** dilute **3.** stigmatized **5.** naturalization **7.** symbol **9.** lethal **11.** brawl **13.** orient **15.** subsidize **17.** surveillance **19.** embossed

Acknowledgments

Picture acknowledgments

Chapter 1: Joel Gordon; *Chapter 2:* Bob Daemmrich; *Chapter 3:* Topham Photos/The Image Works; *Chapter 4:* Monty Brinton, CBS Photo; *Chapter 5:* Lou Requena/AP/Wide World Photos; *Chapter 6:* Tony Freeman/PhotoEdit; *Chapter 7:* Rudi Von Briel/PhotoEdit; *Chapter 8:* Joel Gordon; *Chapter 9:* Judy Gelles/Stock, Boston; *Chapter 10:* Charles Gupton/Corbis/Stock Market; *Chapter 11:* Scott Houston/Corbis/Sygma; *Chapter 12:* Rick Maiman/Corbis/Sygma; *Chapter 13:* John Elk III/Stock, Boston; *Chapter 14:* Drew Crawford/The Image Works; *Chapter 15:* used by permission of Shirley Hanshaw; *Chapter 16:* Stephan Savoia/AP/Wide World Photos; *Chapter 17:* Frank Rossotto/Corbis/Stock Market; *Chapter 18:* Will & Deni McIntyre/Photo Researchers; *Chapter 19:* Joe Sohm/The Image Works; *Chapter 20:* Britt Erlanson/The Image Bank/Getty Images; *Chapter 21:* Bob Daemmrich; *Chapter 22:* Dan Loh/AP/Wide World Photos; *Chapter 23:* Grantpix/Photo Researchers; *Chapter 24:* Photofest; *Chapter 25:* Tom McCarthy/Corbis/Stock Market; *Chapter 26:* George B. Jones III/Photo Researchers; *Chapter 27:* Joel Gordon.

Text acknowledgments

Kiku Adatto. "Trigger-Happy Birthday." From *The New York Times Magazine*, May 14, 2000. Copyright © 2000 by The New York Times Company, Inc. Reprinted with the permission of the author.

American Heritage Dictionary of the English Language, Third Edition. Entries "Teach," "frying pan," "tax," "sneak." Copyright © 1996 by Houghton Mifflin Company. Reprinted by permission from *The American Heritage Dictionary of the English Language,* Third Edition.

Nathan Black. "After a Shooting." From *The New York Times*, March 8, 2001. Copyright © 2001 by The New York Times Company. Reprinted by permission.

Richard Carter. "Weathering Prejudice." From *The New York Times*, August 4, 1991. Copyright © 1991 by The New York Times Company, Inc. Reprinted by permission.

Macarena del Rocío Hernández. "What I Did for Love." From the *Philadelphia Inquirer Magazine*, July 2, 2000. Copyright © 2000 by Macarena Hernández. Reprinted with the author's permission.

Jon Katz. "How Boys Become Men." From *Glamour*, January 1993. Copyright © 1993 by Jon Katz. Reprinted with the permission of International Creative Management, Inc.

Garrison Keillor. "How to Write a Personal Letter." International Paper Company, 1987. Reprinted with the permission of International Paper.

Maria Guhde Keri. "Take Me Out of Their Ball Game." From *Utne Reader*, January–February 2000. Reprinted with the permission of Lone Tout Publications.

Richard Lederer. Excerpt from "English Is a Crazy Language" from *Crazy Language*. Copyright © 1989 by Richard Lederer. Reprinted with the permission of Pocket Books, a division of Simon & Schuster, Inc.

Jon Leo. "When Life Imitates Video." From *U.S. News & World Report*, May 3, 1999. Copyright © 1999 U.S. News & World Report, L.P. All rights reserved. Reprinted with permission.

Odalys Martínez. "Black and Latina—Face It!" From *Latina,* July 2000. Copyright © 2000 by Latina. Reprinted with the permission of *Latina.*

Arthur Miller. "Before Air Conditioning." From *The New Yorker*, 1998. Copyright © 1998 by Arthur Miller. Reprinted with the permission of International Creative Management.

Lucie Prinz. "Say Something." From *The Atlantic Monthly*, October 1996. Copyright © 1996 by Lucie Prinz. Reprinted with the permission of the author.

Joyce Purnick. "Some Truths behind Those Statistics." From *The New York Times*, July 7, 2000. Copyright © 2000 by The New Times Company. Reprinted by permission.

Carolyn Foster Segal. "The Dog Ate My Disk, and Other Tales of Woe." From *The Chronicle of Higher Education*, August 11, 2000. Reprinted with the permission of the author.

Gary Soto. "The Colors." From *A Summer Life* by Gary Soto. Copyright © 1990 by the University Press of New England. Reprinted with the permission of the University Press of New England.

Deborah Tannen. "Gender Gap in Cyberspace." From *Newsweek*, May 16, 1994. Copyright © 1994 by Deborah Tannen. Reprinted with the permission of the author.

Brady Udall. "One Liar's Beginnings." From *Personals*: *Dreams and Nightmares from the Lives of Twenty Young Writers* by Thomas Beller, editor. Copyright © 1998 by Brady Udall. Reprinted with the permission of the author.

William Zinsser. "The Transaction." From *On Writing Well*: *An Informal Guide to Writing Nonfiction,* Sixth Edition, by William Zinsser. Copyright © 1998 by William Zinsser. Reprinted with the permission of the author and Carol Brissie.

Index

Note: Numbers in **bold** type indicate pages where terms are defined.

Index of Rhetorical Patterns